Burke's 4

1. Be awed by the mystery of language

2. Listen well

3. Have a heart

THE RHETORICAL
IMAGINATION OF
KENNETH BURKE

1-62
63-90
91-118
143-170
171-222

Studies in Rhetoric/Communication

Thomas W. Benson, Series Editor

THE RHETORICAL IMAGINATION OF KENNETH BURKE

ROSS WOLIN

University of South Carolina Press

UNIVERSITY OF SOUTH CAROLINA **BICENTENNIAL**

Published in Columbia, South Carolina, by the
University of South Carolina Press

Manufactured in the United States of America

05 04 03 02 01   5 4 3 2 1

Library of Congress Cataloging-in-Publication Data

Wolin, Ross, 1956–

The rhetorical imagination of Kenneth Burke / Ross Wolin.

p. cm. — (Studies in rhetoric/communication)

Includes bibliographical references and index.

"Bib and index."

ISBN 1-57003-404-4 (alk. paper)

1. Burke, Kenneth, 1897– 2. Criticism—United States—History—
20th century. I. Title. II. Series.

PN75.B8 W65 2001

801'.95'092—dc21   2001000829

Acknowledgment is made to the University of California Press for permission
to include in the appendix passages from the first edition of Kenneth Burke's
Permanence and Change.

Contents

Series Editor's Preface

How shall we read Kenneth Burke? Burke (1897–1993) was a monumental figure in twentieth-century rhetorical studies, a critic and theorist of vast erudition, wide curiosity, cranky individuality, comic genius, and grand vision. His major writings, most of them decades old, are still in print. A society formed in his name holds conferences about his work, the great themes of which are part of the vocabulary of every rhetorical critic and theorist. Yet Burke's greatest theoretical contributions are usually discussed in critical essays, exciting an appetite to understand the whole as a coherent system to the degree that it does not resist reduction to mere system.

In *The Rhetorical Imagination of Kenneth Burke,* Ross Wolin explores the ways in which Burke has been "largely misunderstood by even his most ardent admirers," who become lost in Burke's "rearticulations and extensions." Wolin offers another way of reading Burke, studying his ideas in historical and biographical context as they developed through time, and taking into account not only the theoretical ideas but also the social, political, and critical dimensions of Burke's writings. Wolin helps us see how Burke is both consistent and changing, and how an emphasis on either the permanence or the change in his ideas, at the expense of the other, is bound to result in a diminished understanding of his work. The result is an attentive, complex, lively, and thoughtful exposition of the intellectual career of Kenneth Burke.

THOMAS W. BENSON

Preface

Now that the twentieth century has ended, one cannot help being worried about the state of American culture. To be sure, scientific and technological advances have radically transformed American life for the better and promise ever greater marvels, especially in biology, medicine, information technology, and the material sciences. Moreover, the economy is doing well and crime is down. Yet, the disparity between the rich and poor is widening, corporate power is concentrating ominously, social conflict is deepening, and a fractious and litigious society seems ever more unable to meet adequately the increasingly complex ethical, social, and political challenges that these and other cultural trends make all the more pressing. Worse still, the explosive growth of new media technologies and outlets—which for so long has been vaunted to stimulate greater public participation and consensus in civic affairs—seems to be fixed more on celebrity and calamity than on meaningful public discourse. With the twentieth century over, America seems on the verge of being paralyzed by a culture of discord.

These cultural vectors are haunting reminders of the late 1920s and early 1930s. At that time science and technology were ascendant, there was great disparity between the haves and have nots, and an influx of immigrants was making American society ever more diverse. The great crises of the early century—World War I, the Great Depression, and the growth of fascism—caused many Americans to wonder whether capitalism and perhaps democracy were dying. In response to the wrenching of American culture, thinkers from virtually every discipline sought new ways to create common ground, despite the fact that there was little agreement as to the nature of the problems, the values to promote, and which solutions would effect the best results. However, there was agreement on one point: that finding solutions would be difficult because of the complex economic, social, political, cultural, ethical, and epistemological factors that figured into any meaningful attempt.

In the 1920s and 1930s Kenneth Burke was one of many critics attempting to discover better ways to cultivate agreement among persons and groups with profound differences. Born in 1897, Burke left his native Pittsburgh as a teenager to join the New York intellectual scene as a budding poet and novelist. He spent most of his life as a literary critic, using literature, philosophy, ethics, and linguistics to analyze the nature of language and agreement. His goal was social betterment: "towards a better life," he said in his early work; and later, as he grandly put it in *A Grammar of Motives* (1945), *ad bellum purificandum* ("toward the purification of war"). Burke's broad knowledge, penetrating social insight, and keen critical judgment garnered admiration from key figures of the

American literary world in the 1920s and 1930s. In the 1940s and 1950s his renown broadened to include psychologists, philosophers, sociologists, and anthropologists. Even now he is regarded as one of the most intriguing and important literary critics of the twentieth century.

Throughout his career Burke was both praised and criticized, often for related reasons. For one thing, his work covers an extraordinary variety of texts, authors, and theories from virtually all the liberal arts (and even some sciences)—often ranging freely among them. Some readers find Burke rich, stimulating, and provocative; others find him undisciplined and intellectually disingenuous. Burke's politics also brought him praise and censure. Long a leftist, Burke was sympathetic to communism and in the 1920s and 1930s maintained close connections with important members of the communist movement in New York. Yet, in the early 1930s, when he and many others were as close to communism as they would ever be, he still did not join the party and even made public statements that brought condemnation and ridicule from the faithful. Some of Burke's critics admired what they perceived to be political independence and originality; others rebuked what they took to be a profound political failing.

These wildly disparate reactions arose in part because of Burke's intellectual proclivities. A bohemian at heart, Burke was fond of being contrarian. "When in Rome," he said, "do as the Greeks." This is far more complex than just a youthful snubbing of political and social conventions. He was acutely aware of human tendencies to be doctrinaire and to be seduced by self-serving politics. So Burke crisscrossed the liberal/conservative split, trying to find what was right in both camps. Thus, to leftists he sounds too traditional and to conservatives he sounds too radical. Indeed, some of the harshest condemnation comes from those with strong political stances, such as Mike Gold. Burke's contrariness results also in a kind of intellectual bohemianism, what he called a "cut across the bias" of accepted intellectual categories. In *Counter-Statement* (1931), for instance, Burke combines aesthetics and politics; and in *The Philosophy of Literary Form* (1941) he blends linguistics and social psychology. Naturally some readers find this inspiring; others, such as the philosophers Sidney Hook and Max Black, detest what they presume to be a retreat into "suggestiveness."

Despite the wildly varying responses to Burke's theories, the great majority of his readers believe that he must be reckoned with. This is more true today than it has been for decades. One has to be impressed by the fact that almost twenty books about him have appeared since 1982. Indeed, most of his books remain in print, new collections of essays have been issued, and scholarly articles cite him more and more. Perhaps similarities between the first three decades of this century and the final few contribute to this renewed interest in Burke's theories about language and rhetoric. As we meet new challenges that

echo the past, Burke's inquiries into meaning, orientation, faction, communication, and rhetoric are as urgent today as when Burke raised them long ago
and for decades after.

Unfortunately, throughout his career—and even today—Burke has been
largely misunderstood by even his most ardent admirers. The reasons for this are
complicated, and the key ones are referred to above. In fact, much of this book
is an explanation of just how his intellectual and political cut across the bias
confuses and sometimes alienates his readers. In addition, Burke is misunderstood in large part because of two coextensive desires: (1) to explore the great
complexity involved in understanding the roles of language and agreement in
human relations, and (2) to try to make his case in a new way, in the hope that
his ideas would have more impact. (Burke has said that "everything" he wanted
to say found its roots in his first book of criticism, *Counter-Statement*.) Put otherwise, Burke is misunderstood because the very themes he hoped to reinforce
and make more persuasive are actually obscured by his series of rearticulations
and extensions in new intellectual idioms. To make matters worse, as Burke's
career progressed, themes from his early works moved into the background,
becoming masked by increasingly theoretical and philosophical concerns.

An overview of Burke's wide-ranging studies will give some indication of
the difficulty of tracing his ideas. In *Counter-Statement,* Burke explores the
nature of agreement and disagreement in terms of aesthetics and politics. In
Permanence and Change (1935) he approaches these problems in terms of ethics
and communication within organizations. In *Attitudes toward History* (1937) he
uses literary genres to uncover and organize fundamental similarities and differences in ways of thinking during the great epochs of human history. In *The
Philosophy of Literary Form,* Burke returns to the aesthetic, this time using psychological and linguistic theories to explain how "clusters" of ideas and images
form the bases for "identifications." Burke's crowning achievement is a study of
human relations that culminates the theory of "dramatism" as elaborated in *A
Grammar of Motives* and *A Rhetoric of Motives* (and refined in later books). In *A
Grammar of Motives* (1945) Burke focuses primarily on the philosophical and
dialectical dimensions of agreement and disagreement. In *A Rhetoric of Motives*
(1950) he turns to the strategies employed to create, maintain, and modify one's
place in a social hierarchy. In *The Rhetoric of Religion* (1961) Burke speculates
on what the "vocabulary of transcendence" in religious doctrines can tell us
about the nature of language. Burke's last major book of criticism, *Language as
Symbolic Action* (1966), is a collection of theoretical refinements and critical
applications of his theories.

I wrote this book because much of what I have read about Burke ignores important aspects of his thinking. Influenced heavily by the intellectual currents of the

1950s and 1960s, scholars have sought within Burke theoretical and philosophical systematicity that is not there. Worse yet, because of the profoundly fertile observations Burke makes about the nature and characteristics of language in general, many readers have largely ignored the social and political arguments that infuse his work. In short, I believe that the theoretical bias, which favors his later works, distorts what Burke was trying to say. To best understand his later work we have to embrace his early work fully. In addition, much of the contemporary scholarship about Burke departs a great deal from what Burke intended. That is not a problem per se. Burke's ideas are so fertile that they inspire writers in many disciplines on matters far afield from what Burke was interested in. That is because language pervades human experience and Burke has penetrating insight into the nature and characteristics of language. Recently a number of books and articles have tried to synthesize Burke by imposing on him an overarching theory. These attempts are limited in that they use Burke piecemeal, and in any event the Burke that emerges is not the one I see in his work. There is a big difference, I think, between saying "Burke makes me think . . ." and saying "Burke says . . ." I hope that greater clarity about what Burke said will improve both the extensions of Burke's thought and our understanding of Burke himself.

Readers of this book will encounter an approach to Burke that is rare in scholarly literature. I focus on the development of his theories, especially as they appear in the public documents he produced. I principally analyze the relationships between texts, explaining how his ideas developed over time as rearticulations and extensions of previous arguments. A few writers on Burke have used biographical information. I do too. His letters are particularly illuminating as to intent, even though letters have their limitations. On the other hand I largely ignore unfinished manuscripts, unpublished essays and notes, and even a 1930s monograph called "Auscultation, Creation, and Revision," mostly because it was dropped by Burke. Some scholars made much of this monograph after it appeared in 1993, at the end of a long and prolific life. And some made much of other unpublished and unfinished drafts that are floating around. But I am dubious of the value of such material. At the least, since they are not part of the public documents Burke produced, I do not give them equal status to works that clearly have his imprimatur. Some parts of his published corpus that I go into have been largely ignored by the secondary literature. For instance, his earliest essays are hardly ever mentioned. And few writers talk about "The Dictionary of Pivotal Terms" in *Attitudes* or "The Tactics of Motivation" or "The Dialectic of Constitutions" in the *Grammar.* These three pieces are extremely important to an understanding of what Burke is saying.

Also rare in studies of Burke is discussion of the way he was received by his contemporaries at each stage of his career, which I present. For evidence I largely use reviews of his books and his comments in letters about his influence. Together these demonstrate a crucial point: that despite great praise, Burke was largely misunderstood and misused. Burke even complained that others used his ideas without attribution. Stanley Edgar Hyman discusses Burke's influence on a smattering of critics and writers in *The Armed Vision*. Even so, until the 1960s few people actually used his ideas to any great degree. Burke's own statements attest to this. Students of Burke owe William Rueckert a great debt for his thick compendium of reviews, *Critical Responses to Kenneth Burke*. I have found it invaluable. And the immense bibliography in that volume has been indispensable. Paul Jay's *The Selected Correspondence of Kenneth Burke and Malcolm Cowley, 1915–1981* has been helpful as well. I also discuss the theoretical articles that comment and build on Burke's ideas. Some people read Burke with a smile, some with a frown, and a few with an outright scowl. I hope that this book partially clarifies just what leads to these various responses.

Readers of this book will also encounter a number of angles into Burke. I alternate between biography, psychological biography, intellectual history, the impact of critical ideas on Burke, the relationship between art and politics, and Burke as a rhetor—and more, I daresay. That is because the study of Burke perforce draws one in many directions. No single volume could do justice to the complexities and riches of his work. If I were to confine myself to, say, psychological biography, the reader would miss out on a lot. So the reader will get a variety of perspectives on the development of his ideas.

Finally, I would like to clarify who could benefit from this book. For the scholar who is familiar with Burke, this book explores in depth the meaning and significance of key concepts in Burke's thinking and provides a clear sense of how dramatism arose out of Burke's earlier theories about art, politics, and language. For someone who read Burke a while ago, was once familiar with his work, but may have been puzzled by his difficult prose, this book clarifies what Burke was trying to get at in each of his major works. I believe, too, that it is an effective introduction to Burke for those unfamiliar with him: scholars in a variety of fields in the liberal arts and humanities, graduate students and undergraduates, and anyone interested in the liberal arts in general, especially literary criticism and rhetoric.

Acknowledgments

I would like to thank Austin Babrow, Stephen Collins, and Matt McAllister for their advice, in particular for helping me see Burke in a broader context. I am especially grateful to James Hoopes for his gracious and insightful comments while slogging through more drafts than anyone should suffer. Most of all, I am indebted to Thomas M. Conley. The argument I am making reflects what he has been telling students and colleagues for years. His detailed and careful readings of the book at all stages of development were invaluable in helping me formulate my thoughts about Burke and express them more clearly than I would have otherwise. Of course, I take full responsibility for all errors and opinions contained herein.

And thanks to Stephen Crook, of the Henry W. and Albert A. Berg Collection of English and American Literature in the New York Public Library, for his assistance regarding Burke's correspondence with Dr. James Sibley Watson Jr. Barry Blose and Christine Copeland, of the University of South Carolina Press, along with Patricia Coate, supplied indispensable editorial advice. Finally, I would like to thank the Babson College Board of Research for funding that helped make this book possible.

Abbreviations

ATH   *Attitudes toward History*. 1937. 3d ed., 1984.

CS   *Counter-Statement*. 1931. 2d ed., 1968.

GM   *A Grammar of Motives*. 1945. 2d ed., 1969.

Jay   *The Selected Correspondence of Kenneth Burke and Malcolm Cowley, 1915–1981.*

PC   *Permanence and Change: An Anatomy of Purpose*. 1935. 3d ed., 1984.

PLF   *The Philosophy of Literary Form: Studies in Symbolic Action*. 1941. 3d ed., 1973.

RM   *A Rhetoric of Motives*. 1950. 2d ed., 1969.

RR   *The Rhetoric of Religion*. 1961.

LASA   *Language as Symbolic Action: Essays on Life, Literature, and Method.* 1966.

Earlier editions, when used, are indicated in the parenthetical citations and endnotes. See the bibliography for full citations.

PART I

Towards a Better Life through Art, Criticism, and Politics

Kenneth Burke is among a handful of scholars who have shaped profoundly the meaning of "rhetoric" in the twentieth century. He was drawn to the study of rhetoric not for its own sake but because he believed that in rhetoric certain important questions about human relations coalesce. When Burke began publishing criticism in the 1920s, rhetoric played a smaller role in his thinking than it ultimately played decades later. Yet even by the 1950s, when "rhetoric" absorbed his attention greatly, he was still drawn to it more for what its study could tell us about human relations generally than for narrower concerns about what makes a speech effective.

Burke's career falls into three phases, starting in the early 1920s and extending to the publication of *Language as Symbolic Action* in the 1960s. The first phase begins with his fiction, poetry, and criticism of the early 1920s and culminates with the publication of *Counter-Statement* in 1931. In the second phase Burke published *Permanence and Change* (1935), *Attitudes toward History* (1937), and *The Philosophy of Literary Form* (1941). The third phase includes *A Grammar of Motives* (1945), *A Rhetoric of Motives* (1950), *The Rhetoric of Religion* (1961), and *Language as Symbolic Action* (1966). These phases demarcate different emphases in his thinking, though communication is a central theme uniting all three. The first phase, arising out of the allure of bohemianism and modernism in the 1910s and 1920s, focused on the relations between art and politics. The second, profoundly affected by the Great Depression, centered on how communication figures into what Burke calls "cooperative" organizations. The third, prompted by global warfare, consisted of a more general investigation into the dialectics of accounting for human motivation.

Although the three phases are united in that Burke was working out a vision of how communication functions, in the first phase his ideas about communication and human relations were embryonic, as might be expected. This is due in part to the fact that in the 1920s Burke did not write any book-length study. His poetry, fiction, translations, and critical essays appeared in a variety of literary journals, and at the end of the first phase (1931) he published *Counter-Statement,* an anthology of criticism written over the span of a decade. But it is also due to the fact that his adolescent sense of himself as an avant-garde aesthete began to decay in the middle of the 1920s when employment problems and personal difficulties became pressing. The Wall Street crash in 1929 seems to have had a major impact on Burke's view of the world and of himself. In what he called his aesthetic period Burke emphasized aesthetic theory and literary effect, and he only came to focus more coherently on communication in the 1930s. In 1953, reflecting on his early career, Burke said that "*Counter-Statement* shows signs of its emergence out of adolescent fears and posturing, into problems of early manhood" (*CS*, 213). The importance of these early years cannot be overestimated because many of the ideas that occupied Burke's mind for the next three decades found their first expression in the 1920s and early 1930s. "For all the occasional immaturity of some attitudes in . . . *Counter-Statement*," Burke commented, "the book adequately supplies an introduction into [my] later concerns" (*CS*, 219).

Perhaps the best way to understand what Burke was saying in this first phase of his career is to see it as an exploration of several related ideas falling under the theme of "towards a better life." Like many of his contemporaries, Burke believed that American society faced serious problems resulting from a number of factors, one of which was the inability of established thinking and practices to redress long-standing inequities and the problems resulting from new social, political, economic, and technological conditions. Taking a view that might seem less sensible today than it would have to a critic in the 1920s, Burke held that art is a mode of survival that leads to a better life. He believed that the artist, by disposition, is antinomian, someone who questions the status quo. He believed that an awareness of aesthetics will help even those who are not artists see things differently than the ordinary person, leading to greater insight about human experience. In this way art and politics converge. So throughout the first phase of his career Burke explored different ways in which the aesthetic and the political overlap.

One way in which art leads toward a better life is through the institutions of art and criticism. Unlike some of his contemporaries, Burke did not believe in a "pure" art, art for art's sake. Nor did he believe that art needs to be justified as practical or useful. Art, he said, is important because art deals with "the constants of human nature." Furthermore, human expression always to some degree has aesthetic elements. In these senses art is "equipment for living." The same holds true for criticism, which is something of a counterpart of art. In *Permanence and Change,* Burke even says that "all living things are critics." To be engaged with the world is to be critical.

By the time Burke was writing new essays for *Counter-Statement* he had become increasingly convinced that art and criticism should lead people toward specific goals. He was troubled by industrialism, efficiency, capitalism, increased consumption, and other "dominant factors" in American society.

Eschewing the agrarian solution and the values of optimism and practicality favored by the bourgeois, he championed the bohemian aesthetic of inefficiency, dissipation, and nonconformism. Whether or not we accept Burke's particular aesthetic tastes, we must realize that he conceived art and criticism as having profound political and ethical implications. And so we cannot properly understand his later works unless we recognize the purposes Burke believed aesthetic criticism should serve.

Another idea associated with "towards a better life" is form, or what makes art function as art. As with many of his modernist contemporaries, art and criticism for Burke were matters of aesthetic form. But whereas many modernists saw form as something distinct from and even opposed to content, Burke believed that form and content merge. Moreover, as will be discussed in chapter 2, Burke conceived of form not as a characteristic of the object or text under study, but as a psychological relationship between audience, artist, and artwork. Form is the creation and satisfaction of "expectations" in the audience. Art is distinguished by the complexity and significance of its forms. (Thus, viewing a Cezanne painting is formally more interesting and significant than ordering a pizza.) Since the creation and satisfaction of expectations are affected by our experience of the world—and are often directed precisely toward affecting our experience—form has political and ethical implications too.

A third idea associated with "towards a better life" that arises out of the previous two is rhetoric. If art is equipment for living and is directed toward manipulating our expectations, then art is to a great degree a matter of rhetoric, of persuasion about matters of social and political concern, and of the values that we hold dear.

These ideas about art may not seem strange to us today, but in the heyday of modernism they were quite objectionable to some. In fact, overall, Burke was harshly criticized by political activists, philosophers, and art critics. The two chapters that comprise part 1 show how the first phase of Burke's career culminated in a theory that combined art and politics. Chapter 1 will cover Burke's life as a young man in Greenwich Village hoping for success as a novelist and poet and ultimately turning to criticism as his main literary vocation. Chapter 2 covers *Counter-Statement,* explaining how it developed and set the ground not only for the next phase of his career but for all the work that followed.

1

The Formation of a Critic

In the second decade of the twentieth century—as the European war raged on; as relations with Mexico deteriorated nearly to armed conflict; as calls for prohibition and woman suffrage spread across the nation; as corporations monopolized, price-fixed, and restrained trade; as antitrust suits filled court dockets; as strikes all over America paralyzed mining, the railroads, and other industries; as Americans witnessed Red Scares and the most powerful socialist movement yet—a group of promising and eager Columbia College students participated in a small literary society called the Boar's Head. Supervised by a respected professor, John Erskine, these "very soulful" students would meet to read aloud their artful poems and receive polite criticism from their peers. Matthew Josephson, attending his first meeting sometime around November 1916, listened carefully to the fledglings. He was not happy. Poem after poem, he became increasingly irritated by "old tags about Grecian nymphs and mythical heroes or scraps of moonlight and fading roses and other such sentimental properties." Then "a short, thin, bespectacled youth of pale and intellectual appearance, and a shock of black hair, spoke forth in very different voice from the others; he was a young *révolté* reading harsh unrhymed verses that described a dream carrying overtones of repressed and melancholy sexual desire!"[1] Josephson was delighted. But Erskine was not. As the scandalmongering rebel finished, the professor "at once rounded upon the poet," defending the genteel tradition and deriding experimental free verse. When Josephson came to the stranger's defense, the professor turned on him, "shouting that Freud was but a charlatan." The two young men of course could not hold their own, and when the meeting was over, as their peers left the room, they defiantly exited through the window. That nineteen-year-old *révolté* was Kenneth Burke.

Burke started his career as did many other aspiring litterateurs of the generation born around the turn of the century. In the 1910s he made his way to New York and immersed himself in the vibrant literary world of Greenwich Village. By the 1920s Burke wrote poems and fiction for the "little magazines" and was working on a novel. His poetry and fiction were experimental, influenced by modernist French and German literature, and were well received. Unfortunately, then as today, poetry and fiction to Burke's taste did not pay well, if at all. To provide a meager income Burke wrote book reviews and translated essays and modernist German fiction into English, including several works by Arthur Schnitzler, the introduction to Oswald Spengler's *The Downfall of Western Civilization,* and Thomas Mann's "Tristan" and "Death in Venice." In

March 1924 Burke became an editorial assistant at the *Dial*, at the time America's premier literary journal (by some accounts, the best literary journal of the century). Toward the end of the 1920s he wrote music criticism for that influential magazine.

Despite Burke's intention to be a poet and novelist, poetry and fiction represent a relatively minor part of his career, at least by quantity. Although he continued to write poems and fiction for most of his life, his output was fairly small: one book of poetry, one novel, and one collection of short stories. Most of those were published initially between 1924 and 1932.[2] Indeed, his fiction and poetry have been dwarfed by his literary criticism, which includes hundreds of book reviews and essays, some of which are collected in seven of his eight major books of literary criticism. Burke's career in criticism started off strongly. His reviews were well regarded, and his early essays were considered incisive, sometimes brilliant. It is as a literary critic that he has without question made his mark as one of America's great twentieth-century men of letters. Burke's first major critical work is *Counter-Statement* (1931), a collection of essays and reviews written and revised between 1921 and 1931. Since its reissue by the University of California Press in 1968, *Counter-Statement* seems to toss around the backpacks of a good many graduate students taking courses in contemporary rhetorical theory, and it even appears on the book lists of some undergraduate courses. Yet overall, *Counter-Statement* has been largely ignored by more-advanced scholars. Indexes of scholarly citations demonstrate that scholars overwhelmingly favor his later works, especially *A Grammar of Motives* and *A Rhetoric of Motives*. Even worse, his early essays and books are on the whole disregarded.

This may not seem to be a problem. Perhaps the books of what he called the "*Motivorum* project"—*A Grammar of Motives* and *A Rhetoric of Motives*—are more insightful and important than the early work. I do not believe this to be the case, for the *Grammar* and the *Rhetoric* are outgrowths of *Counter-Statement, Permanence and Change, Attitudes toward History,* and *The Philosophy of Literary Form.* I consider the *Grammar* and the *Rhetoric* to be rearticulations, extensions, or modifications of the earlier books. In fact, Burke supports this view: "*Permanence and Change,*" he has said, "in effect takes up where *Counter-Statement* left off" (*PC,* 302–3). In "Curriculum Criticum," Burke's explanation of the "'curve' of development" of his "position" from *Counter-Statement* to the *Rhetoric,* he describes *Attitudes toward History* as a "companion volume" to *Permanence and Change* ("not just a sequel, but in one respect an early revision").[3] *The Philosophy of Literary Form* continues the rearticulation, he says, acting as "a summarization of the author's notions about the symbolic function of literary forms" (*CS,* 217). And Burke has even recognized that "for all the occasional immaturity of some attitudes in his *Counter-Statement,* the book adequately supplies an introduction into his later concerns" (*CS,* 219). All these statements suggest that Burke realized the profound debt his later work owed to its forebears, especially *Counter-Statement.*

A simple question can be posed: What was Burke trying to do with *Counter-Statement?* The answer does not come easily, for *Counter-Statement* is the culmination of Burke's decade-and-a-half struggle to conceive and adapt sophisticated ideas to a complex and rapidly changing intellectual, social, and political milieu. If the socially and politically tumultuous world of Burke's adolescence is not viewed as enough to prompt a brilliant and humane young man to retreat from the simple and self-serving positions then so common, Burke's world fifteen years later—the Wall Street crash, the Great Depression, the "Soviet experiment," the beginning of "the heyday of American communism," the rise of European fascism—prompts even greater misgivings.[4] By 1931, in an America rapidly falling to the nadir of the Depression, Burke felt a strong need to speak against "principles" championed as the bases for solutions to contemporary problems. Burke alludes to this in the preface to the first edition of *Counter-Statement,* when explaining the book's title: "Perhaps it should be said, by way of preface, that this book does not set itself up as an 'attack.' It deals but secondarily and sporadically with refutation. We have chosen to call it *Counter-Statement* solely because—as regards its basic concerns and tenets—each principle it advocates is matched by an opposite principle flourishing and triumphant today. Heresies and orthodoxies will always be changing places, but whatever the minority view happens to be at any given time, one must consider it as 'counter.' Hence the title—which will not, we hope, suggest either an eagerness for the fray or a sense of defeat" (*CS,* vii). The answer to the seemingly simple question becomes even more difficult because of the complex and vibrant literary culture to which he spoke. Reacting against the nineteenth-century *ars gratia artis* conception of aesthetics and its twentieth-century counterparts (following somewhat the lead of European modernists and the American avant-garde), Burke, as did some of his contemporaries, rejected the idea of "pure" art and sought to establish a socially and politically driven aesthetic. Numerous theories of art were prevalent in the New York literary world of the 1920s, complicated by political affiliations and social and economic subcultures that caused a proliferation of perspectives. And the vibrant literary culture was all the more balkanized due to the industry of modern literary production. In the 1920s and early 1930s the chief outlet for modernism was the little magazines (one bibliography lists well over two hundred founded between 1920 and 1931).[5] Getting published in little magazines was not easy; poor funding (the magazines often struggled just to pay the printer), continuously shifting intellectual and political allegiances, and even government harassment and censorship made success shaky.

The answer to the question is complicated as well by characteristics of *Counter-Statement*. The book is a collection of essays written for different purposes and audiences. Some essays stand alone; others are companion pieces; still others are attempts to make an anthology cohere into a book. Moreover, the essays were written over the span of a decade, Burke's formative period as a critic—when he was as much figuring out what to say as how to say it. Further complicating matters, Burke constructed *Counter-Statement* to meet three ends. In a telling letter to Malcolm Cowley he reveals his "Critic's Credo," the agenda and organizing principle behind *Counter-Statement:* "This Critic's Credo should contain (a) an apology for art in the light of any current doctrines which might seem to discredit art, (b) A rhetoric, an analysis of the processes by which a work of art is effective, and (c) a program, a discussion as to what effects might be desirable at the critic's particular time in history" (Jay, 198). Unfortunately, Burke provides few clues in *Counter-Statement* that would indicate his credos. Burke even confuses the reader by separating essays that fall under the same heading. The obvious reason for the structure of the book is to present the essays in chronological order, based on when they were written, which parallels Burke's developing ideas. Even so, the structure emphasizes the interpenetration of the credos; Burke tells Cowley that they "will be found to merge into one another" (Jay, 198). The complexities involved in understanding *Counter-Statement* are evidenced by its critical reception. Scholars today who pay attention to *Counter-Statement* cite mostly the preface, "Psychology and Form," and "Lexicon Rhetoricae." Though they speak highly of *Counter-Statement,* ignoring most of the book seems to belie the praises. But even in the 1930s, when most reviewers frequently mentioned the majority of the other essays, including "Program" and "Applications of the Terminology," *Counter-Statement* was hardly well received. Most reviews were harshly critical—and the book hardly sold.

In short, any attempt to understand *Counter-Statement* immediately catapults us into an examination of how Burke adapted to the literary and political scene in New York from his arrival there in the middle 1910s through the publication of *Counter-Statement* in 1931. The question What is Burke trying to say? begs us to ask first, Who is Kenneth Burke?

For a twentieth-century man of letters who published hundreds of essays, book reviews, and translations, one volume of poetry, two volumes of fiction, and nine volumes of criticism; for a man who taught at colleges and universities for nearly half a century (including the New School of Social Research, the University of Chicago, Bennington College, the University of California, Harvard University, Pennsylvania State University, and Wesleyan University); for a Guggenheim Fellow, a member of the National Institute of Arts and Letters (1946), a member of the Princeton Institute for Advanced Study (1949), a Fellow at the Center for

Advanced Study in the Behavioral Sciences (1957–58), a member of the American Academy of Arts and Sciences (1967), a recipient of the Gold Medal for Belles Lettres and Criticism from the American Academy of Arts and Letters (1975) and the National Medal for Literature (1981), Kenneth Burke had quite an unexpected educational background. Never having obtained a college degree (in fact, he spent only three semesters in college), Burke taught himself through broad and voracious reading and by immersing himself in the literary and political world of New York.[6]

Born in 1897, Burke even as a teenager was avidly interested in literature.[7] While attending a Pittsburgh high school—along with Malcolm Cowley and James Light, who were friends—Burke was part of a literary crowd that rebelled against the school curriculum and the adolescent interests of other students. Burke also rebelled against his parents, who urged him to give up literature and enter a career in banking.[8] When he moved with his family to New Jersey at age eighteen, Burke wasted little time advancing his literary career: mornings were devoted to writing stories, poems, essays, fables, and plays ("all of them lopsided, brilliant, immature," according to Cowley).[9] Burke also frequented Greenwich Village, ambitiously cultivating literary connections. He was quick, for example, to become friendly with the British writer Louis Wilkinson and, through him, Theodore Dreiser. In his earliest letters to Cowley, Burke expressed excitement about making literary acquaintances and that he hoped to capitalize on those connections. In November 1915, for instance, he wrote of his happiness that "between Wilkinson and Dreiser I shall certainly have access to the publishers I want if I ever have a book." He wrote that he was "very anxious to meet Mencken, and am going to try my best to do it" (Jay, 12). Burke's desire to use literary connections to help make his mark would continue for several years. In a September 1917 correspondence, for instance, he complains to Cowley about not being able to get his work into print: "I can continue on in the same disdainful obscurity that I lived in last year," he says, "with the one heaven-sent difference that I know now where the people are I want to meet, and can meet them if I want" (Jay, 53).

Burke's interest in literature grew when he entered college. In spring 1916 Burke spent a semester at Ohio State University, where he studied modern literature and philosophy and was introduced to the serious study of Thomas Mann and Sigmund Freud. In his short time there Burke was quite active with literary matters. He helped edit an Ohio State literary magazine, the *Sansculotte,* which published some of his work (a translation of Alfred Mombert's "Lullaby," one short piece of fiction, and ten poems). Dissatisfied with the limitations of studying at Ohio State, Burke after one semester moved back to New Jersey, intending to enroll at Columbia College, on the Upper West Side of Manhattan. After returning to the East Coast, Burke continued his readings in literature and philosophy, and seemed to be drawn more toward writing fiction than poetry (he reported frustration with getting his poems published; he also had several novels in the works).

From 1910 to 1920 Columbia was an exciting place to study. The faculty included, among other notable figures who predated Burke's matriculation in 1917, Charles Beard, Franz Boas, J. McKeen Cattell, Henry Wadsworth Longfellow Dana (Longfellow's grandson), John Dewey, Max Eastman (an instructor in philosophy, 1907–11), John Erskine, Leon Fraser, Brander Matthews, James Harvey Robinson, Joel Spingarn, and George Woodberry. Columbia also boasted students who would become well-known intellectuals. For instance, by the time Burke arrived, Randolph Bourne (a former graduate student at Columbia) lectured occasionally on campus. In 1917 the student body included Irwin Edman, Joseph Freeman, Louis Gottschalk, Louis Hacker, Matthew Josephson, Richard McKeon, and Frank Tannenbaum. Most of the excitement at Columbia centered on politics. Alive with debates about America's role in the war, the campus was a center for antiwar protest. Three professors were fired in 1917 for unpatriotic activities (Cattell, Dana, and Fraser), and Beard, in protest, resigned. Many students were involved in political debate, and on the whole the student body opposed intervention. Some students were even arrested for subversion. Despite all of this going on around him, Burke was far more interested in literature. Unfortunately, the college (and the Upper West Side of Manhattan) lacked an exciting social/literary culture. Burke was dissatisfied and sought other ways to advance his interests. He and Josephson "increasingly isolated themselves from the mainstream of student activity and focused their attention on writing."[10] Burke and Josephson also spent much of their free time with Edna St. Vincent Millay and her friends in the Village, where they immersed themselves in the literary culture they prized and experienced vicariously the bohemian lifestyle they admired.

While Burke was downtown the rich, aesthetic world of Greenwich Village offered experiences that made him question the education he was receiving uptown. In the Village, Burke spent a lot of time visiting a high school friend and his wife, who had moved from Pittsburgh. Jim and Susan Light rented a large apartment they dubbed Clemenceau Cottage because Georges Clemenceau once lived there in exile. The visits to Clemenceau Cottage gave Burke access to a social/literary culture that Columbia lacked and offered him a wide range of intellectual and aesthetic contacts. The Lights rented rooms to the poet Djuna Barnes and to the photographer Berenice Abbott. Dorothy Day, journalist and feminist, lived in the apartment downstairs. The Lights were also friendly with Eugene O'Neill and Floyd Dell, contributing editor to *The Masses*. Dell's connection with the Lights may have been an important influence on Burke. Dell was one of the first New York intellectuals to discover

Freud, and he promoted psychoanalysis to the Greenwich Village community. Visiting the Lights may also have provided another important influence on Burke. Jim Light was a member (and eventually director) of the Provincetown Players, and through him Burke became friendly with the troupe. As a note of interest, Mike Gold, who would later become the highly influential editor of *New Masses,* wrote three plays for the troupe, was friendly with Eugene O'Neill, and read Tolstoy with Dorothy Day.[11] The exciting literary culture led Burke to be "horrified at the realization of what college can do to a man of promise" (Jay, 56)—so much so that he did not plan to finish the year. "I am not going to bother preparing for the final exams," he wrote Cowley in 1918, and added further, "indeed, I shall not take them." Burke had come to feel that school was a waste of time and that learning could be more valuable on his own. "No," he told Cowley, "school is over; from now on begins my academic career, the time has come for study" (Jay, 57–58).[12]

While Burke was at Columbia and frequenting the Village, his disgust with higher education was matched by his distaste for the pretensions of the literary world he hoped to enter. Of course, his dislike of literary conventions was obvious as early as 1916 when he delivered that heretical poem to the Boar's Head. At Columbia he became highly critical of literary culture too, feeling that nepotism and aesthetic conservatism undermined literary progress. Sometime between 1917 and 1918, for instance, Burke, Cowley, and Josephson formed what they called the Anti-Logrolling Society, an informal group of three established as "a challenge to the vices of puffing and mutual admiration already manifested in the small literary world of New York." Hoping "to prevent each other from developing too much self-esteem," a problem they believed to be prevalent among the literary crowd, they planned to "ruthlessly evaluate" each other's work in order to keep themselves in line.[13] After deciding to leave Columbia, he immediately began producing his best work thus far. Within six weeks Burke was working on "The White Oxen" and was pleased with his progress, and a month later the first draft was finished (Jay, 60, 64). Eventually *The White Oxen and Other Stories* would be well received by critics.

Upon deciding to quit Columbia, Burke made a second courageous decision: "I shall get a room in New York and begin my existence as a Flaubert" (Jay, 56). While it is probably too much to say that he became a Flaubert, he did eventually get a room in Greenwich Village, moving into Clemenceau Cottage. Burke's new life, sustained principally by a poverty-line stipend from his father (given in lieu of tuition), was his strongest taste yet of the bohemian world. He shared an apartment with an actor/director, a poetess, a photographer, and an odd assortment of other characters ("two old women with beards, an idiot boy, and an Australian draft evader").[14] Burke's close friend Josephson, equally disenchanted with Columbia, often avoided the uptown dormitories and stayed overnight downtown. By moving to the Village, Burke was now steeped in bohemian culture—with its poets, novelists, artists, syndicalists, anarchists, and feminists and its coffeehouses, beer halls, and soirees. He was able to establish and maintain a great variety of literary connections. In the Village, Burke was a close friend of Cowley, Josephson, and Hart Crane, and after a few years he became friendly with, or at least knew, a great assortment of literary figures: Gorham Munson, Slater Brown, Amy Lowell, Conrad Aiken, Edna St. Vincent Millay, e.e. cummings, John Dos Passos, William Carlos Williams, Waldo Frank, Paul Rosenfeld, Van Wyck Brooks, Carl Sprinchorn, Robert McAlmon, Robert M. Coates, John Wheelwright, Allen Tate, and numerous others. Burke was also nearer to the coteries gathered around famous figures such as Max Eastman, Gertrude Vanderbilt Whitney, and Mabel Dodge. Burke's involvement with these groups was no doubt limited, but news of what went on each night among the big names spread throughout the Village by the next day.

During these years there was much social turmoil in the United States. Throughout the nation prohibition was spreading and woman suffrage was hotly debated. (The Village had long been a center for speakeasies and feminism.) But the labor movement had the most direct impact on Americans. All over the country labor disputes flared, some even sparking race riots, such as those in East Saint Louis and Houston. Shortly before Burke arrived at Ohio State in 1915, striking steelworkers in Youngstown rioted; they burned and looted the business district, causing eight hundred thousand dollars worth of damage. And in East Pittsburgh in 1917 an unsuccessful strike at a Westinghouse plant sparked rioting that forced the governor to call out the state militia. Coal miners, copper miners, petroleum workers, ironworkers, boilermakers, machinists, rail workers, shipyard workers, longshoremen, lumber workers, garment workers—men and women in all trades—demanded better pay and better working conditions (an eight-hour workday was a common demand). One labor dispute evolved into a crisis when the four railway brotherhoods went on strike, halting rail service nationwide. Fearing a nation at war becoming paralyzed, President Wilson intervened in the negotiations and publicly endorsed the brotherhoods' chief demand, an eight-hour workday. When railroad management rejected the proposal, Congress passed the Eight Hour Bill (which was soon ruled unconstitutional). Rail service was so vital to the war effort that, toward the end of 1917, Wilson placed the railroads under government control. New York was the scene of many strikes, particularly in the garment and mass transportation industries. By the end of July 1916, for instance, a strike of street railroad workers north of the city spread to New York, stopping surface and elevated lines.

As the country mobilized for war—precipitating more vocal and organized protests from socialists and pacifists—the government acted quickly to quash violent and even nonviolent dissent. On 22 July 1916, for instance, a bomb exploded during a preparedness parade in San Francisco, killing eight people and injuring forty. Tom Mooney, a radical labor leader, was eventually convicted and sentenced to death for the bombing, becoming a symbol of governmental harassment of dissidents and sparking worldwide protests (the death sentence was commuted to life imprisonment). Sometimes government harassment netted innocent persons. Prompted by the Mooney affair to investigate radical organizations, federal agents raided Industrial Workers of the World (IWW) headquarters in twenty-three cities on 5 September 1917, arresting Bill Haywood and 166 others. Many of those arrested were hardly involved in radical politics, some doing nothing more than clerical work for the IWW.[15] The government crackdown on nonviolent protest was even more disturbing. On 15 June 1917, for instance, Emma Goldman and Alexander Berkman (editor of *Blast,* an anarchist paper) were arrested for interfering with military registration and charged with violations of the Conscription Act. In a celebrated case of harassment of nonviolent dissidents, officials were disturbed by a two-hour speech delivered by Eugene V. Debs in Canton, Ohio. Although he hardly mentioned the war, he was arrested for violation of the Espionage Act, convicted, and sentenced to ten years.[16] The government did not limit its harassment to radical demonstrators, nonviolent protesters, and speech makers. In 1918 the government twice prosecuted Max Eastman, Floyd Dell, and Arthur Young, editors of *The Masses,* for publication of dissident cartoons, poems, and editorials (even though, curiously, Eastman and Dell supported the war).[17] Prosecutors in both trials charged the editors with violations of the Espionage Act and failed to secure convictions.

During this era of social and political unrest, and especially after enrolling at Columbia, Burke became more interested in politics. His earliest letters to Cowley, before Columbia, spoke mostly about literary matters, philosophical speculations, the exciting literary scene, and career objectives; however, after enrolling Burke started to write about politics, principally America's role in World War I. In May 1917, shortly after America's declaration of war against Germany, Burke wrote disparagingly about the war effort, called himself an "internationalist," claimed that the anticonscription movement was basically sincere, and suggested that the government's rationale for war was illusory. Realizing that he was being drawn to the Left, Burke at one point said, "I hope to God this war is over soon—else I may become quite rabid on these matters and all my pride of my nationality may avail me not at all" (Jay, 37). By 18 September 1917 Burke called himself "more or less" a socialist (Jay, 52).

As much as Burke was drawn to the Left, he did not go far in that direction. After the declaration of war Burke and Josephson "resolved to try to impede the American war effort" and joined the Guillotine Club, a new socialist and pacifist organization in the Village.[18] In July 1917, Josephson recalls, the Guillotine Club had just turned radical and gone underground. Their second meeting was secret, and Burke and Josephson ventured out at night to the club's well-publicized clandestine meeting, held in a beer hall. They were stopped at the door and interrogated in turn. Both of the would-be radicals were denied entrance: Burke because he refused to kill for the movement, and Josephson because he refused to accept the club's authority blindly. The two young men wandered off into the night disillusioned by the simple-mindedness of radicalism.

Burke's frustration with radicalism that night would not be unique. Throughout his life Burke argued for substantially improving American government and society; however, he always kept a distance from the more radical leftist groups. Burke often suggested that political groups seldom recognized that social, political, and economic structures develop precisely because they serve real human needs. In rejecting the political and economic structures of the status quo, radical groups are as likely to ignore the virtues of the current system as the conservatives are to deny the benefits of radical change. Both sides typically construe the situation through false dichotomies that perforce dismiss the other. For instance, as much as Burke felt great sympathy for agrarianism and disapproved of industrialism, he believed that by setting itself as the *opposite* of industrialism, agrarianism ignored the very real and necessary adjustments to modern society offered by industrialism (see, especially, *CS,* 108). And as much as Burke criticized American capitalist society, he detested the inability of socialists, communists, and radicals to see that certain capitalist structures usefully served very real needs. In Burke's view, business and private property were not all bad. Burke was particularly irritated by the stifling orthodoxy of radicalism. This is precisely the root of "bureaucratization of the imaginative," the central idea of *Attitudes.* In that book Burke argues that imaginative and creative approaches to solving social problems tend to become more rigid and less effective as they evolve into standard practices in business and political organizations. Burke's feelings toward communism were motivated in part by his distaste for orthodoxy. Though in the 1930s Burke was sympathetic to communism, he was quite suspicious of the Communist Party, approving only of the *goals* of communism, not the policies and practices of the organizations established to realize those goals.[19] In sum, during Burke's early years in New York, as much as he may have been attracted to and investigated more radical thinking, he ultimately rejected radicalism because it suffered from some of the same disturbing features from which capitalism suffered. In any event, Burke was much more interested in literature.

While the nation suffered the social and political distress of the 1920s, the avant-garde literary world was changing. When Burke first moved to New Jersey as a teenager with his family in the middle 1910s and started to frequent the Village, imagism and the poetry of Ezra Pound had already been firmly established. By the time Burke entered Columbia, Amy Lowell had succeeded Pound as the saint of imagism and many young poets were busily crafting poetic structures and rhythms around their pet images. While at Columbia, Josephson met Lowell and became something of a disciple.[20] Like many young poets (and Lowell), however, Josephson soon abandoned imagism and heeded Pound's call to follow the modern French move to pure poetry.[21] By 1919 both Cowley and Josephson were staunch advocates of French modernism. Burke had long been interested in French literature, both classical and modern, but did not heed the call, for he disapproved of Americans following the French lead. Despite being captivated by French literature, Burke held a vague distinction between being "French" and having "Frenchiness"—a difference, he said, between "Baudelaire" and the "Baudelairians" (Jay, 64). As he would later suggest with "bureaucratization of the imaginative," Burke believed that ideals are often profoundly miscast when applied at large by many people to concrete circumstances. But there was more to his rejection of the French. As much as Burke may have admired the pure poetics and sophisticated literary techniques of the modern French and believed that American culture was seriously imperiled by the lingo of journalism and advertising, he also felt that Americans should not simply adopt French values and style. "Our danger lies," he said, "not in borrowing the French, but in borrowing fatuously and injudiciously" (Jay, 64). A few years later Burke made essentially the same point when he urged Cowley to give up his interest in Dada (Jay, 131–34).

As exciting as the literary world was for Burke in his first years in New York, it was not without its frustrations. In the 1910s Burke had been a headstrong and callow amateur trying to penetrate New York's literary scene. Though considered promising by some, he had published little. And although he had managed to gain some professional experience by writing anonymous book reviews for the *New York Times* and journals, he was nonetheless an inconsequential figure. As the spring of 1919 approached, Burke became frustrated: he had trouble getting into print (in 1918 and 1919 he had only two publications), his friends had been drawn too much toward French modernism for his taste, and wartime inflation nearly doubled prices while writers' salaries rose little. Despite his marriage to Lily Batterham in May 1919, Burke had become bored and "melancholy, world-rejecting." With all his frustrations, Burke was "ravished" by the idea of living rustically. Feeling that by living as cheaply as possible he could concentrate on writing, in spring 1919 Burke moved with his wife (and one hundred dollars) far upstate to Candor, New York. Burke did live cheaply. Josephson, who visited for a week in June, told of how he and Burke "smoked out a woodchuck and Burke slew him with an axe. . . . On another occasion we made a rather crude job of trapping a big river turtle, which we consumed in the form of a soup."[22] While upstate Burke was able to overcome his melancholy and advance his literary interests. He reported reading Rémy de Gourmont and Thomas Mann, and studying Latin (Jay, 66–67).

Burke's return to the Village in fall 1919 marked his entry into the literary scene as a significant figure, for he then began association with the *Dial,* which was to become perhaps the most celebrated literary journal of the century. Prior to his association with the *Dial,* Burke had trouble getting published in part because of his interest in experimental fiction. Not only were most of the established journals run by a small, relatively close-knit group of writers and editors who were not particularly receptive to experimental work by unknowns, there were few minor journals that would publish experimental verse and prose. The *Dial* offered an outlet to writers of special talent. "An ancient and honorable name in American magazine annals," the *Dial* had a tumultuous history. The publication had been founded in Cambridge, Massachusetts, in 1840 by Ralph Waldo Emerson, Margaret Fuller, and others, and its editors had rejected commercial success in favor of maintaining high aesthetic and intellectual standards.[23] After failing financially the *Dial* had expired in 1844 but was revived in Chicago in 1880 as a competent but unimaginative review of literature. When Martyn Johnson took over the magazine in 1916, it changed "from an academic and imitative monthly to a serious critical review." In 1918 the *Dial* moved to New York and took on an editorial staff that included George Bernard Donlin, Harold Stearns, Scofield Thayer, Clarence Britten, John Dewey, Thorstein Veblen, and Helen Marot. "Under them," observes Hoffman, "*The Dial* became an organ of liberal opinion, in direct competition with *The Nation* and *The New Republic.*"[24] During Johnson's tenure the *Dial's* liberalism sought to advance American culture through the study of its literary traditions: "The Martyn Johnson *Dial* had sponsored the sort of criticism that was advanced by *The Seven Arts* group. It was a liberal criticism, a criticism that diligently explored the American literary heritage, ancient and contemporary, for its ideas, attitudes, and philosophies. It was not criticism of literature from an aesthetic or technical approach at all, but simply an estimate of American thought as revealed in literature. The purpose was to examine the national literary accumulation, to estimate it from a liberal point of view, to suggest what should be retained and what should be discarded. In short, the purpose was to discover the foundation on which to construct the American future."[25] In 1919, facing financial troubles and simply tired from trying to make the magazine successful, Johnson sold out to Scofield Thayer and Dr. James Sibley Watson Jr. The Thayer-Watson *Dial* was very different from the journal's previous incarnations. Believing that the American agenda of the *Seven Arts* had largely been met and that the future of criticism lay in better understanding how artistic expression in general differed from other forms of expression, Thayer and Watson redefined the critic's role from that of an analyst of the American literary heritage to that of an analyst of artistic structure, form, and technique. Although the new *Dial* covered several art forms, the emphasis was clearly on literature. Furthermore, Thayer and Watson broadened the critic's compass, expanding the *Dial* beyond traditional American literary forms to European poetry and prose and to experimental literature. They "labored to make their magazine an international organ which would represent and address men everywhere."[26]

Watson was to become a profound and seminal influence in Burke's life, though much about this is unclear. We do know that Watson was in large part responsible for the *Dial*'s interest in Burke as a young writer and critic. And in early 1924, when the *Dial* needed to replace an editorial assistant, Watson pressed for Burke; he said, "Please bind him with hoops if possible."[27] Four years later Watson chose the recipient of the "*Dial* Award," a prestigious honor given for distinguished service to American letters. It came with a two-thousand-dollar prize, no mean sum in the late 1920s. Previous winners had been Sherwood Anderson (1922), T. S. Eliot (1923), Van Wyck Brooks (1924), Marianne Moore (1925), e.e. cummings (1926), William Carlos Williams (1927), and Ezra Pound (1928). For the final award—the magazine ceased publication in 1929—Watson chose Burke. Watson's impact went well beyond providing Burke with an outlet and recognition; he was also a major influence on Burke's early intellectual development. Frequently contributing to his own magazine, sometimes under the pseudonym "W. C. Blum" and sometimes anonymously in the "Comments" section, Watson wrote with a scope, stance, and style that Burke emulated.[28] Burke even suggested that Watson provided him with the concept of "identification," the nucleus of *A Rhetoric of Motives.*[29] More important, throughout decades of often weekly correspondence Burke turned to Watson for intellectual inspiration, criticism, advice, and emotional and, at times, financial support. Watson also at times offered medical advice and even prescriptions. One significant indication of Watson's influence is that Burke dedicated three of his books to his mentor and friend: *The Philosophy of Literary Form* to J. S. Watson Jr., *A Rhetoric of Motives* to W. C. Blum, and *Language as Symbolic Action* to "J. Sibling W."[30]

The *Dial* was a great vehicle for Burke's fiction, especially since after his return from upstate New York he had begun to write with great vigor. By the summer of 1920 Burke had several stories in progress or recently published. In June he reported to Cowley that he was working on a trilogy that would include "The Birth of Philosophy," "The Dungeon," and "The Anatomy of Sensation"; and one month later he finished revising "The White Oxen" (Jay, 74, 75). Burke also managed to get a few more stories published. Publication of the new *Dial* began in January 1920, and one of his stories ("Mrs. Maecenas," later included in *The White Oxen,* 1924) appeared in the third number (March 1920). Burke followed this with two stories in the July number ("The Excursion," also published in *The White Oxen,* and "The Soul of Kajn Tafha"). Burke was encouraged by these successes, and in a spurt of fiction writing that would last for two years after his summer in Candor in 1919, he wrote many stories for publication in the *Dial* and other little magazines (*Little Review, Manuscripts, Secession, S₄N, Broom*) and later collected in *The White Oxen.* Burke's rustic summer helped him get over the literary paralysis of 1918 and 1919. (Burke was quite productive in later rustic retreats. When living in North Carolina during the summer of 1920 and in Maine during the spring and summer of 1921, he wrote most of the stories published in *The White Oxen.*) But being able to produce would not have mattered if the *Dial* had not provided Burke a forum for his stories.

The *Dial* was also a great vehicle for literary criticism, which toward the end of the decade Burke began to pursue more seriously. Sometime in 1919 or 1920 he started writing anonymous book reviews for the *New York Times, Export Trade,* and the *Literary Review of the New York Evening Post.* Although these reviews were not intended to be particularly sophisticated, he was glad for the assignments because they were part of the process of penetrating the literary scene and, more important, provided some income. But Burke disliked short newspaper reviews, preferring criticism that reflected his personality, ideas, and vision. This is made clear in his correspondence with Cowley from January 1921. Having impressed the editors of the *Times* with his short, anonymous reviews, Burke was given the chance to write a longer review with a byline. He reasoned that he ought to mimic the style of the *Times* to get the longer review published. "Of course, I was very careful," he told Cowley, "and wrote something which I thought was excellent *New York Times,* without a word of K. B." (Jay, 78). The review was published, but Burke was troubled when he saw his name on material not fully his own. He was glad to ape the *Times* but did not want his name associated with such pieces. "I had hoped for a lovely anonymous corner on the *Times,* where my whole concern would be with writing *New York Times,*" he said, "but I simply refuse point blank to begin crapping on my signature" (Jay, 78). Decades later, in the 1960s, the women's magazine *Mademoiselle* offered to pay Burke several thousand dollars just to use his name on an article about career choices for women. Burke refused, choosing to write the article himself, even though he was not particularly interested in doing so. Burke found the *Dial* and other literary journals in the 1920s attractive in part because he could publish literary criticism to his taste. In 1920 Burke's first review for the *Dial* appeared in the April number (a review of John Cournos's *The Mask*). Thayer and Watson liked his work and in the next few years published more of his book reviews and even some essays. The *Dial* was not Burke's only avenue. In the second half of 1920 he reviewed books by James Huneker, Waldo Frank, and Floyd Dell for the *Literary Review of the New York Evening Post.*

In the 1920s Burke's criticism quickly grew more sophisticated and comprehensive. "I am thinking," he wrote Cowley in July 1920, "of hatching up some sort of a club-article on Eliot, Williams, and Masters." His passion for criticism grew so strong that he was itching to write about certain topics. At one point Burke warned Cowley, "If you don't soon write me that you have begun your essay on Laforgue, I am going to snatch it out from under you" (Jay, 75).[31] Burke's new passion included general questions about literary theory. For a while he and Cowley had been discussing the "literary movement" they were creating, trying to pin down more precisely what they were up to. Throughout these discussions Burke generally remained less assertive than Cowley. However, by September 1920 he became more sure, declaring, "We at last have a school, a school, my friend, which lives with the throbbing of our hearts. Our school is INTEGRALISM, the emphasis of the unit, the vision of art as a succession of units, or integers. . . . By striving for essences, by attempting to fix one entire facet of approach in a few sentences, we thus attain a unit, so distinct that it almost gains complete independence of the form as a whole. These units fall together exclusively by emotional laws" (Jay, 77). Burke and Cowley were so sure of themselves and their "school" that they decided to go public and plotted to get Margaret Anderson, editor of the *Little Review,* to dedicate one issue to their "literary movement." Of course, nothing came of that.

As 1920 neared an end and the new year began, Burke started to display the sophistication of the critic people know today. In January 1921, for instance, he wrote to Cowley that he was "meditating a grand series of articles, each dealing with some phase of our great classical revolution" (Jay, 79). The first article, "Some Aspects of the Word," arguing for the "un-musicality of literature," was done. Next would be "The Logic of a New Classicism," which would chart the relations between current cultural conditions and "the former great classical wave in Europe" (Burke's rationale for drawing this analogy was a somewhat Spenglerian belief that "social and intellectual conditions are manifestations of the same underlying tendency"; see Jay, 80). It is not known if these unpublished essays were ever reworked and published, but the topics indicate more sophisticated critical interests than was previously seen in Burke. As Burke began to think more seriously about literary aesthetics, he started to see the social, political, and philosophical dimensions of art. "If I could afford it," he wrote Cowley, "I should give up belles lettres entirely and go in for a few years of niggling with pure ideas. It seems to me, for instance, that the art-process is much more interesting than any work of art, and that art seen from a philosophic standpoint begins to have more appeal than when seen from merely artistic standpoints of excellence and interest. This, certainly, is a dire confession, and probably marks my destruction as a writer of prose fiction" (Jay, 80).

Perhaps Burke's growing interest in criticism stemmed from satisfaction with his first major critical essay. "Approaches to Rémy de Gourmont," the lead article in the February 1921 *Dial,* was intended to rehabilitate de Gourmont's literature among the literary Left in New York. Burke saw the problem this way: whereas de Gourmont was ignored because he seemed to be part of the old school Burke's readers were reacting against, he was actually "one of the finest writers of his century" in part because he followed principles that were modernist ahead of their time. "My point," said Burke, "is simply to emphasize the free basis on which de Gourmont began his writing, and what opportunities it might offer to an active mentality."[32] Unfortunately, this essay has been largely overlooked by readers of Burke today. "Approaches" not only analyzes de Gourmont insightfully, but it also reveals that Burke was beginning to look at art more philosophically.

The essay is divided into four sections, each representing a different way to understand de Gourmont. Section 1 points to the two factors "which insured the liberty of his writing" (127): de Gourmont's cloistered, bookish life and the combination of three characteristics that, enigmatically, mutually reinforce each other (a profound urge to express himself, a championship of decadence, and a worship of art for art's sake). Burke uses a rough biographical sketch to show that de Gourmont's *ars gratia artis* was a natural extension of this cloistered man's decadence. Section 2 explains how de Gourmont used the technique of "dissociation" to break down assumed singular ideas into conflicting subparts creating complex ambiguities that gave his work "a cautious equilibrium." (For example, "his conception of the intelligence as a disease or an error" was balanced with "his enthusiasm over the beauty of a perfectly functioning intelligence").[33] Section 3 argues that de Gourmont's reliance on standard literary themes (such as licentiousness and blasphemy) and seeming lack of style are actually stylistic manifestations of a profoundly individual (and psychological) capacity "for treating subtly and intelligently of everything" (135). Section 4 presents an older de Gourmont in decline, his final works representing "the magnificent ruins of a great intelligence" (137). Although he realized great inspiration from his cloistered detachment from life, de Gourmont's intelligence failed, Burke argues, when the gravity of World War I undermined his detachment (de Gourmont turned to "patriotic dogmatizing"). Yet even in his decline, Burke points out, de Gourmont did not fully lose his incisiveness. Though he no longer built contradictions through dissociation, he at least always qualified his partisan views. Contradiction, says Burke, became "modification."

"Approaches" is a subtle and complex essay. Wanting to stake out a place for de Gourmont in the hostile 1920s, Burke shows that he actually has much in common—intellectually and aesthetically—with those who ignore or disdain him. de Gourmont was a passionate decadent, and decadence was spiritually at one with the bohemian credo. Moreover, de Gourmont tried to undermine the most essential and stable conceptions basic to his culture. By showing de Gourmont to be a masterful technician, Burke suggests that de Gourmont was as interested in literary technique as were the modernists in the 1920s. Each section of the essay was probably enough to win the day, yet Burke decided to present all three. Offering several "approaches" instead of affirming one single "truth" is not only an adaptation to a multiform audience, but a demonstration of Burke's belief in a multiplicity of views—an important component of sophisticated bohemian culture. Yet in "Approaches," Burke does much more than simply stake out a place for a neglected author; he diagnoses a contemporary malaise and prescribes a corrective. The fourth section, in contrast to the excited appreciation of the other three, portrays a literary mind wracked by political concerns. The problem is not, Burke claims, that de Gourmont had political interests; rather, in the face of political crisis de Gourmont sublimated his creative spirit. Consequently, he lost the very characteristic that enriched his literature profoundly. Burke is not suggesting that literature is superior to politics or necessarily sullied by it. He is saying that literary concerns and politics mix well until political concerns overwhelm aesthetics. Simply put, one can go too far. This point is reinforced by Burke's inclusion of section 4 with the other three. The last section, after all, is not simply an addendum that concludes the biography, but another "approach" to Rémy de Gourmont.

The essay on de Gourmont is a powerful cautionary tale. For one thing, Burke may even be suggesting that de Gourmont's later aesthetic shortcomings were a *natural* development that men and women of intellect must resist. Notice that Burke incorporates two developmental patterns. First, there is the roughly chronological biography from early life to too much life and then death. This is matched with a historical parallel: antecedents of decadence, decadence in its prime, then decline. A second developmental pattern follows the classical rhetorical stases, questions used to locate the essence of a dispute. The first stasis— "Does it exist?"—is answered by positing the existence of a decadent fever of innovation. For the second stasis—"What do you call it?"—Burke answers, "dissociation." For the third stasis—"Of what sort is it?"—Burke suggests the style using "*just* values and *exact* appellations." And for the fourth stasis—"Is this the right forum for judgment?"—he shows that politics is good until it intrudes too far into aesthetics. Without making too much of the existence of this pattern, the point overall is simply that Burke uses developmental patterns cleverly to establish that a life that connects art to living has characteristics and tendencies that may not readily be seen. For Burke, a *meaningful* literary life—even when detached, as for de Gourmont—contains the ingredients of its own destruction. If aesthetic ruin is built into the process of creativity and is even a natural outcome of living an aesthetic life, Burke is warning his contemporary modernists that they may end up in ideological and aesthetic collapse despite their hopeful pretensions otherwise. Still, de Gourmont's life is a tale of redemption. Perhaps because he was a great writer he did not yield fully to his own tragic flaw. He may have been unable or unwilling at the end of his life to point out such penetrating contradictions, but he still qualified his patriotic beliefs. Moreover, as Burke indicates near the end of section 4, perhaps de Gourmont's later excesses were but a *temporary* adjustment to prevailing circumstances. There is evidence, Burke suggests, that de Gourmont might have transcended his faults had he outlived the war. There is the question of whether Burke also believed the danger to be even greater for his contemporaries because most of them simply were not great artists. In the essay on Flaubert, Burke distinguishes between those who are admitted after knocking on the door and those who are not. Burke's charge to his contemporaries is clear: Follow your current course and literature is lost. Learn from de Gourmont and maintain that cautious equilibrium. Learn that literature and politics mix only so far—but if they do not mix correctly, at least we each have the ability within to reestablish equilibrium.

In the first half of 1921 Burke published "Approaches to Rémy de Gourmont" and a few book reviews for the *Literary Review of the New York Evening Post,* the *Dial,* and the *Freeman.* He did not publish a single story or poem. While it might seem that he gave up belles lettres, he in fact did not. Within three months of telling Cowley that he might switch to criticism, Burke moved to Monson, Maine, to spend the late spring and summer concentrating on his short stories. He told Cowley that fiction is "what I am trying to write, and what I put most into" (Jay, 86). And write he did. By the end of that fertile summer Burke had written ten stories that he later published in little magazines and then collected in *The White Oxen.* However, Burke worked so hard on the stories that by the end of the summer he was exhausted and thought he might return to criticism. Criticism was appealing because Burke realized that fiction would not provide the kind of income he would need after returning to New York City in the fall. "Already I have begun getting my hack in shape," he wrote Cowley from Maine (Jay, 99). Burke set to work on some authors he had long admired and studied: Thomas Mann, André Gide, Gustave Flaubert, and Walter Pater (Jay, 99, 102–3).[34] His new efforts resulted in two essays that have been largely overlooked by scholars. This is unfortunate, for not only are the essays insightful about their subjects, they reveal a lot about Burke's assessment of his literary milieu as well. The essays were written in the summer and fall of 1921 and concern Flaubert and Pater.[35] Burke's interest in Flaubert was especially strong. "*Dial* or no *Dial,*" he told Cowley, "I must write on Our Flaubertian Inheritance" (Jay, 99). Burke wanted to write about Flaubert, whom he called a "critical" artist, in order to "show how the art-to-conceal-art aesthetics is so poorly fitted to his type of accomplishment. The reason for this is that the concern with processes is the most vital phase of the critical artist, whereas the art-to-conceal-art aesthetics demands a complete covering of the tracks of these processes" (Jay, 99). Burke published "The Correspondence of Flaubert" in the February 1922 *Dial*.

Like "Approaches," "Flaubert" is as much about Burke's literary milieu as about its ostensible subject. This becomes clearer as the essay progresses, but the earlier sections, which may seem merely background about Flaubert's life, are central to Burke's point. The essay begins with a description of Flaubert's disgust upon finding out that Balzac was interested in literature solely "to procure for him some considerable social station, to make him a Parisian celebrity."[36] Flaubert, Burke observes, "was certainly one of the *tour d'ivoire* school of writers" who believed that "art was not something to pick up and lay down . . . it was something to live in" (147). Burke goes on to describe how Flaubert displayed in his adolescence a precocious and passionate exultation of pure aesthetics. But before Burke gives his catalog of six features of Flaubert's *tour d'ivoire* adolescence, he makes a telling remark. "Flaubert at eighteen," he says, "had all the earmarks of a promising young genius in revolt against Ohio, destined to come to New York and get a job with some advertising agency" (148). The reference, of course, is to the litterateurs who loaded onto buses and trains for Greenwich Village, starry-eyed and idealistic, most of whom failed as fiction writers or at least could not make a go of it without supplemental income. "This may not be the adolescence of everyone," Burke says, "but it is certainly the adolescence both of those who knock and are admitted and of those who knock and are not admitted" (149). The reference to Village bohemians of the 1920s is unmistakable, and Burke strengthens it by mentioning the outrage caused by Flaubert's treatment of political issues and the charges of obscenity and paganism against him. This is clearly a reference to the outrage, aesthetic and moral, caused by the great offenders of the 1920s, the bohemians.

As in the essay on de Gourmont, Burke uses his subject to caution literary modernists of dangers inherent in their approach to life and art. This time biography enters through the correspondence of Flaubert's youth. "The most striking implication of the letters with respect to his art-methods," Burke argues, "is that his emotions are paralyzed by his intelligence" (151). In other words, "it is simply that he was trying by the exercises of processes which were primarily intellectual to write under an aesthetic whose processes were primarily intuitive" (152). If Burke wanted merely to say that intuitive writing is undermined by modernist technique, he need not have used Flaubert to point this out. But writing of Flaubert gave him an occasion to mention *specific* emotions. Burke's peculiar catalog of Flaubert's adolescent responses to the world reflects aesthetic excesses among literary modernists. "The cult of the illicit" is not merely a reference to the forbidden in general, but a reference to the particular improprieties of the Villagers—and so on with "the cynicism of analysis," "diffusion, frustration, renunciation," "exuberance of conceptions, intoxication of talk, love of plenitude," "escape," and "insanity" (148). Burke is referring more to his contemporaries than to Flaubert. The problem Burke notices is far more important than a disparity between the aesthetic of one literary genius and his methods. Flaubert, like many bohemians of Burke's day, led an emotionally vital life at odds with the aesthetic demands of his method. "The final testimony of the letters," says Burke, "seems to be that Flaubert never succeeded in arriving at an aesthetic amenable to his temperament" (150). Burke is thus arguing by analogy that the 1920s bohemian lifestyle could draw one into, and inure one to, a perspective that was antithetical to modernist aesthetics. By starting analytically with, and focusing predominantly on, the *correspondence* of Flaubert, Burke frames the mismatch between creativity and method with distinctly nonaesthetic elements, giving the argument a political flavor. In a way, "Approaches to Rémy de Gourmont" and "The Correspondence of Flaubert" make the same point. Both Flaubert and de Gourmont failed, Burke argues, because they subscribed too fully to a cult of technique: de Gourmont could not modify his aesthetic when he lost the detachment necessary for it to succeed; Flaubert never had sufficient detachment in the first place. Flaubert never had his aesthetic in the first place. Burke is suggesting that when technique or process becomes so refined, an artist so technically able, and the technical imperative so strong, technical achievements may supplant communication as the motive force behind art. Commenting on "Correspondence" two years after it was published, Burke made a point that seems to characterize both essays: "I plead that the artist, immersed in his subject matter, finally shoots over the top—that of a sudden things which had been tools suddenly become aims" (Jay, 158). In the cases of de Gourmont and Flaubert, this misdirection was not merely an abstract academic problem; it found its source in the personality and lived experience of the authors.

"Notes on Walter Pater" is neither as sophisticated nor as developed as the essays on de Gourmont and Flaubert. The title aptly suggests its contents: six sections, ranging in length from one-half page to two pages, each briefly sketching some aspect of Pater's aesthetic and together resulting in one loose argument. Burke suggests that whereas de Gourmont and Flaubert ultimately failed, Pater succeeded. Burke begins by observing that "man, once he became man, has remained a constant, 'progress' being a mere change of emphasis, a stressing of some new phase of this constant" (53). Pater, a "deeply contemporaneous" artist, "assumes a certain lasting value in that he has touched the constant of humanity" (53). Burke shows keen interest in how Pater conveys the "resolution of his times." He finds in Pater a style that is "delicate," "tentative," "leisurely"—a focus on overtone rather than tone. This delicacy and interest in overtone are precisely Pater's successes, which the modernists of Burke's day did not achieve. The modernists, Burke argues in "Approaches" and "Correspondence," did not match aesthetic intent with aesthetic practice. In contrast, Pater's art "is a perfect co-ordination between impetus and execution" (53). Pater also desired to speak about contemporary problems and wrote with a highly refined technique ("he wrote . . . as a scholar, interested vitally in the mechanism of his sentences, using words with a greater philological accuracy" [55]). Unlike Burke's contemporaries, Pater exhibits balance between intent and practice; he was not interested in particulars for themselves but as "correlations with the general"—as relations to "the culture and traditions of whole peoples" (56). This is the first point that Burke directly addresses specific contemporary problems. He mentions woman suffrage, the forty-four-hour work week, and starting a traction company in Idaho. Pater, Burke suggests, is a better modernist than the 1920s avant-garde because he transcends the immediate political situation by correlating contemporary problems with "constants of humanity" and has a technique that best suits such a transcendence. In a way, Burke argues, Pater's match of impetus to execution transforms literature so that ideology becomes neither the starting point nor the end of literature; it becomes the *means* of literature. According to Burke, "it was this same love of the overtone which gave Pater's use of ideology its flavor of beauty, rather than of argument. For he treated ideas not as something to convince, or to startle, but as horizons, or skillful situations, or developments of plot, in short, as any other legitimate element of fiction" (57). That is Pater's power as a writer. And that, Burke says, is what Pater can teach contemporary literary modernists.

"Approaches to Rémy de Gourmont," "The Correspondence of Flaubert," and "Notes on Walter Pater" constitute a tremendous critical debut. But these works were just those parts of his critical turn in 1921 that made it to the public. Burke also devoted more serious thought to important questions about the nature and function of criticism than he had for a while. The range and depth of his thinking is impressive, if not startling. For instance, disturbed by a symposium on "The Function of Criticism" in the *New Republic,* Burke complained to Cowley that it was a "general rehashing of impressionism; absolutely not a word of aesthetics" (Jay, 102). Modern literary criticism was deficient, he felt, because the critics were not saying anything valuable about criticism itself. To fill the vacuum, Burke was "planning an inventory of literary currents, to take up such things as realism, romanticism, decadism one by one and maintain their bankruptcy" (Jay, 102). Burke became interested in philosophical aspects of criticism too. For instance, his interest was piqued by whether art or aesthetics comes first (a question that de Gourmont raised). Burke also pondered over such matters as the distinction between the relative and the absolute, and the relation of literature and criticism to ideology. After complaining about vagueness in literature, Burke excitedly told Cowley that he had come to a realization that "the *means* of literature is ideological clarity" (Jay, 103). This sentiment was echoed a few years later in a review of V. F. Calverton's *The Sociological Imagination,* in which Burke argued against "causation" theories of literature.[37] Causation is Burke's rubric for Marxist literary criticism. He pointed out that for Marxists, one "means" of ideology is literature.

Burke's turn to criticism was marked by two important characteristics. First, he began to consider finer points of aesthetic theory. Previously he had largely spoken of broad trends and general relations (for example, that current critics were too impressionistic). With the essays on de Gourmont, Flaubert, and Pater he began to develop specific, detailed aspects of literary aesthetics. For instance, in "Correspondence," Burke explored how technique fits aesthetic vision. More significantly, Burke posited a specific philosophical basis for aesthetics. He had already come to believe that the Absolute and the Relative lie at the center of aesthetics. In "Pater," Burke commended him for "having really penetrated the implications of Relativism" (58). Such themes came to a head in a letter to Cowley, dated 30 October 1921, in which Burke suggested that "form" could be the root of an aesthetic: "As to the old ideal of the welding of form and matter, it is linked with the search for the Absolute. The search for the Relative involves the triumph of form over matter, for it is relations which always give matter a new complexion. Thus, we accept this much as axiomatic: Art in the deepest sense is always contemporaneous, that is, parallels the general complexion of the times. . . . Accepting that much as axiomatic, we must accept the triumph of form over matter as the channel of art" (Jay, 103). A commitment to form as the basis for art shifted the philosophical foundation of aesthetics from metaphysics to the philosophy of history. Burke mentioned Spengler's philosophy of history as a possible basis for a new aesthetics. But it would be wrong to call Burke a Spenglerian. He may have adopted a Spenglerian perspective in the loosest sense, by seeing developmental patterns in history, but the similarity does not go far. This is evidenced by Burke's non-Spenglerian dissatisfaction with a few of his stories: "a work of art is that which becomes something else, but [*sic*] natural, rather than logical, progression. (. . . There is nothing *logical,* for instance, in a pod following a blossom, or a fever following germs in the intestines. Yet the art processes should evolve in just this way.) This same principle of something becoming something else would be reproduced in both the broad outlines of the story, the layout of the subdivisions, the paragraph—and ideally, I suppose, even the sentence" (Jay, 90–91). Burke would soon see even deeper problems with Spengler. His 1926 review of *The Decline of the West* would be rather critical of Spengler's "cultural subjectivism and aesthetic defeatism" and the implication that modern art is inferior to art of previous cultures.[38]

The second important characteristic of Burke's turn toward criticism is the development of a particular rhetorical strategy for appealing to an audience that might otherwise reject his attack upon them. It is no coincidence that each of the three essays analyzes a particular literary figure in order to address more general contemporary literary problems. "Why don't you, by the way, adopt my system of propaganda?" Burke wrote Cowley. "That is, hitching one's theses to the name of accepted past writers. People who will turn aside from a general article will read something on a specific man, especially if it has a few dates thrown in, and the name of his mistress. I find the thing working out very satisfactorily" (Jay, 112). One should keep in mind that, as much as Burke made a great critical turn in 1921 with the essays on de Gourmont, Flaubert, and Pater, and by speculating about the nature and function of criticism, he did not abandon fiction or principally become a critic. As was pointed out earlier, Burke at this time was writing several stories, which he did for more than just pleasure. He longed to publish in the right places. In May 1921 Burke complained to Cowley that Williams wanted only his criticism and poetry for *Contact*. Worse yet, the *Dial* also ignored his fiction. Burke was especially interested in placing a story in *Contact*, "both because I should like to see it appear there and because I should like to slobber on that bastard buttock-licking *Dial,* so that they would be properly bullied into taking some of the stories I shall write this summer" (Jay, 86).

At this time Burke was avidly cultivating literary contacts. For instance, as early as January 1921, largely because his reviews for the *Dial* had made him more visible, Burke spent an afternoon in the country with William Carlos Williams (Josephson and Robert McAlmon were present as well).[39] Burke made a good impression on Williams, which, in combination with the appearance of "Approaches" soon after, certainly had something to do with Williams's publication of Burke's work in *Contact,* the magazine started in 1920 by Williams and McAlmon and edited by them. In May 1921, just a few months after that meeting, Williams accepted one of Burke's essays for publication and intended to run a poem as well.[40] Williams, by the way, was a good friend of Margaret Anderson. Shortly after Burke met Williams, Anderson published one of Burke's stories, "David Wasserman," in the *Little Review* (Autumn 1921), and a year later another was published there.[41] At about the same time, in May 1921, Burke was also sought out by Paul Rosenfeld, who "came around the other day to ask me to contribute to a sort of pamphlet-magazine, to be my own editor, and to associate with Rosenfeld, Waldo Frank, and

Sherwood Anderson" (Jay, 79). Burke was rather surprised by Rosenfeld's proposal, for Rosenfeld, Frank, and Anderson were key members of the *Seven Arts* group that Burke and his friends had disliked. Nonetheless, Burke submitted a short story, "Olympians," which was published in the first issue of *Manuscripts* (February 1922), a short-lived and irregular magazine that was edited and published by its contributors, and which featured work by Williams, Frank, Burke, and others (that issue printed another short story by Burke, "Scherzando").[42]

The creative momentum Burke achieved in 1921 grew in 1922. In just one year Burke published seven pieces of fiction (in *Secession, Manuscripts,* the *Little Review,* and S_4N), three poems (in *Contact, Secession,* and S_4N), three essays (in the *Dial,* the *Freeman,* and the *Literary Review*),[43] ten book reviews with bylines (in the *New York Times Book Review,* the *Dial,* the *Freeman,* and *Vanity Fair*), and four translations (including, with Scofield Thayer, part of Thomas Mann's "Tristan" in the *Dial*). It is true that most, if not all, of the stories were written in the previous year, as was the major critical essay (the other two were quite short).[44] Even so, Burke had a lot of creative energy that went into editing and critical speculations. By January 1923, he reported, most of his time was spent editing (Jay, 133).

It is hard to say with certainty why Burke turned to criticism, but some reasonable guesses can be made. First, Burke was not optimistic about his career as a fiction writer ("I may as well decide for good and all," he wrote Cowley, "that my stories are doomed" [Jay, 79]). Second, this was a period in which Burke, like many of his literary friends, searched for a literary voice. In fact, his once fairly cohesive circle of like-minded writers began to break up. One fracture line developed because many of Burke's contemporaries had moved to Paris and other literary centers in Europe. Burke stayed in America, out of touch with the literary scene across the ocean. As these temporary expatriates became acquainted with European letters, they were seduced by surrealism and Dada, movements that left Burke cold.[45] Third, Burke's literary colleagues began to form their own alliances, setting divergent agendas that created factions and initiated heated squabbles. Burke did not like this at all. But perhaps the main reason for the change was that Burke became an associate editor for *Secession* and developed a closer relationship with the *Dial*. Despite the fact that it lasted only two years (eight issues) and had a low circulation of only 500 copies per number (including 350 distributed gratis), *Secession* was enormously influential on the literary scene.[46] Each of the first three issues was reviewed at length by the *Nation,* the *Dial,* the *Double Dealer,* the *Little Review,* the *Nation and Athenaeum,* the *New York Times,* and the *Criterion*. Burke got involved with *Secession* because it presented a unique opportunity both to gain exposure and to advance the kind of literature he admired (Burke said that he even felt a "responsibility" to work there). He did get some exposure: in little more than a year *Secession* published four of his stories and one of his poems. Even so, Burke was hired chiefly for his critical skills as an editor.

The genesis of *Secession* illustrates the kinds of problems Burke struggled with in the early 1920s. *Secession* emerged because the time was right. But if its origin were traced to specific acts by specific people, Malcolm Cowley, Gorham Munson, and Matthew Josephson were responsible for its creation.[47] For some time Cowley had been saying that a few young writers opposed to both orthodox literary traditions and the aesthetics of Theodore Dreiser and H. L. Mencken were on the verge of creating a new literary movement. Toward the end of 1921, with Slater Brown, Kenneth Burke, e.e. cummings, Foster Damon, and John Dos Passos achieving some success, Cowley was even surer that the dawn of a new literary movement was imminent. But the movement remained inchoate. These young writers were still largely unknown and had difficulty getting into print. With this in mind, Cowley fashioned a manifesto for this "Youngest Generation," proclaiming in the *Literary Review of the New York Evening Post* that a new generation of young writers had arrived.[48] This new generation was opposed to orthodox literary traditions, was left cold by the "enthusiasms" and controversies inspiring established writers, and was interested in modern French literature (especially Flaubert and de Gourmont), literary form, simplification, and experiment.[49] As much as he was able to draw these similarities, Cowley did admit that this movement lacked "an organized body of opinion" and "solidarity" because it was emerging through the efforts of like-minded writers, working individually, who followed the same general "habits of thought." The movement, he felt, needed some kind of focal point so that it might jell and mature. A literary magazine such as *Secession* could be the voice of this Youngest Generation.

In the "Fledgling Years," Gorham Munson says that Cowley's article brought "to a sharp focus" his own ideas for an alternative to the kinds of little magazines then prevalent.[50] Munson conceived *Secession* as a forum for the literature and criticism of these young experimentalists, but it was also to be managed differently than most other literary journals. Finding "personal" magazines (those run by demagogic editors, such as the *Little Review*) too aggressive and intellectually idiosyncratic, and finding "anthological" magazines far too indiscriminate and injudicious in their magazine mentality, Munson ran *Secession* by editorial committee. *Secession* was intended to last only a couple of years and ran only from spring 1922 to April 1924. It was edited by Munson the entire time, with Josephson coediting from August 1922 to January 1923 and Burke from January 1923 through September 1923. From the start, Munson's influence on *Secession* was pervasive. He established its mission, determined who and what would appear in the magazine, and chose his coeditors. His most important deviations from Cowley's sketch were the inclusion of other important young writers in the Youngest Generation and the expansion of the magazine's interests to include Dada and other modern French writers (Munson's Youngest Generation also included Donald B. Clark, Cowley, Hart Crane, Waldo Frank, Matthew Josephson, Marianne Moore, Wallace Stevens, Mark Turbyfill, W. C. Williams, and Yvor Winters; his French writers included "certain allied Frenchmen, Guillaume Apollinaire, Louis Aragon, André Breton, Paul Eluard, Philippe Soupault, and Tristan Tzara").[51] Munson was also chiefly responsible for wooing Burke to the staff. After adding Josephson as an editor, Munson realized he needed a third editor not only to get the work done, but also to give him a tie-breaking advantage over Josephson in editorial decisions. His first choice was Burke, who joined *Secession* as an editor for the fourth number, with editorial duties commencing half a year before his first issue.[52] *Secession* may not have been as purely group driven as Munson envisioned, but it seems to have been significantly different from other literary journals of the time.

Secession offered Burke great opportunities, both intellectually and professionally. Yet from the start Burke had an uneasy relationship with this new and broad-minded journal. Long before *Secession* appeared, Burke had strong reservations about Munson's influence. "I have my doubts," he told Cowley, because "people are asses, to speak of getting out a magazine with Tristan Tzara and Malcolm Cowley, as though the two were quite synonymous" (Jay, 79). Burke echoed this feeling a year and a half later when he said that he was "long and stubborn about going into *Secession,* because for some reason or other [he] felt it as a responsibility." Burke did not want "to be connected with just one more piddling paper" (Jay, 125). Uncomfortable with what the magazine was doing, Burke sought to redirect its mission. When Munson first approached Burke about joining as an editor, Josephson recalls that Burke "would have no part in our Dadaist experiments or in our proposed exegesis of the Machine Age. . . . Burke was hell-bent on leading American literature and criticism back to the true path of Spinoza and Goethe, his literary idols of the moment."[53] Burke did, however, sign on, telling Cowley privately that he wanted to turn Munson's yapping into a toothy bite. "What do you think of a pamphleteering drive on the various New York critical diseases, a dogging of the liberals?" he asked Cowley. "Or, over against this, are you for a magazine of pure letters, without polemic . . . ?" (Jay, 124).

Polemic was important to Burke, but he was interested only in the right kind of polemic. *Secession,* unfortunately, cultivated improvident disputes. First, Munson aimed his gun at the wrong targets. In the early issues he unwisely derided several contemporary writers, critics, and little magazines, particularly the *Dial,* for not departing far enough or vigorously enough from American literary traditions. Regardless of the validity of his criticisms, the *Secession* writers remained powerless upstarts. Even before Burke signed on, he felt compelled to disavow the "anti-*Dial* stuff " to Gilbert Seldes, then an associate editor of the *Dial* (Jay, 119). Second, *Secession* caused rifts and infighting among Burke's friends. For example, disagreements between Munson and Josephson arose at the start, which in part prompted Munson to add Burke to the staff, hoping for good advice and a rubber stamp. Munson's plan notwithstanding, Burke questioned his literary tastes and intellectual abilities, and thus he was not a yes-man. Tensions between Munson and Josephson came to a head when Josephson altered an issue against Munson's wishes. Then in January 1923 Josephson left *Secession* for *Broom,* where Cowley was an associate editor. Cowley played an interesting role in *Secession.* He was never officially connected with the magazine, but behind the scenes and unbeknownst to Munson he helped Josephson and Burke edit the magazine. Although reports conflict, soon after Josephson left *Secession* he and Cowley altered the fifth number of *Secession* after Burke and Munson had sent it to the printer. These squabbles infected the Youngest Generation until the group fractured according to individual members' affiliations with either *Secession* or *Broom.* The problem got so bad that a fall 1923 meeting of the two factions, intended to settle differences, ended up making tensions worse—leading eventually to a fistfight between Munson and Josephson. Though Burke seems to have remained somewhat distant from these disputes, refusing to ally himself explicitly with any faction, the conflicts took their toll. He remained with *Secession* less than one year, leaving Munson to produce the final two issues alone.[54]

As Burke became disillusioned with *Secession,* literary wrangling, and his Francophile friends, his relationship with the *Dial* grew stronger. In May 1922 he wrote to Cowley that he, Watson, and Seldes had "worked out the details of " his joining the *Dial* as an assistant editor, temporarily replacing Sophie Wittenberg from July until November (Jay, 119). As matters turned out, Burke did not replace Wittenberg until March 1924, when she left the *Dial* upon marrying Lewis Mumford. Burke's editorial relationship with the *Dial* before March 1924 is not fully clear. Though he had no official place in their offices in 1923, he did work for Thayer and Watson. Several of Burke's 1923 letters to Cowley, the earliest dated 18 January, include headings from the *Dial* offices. Moreover, *The Time of the Dial* contains a 21 February 1923 letter from the "Editorial Department" of the *Dial* signed by Burke. Also printed is a 1 March 1923 letter from Paul Strand to "Mr Kenneth Burke, Editorial Department, The Dial." Even after he became an assistant editor in 1924, his work for the *Dial* was "spasmodic" until 1927.[55]

During this period Burke's ideas about art began to take form. For one thing, he began to conflate art and criticism. He suggested, for instance, that "a marked critical tendency will be found in any of our significant writers" (Jay, 112). Burke began to reject the idea that criticism was just the study of literature, realizing that criticism was necessarily part of art. Burke thought that to produce good literature an artist needs a substantial critical sensibility and should integrate critically derived elements into his or her artwork. According to Burke, "this critical tendency must necessarily manifest itself in a more or less carefully elaborated aesthetic programme" (Jay, 112). Burke's conflation of art and criticism, however, neither abolished the distinction between art and criticism nor reduced one to the other; rather, he suggested that the goals and methods of art and criticism *overlap*. It could be said that Burke's work in the early 1920s was a struggle to define the meaning of the overlap, to determine its scope, and to assess its impact on other disciplines. In the early 1920s Burke also began to recognize the powerful influence of communication on artistic production. He long held, as did many others, the unremarkable idea that art is a special kind of activity that by its very nature puts special demands on the artist. But as early as February 1922, unlike many of his young contemporaries, Burke began to specify that quality and consider the demands it puts on the artist. First, he came to see the sociological aspects of the artist's ability to communicate. Aesthetic appreciation, Burke argued, is not widespread. Nor does society have a single, stable, communal aesthetic. To make matters worse, only a few people have natural talent for aesthetic appreciation, and only some of the rest could be taught to achieve it; the great majority of people, Burke said, are "unsensitive to aesthetic values."[56] "Art," he believed, "is the possession of the initiated" (Jay, 111). Burke was even pessimistic about his own chances of gaining wide influence. "The public is stupid," he told Cowley; "if one is successful there is something wrong" (Jay, 122). If the audience is difficult to reach, the artist's message makes matters worse. Burke believed that good works of art invent new aesthetics. By its nature, art engineers its own frustration.

According to Burke, the critic needs to be profoundly sensitive to current intellectual, social, and cultural conditions. In May 1922, in a letter to Cowley, Burke explained that the critic must tailor his argument to the audience. After commenting that he detested Paul Rosenfeld, thought *Vanity Fair* "a symbol of smart nonsense," "clamored against" Waldo Frank, and rejected Van Wyck Brooks's praises, Burke wondered whether his own critical strategies needed reassessment: "Just what one should do I do not know. One must not toady; and on the other hand one must not cut off his revenues with an unnecessary vandalism. My solution is to attempt a more constructive type of criticism, not merely to attack the existing, but to build up a counter-structure. Of course, we have always done this to a degree. My method now would be to minimize the attack and emphasize the counter-structure. Thus, I do not modify my attitude, but modify my method. Tell me, is this lousy opportunizing? I do not think so. The important thing is to round out one's own conception of intellectual excellence, to develop a consistent and synthetic system of approach. This can be done without growling" (Jay, 119). Of course, being sensitive to current conditions means more than simply figuring out how to say what you

Criticism stems from rhetoric

want to say without losing your job. It also involves speaking *for* your society. In addition to being troubled by American politics, Burke became concerned about other factors that affect Americans' basic attitudes. For instance, he complained about "the *complacent* superficiality" of "our contemporary journalists," a reference to a pathology that he feared was infecting the general population (Jay, 127). He also complained that Americans lacked a "richness in certain specific emotions. . . . the richness which makes for peasants, household gods, traditions" (Jay, 131). Burke even wondered whether there were any "'promise' . . . in America," believing that persons such as Van Wyck Brooks (as opposed to Josephson) showed promise because they "get more pleasure out of being right than out of carrying an issue" (Jay, 133).

As Burke was in the process of placing communication and criticism at the center of aesthetics, he latched onto the idea of "rhetoric." Though it makes sense, this comes as a surprise because Burke seldom used the word before and certainly not as a basic principle of aesthetics. Moreover, "rhetoric" was hardly a term common to the intellectual world of the 1920s in general or Burke's literary crowd in particular. Rhetoric seems to enter aesthetics through its relations with criticism. "Do you know," he asked Cowley, "that criticism is a subdivision, not of dialectics, but of rhetoric? By which I mean that we must all vituperate and deify, and the one with the cleverest tricks wins. For there is no ultimate element on which a critical system can be based" (Jay, 112). In this February 1922 letter Burke spoke of rhetoric generally, with no inkling of any particular rhetorical theory. At the time Burke was working on an essay titled "The Priority of Forms" and arguing that form is prior to matter and "bring[s] out the best possibilities of matter" (Jay, 113). However, Burke was careful to eschew universal notions of forms, especially Platonic ideals, for he did not want to ground art in metaphysics. "I emphasize," he said, "that my aesthetics is not metaphysical, but psychological." Burke told Cowley that, unlike Dostoyevsky, "I situate the psychology in the forms" (Jay, 114). There is a danger in making too much out of these spare comments, but there is in fact an important difference between "form" in this discussion and the way he talked about it in October 1921. In the 1921 letter Burke argued for "the triumph of form over matter as the channel of art" (Jay, 103). In both discussions "form" meant basically the same thing—a channel for art—but Burke introduced the term for different reasons. The idea of form entered the 1921 discussion because, in contemplating the possibility of a priori art, Burke was led to the Absolute and the Relative: "As to the old ideal of the welding of form and matter, it is linked with the search for the Absolute. The search for the Relative involves the triumph of form over matter, for it is relations which always give matter a new complexion. Thus, we accept this much as axiomatic: Art in the deepest sense is always contemporaneous, that is, parallels the general complexion of the times" (Jay, 103). Burke believed that being "contemporaneous" meant seeking the Relative, wherein form triumphs as the channel of art. And at that point in his life Burke thought that the relative/contemporaneous foundation of aesthetics might be a Spenglerian philosophy of history. When he discussed rhetoric in 1922, form arose because communication became a central problem when art and criticism were conflated. From 1921 to 1922 Burke shifted from an abstract, philosophical point of view to a more sociological perspective. That may be why form at first led Burke to philosophy, whereas later form led to social functions such as those in drama: "We must, perhaps, assign to criticism a two-fold purpose. Technically, it is a guardian of the forms; and also, it fights the old battles of subject matter. It worries over the possibility of categorical judgments, of whether philosophical subject matter for instance, is categorically superior to farce, so that the acme of philosopher-poet would be superior to the acme of farce-writer" (Jay, 114). In any event, Burke's turn to rhetoric makes sense. He hoped that art would be oppositional or even polemical. Therefore, a theory of art probably ought to be based on concepts arising out of controversy, dispute, faction, and difference. Rhetoric fit beautifully.

Despite the natural affiliation between rhetoric and Burke's purposes, it also seems quite obvious that Burke's literary milieu greatly influenced his interest in the relationship between rhetoric and aesthetics. The differences between the *ars gratia artis* crowd and the young modernists, the problems Burke had getting published, the wrangles centering around the *Seven Arts* group, the tensions that developed between *Secession* and *Broom,* dissension within the *Secession* group—all occurring in an era of social turmoil and censorship—made rhetoric seem to be a sensible basis for aesthetics.

Rhetoric was Burke's most important discovery, for it occupied his mind for the next half-century, impressing its indelible mark, directly and indirectly, on all his criticism. Burke took a long time to discover rhetoric and even longer to embrace it fully. When he discovered rhetoric after seven years on the New York literary scene, rhetoric was but a vague notion. Just three years later (1924) that vague idea had become more distinct, for Burke had written his first essays featuring a rhetorical perspective, "Psychology and Form" and "The Poetic Process."[57] Even in those Burke was tentative about rhetoric: though a rhetorical perspective pervades them, the term "rhetoric" only appears once in "The Poetic Process" and never in "Psychology and Form," the more important of the two.[58] Actually, Burke was unsure about "Psychology and Form." Writing to Alyse Gregory in late 1924, he admitted that he was "tremendously indebted to The Dial" for accepting the essay for publication. "Had you refused it," Burke revealed, "I should not even have tried to place it elsewhere."[59] By the time Burke was finishing *Counter-Statement* in spring 1931, he was surer about rhetoric. Its role in "Lexicon Rhetoricae," an extension of "Psychology and Form" and "The Poetic Process," cannot be overemphasized. Moreover, "Applications of the Terminology," the final essay of the 1931 edition, ends with a two-page discussion of rhetoric.[60] Leaving the reader of *Counter-Statement* with rhetoric as a final thought was no accident. As Burke moved on to *Permanence* and *Attitudes,* rhetoric played an even greater role.[61]

Burke never developed a systematic rhetorical theory, despite his many fertile ideas about rhetoric. He would wait about a quarter of a century, until *A Rhetoric of Motives* (1950), before going into the history of rhetoric in detail—and even there no theory emerges. In all his books Burke *used* rhetoric as a way to articulate something more basic, something central to aesthetics, criticism, communication, social structures, and political organizations. Perhaps it was not until the *Grammar* and the *Rhetoric* that Burke fully realized—and could fully articulate—the place rhetoric held in what he had been talking about all along. Even so, rhetoric was secondary to the broader goals of the *Motivorum* project. There Burke suggests that understanding the ways motives are manifested in messages is central to understanding human relations. And rhetoric is essential to that. In short, Burke's entire career could be viewed as a struggle to locate and clarify the role of rhetoric.

Put otherwise, throughout his career Burke struggled to say something, articulating his ideas differently in new social and intellectual milieus. Just how did he adapt to new situations? In *Counter-Statement,* Burke argues for a political aesthetic. In *Permanence* he offers a psychologically based view of interpretation, transition, and orientation. In *Attitudes,* Burke investigates the functioning of symbolic forms in organizations and political communities. In *Literary Form* he develops a psychological aesthetics. In the *Grammar* and the *Rhetoric* he defines the outlines of a "philosophy" and "rhetoric" of motives attribution. And later, in *The Rhetoric of Religion* and *Language as Symbolic Action,* Burke continues developing his rhetoric of motives, returning to literary criticism. What Burke writes about in each of his books should not be looked at independently of his other books. And since the *Grammar* and the *Rhetoric* dominate the understanding of Burke, looking carefully at his early work is imperative, for the motives books cannot be understood and fully appreciated independent of them. What that "something" is that Burke spent so many years trying to articulate has still not been clarified, and for the moment it will not be. Borrowing a conceit from Burke's *Grammar,* this book as a whole is an investigation of, and amplification on, that "something."

Counter-Statement
Aesthetics, Meaning, and Social Reform

Published in 1931, *Counter-Statement* contains eight essays written over the span of a tumultuous decade. At the beginning of those ten years America had been recovering from World War I and dancing the Charleston; by the end the Wall Street crash was history and the economic breakdown of the Great Depression had commenced in earnest. As the country continued to urbanize, immigrants from Eastern Europe transformed large urban centers. New York, now America's first world-class cosmopolis, experienced an influx of writers, artists, and intellectuals of all sorts, many of whom came for the bohemian life in Greenwich Village. Long a center for the Left, New York also became the place to be for social critics, philosophers, labor reformers, political activists, and many others disaffected by capitalism. As the 1920s progressed, governmental pressure and other factors crippled the largest socialist movement America had yet seen. Some of the more radical leftists turned to communism, and many more flirted with it. While these changes were taking place, university education expanded and democratized.

The decade from 1920 to 1931 was tumultuous for Burke as well. In 1920 he was unknown, hanging around Greenwich Village hoping to make it as a poet and novelist. But fiction writing hardly placed food on the table; Burke had to scramble to make ends meet. In the 1920s he managed to survive by translating, writing book reviews, and working as an editor for the *Dial*. Unfortunately, those activities did not afford much security—especially since, after 1925, Burke's place at the *Dial* was shaky. Late in the year editor Scofield Thayer fired him. Despite intervention by supporters (which kept him on there until 1926) and Burke's eventual full return to the *Dial* in 1927, employment there was never again as secure as it had been before the winter of 1925. At a low point, when Burke left the *Dial,* he took a full-time position at the Laura Spelman Rockefeller Memorial Trust to do research on drug addiction (he was there for a year and a half). A year after he left the Rockefeller Trust, with the *Dial* on the decline and about to fold, Burke took a full-time position at the Bureau of Social Hygiene (from October 1928 to the middle of 1930) researching the relations between drug addiction and crime. All the while Burke managed to do some part-time editing at the *Dial* and a little writing, but an exhausting schedule diminished his output dramatically. If employment problems were not enough to make things difficult for this man of letters, Burke had personal difficulties too. While working at the Rockefeller Trust and the Bureau of Social Hygiene, Burke had focused what little time he had on translations, book reviews, and music criticism. But in the late 1920s, as his marriage deteriorated (he eventually divorced his wife and married her sister), Burke returned to fiction. From 1928 to 1930 he published ten "declamations," short pieces of fiction that formed the basis for his second book, the novel *Towards a Better Life* (published in 1932). His fiction, Burke later said, helped him work through the difficulties of his first marriage. It is not surprising that *Towards a Better Life* was a torture to write. Yet this was not the first time Burke had trouble writing. From time to time he went though periods of what he called "aesthetic paralysis." As 1931 approached, Burke became increasingly isolated from his literary colleagues and, in general, withdrawn. This once aspiring poet and novelist had relegated poetry to a hobby, had turned to fiction for therapy, and was on the verge of abandoning fiction altogether.[1] Despite having become one of the most promising literary critics in New York, by the end of 1932 Kenneth Burke was near a nervous breakdown.[2]

As the decade wore on, but especially after the Wall Street crash, Burke became increasingly disturbed by America's social problems, which stimulated his interest in politics. As was indicated in chapter 1, Burke was not political in the ways some intellectuals were in the 1920s and early 1930s. He did not become a member of political organizations, rally, organize, or demonstrate. Suspicious of political organizations, Burke settled for theory and writing. Referring to the communist groups of the early 1930s, he told Cowley in 1932, "I am not a joiner of societies, I am a literary man" (Jay, 202). He was so keenly interested in aesthetics at that time that he called it his "aesthetic period." But Burke was no pure aesthete. He used aesthetics to address social and political problems. Even his early essays (on Gustave Flaubert, Rémy de Gourmont, and Walter Pater) have social and political colorations. For an understanding of just what Burke is getting at in *Counter-Statement,* the work should be viewed and understood as the product of this tumultuous decade. Burke's "counter-statement" was borne of personal and cultural upheaval.

Two readers of Burke, Frank Lentricchia and Jack Selzer, take *Counter-Statement* to be part of the modernist debate.[3] This is no doubt correct and helps to contextualize his theories and politics. Yet each of these authors casts the "debate" uniquely: Lentricchia sees it as polemical, and Selzer calls it a "conversation." To be fair, both have their own concerns: Lentricchia, to use Burke as a model for the literary-social critic of the 1980s (who emerged out of the modernist tradition); and Selzer, to recognize the role modernism played in Burke's life from 1915 to 1931. As such, both authors highlight what best serves their needs. But they obscure a central feature of Burke's thinking, one that echos throughout his entire corpus: entreaty, invocation, exhortation, even beseechment. *Counter-Statement* is not quite polemics and not just part of a conversation. More than just another modernism, it is a call to attend to the ways we use language to build social structures, a call to use rhetoric and communication as framing devices and intellectual foils for exploring the murky realm where language, philosophy, social life, and political ideology exist as one—before disciplines cleave them apart—and a call to see the extent to which language and politics are profoundly of a kind. If this is not apparent from reading *Counter-Statement* alone, it is unmistakable in light of Burke's career development after 1931. *Permanence and Change* (1935) and *Attitudes toward History* (1937) become increasingly pressing, at times almost frantic. By 1945, when he published *A Grammar of Motives,* the agitation arising out of the darkest moments of the Great Depression had faded, but the urgency largely remained. This is because Burke's entreaties in *Counter-Statement, Permanence,* and *Attitudes* had been ignored. And the cultural vectors that he had cautioned against for so long to some degree contributed to global warfare.

Ignored by whom? The answer might naturally seem to be "modernists," writers in the tradition of literary modernism, and social critics and philosophers more generally. Yet that would be misleading, for over the course of his long career Burke's most penetrating and often harshest critics—those who struck at the core—were by and large men such as Granville Hicks, Harold Rosenberg, Sidney Hook, John Crowe Ransom, Max Black, Abraham Kaplan, and Richard Chase. In the early years Burke may have addressed modernists, even using their categories and concepts, but he also hoped that a much broader set of intellectuals—the so-called "New York intellectuals"—would be wary of certain habits of mind and would incorporate the study of literature into their methods of addressing social and political problems. One complicating factor is that the New York intellectuals were divided roughly into two groups with different theoretical and political underpinnings, the academic intellectuals and the literary intellectuals. More detail will be provided later in this chapter. At this point it can be suggested that casting Burke as part of a modernist polemic or a modernist conversation obscures both the audience to which Burke spoke and the reason he addressed them. Such casting does not lead to an understanding of why *Counter-Statement* received such harsh criticism. As much as the force of Burke's criticism made him someone to reckon with, little came of *Counter-Statement*. The book did not sell well, and Burke lamented the fact that no one seemed to adopt his ideas or acknowledge his influence. Literary critics would praise his essays and perhaps incorporate an idea here or there into their own work, but in the 1920s and early 1930s no theorist accepted or developed Burke's positions. At best, he was a foil for their work. One of the great puzzles in understanding Burke's legacy is the fact that despite the highest praise from scholars in many disciplines, it was not until the 1960s that his ideas started to be used broadly—and even so, there are questions about how he was used even by his most ardent admirers. So at least from Burke's perspective, the answer to the question Ignored by whom? is, Pretty much everyone.

If *Counter-Statement*'s critical reception in the 1930s is any indication, Burke's contemporaries had trouble understanding him. In general, reviewers of *Counter-Statement* complained that he was ambiguous and offered separate, if not conflicting, messages. Though most reviewers praised some aspect of the book, they certainly missed Burke's basic point and harshly criticized him on inappropriate grounds. This occurred despite an enormously useful preface in which Burke quite clearly explains his intent and central points, placing the book within an intellectual and social context. What was *Counter-Statement* meant to counter? What was the nature of Burke's oppositional stance? And why was Burke misunderstood and harshly criticized? The answers to these questions are complex and involve a variety of factors, but there is one pre-dominant cause: Burke's audience was diverse, and what he wanted to say did not easily fit into the heterogeneous intellectual traditions he faced. A detailed look at the text will aid a clearer understanding of this. The rest of this chapter is divided into two main sections. The first examines the argument of *Counter-Statement,* as published, taking special notice of how *Counter-Statement* is an adaptation to the social and intellectual milieu of the late 1920s and early 1930s. The second section will examine some reviews of *Counter-Statement,* pointing out how Burke's adaptation to his milieu was largely ineffective.

Counter-Statement is complex, sometimes obscure, and often puzzling. As in most of his criticism, Burke uses esoteric concepts and arguments by analogy and allusion. He lumps together language, literature, art, method, social problems, and political ideology and practices, often meaning some or all when talking about any one of them. The essays in *Counter-Statement* were written for different purposes over the span of a decade. The early essays emphasize aesthetics. For instance, in "Psychology and Form" (written in 1924) Burke argues that form is not a struc-tural feature of the artwork, but a psychological state combining the artwork, artist, and viewer. By 1931 the Depression led him to emphasize politics and social pol-icy. "Program" and "Applications of the Terminology" are virtually political tracts. But Burke did not shy away from merging literature and politics. In discussing lit-erary technique, he branches off into a long digression about a social or political problem; likewise, in the middle of a section on some political issue, he wanders off into poetics, symbology, or literary method. For example, in concluding a dis-cussion of Rémy de Gourmont, Burke argues that de Gourmont's turn to war propaganda resulted from the weakness of his aesthetic. This was by all means an aesthetic judgment by Burke, but it was also a comment on the potential weak-ness of propaganda as a political tool. Burke even combined aesthetics and politics more directly. For instance, what might be made of a comment such as "the aesthetic . . . would be driven back to democracy," which appeared in a section on fascism, democracy, and industrialism (*CS*, 114)? Incidentally, readers of *Counter-Statement* today might have a better feel for such statements if they fully appreciate the anxiety and urgency that molded criticism written during the Depression.

Counter-Statement begins with "Three Adepts of 'Pure' Literature" (*CS*, 1–28), an examination of the lives and aesthetics of Gustave Flaubert, Walter Pater, and Rémy de Gourmont—each purported to have developed a unique "pure" or "perfect" art, and each having to some extent failed in his attempt. This essay is a revision and combination of the three essays discussed in the previous chapter: "Approaches to Rémy de Gourmont" (1921), "The Correspondence of Flaubert" (1922), and "Notes on Walter Pater" (1924). But it is not merely an agglomeration of those essays. There are important differences between the *Counter-Statement* essay and the earlier versions, which will be discussed later in this chapter. According to Burke, Flaubert "never succeeded in arriving at an aesthetic amenable to his temperament," in part because "his medium was not adapted to the effects he most desired" (*CS*, 5, 6). "Despite his many art-to-display-art preferences," Burke comments, "he was attempting to write under an art-to-conceal-art aesthetic" (*CS*, 7). Flaubert's chosen medium, the novel, contributed to this imperfection, Burke says, because "The novel makes of literature the verbalization of *experience,* the conversion of *life* into diction—whereas Flaubert, with his pronounced interest in the absolute effects of art, would make of literature the *verbalization* of experience, the conversion of life into *diction*" (*CS*, 7). Burke concludes the section on Flaubert by pointing out that Flaubert's choice of the art-to-conceal-art aesthetic led him to avoid some of the resources of language ("avoidances of too many *of*'s, avoidances of ambiguity to do with the antecedents of pronouns, avoidances of phrasing unsuited to his respiration, avoidances of vowel combinations awkward to the tongue" [*CS*, 9]). Burke reminds us that contemporary aesthetics would unwisely applaud this.

In contrast, Pater's art marks a "superior adjustment of technique to aesthetic interests," for, unlike Flaubert, he "shaped prose fiction to his purposes" (*CS*, 9). That "shaping" lies in Pater's integration of critical elements into his fiction, a characteristic that Burke admired. Nonetheless, Pater's aesthetic is flawed. "Art to Pater," Burke says, "was 'not the conveyance of an abstract body of truths,' but 'the critical tracing of . . . conscious artistic structure'" (*CS*, 12). Pater leached any argumentative force from ideas. "He treated ideas not for their value as statements, but as horizons, situations, developments of plot, in short, as any other element of fiction" (*CS*, 14). He used ideas and human problems as fodder and was unable to see beyond the realm of artistic effect. "If, by the doctrines of his century, the dignity of man in nature had been prejudiced atrociously," concludes Burke, "the predicament meant hardly more to Pater than an added incentive to proclaim the dignity of man in art" (*CS*, 15).

Burke says that to Rémy de Gourmont, "art was 'justified' because art was an appetite—in being desired it found its ample reason for existence. Art did not require defense as an instrument of political or social reform. Art was purely and simply a privilege" (*CS*, 16). "Theoretically without external obligations, at liberty to develop his medium as he preferred," de Gourmont produced literature as he liked, seemingly freed by his pure aesthetic (*CS*, 17). Yet, Burke argues, the freedom was an illusion. de Gourmont, like all artists, was still bound by his history. A leper and recluse locked and shuttered within his rooms, "living almost exclusively with books," he produced a literature rich with association, symbol, and dissociation. His literature, influenced by his dreadful plight, "maintained a conflict of attitudes which gives his work considerable liquidity" (*CS*, 20). As circumstances changed, so did his aesthetic. de Gourmont's pure aesthetic faltered during World War I—whereas "the godlessness of his youth was freedom, his god became attachment" to patriotism (*CS*, 26).

Burke's main point is that all three "adepts" failed to produce a pure art. Flaubert's aesthetic did not match his intention; Pater's aesthetic sapped ideas of their real value; and de Gourmont's aesthetic was too steeped in personal history to be anything near "pure." It is true that Burke found aspects of each of these aesthetics attractive. Overaestheticizing Burke might lead to the assumption that these writers were his heroes and that Burke even took de Gourmont for a role model. This is the opinion of Selzer, who emphasizes an aesthetic Burke conversing with modernists at the expense of Burke's social and political interests.[4] In fact, as shall be shown later in this chapter, there is much to commend Selzer's view, for Burke drew inspiration from de Gourmont's ideas about dissociation. Nonetheless, in the end de Gourmont's aesthetic failed for the same reason that Flaubert's and Pater's failed: there cannot be a "pure" art.

"Psychology and Form," the second essay, was written originally in winter 1924 and is the most widely cited essay in the collection (perhaps of Burke's entire corpus).[5] Its place in the development of Burke's ideas cannot be overemphasized because it establishes the central principle of Burke's aesthetic, which is reflected in most of his criticism for the rest of his career (Jay, 290). It is important biographically because Burke "personally" found the essay quite "fertile" (Jay, 233). Burke wrote "Psychology and Form" as a corrective for a modern "derangement of taste" fostered by the growth of science. "Scientific criteria," which emphasize the conveyance of information at the expense of emotional or spiritual factors, Burke argues, have been "unconsciously introduced into matters of purely aesthetic judgment" (*CS*, 31). In the modern world, he says, the artist lays "his emphasis on the giving of information—with the result that art tends more and more to substitute the psychology of the hero (the subject) for the psychology of the audience" (*CS*, 32). Modern aesthetics, Burke points out, has been seduced by the cult of science and lacks an interest in, a theoretical understanding of, and techniques for maintaining the proper balance between the informational imperative and the emotional imperative.

The principle behind the reestablishment of a proper balance is Burke's concept of "form." Form is not, in his view, simply a structural feature of an artwork, but a psychological *relationship* between the artwork, viewer, and artist. Form exists when the artist styles the artwork so that it stimulates expectations in the viewer and then satisfies those expectations. Burke calls this stimulation and satisfaction an "emotional curve." When an artwork has a "proliferation" of emotional curves, Burke says, it has "eloquence," which "is simply the end of art, and is thus its essence" (*CS*, 41). By redefining "form," Burke has turned the focus of aesthetics away from realistic portrayal as an *end* in itself to realistic portrayal as a *means* for rhetorical effect. Burke explains this by suggesting a difference between the "psychology of information" (as in a scientific description of a tree) and the "psychology of form" (as in a poem about a tree). This distinction, says Burke: "involves a definition of aesthetic truth. . . . Truth in art is not the discovery of facts, not an addition to human knowledge in the scientific sense of the word. It is, rather, the exercise of human propriety, the formulation of symbols which rigidify our sense of poise and rhythm. Artistic truth is the externalization of taste" (*CS*, 42).

"The Poetic Process," the third essay in *Counter-Statement,* was written as a companion piece to "Psychology and Form" at the same time, in winter 1924.[6] Burke intended to explain how form figures into the process of an artist's literary creativity. Burke begins by pointing out that people naturally respond to patterns and that events and emotions are experienced as patterns. There are, he says, certain "innate forms of the mind" endowed with "the 'potentiality for being interested by certain processes or arrangements,' or the 'feeling for such arrangements of subject-matter as produce crescendo, contrast, comparison, balance, repetition, disclosure, reversal, contraction, expansion, magnification, series, and so on'" (*CS*, 46). Art, Burke argues, is a "particularizing" or "individuating" of human experience by mimicry of its patterns in an artwork. The artist achieves such mimicry by imbuing an artwork with "form." In this essay, "form" means basically the same thing as it did in "Psychology and Form," but Burke now refers to form more as a type of self-expression that fills out with subject matter a pattern that aptly conveys a specific mood or experience (*CS*, 51–52). "The poet," he says, tends "towards two extremes, or unilaterals: the extreme of utterance, which makes for the ideal of spontaneity and 'pure' emotion, and leads to barbarism in art; and the extreme of pure beauty, or means conceived exclusively as end, which leads to virtuosity, or decoration" (*CS*, 55–56). The mystery of art, Burke suggests, lies in its resolution of our appetite for self-expression and our need for using technique to appease that appetite: "in that fluctuating region between pure emotion and pure decoration, humanity and craftsmanship, utterance and performance, lies the field of art, the evocation of emotion by mechanism, a norm which, like all norms, is a conflict become fusion" (*CS,* 56). This fusion is realized, Burke argues, in the creation of a symbol. Yet this fusion does not allow us to escape conflict, for the symbol itself creates discord. "The symbol faces two ways," says Burke, for not only is it a "generative force" that "demands a *logical* consistency" within the emotional field of the artwork, but the symbol "also applies to life, serving here as a formula for our experiences, charming us by finding some more or less simple principle underlying our emotional complexities" (*CS,* 61).

"The Status of Art" is an attempt to cure a pathology concerning the status of art in the 1920s. Burke argues that various defenses of art actually undermine its place in human affairs. One such defense is the *ars gratia artis* aesthetic. Burke observes that "in the nineteenth century, when much was brought into question, many things previously called good had to be defended—poetry among them. Wherefore the slogan of *Art for Art's Sake* which, though it was often pronounced with bravado, clearly had about it the element of a 'justification'" (*CS,* 63). With advances in science and technology in the twentieth century, art's justification had turned sour, for "uselessness," once a virtue, rankled the modern temper. According to Burke, attempts to justify art because of some kind of special instinct in the artist just makes matters worse. A second defense of art argues that art is "amoral" or "unmoral." This also undermines the position of art in a technological age, for it implies "once again the ineffectiveness of art" (*CS,* 66). The third defense, called here the "bohemianization" of art, arises out of the second. When bohemians co-opted art in their conflict with the bourgeoisie, "the alignment was greatly to the detriment of art, as many trivial artists, and even some artists of rank, chose to exploit this division by making their opposition more picturesque than ominous" (*CS,* 68). The bohemianization of art led to mystifying symbolist techniques and the development of elitism in literary values. Burke goes on to argue that as deleterious as these justifications of art are, the most insidious are the "causation" defenses based, for instance, on psychology, economics, and history (*CS,* 72–89, especially 80). These "place art as a kind of by-product, the result of more vital and important forces" (*CS,* 72). As such, art loses much of its meaning, simply being "futile" reflections of deeper factors of human experience. Perhaps the key point here is that in all these defenses art becomes profoundly disconnected from life. Burke goes on to argue that for the status of art to be rehabilitated, there must be recognition that art does not need to be defended: "We advocate nothing, then, but a return to inconclusiveness. A century of 'refutations' is salutary at least in emphasizing the fact that art has not been 'refuted.' . . . [Art] needs no 'dignity' beyond the mere zero of not being glibly vilified. To the artist, the belief that the ways of influence are devious and unpredictable, and that 'anything can happen,' should be sufficient justification for devoting himself to his purely aesthetic problems, solving them according to his lights, and letting all other eventualities take care of themselves" (*CS,* 91). "The Status of Art," it should be noted, was not Burke's first attempt at such a cure, for this essay borrows heavily from three of his book reviews published in 1925 and 1926. In "On Re and Dis," a review of V. F. Calverton's *The Newer Spirit,* Burke argues that Calverton's "sociological" criticism erred by transforming "environmental" criticism into "causation" criticism.[7] Much the same point is made in both pieces, with "The Status of Art" incorporating about two paragraphs of the earlier essay verbatim.[8] In "A New Poetics," a review of I. A. Richards's *Principles of Literary Criticism,* Burke supports Richards's analysis of the "problems of artistic excellence in an age of practical, economic ills."[9] And in "A 'Logic' of History," a review of Oswald Spengler's *The Decline of the West,* Burke attacks the "cultural subjectivism and aesthetic defeatism" in Spengler's analysis of cultural cycles, deploring its implication that modern art is inferior to art of previous cultures.[10] Burke incorporates verbatim approximately two-thirds of "A 'Logic' of History" into the *Counter-Statement* essay.

In "Thomas Mann and André Gide," *Counter-Statement's* fifth essay, Burke again questions apologists of art. This time he questions the value of judging literature by the extent to which it celebrates virtue and derides corruption. Both gauges miss the point of artistic creation. Art, he says, prevents society from falling too easily into the often self-realizing traps of celebration and derision. The most basic function of art, he suggests, is "questioning," a refusal to submit to the normative, prescriptive terms of the protectors of virtue and classicism. Burke celebrates Mann and Gide, who both "maintain 'the Bohemian, the ironic and melancholy, the unattached, the grimly humorous, the innocent, the childish,'" for they resist the detractors of art (*CS,* 106). But, more important, Mann and Gide try "to make us at home in indecision . . . to humanize the state of doubt" (*CS,* 105). This inclination provides us with "the corrective of a disintegrating art, which converts each simplicity into a complexity, which ruins the possibility of ready hierarchies, which concerns itself with the problematical, the experimental, and thus by implication works corrosively upon those expansionistic certainties preparing the way for our social cataclysms" (*CS,* 105).

In "Program," Burke "speculates as to which emotions and attitudes should be stressed, and which slighted, in the aesthetic adjustment to the particular conditions of today" (*CS,* 107). Burke believed that in the late 1920s and early 1930s mechanization, urban growth, capitalism, and science were causing a cultural crisis in America. These cultural factors contributed to a malaise that promoted simple answers to complex questions, often by casting situations into simple dichotomies. Burke maintained that the artist was in a unique position to understand, question, and take a stance on large-scale cultural conflicts because art is simultaneously atemporal and historical (it deals with "the constants of humanity," yet is a "particular mode of adjustment to a particular cluster of conditions" [*CS*, 107]). With that the case, Burke sketches predominant social factors affecting the artist and how the artist ought to respond to them:

(1) The tension between agrarian and industrial forces. The agrarian-industrial conflict, Burke argues, arises from large-scale social transformation. Conditions that stimulate industrialism and stem from the growth of industry exist along with agrarian elements. "The artist, who is seeking to adjust a vocabulary to a situation," says Burke, "is necessarily sensitive to both the surviving and the emergent factors in the situation" (*CS*, 108).

(2) The indeterminate position of the artist. The artist, sensitive to both surviving and emergent factors, sees the good and bad in both sides of a conflict. His sympathy for both sides leads him to reject the bifurcation, supporting instead "an emphasis to which the contemporary public is not accustomed" (*CS*, 110). Thus the artist "will budge, rather than flatter, his audience" (*CS*, 109).

(3) The tension between practical and aesthetic imperatives. "In so far as the conversion of pure science into applied science has made the practical a menace," Burke argues, "the aesthetic becomes a means of reclamation" (a "corrective of the practical"; the aesthetic as a "modernized version of the earlier bourgeois-Bohemian conflict" [*CS*, 110–11]).

(4) The effect of mechanization on unemployment, leisure, overproduction, and underconsumption. Mechanization, causing overproduction and unemployment, Burke argues, will eventually force some kind of redistribution of wealth from industrialists to the workers.

(5) The destabilization of traditional political categories (conservative and liberal), caused by the shifting character of political and economic structures.[11] As norms change, the new becomes tradition; hence, a call to return to the old order can be attacked as "radicalism." Burke says that this is precisely a source of misunderstanding in the debate over agrarian and industrialist values and politics.

The next-to-last essay of *Counter-Statement*, "Lexicon Rhetoricae," is the longest of the collection, comprising more than one-quarter of the 212 pages that make up eight essays.[12] Burke calls it the volume's "set-piece" and gives it the subtitle "Being a Codification, Amplification, and Correction of the Two Essays, 'Psychology and Form' and 'The Poetic Process'" (*CS*, 123). He wrote "Lexicon Rhetoricae," he says, in order to build "a kind of judgment machine, designed to serve as an instrument for clarifying critical issues (not so much for settling issues as for making the nature of a controversy more definite)" (*CS*, ix). Although Burke calls the lexicon a "critical machine," he is exaggerating a bit—it certainly does not provide a systematic method. It is rather "an attempt to schematize many critical concepts which have been more or less vaguely in the air since psychology took the place of metaphysics as a foundation for aesthetic theory" (*CS,* ix). His lexicon "seeks to perform this function by working out a set of 'pivotal' or 'key' terms for discussing the processes of literary appeal" (*CS,* ix). In doing so, Burke turns previously vague speculations into a more or less coherent statement. In a letter written three decades after the publication of *Counter-Statement,* Burke reaffirms the value of his lexicon: "As for stuffo [*sic*] on relations between artist and society, I guess I said more about that subject in *Counter-Statement* than anywhere else. In fact, I think that every article in that book ends on that theme. And though now I'd temper it with age . . . I guess that, by and large, I'd still subscribe to the same position. Perhaps the last few pages of the 'Lexicon Rhetoricae' (sections 38 and 39) sum it up best" (Jay, 342).

In the first two sections ("The Nature of Form" and "The Individuation of Forms") Burke further explains what form means and shows how it functions in a variety of situations. He then discusses in great detail the implications of his definition of form. Earlier it was noted that Burke saw form not as a structural feature of an artwork, but as a psychological relationship involving the creation and satisfaction of expectations. This is not simply a matter of pleasure and preference. In fact, Burke argues that the audience is deeply steeped in a culture and community that affects every aspect of the expectation-satisfaction curve, including the manner of presentation and defining, limiting what is intellectually, socially, and politically acceptable and preferable. Hence, one implication of casting form as he does is that context, interpretation, ideology, persuasion, power, and artistic truth become essential elements of art, not subsidiary or even concomitant factors. This perspective may be commonplace today, but it was a "counter-statement" to Burke's audience in the 1920s. The emphasis on persuasion being at the center of art was particularly novel.

Much of what Burke has to say about the artist and society coalesces in the idea of the "symbol." He discusses the symbol in "The Poetic Process," but there the discussion is principally technical (*CS,* 56–62). In the lexicon Burke now moves well beyond defining the symbol as a verbal manifestation of experience. He sees the symbol as a cultural force, arguing that symbols serve various functions relative to situations: symbols help us interpret situations; they favor the acceptance of situations; they act as "correctives" by promoting things that current situations lack, by stimulating moral emancipation. Whereas "The Poetic Process" details the options an artist has to represent a pattern of experience, Burke now primarily analyzes how the symbol merges the individual and environment, transcending both. It is no coincidence that Burke's discussion of the symbol begins in the section "Patterns of Experience" and spills over into the next section, "Ritual," where he treats such matters as ideology, eloquence, categorical appeal, and aesthetic truth. Finally, it is important to point out that the lexicon, as much as it is retrospective, foreshadows Burke's later books. The essay ends with a section titled "Universality, Permanence, Perfection." Permanence, of course, is a principal concern of his next book, *Permanence and Change*. And perfection becomes a vital (though largely unrecognized) component of Burke's *Grammar* and *Rhetoric*.[13]

Burke concludes *Counter-Statement* with "Applications of the Terminology," a prophylactic. Throughout the book Burke points out that literary technique and "dealing with life" are often conflicting goals of art. This conflict finds its purest expression in the relationship between the absolute and the relative. In "Applications," Burke argues that aesthetics ought not come down on one side or the other. The artist, he says, need not choose between technique and social utility, for art necessarily deals with both technique and important questions of human experience. The problem of aesthetics, Burke suggests, is understanding how artistic technique and social purpose, two seemingly separate realms, overlap and blend together. Interestingly, "Applications" concludes with two pages about rhetoric, for when technique and social purpose are blended, Burke points out, appeal becomes the center of art.

Though all the essays in *Counter-Statement* treat the same themes, the emphasis in each varies. Some are primarily about literary movements and the status of art in society; others explain the technical workings of art; still others explore the social and political factors salient to the production of art. Grouping the essays of *Counter-Statement* in this manner makes it quite apparent that Burke succeeded in designing the book to fulfill the three goals of his "Critic's Credo" outlined for Cowley in October 1931. As was pointed out in the previous chapter, the credo contains an apology for art, a rhetoric, and a program.

The apology consists of "Three Adepts," which attacks the *ars gratia artis* conception; "Mann and Gide," which attacks moralist gauges of art; and "Status," which attacks utilitarian views of art. Clearly, Burke is arguing that the aesthetic legacy of the nineteenth century, and its twentieth-century counterparts, is bankrupt and impedes the advancement of literature and literary theory. These three essays "clear the ground" for new theory. Much of the apology was written well before 1931 and was modified for publication in *Counter-Statement*. The modifications indicate the extent to which Burke changed in the 1920s. We see this in the way "Three Adepts" is different from the essays from which it is derived—"Approaches to Rémy de Gourmont," "The Correspondence of Flaubert," and "Notes on Walter Pater." "Three Adepts" is basically the same as the earlier essays and utilizes large verbatim chunks of each; yet there are important differences. For instance, Burke has updated the earlier essays to reflect better the milieu of the late 1920s and early 1930s. Some passages included in the earlier version are deleted from the revision, marking a shift in the fashion of aesthetic debate (for instance, two paragraphs about Henri Bergson on page 152). And there are similar additions to the revision (for instance, comments about James Joyce and Gertrude Stein [CS, 24]). Yet far more important are the modifications that demonstrate a change in tone. The exciting, vibrant literary world Burke saw in the late 1910s and early 1920s was withering. Fewer new magazines were coming out in the late 1920s, and many had died (the *Dial* folded in 1929). Many young writers who earlier seemed destined to be poets and novelists turned to journalism and advertising—forced there by a lack of talent, a lack of success, fewer publishing outlets, and/or the downturn of the economy. Moreover, Burke had become increasingly disillusioned about fiction as a vocation. So in revising "The Correspondence of Flaubert" for inclusion in "Three Adepts," Burke deleted the comment about Flaubert having "all the earmarks of a promising young genius in revolt against Ohio." This may be a fairly minor deletion in the larger context, but it changes the tone. The reader of "Three Adepts" gets a muted condemnation of the bohemian aesthetic of the 1920s, one less directed at personal lapses. Burke could hardly be blamed for toning down the personal attack at a time when so many men and women were helpless before social and economic forces they could not understand, much less flourish within.

The argument could be raised that from the early 1920s to 1931 Burke changed his point and so did not need to make such references. Of course his ideas developed, but he did not change his mind regarding the basic point. For instance, in the section on de Gourmont in "Three Adepts," Burke says that "suddenly de Gourmont needed his god; and since the godlessness of his youth was *freedom*, his god became *attachment*" (*CS*, 26; emphasis added). Burke puts it this way in "Approaches": "since the godlessness of his youth was *mobility*, his god became *certainty*" (137; emphasis added). In the 1920s Burke associated mobility with certainty; in the 1930s, he turns to freedom and attachment. Burke adapts his message for a Depression-era audience. Mobility—where would one go? As the great migrations of farmers, rural residents, and workers of all sorts bore out, it did not much matter. Perhaps a Hooverville was better than a derelict farm in dusty Oklahoma, but jobs were still scarce for the neediest wherever they went. Certainty—what could one be sure of? Certainly not certainty. If ever there was a time in which "all that is solid melts into air," it was then. For people who had lost much there was at least the chance to stand up for their beliefs. It is easy to understand why the Depression was perhaps the most politically active period in the twentieth century. It is no wonder that in "Three Adepts" Burke hints that the writers around him should take a political stand, a position made more explicit in "Program." On the whole, though, "Three Adepts of 'Pure' Literature" still condemns pure aesthetics in much the same way as do the three essays from which it was derived.

Another interesting aspect of *Counter-Statement*'s apology is how Burke avoids the very language that in other circumstances might help him make his case. For a long time Burke had been interested in the relations between the absolute and the relative, championing the relative to a world that prized absolutism. (Of course, he was not a *relativist* as the term then was largely used, since he was not a global relativist.) Yet in "Three Adepts" Burke carefully avoids even implying relativism. When starting to write this chapter, I thought of *Counter-Statement* as a rhetoric of contemporaneity—that in works written through 1931 Burke develops a way to treat the contingent while avoiding rampant subjectivism (or, far worse, solipsism) on the one hand and absolute idealism on the other. I imagined that he articulates that fluctuating region between the absolute and the relative. I still believe that; however, in works written at the end of the *Counter-Statement* decade, Burke expresses less fervor for the contingent and the relative. He actually excludes ideas about contemporaneity from parts of *Counter-Statement* where they would be expected. For example, the most interesting parts of "Pater" are those that treat contemporaneity, impressionism, and relativism. In adapting "Pater" to "Three Adepts," Burke to a large degree cut out explicit mention of these ideas.[14] Other examples are the deletion of Pater's favoring of overtone and de Gourmont's maintenance of a "cautious equilibrium." In short, in a world falling apart, a chant for the tentative or the subtle or the contingent or the changing would hardly sound right. Still supporting the relative, Burke had to recast his message in ways that would be more effective.

The "rhetoric" credo of *Counter-Statement* is contained in "Psychology and Form," "The Poetic Process," and "Lexicon Rhetoricae." We see in these essays the same kind of adaptation to the milieu of the 1930s. "Psychology and Form" and "The Poetic Process" were written in winter 1924, though both have roots farther back. They deal mostly with technical aspects of aesthetics. "Lexicon Rhetoricae," written much later, starts with technical matters but soon gets into the role of art as a social force and the impact of form-as-experience on other concepts typically associated with "experience." For example, in a technical section on the individuation of forms, Burke launches into a discussion of ideology (*CS*, 146–47). Burke does not say things in "Lexicon Rhetoricae" that contradict the earlier essays, but the emphasis has changed. We see this in a selection from "Three Adepts" that is used in "Lexicon." "Three Adepts" includes a paragraph in which Burke uses Stendhal and Victor Hugo to explain the meaning of "pure aesthetic" (Stendhal's "greatest ambition," observes Burke, "was to write sentences which could make the reader forget them as sentences" [*CS*, 8]). In "Lexicon" Burke presents a similar passage in the section on "The 'categorical appeal' of literature," but instead of exemplifying a pure aesthetic, Burke uses Hugo to argue that the possibility of eloquence is evidence that literature is profoundly important to lived experience (*CS*, 167–68).

The third of the three credos, the "program," consists of the essays "Program" and "Applications of the Terminology." The date of composition of "Program" is unclear, but its marked difference from most of the other essays of *Counter-Statement* suggests that it was written later. Also, in the 1967 addendum to "Curriculum Criticum," Burke says that "the particular conditions of today" that "Program" addresses are the conditions of 1931 (*CS,* 224).[15] It can also safely be said that "Applications" was composed rather late. Writing to Cowley in June 1931, Burke said that he was going "to finish up the closing three thousand or so words of *Counter-Statement* this week" (Jay, 193). That works out to be about the last nine pages of "Applications."[16]

"Program" and "Applications" are different from the rest of *Counter-Statement* chiefly because of their strong political content. The sketch of "Program" provided earlier gives some indication of the kinds of political issues that interested Burke; but it does not indicate how far to the left his politics had drifted. Burke's questioning of industrialism, for instance, was not a call for the return to purely agrarian society. Though he did like much that the agrarians stood for, he fully realized that an agrarian society could not meet the needs of contemporary America. Put another way, he was sympathetic to agrarianism but suspicious of the agrarian philosophy of the *I'll Take My Stand* movement. Moreover, industrialism in theory was not the problem; rather, America suffered, Burke felt, because of its particular kind of industrialism and the political structure that supported it. In the section on "fascism-democracy," after presenting a convincing attack against industrialism (especially in a Fascist state), Burke offers a counter view: "'Discourage' industry? We have seen how industry, alas! can be only too drastically discouraged. And if one would undermine the basic props of industry, he must be sure that the masses are not crushed in the fall. It is obvious that industry cannot be discouraged without the spread of misery among millions unless the democrats take to the generous spending of the industrialists' fortunes. The redistribution of wealth by some means—nationalization, or income and inheritance taxes, or some such—is an important political and economic implication of an 'anti-industrial' aesthetic" (*CS,* 115).

Such language indicates that Burke had clearly adopted the terms and commonplaces then current among socialists and communists. This is, after all, the first instance in which Burke speaks of fascism in his critical essays. And the preoccupation with the worker and associated ideas is a mark of the times. We also see in "Program" discussion of the bourgeois-bohemian conflict (for example, *CS,* 111–12 and 119). In "Applications," additionally, Burke speaks of the "proletarian attitude" (*CS,* 189). Of course, at this stage Burke could hardly be called a socialist or even a communist. It is true that Burke was attracted to socialist and communist ideologies, but what socialist or communist of that era could even hint at support of industrialism within basically sound capitalist structures? Far worse, Burke repeatedly suggests that his program is highly contingent—it would work for today, but perhaps sometime later conditions would change such that new "emphases" would require a different program. He says this, for instance, in the following passage from "Program": "This Program would not, let it be repeated, sum up the absolute, unchanging purpose of the aesthetic. It would define the function of the aesthetic as effecting an adjustment to one particular cluster of conditions, at this particular time in history. . . . The artist who wrote a novel called *Vive the Dole* would, most probably, find that his work died with the death of the specific situation for which it was written" (*CS*, 121). Hardly a single committed socialist or communist of the 1930s would agree to that, not just because it goes against the creed, but because it could provoke the wrath of political compatriots. Burke's adoption of such terms and commonplaces indicates not only his deep concern for certain issues and certain ways of thinking about them, but a compulsion to use the language of his audience.

An interesting aspect of *Counter-Statement* is the significance of offering an apology, a rhetoric, and a program. First, the distinctions among them are not clear-cut. For one thing, the apology strongly suggests social and political change, albeit at a high degree of generality. And as much as the rhetoric is aesthetic and the program political, these are matters of emphasis, not absolute differences. Rhetoric by nature combines art and politics, if rhetoric is understood to be anything other than pure decoration (and even then it could be argued that the criteria for decoration are social constructs). Furthermore, politics in the way Burke conceives it is closely allied with aesthetic practice. It is important to realize too that the offering of a rhetoric and program is itself an apology for art. Why posit a rhetoric and political application for art if not assuming that art is justified? Of course, the apology is more important for its particular justification of art; and the rhetoric and program, in their apologetic aspects, further the sociopolitical view that art is, as Burke said much later, "equipment for living." Burke recognized the interpenetration of the credos when he told Cowley that they "will be found to merge into one another" (Jay, 198). The overlap of the credos accentuates Burke's identification of art with politics. If art is a means for coping with a world often greatly at odds with the needs of people, social and political change must be accompanied by aesthetic change. Perhaps this is why Burke used a chronological pattern for the book rather than grouping the essays together for each credo. "These essays, read in their present order," he says, "should elucidate a point of view" (*CS*, viii).

Burke's style of argumentation—suggestive, cryptic, enigmatic—contributes to the difficulty some readers have with *Counter-Statement*. As much as Burke is often clear and forceful, he also uses slogans, aphorisms, analogies, etymological arguments, rhetorical questions, hyperbole, and drastically reductionist claims. For example, in "Psychology and Form" a major argument for his redefinition of form is an example from *Hamlet* I:iv, when the prince first confronts the ghost of Claudius (*CS*, 29–32). And in "Thomas Mann and André Gide" the thesis statement is a metaphor: after contrasting a clenched fist to a comfortably drooping hand, Burke says, "it is with such opening and closing of the hand that this essay is to deal" (*CS*, 92). He constantly argues by implication, letting overtone mean as much as explicit statements. Moreover, Burke is often less interested in making clear-cut distinctions than he is in trying to understand how ideas shade into one another. Of course, there is much good in that, but it can make already difficult material even harder to understand. Much later in his career, in a different context, Burke goes so far as to make the avoidance of neat distinctions a goal: "what we want is *not terms that avoid ambiguity,* but *terms that clearly reveal the strategic spots at which ambiguities necessarily arise*" (*GM*, xviii).[17] There are also places where Burke is less than forthright because there was good reason to be prudently evasive. For instance, in "Program" his politics suggests socialism or communism, but he never quite commits himself to any clear political affiliation. In the section on "Fascism-democracy" Burke argues that "the aesthetic would seek to discourage the most stimulating values of the practical, would seek—by wit, by fancy, by anathema, by versatility—to throw into confusion the code which underlies commercial enterprise, industrial competition, the 'heroism' of economic warfare; would seek to endanger the basic props of industry" (*CS*, 115). Burke wanted to avoid being labeled a fellow traveler: he did not embrace any particular socialist or communist organization and feared that being associated too closely with any political group could limit his chances of getting published. Worse yet, he could be out of work, with few prospects. Political affiliation also could affect a writer's social contacts, and one had to have the right contacts to get published regularly, to receive good critical reviews, to be offered editorial opportunities, and to maintain a good reputation in the literary community. Literary memoirs from the era are very much a chronicle of such shifting associations and their consequences.

As much as Burke is often suggestive, he also tends to make puzzling connections and go off on what seem like long digressions. We must remember that when *Counter-Statement* was written Burke was known as a music critic, a poet, a novelist, a literary critic, and a former editor of *Secession* and the *Dial*. Yet his first book of literary criticism discusses agrarianism, industrialism, psychoanalysis, fascism, unemployment, "the dole," economic causation, determinism, religious conversion, Oswald Spengler, Karl Marx, Jean-Jacques Rousseau, Charles Darwin, Plato, Epicurus, Friedrich Nietzsche, and more. At the end of "The Poetic Process," for example, after discussing the nature of the symbol, Burke adds: "The symbol faces two ways, for in addition to the technical form just mentioned (an 'artistic' value) it also applies to life, serving here as a formula for our experiences, charming us by finding some more or less simple principle underlying our emotional complexities. For the symbol here affects us like a work of science, like the magic formula of the savage, like the medicine for an ill" (*CS*, 61). And when discussing "the status of art" Burke argues that the best art is often art that the majority abhors, and he then turns to an analysis of causation theories (*CS*, 77–80) and determinism (*CS*, 80–82). Even reviewers of *Counter-Statement* commented on its breadth.

Many of the qualities of *Counter-Statement* come into clearer focus if we recognize that, although Burke addressed literary modernists, his audience was primarily the New York intellectuals of the late 1920s and early 1930s. We shall see that, contrary to currently held popular notions, the New York intellectuals were not a single group with one vision of intellectual progress; rather, they were a disparate group that followed two very different ideas about the role of art, intellect, and politics in society. (Moreover, despite being just one of several groups of intellectuals at work in New York, they were so influential that they dominated the New York intellectual world.) The New York intellectuals came of age in a rapidly changing era. During the 1920s and early 1930s great social events and cultural trends profoundly changed the way people thought about the world. The horrors of World War I demarcated a new horizon in humanity's capacity for conflict, terror, and organized destruction—and the "sausage factory" utterly shattered pretensions of human nobility and value. Economic problems in Europe, compounded by political upheavals and a general loss of faith, stimulated a great emigration of Eastern Europeans to the United States in general and New York in particular. Large numbers of marginalized immigrants passing through Ellis Island fueled the growth of ghettos on the Lower East Side and in Hell's Kitchen, aggravating the already inhumane exploitation of workers. The stock market crash and the Great Depression just exacerbated the situation.

As a result of all this social and economic upheaval, many intellectuals came to believe that political action was necessary to fix the grave economic and social problems America faced. They turned to socialism. As conditions worsened in the 1920s, but especially after the Wall Street crash, socialism increasingly seemed impotent, and many intellectuals in New York, especially Eastern Europeans, turned to communism. Principally middle-class, well-educated, and Jewish, they imbued communism with an intellectualism long missing from the politics of the Left. Some sought out forms of communism that used historical trends as the ground for political change. Others found forms of communism based on broader philosophical principles. But on the whole these intellectuals needed to justify communism on grounds more secure than simple notions of equity or a generalized betterment. As the New York intellectuals got more political, art became more important and aesthetics took on a decidedly political color. Art began to be seen as an important source of social change because it was considered the best medium through which the masses could be enlightened and galvanized for social action. The visual and performing arts were especially important here, but many intellectuals of the 1920s and 1930s understood the limitations of these art forms. Literature, especially the proletarian novel, was thought to be superior to other art forms as a way to reach the masses: not only was it relatively cheap and widely accessible, but the novel was believed to appeal better than high art to a popular audience.

Thomas Bender offers an excellent analysis of the New York intellectuals.[18] Bender argues that starting in 1750 New York's intellectual life developed in three phases, each characterized by different models or traditions that New Yorkers looked to for their "intellectual charters" (xiv). During the first phase, "civic culture," which lasted from the 1750s to the 1840s and was modeled after Enlightenment Edinburgh, intellectuals "embraced values of cosmopolitanism (along with civic and national pride), humanism, and classicism. . . . it was not oppositional or anti-bourgeois" (36–37). "Literary culture," the second phase, which lasted from the 1840s to the 1880s, was modeled after Parisian intellectual life. During this phase class affiliation and purely political machines were rejected as means for social benefaction. Instead, literary intellectuals believed that disinterested intellectual freedom, manifested in cosmopolitan aesthetic advancement and criticism, was the way to improve society. Literary culture found its strongest statement in the bohemian intellectuals of Greenwich Village (for instance, Randolph Bourne and Floyd Dell). "Academic culture," the third phase, lasting from the 1880s to at least the late1980s (when Bender's book was published), was modeled after "the German research university . . . [where] intellectual discourse would be purified and the authority of the intellect justified" (xv). Academic culture held that the rigors of philosophical analysis will remove the chief obstacles (confusion, emotion, and partisanship) that undermine effective decision making for solving social problems. A coherent and sympathetic new order could be formulated, academic intellectuals believed, if only "the force of reason" could prevail. Key figures of academic culture in Burke's milieu were Charles Beard, Morris Cohen, John Dewey, Sidney Hook, Harold Leask, Wesley Mitchell, and Thorstein Veblen. In the 1920s and early 1930s all three broad intellectual charters were still quite alive—though the New York intellectuals Burke addressed were largely members of literary or academic culture. Civic culture was quite active in New York but virtually nonexistent in the Greenwich Village community. Civic intellectuals, on the whole, were wealthy patrons of the arts who lived on the Upper East Side. They prospered socially and financially under the status quo, supported the social and political structures that maintained their wealth and influence, and were more interested in the purely aesthetic aspects of contemporary art. The literary and academic New York intellectuals were generally antibourgeois, suspicious of prevailing social and political structures, and engaged in their own ways of bringing about changes that they hoped would alter the prevailing order. It is true that civic intellectuals influenced literary production in the United States, but they had little to do with the avant-garde literary world downtown, especially as it became more politicized.

The community Burke addressed thus chiefly comprised adherents to two different intellectual traditions. The distinction between the two camps was not absolute, but there were clear differences of emphasis. The literary bohemians lived principally in a Greenwich Village subculture. Most interested in literary method and experimentalism, they believed that aesthetic progress would alter culture and thereby induce social reform. Literary bohemians were political and dabbled in organizing and rallying, but they were in general naive and far more interested in simply writing novels, short stories, and poems. Academic intellectuals were not as concentrated in the Village, some having strong ties to Columbia University on the Upper West Side. Academic intellectuals such as Sidney Hook were intensely interested in philosophical analysis, often using Karl Marx, Vladimir Lenin, or some other political economist, historian, or philosopher as the foundation for criticizing American society. Some became intensely political but preferred armchair politics to rallying. When academic intellectuals got involved in political action, it was usually low-level work, although a few became strategists for leftist groups. They were especially adept at writing essays, engaging in debate and conversation, and advising political leaders. Burke tried to "cut across the bias" of this division by writing a speculatively driven political aesthetic (or an aesthetically driven speculative politics). In trying to subvert traditional ways of thinking, Burke lumped together aesthetics, literary method, social problems, and politics. He constantly drew connections between seemingly separate realms in an attempt to show that one realm naturally and "logically" leads to another. In fact, Burke explicitly said that his "Program" was an attempt to make such a connection. "'Program,'" he said, is "a hypothetical translation of Bohemianism, or Aestheticism, into its corresponding political equivalents, as though one were proposing planks for the platform of a national 'Art Party'" (*CS,* xiii).

Counter-Statement is replete with examples of Burke's subversion of the distinction between literature and politics. In "Three Adepts," for example, Burke added to his treatment of de Gourmont a section on the role of art "as an instrument of political or social reform" (*CS,* 16). Moreover, to balance the social/political and literary aspects of "Three Adepts" better, Burke at several points chose not to include passages on literary technique that were included in the original articles from which "Three Adepts" was culled (compare, for instance, *CS,* 25, and "Approaches," 135–38). In "The Poetic Process," for example, in a discussion of self-expression, Burke says that "one man attains self-expression by becoming a sailor, another by becoming a poet" (*CS,* 53). In the next paragraph he comments that "Napoleon attained self-expression by commanding an army" (CS, 53). Burke was clearly trying to say that "self-expression," as a motive, pervades all of life (and, by implication, that methods we use for analyzing self-expression in literature apply outside of it). There are also cases where Burke more extensively bridges the division between literature and politics. In "The Poetic Process," for example, after a discussion of the symbol, Burke turns to the relationship between the "power" of the symbol and the appeal of theories of history or science (CS, 58), then shifts to a discussion of the appeal of the technical presentation of symbols, and then shifts back to social aspects of literature (CS, 59–62). In fact, in "The Status of Art" Burke quite cleverly frames the essay as a discussion of rationales for art, but the various "justifications" of art are actually condemnations of the transgression of certain ways of thinking beyond their proper purview. Another excellent example occurs at the end of "Thomas Mann and André Gide," where Burke quite clearly argues that certain modernist aesthetic principles (irony, novelty, experimentalism, vacillation, the cult of conflict) ensure that we do not allow our habits to hurt us (CS, 104–6).

In conflating art and politics, Burke writes sometimes like a literary bohemian and at other times like an academic intellectual. He shifts between elaborate literary analyses of texts and philosophical or political speculations. A literary Burke is seen in discussions of "psychology" in *Hamlet* (CS, 29–31); symbolism in *Death in Venice, Tonio Kröger*, and *The Immoralist* (CS, 92–96); "climactic arrangement" in Oscar Wilde, William Wordsworth, and Jean Racine (CS, 135–38); and objectivity and subjectivity in William Shakespeare (CS, 195–97). Much of "Three Adepts of 'Pure' Literature" and "The Poetic Process" displays the literary Burke. The academic Burke emerges in the discussions of Spengler in "Status" (CS, 81–89), conscientiousness and corruption in "Thomas Mann and André Gide" (CS, 99–102), ideology in "Lexicon Rhetoricae" (CS, 146–149), and in much of "Program" and "Applications of the Terminology" as well. On the whole, Burke fit better into the expectations of his literary bohemian audience. One indication of this is the fact that the literary bohemians were far less critical of Burke than were the academic intellectuals, who dismissed or even spurned him. Even so, the literary bohemians had a lot of trouble understanding what Burke was trying to say.

A brief examination of some 1930s reviews of *Counter-Statement* demonstrates that Burke's audience, on the whole, failed to understand him. For the most part the critics tended to categorize him according to the particular intellectual tradition to which they adhered. Literary bohemians thought Burke was writing about literature or art. Academic intellectuals thought he was writing about philosophy or politics. Reviews by Gorham Munson, John Chamberlain, Granville Hicks, Isidor

Schneider, Harold Rosenberg, and Joshua Kunitz are particularly relevant because these reviewers were well known and influential when *Counter-Statement* was published, because their reviews were published in journals thought to be important by Burke's audience, and because their reviews are thoughtful analyses representative of the kind of thinking of Burke's audience. These reviews suggest that Burke's audience failed to see his cut across the bias.

Gorham Munson wrote an early review covering some of Burke's fiction and several essays later collected in *Counter-Statement*. Munson describes Burke's theoretical perspective as "the purest estheticism."[19] He then questions a "crevice in Burke's theory . . . [that] lets in more than the theory can contain." This "letting in," he says, begins with a distinction between form and subject matter. Munson says that according to Burke both are necessary for art, which Burke calls a "process of individualization." But, Munson argues, if we distinguish between form and subject matter, we must recognize the "necessity" of "objectivity and consciousness concerning" both form and subject matter. If that is so, according to Munson, Burke errs in privileging form over subject matter: his "endeavor to make form the major element in art is simply the endeavor to choose between two necessities, which is impossible." On the face of it, the argument makes sense—if Burke does what Munson claims. But Munson misunderstood Burke. Nowhere does Burke say we should choose between form and subject matter; in fact, Burke's point is that form is deeply connected with subject matter. There is no privileging of form because the moment one considers form, subject matter is already to the fore. Talking about form is necessarily talking about subject matter (and, for Burke, vice versa). Burke does focus on form greatly, but as a way into subject matter, not ignoring it. Munson, coming from traditional aesthetics, could hold a form-matter distinction so strongly that he cannot conceive its corruption.

In a 1931 review of *Counter-Statement,* John Chamberlain comments that "Psychology and Form" is "startlingly brilliant—the best in the book, and the most effective, by far," whereas other essays "date badly."[20] He praises and highlights the discussion of form and believes that Burke's case for the "rehabilitation" of rhetoric is "irrefutable." Chamberlain's review contains two features of special interest. First, Chamberlain's acceptance of Burke's rehabilitation of rhetoric (one-half of the review) is based on an attack of the "cult of simplicity" endorsed by the "claimant followers of Ernest Hemingway." Chamberlain argues that Hemingway was an expert rhetor. This review is a bit odd, for Chamberlain's main purpose seems to be to use Burke as an occasion to say something about Hemingway. Chamberlain never explains what the attack against Hemingway tells us about Burke or *Counter-Statement*. The second feature of special interest is Chamberlain's rejection of Burke's "cult of vacillation" as "sophistical."[21] He claims that "vacillation, in a society in which the principle of vacillation is about the only principle flourishing, is self-defeating." That may be true in general, but it does not fairly represent what Burke is saying. Burke supports the cult of vacillation as a counterpart of the cult of the absolute; vacillate when faced with absolutes, not for the sake of vacillation itself. They are not separate choices for Burke, but a dialectical pair in which vacillation is a response to absolutism. All Burke really means is that we should not adopt "certainties" too quickly.

In the *New Republic,* Granville Hicks considers "Psychology and Form" and "The Poetic Process" the "backbone of the book," with the rest of the essays detailing the implications and applications of their basic principles. Hicks questions "the actual value of this set of principles for critical purposes."[22] Hicks believes that in Burke's scheme one cannot criticize an artist's mood (the genesis of artistic effort), the artist's choice of symbol for dealing with the mood, or the artist's "individuation of the symbol, the choice of details to body it forth, except with relation to the symbol itself." These criticisms stem from Hicks's view that, for Burke, "the only proper concern of the critic is technique." The heart of Hicks's criticism is the claim that Burke's understanding of literary composition and literary appeal does not allow the writer or critic to be sensitive to "the needs which his symbol is to meet for his readers." Hicks does recognize that Burke addresses this in "Applications of the Terminology," but he complains that the treatment there is "half-hearted." In Burke's view, he complains, the central element is eloquence. Hicks believes that the ends of eloquence and social responsibility are at odds—that in seeking one, the artist will "sacrifice" the other. He dismisses "Program," the essay that chiefly argues for Burke's social agenda and art's integral role in attaining desirable social ends, by claiming that "'Program' outlines social views derived from his critical system, not social views from which his system is derived." The following issue of the *New Republic* printed both Burke's response and Hicks's rejoinder. Burke complains that Hicks suffers "from a misunderstanding of my purposes," confusing *Counter-Statement's* rhetoric and program.[23] According to Burke, Hicks's charge that Burke cannot criticize an author's mood or symbol applies only to the rhetoric of *Counter-Statement* (where he discusses only "*how effects are produced*"), not to the program (where he discusses "*what effects should be produced*"). Burke goes on to say that Hicks mistakenly assumes that he is only interested in technique. In defense, Burke quotes from "Program": "A system of esthetics subsumes a system of politics." In the rejoinder Hicks admits that he misrepresented *Counter-Statement* but says that his "estimate of the book" still stands.[24] He still maintains that Burke is chiefly interested in method and that "'Program' . . . merely describes the social attitudes of a man who is principally interested in technique." Burke's view, Hicks argues, is fundamentally at odds with effective political judgment and action. As with the other reviews, Hicks suffers from intellectual compartmentalization of thought. There is literature, and there is politics. He cannot see that Burke is arguing a position that cuts across the bias of traditional disciplinary boundaries, that he is arguing for a melding of aesthetics and politics.

Isidor Schneider also considers "Psychology and Form" and "The Poetic Process" the two central essays of *Counter-Statement*. Yet, unlike Hicks, he believes that they give the book "revolutionary importance."[25] Schneider latches onto Burke's rejection of pragmatist criteria for assessing the value of art and then decries the "failure" of "Program." This essay, he says, "proceeds to do the thing his own work has most explicitly forbidden—to provide the writer with a purpose" (25). And he faults *Counter-Statement* precisely because of the tentativeness and skepticism that Burke champions. According to Schneider, "the writer works best when working from conviction even when it is only a temporary one" (25). Again, here is a critic who has misunderstood Burke. If anything, "Program" and "Applications" do provide a purpose for the writer. How is it that Schneider assumes that Burke forbids any purpose, especially political ones? Perhaps Schneider, like Hicks, sees no relation between rhetoric and program, and emphasizes literary technique above all else. This is understandable in a person not used to thinking of artistic technique as inherently political.

Harold Rosenberg, writing for *Symposium,* notes that *Counter-Statement* is "characterised by an antipathy for ordinary ideas not only of the sublime but of the sublunar and subliminal as well."[26] Like other critics, Rosenberg believes that Burke mistakenly focuses on technique: "he bases true criticism not upon that acceptance of a work which depends upon a personal sympathy with the symbol used, but upon a technical understanding of and admiration for the craftsman-skill with which the artist constructs his symbol" (117). This is unacceptable, Rosenberg argues, because, while we ought to judge which emotions are "profound and serious," Burke "has a theory about 'universal experiences' which makes it possible for all emotions to be 'profound and serious'" (117). Rosenberg goes on to suggest three further failures of *Counter-Statement*. First, he complains that Burke's notion of form and related discussions offer "a theory of method . . . so abstract that it depends for its value on the individual using it" (118). This invites an ugly relativism that might, Rosenberg fears, lead to a critical sense that would praise "a Broadway hit." Second, he complains that Burke does not offer "a true description of poetic method" (118). Third, he complains that Burke "has accepted a too naïve form of the artist as craftsman and communicator idea," rejecting Burke's claim that there are psychological universals, and in consequence rejecting his reliance on them as a primary source of artistic invention (119). Rosenberg may be right that form is abstract and individual, but that is precisely Burke's point—there is a tremendous "individual component" about form. Yet this individual component, Burke would argue, does not lead to relativism. Burke's interest, in fact, is in the connection between individual and universal factors.

Of all the reviews of *Counter-Statement,* one by Joshua Kunitz gets closest to what Burke is talking about. "The fundamental postulate of Marxism," says Kunitz, "is that *existence determines consciousness.*" Moreover, he says, "ideological changes and conflicts are ultimately traceable to material changes."[27] Kunitz then distinguishes between specious Marxism (based on a "vulgar materialism") and "true" Marxism (which accepts the idea that the superstructure has an "organizing role in the class struggle"). Burke, he points out, attacks economic determinism by debunking the causal theory behind materialist theories of art, a grievous error that confuses determinism with causation. An attack on causation, he says, ends up being an attack on the vulgar materialist, a straw man. Kunitz has hit upon a glaring weakness in Burke's understanding of Marxism. Yet Kunitz does admit that "the fault is not wholly Burke's." Burke, he says, is "fighting the 'detractors of art,' . . . the V. F. Calvertons." Unfortunately, Kunitz does not make nearly enough of this. He ignores the fact that Burke is not writing sophisticated political theory but rather is responding to the views and politics popular in general and arising among literary bohemians in particular. Despite the presence of sophisticated academic intellectuals in his audience, Burke's politics was not meant to be analytically rigorous; rather it was suggestive of the political direction aesthetics ought to take. "I did not expect to win *literal* adherents," Burke tells the reader of "Program," "yet I believe you might find it serviceable, if you will take it . . . but as an impressionistic portrait of the motivational tangle that besets our nation" (*CS,* xiii). Kunitz, in the end, might be right. Perhaps political heuristics of Burke's sort were inappropriate for the 1920s and early 1930s. But Kunitz nonetheless misses the more fundamental point. His remarks make more sense *within* the Marxist debate than they do from without. Burke, I suggest, is talking from without. Within Marxism, the difference between orthodox and vulgar Marxism is great, but when the field is enlarged, that difference is smaller and less important.

Kunitz also attacks the section "Alignment of Forces" in "Program," deeming it an "essentially innocuous and petty nihilism" full of "spitefulness" (20). He assumes that Burke's negativism is a "positive" philosophy or aesthetic, that Burke champions negativism for its own value. Clearly, that is not the case. "Practical-aesthetic," the section immediately preceding "Alignment of Forces," shows that Burke sets up the negative aesthetic as a corrective to the practical (i.e., a "means of reclamation"). Under other circumstances Burke would offer a different aesthetic as a corrective. This is not unlike the argument Chamberlain made about the cult of vacillation. The real question here is whether or not, in capitalist-industrial society, there can ever be other circumstances. If there cannot, Burke's negativism might not merely be a contingent corrective, but a perpetuity that amounts to a positive philosophy. However, Burke's negativism is *more* than a corrective to the practical. It is also a skepticism in the face of self-righteousness. Loyalty, energy, self-discipline, creativeness, and joy—attributes Kunitz champions—are admirable ideals, but Kunitz's vision is at once utopian and myopic. He misses the fact that seemingly positive values can sometimes be harmful. Kunitz does not praise "loyalty" and "energy" in the abstract but "loyalty to the revolution" and "energy for the revolution." To many American Marxists of the 1930s, under the direct influence of the American Communist Party, such "loyalty" and "energy" merely meant the slavish following of doctrinaire orthodoxies. In *Counter-Statement*, Burke lamented, "our fellows want the seasoned stocks and bonds of set beliefs" (*CS*, 106). It is easy to imagine that Burke and Josephson thought something like this as they wandered off into the night, disillusioned by that radical group's demand for blind obedience.

These reviews represent the kind of thinking among Burke's audience and suggest why *Counter-Statement* was routinely misunderstood. Munson, Chamberlain, and Schneider, emphasizing the literary, attacked the literary elements of Burke's ideas. Rosenberg, the art critic, read Burke as theorizing aesthetic technique. Hicks, a parlor socialist, virtually ignored the aesthetic dimensions of *Counter-Statement* and focused on the political issues. Kunitz, with a more philosophical mind than Hicks, added a philosophical justification to his political attack. In fact, Burke tried to cut across such boundaries by combining these interests in a new way. The critics, habituated to their own perspectives, ended up missing the syntheses Burke was attempting and attacked him without really understanding him. This would prompt Burke to try to make his point again, casting his message in terms drawn from psychology, sociology, and anthropology. The result was *Permanence and Change*.

PART II

The Tactics of Conflict and Cooperation

————————————————————————————————— ■

With *Counter-Statement*, Burke united aesthetics and politics into a fairly coherent position that attacked prevailing theories of art, posited a psychological aesthetic centered on "form" and "eloquence," and suggested the political principles that his aesthetic should cultivate. Most important for those concerned about the development of his ideas, he came to believe that aesthetics is fundamentally rhetorical. This culmination of a decade's worth of literary and sociopolitical theorizing was not well received by his critics. One complaint was that his theories were too aesthetic and not sufficiently political; another was that his political emphasis detracted from his aesthetics. To make matters worse, few recognized the essence of Burke's argument: that the study of communication is central to surviving our grave problems and gaining something from fractious and futile debate. More misunderstood than disagreed with, Burke had virtually no impact outside of a small circle of friends and admirers. Yet he decided to continue making his case.

In the second phase of his career, having faced the disappointing critical reception of *Counter-Statement,* Burke cast his ideas about language and politics in terms of his developing thoughts on communication. In particular, he focused on the relationship between communication, social problems, and what he called "political" organizations (that is, governmental structures and commercial enterprises). Burke continued to believe that a failure to communicate effectively was sometimes the source of faction and dispute, and that understanding communication better would help America solve its problems, or at least allow us to live relatively amicable lives. A call for more and better communication is common today, yet even in its more sophisticated manifestations—as in some calls for more "dialogue" between the races—the call is not nearly as complex as Burke's approach. Today the problem is perceived as one of simple translation: two groups speak different "languages," and getting each to understand the other is the key. The current debate over bilingual standardized testing in English and "Ebonics" is just one instance of difference largely seen as a problem of translation. Closer to what Burke was trying to get at are the claims today that blacks in the United States live in a very different world than whites and that race relations would improve if whites were to understand the black experience. More communication between the races, some believe, would lead to common understanding. Burke, if he were alive today, would certainly not dispute this sense of communication, for it is an important part of social life.

But what Burke meant by communication was much more complex. In regard to *Permanence and Change* (1935), Burke stated that his concerns were "communication, interpretation, orientation, integration, coöperation, transformation, simplification" (*CS*, 214). Burke saw these not merely as matters of persons taking the time to talk and listen to one another, but as problems that arise out of the nature of language and meaning. *Permanence, Attitudes,* and *Literary Form* show that the chief problem of language and meaning arises not out of different languages spoken by, say, different racial groups, but by a universal problem of meaning: the belief that there is a neutral language, devoid of emotion, which is the ideal basis for communication because its clarity prevents misunderstanding and the irrationality of emotion from entering into discussion. Eschewing this "semantic" ideal for all but some specific scientific uses, Burke argues that social and political problems are best treated with what he calls the "poetic" ideal, language that is emotionally "weighted." In this view, dealing with social and political problems requires a language that allows otherwise different or even contradictory statements to exist side by side. To consider human experience fully, Burke says, we must recognize that experiences and ideas can be described differently. Burke's fullest treatment of this issue appears in his essay "Semantic and Poetic Meaning" in *The Philosophy of Literary Form*. In *Counter-Statement,* Burke says that art deals with the "constants of humanity" and "universal experiences" (that is, the "various kinds of moods, feelings, emotions, perceptions, sensations, and attitudes discussed in the manuals of psychology and exemplified in works of art" [*CS*, 149]).

Burke's approach to communication in the second phase of his career began with these constants of humanity. *Permanence* starts with the idea that communication is affected profoundly by "orientation" (perspective arising out of experience). Burke goes on to say that large-scale governmental and business structures have led to pathological cultural orientations that have resulted in an "ethical confusion" that needs to be corrected by the adoption of new political principles and sociopolitical structures. Although there is overlap between Burke's sense of communication and the kind mentioned earlier, Burke is really talking about something different.

By the time Burke was writing *Attitudes toward History* (1937), he had shifted his focus from "communication in terms of ideal coöperation" to "patterns of conflict typical of actual human associations" (*CS*, 216). *Attitudes* is a difficult book because it has a frenetic quality resulting from the frantic concerns out of which it arose. Its three parts approach the problem of conflict in very different ways. Part 1 covers what Burke calls "frames of acceptance" and "frames of rejection," using literary genres to explain how we build perspectives or orientations for interpreting the world. In part 2 Burke argues that the great epochs of Western history can be explained in terms of acceptance and rejection frames. And in part 3 he examines how interpretive frameworks arise out of social routines and rituals. The "Dictionary of Pivotal Terms," the set piece of part 3, amounts to an inventory of interpretive and argumentative strategies used in organizations. In the end, Burke's interest in actual organizations led him back to a more direct consideration of rhetoric, albeit characterizing "rhetorical form" more specifically than he did in *Counter-Statement*.

In *The Philosophy of Literary Form* (1941) Burke returned to the consideration of language and aesthetics in general. *Literary Form,* a collection of long and short essays, book reviews, and incidental pieces, he says, is "a summarization of [his] notions about the symbolic function of literary forms" with a "stress . . . upon the work in its internality" (*CS,* 217). Yet this return is not a retreat. His view of aesthetics and language, affected by his developing ideas about communication, is even more psychologically oriented than *Counter-Statement* and retains the social and political emphases of his *Counter-Statement, Permanence,* and *Attitudes* (though his politics had changed). In "The Philosophy of Literary Form" Burke makes the case for the idea of "symbolic action," a concept that fuses the political, aesthetic, and rhetorical into a unity only approached in his earlier writing. Treating a work in its internality, in Burke's view, is treating it in its "external" sociopolitical sense.

In all three books from the second phase of Burke's career he continues to assume that study of the nature and uses of language—especially aesthetic language—is a way to understand how values operate in human society. By focusing on communication Burke develops a more sophisticated blurring of the distinctions between art and politics that he began to undermine in *Counter-Statement*. At the same time, "rhetoric" continues to be developed in more complex ways. In the second phase Burke also comes to a clearer sense that the various issues he treats are part of a wider concern he has about human relations in general and motivation in particular. In fact, Burke said that in *Permanence* he "widened his speculations to include a concern with problems of motivation in general"—a concern that emerges in *Attitudes* and *Literary Form* as well (*CS,* 214). As such, the second phase of Burke's career is something of a transition to *A Grammar of Motives* and *A Rhetoric of Motives,* in which Burke begins to recast his whole argument again.

Part 2 of this book contains three chapters covering *Permanence and Change, Attitudes toward History,* and *The Philosophy of Literary Form* in turn. Each of Burke's books, it will become clear, is his attempt simultaneously to develop his ideas and recast them to an audience that finds it difficult to understand or accept his cut across the bias of accepted concepts and categories.

Permanence and Change
Ideals of Cooperation

■

The unprecedented social despair of the Great Depression compelled many New York intellectuals to question the American political landscape and their place in it. Accepted ideas and institutions had failed, and because there seemed to be no sure direction for fixing America's problems, they held little hope for the future. Believing that capitalism was on the verge of utter collapse worldwide—and that its vaunted ability to resuscitate itself was a feeble, vain, and morbid hope—many intellectuals turned to the Left for an ideology and politics that could address contemporary problems effectively. For some the conversion to socialism or even communism was immediate and complete; for many, it was tortuous. As a result many new movements proliferated, rapidly mutating and combining and dissociating with one another, and the ferment dazzled even the best minds. This virtual riot of new ideas caused a profound crisis of faith among intellectuals. As intellectual instability deepened and spread, Burke became convinced that without the sort of redefinition and readjustment of emphasis he lays out in *Counter-Statement,* real reform in America would be impossible. Burke's solution—cutting broad strokes across the traditional boundaries between aesthetics, politics, and psychology—was as radical as the situation that begot it, repudiating accepted thinking about social problems. The profound change of consciousness that must take place when treating art *fundamentally* in terms of overproduction or fascism cannot be overemphasized. Nonetheless, Burke believed that if his readers understood his cut across the bias, they would see the limitations of the status quo, adopt his politicized aesthetic and sociopolitical program, and thence be better prepared to make the right choices. Yet *Counter-Statement* failed precisely because his audience was not disposed to understand or accept his intellectual challenge. In fact, *Counter-Statement* had virtually no impact at all, for which Burke blamed the book's theoretical abstractness. "I guess Americans simply will not read philosophy as such," he wrote Cowley as he was working on *Permanence,* "and since I want to be read, I must again bestir myself to find the rephrasing of my position that might ring the bell" (Jay, 209).

Permanence and Change: An Anatomy of Purpose was published in 1935, the bulk of it composed in 1932 and 1933. According to Burke, it "was written in the early days of the Great Depression, at a time when there was a general feeling that our traditional ways were headed for a tremendous change, maybe even a permanent collapse" (*PC,* xlvii). Perhaps those fears were so strong that Burke felt compelled to make a faster, more sustained attempt at getting his message across, and he produced a single book in a few years rather than an anthology in seven. "On Interpretation" (part 1 of the book) was published in the February 1934 issue of *Plowshare,* but there is no evidence to suggest that Burke wrote it as a separate essay. Even if he did, it flows seamlessly into the book as a whole. Part 2 ("Perspective by Incongruity") and part 3 ("The Basis of Simplification") were certainly written exclusively for *Permanence.*[1] But *Permanence* is not merely a reiteration of *Counter-Statement;* it is an extension and rearticulation. "Perhaps one drops nothing," he wrote Cowley in 1934, but rather "one simply, as he matures, finds that he must take more into account. . . . I think that everything in [*Permanence*] was implicit in my essay on 'Psychology and Form.' . . . I have simply extended a criticism of art until it included areas of production which do not happen, in the language of common sense, to be called art" (Jay, 209). In particular, Burke included aspects of the social sciences that he considered vital to understanding what holds human communities together. Commenting on the differences between the two books, Burke notes that although "*P&C's* 'literary' beginnings are apparent . . . the 'literary' inheritance from Flaubert involves no 'disjunction.' For a concern with the proprieties of style leads quite 'naturally' into such matters of human relations in general as the social sciences center on. And the 'personal' aspects of style lead to psychology of one sort or another" (*PC* [1984], 303). Even fifty years after the publication of *Permanence,* in the afterword to the third edition of the book, Burke still maintained that the book "in effect takes up where *Counter-Statement* left off " (*PC* [1984], 303). Burke's extension and rearticulation of *Counter-Statement* were adaptations to the social, political, and intellectual climate of the early to middle 1930s, a response to changing relationships between art and politics, new notions about the role of philosophy in social thought, and the impact of psychology on speculations about human problems.

In the 1920s and early 1930s the distinction between once separate disciplines began to erode. For one thing, in the 1920s art and the avant-garde had an enormous influence upon literary culture in general and upon the literary scene in New York in particular. Cubism, the Bauhaus, futurism, surrealism, Dada, atonal music (the list goes on), and new literatures (James Joyce, French and German modernism, realism, the proletarian novel) stimulated much cross-fertilization and aesthetic growth in a variety of art forms. By the early 1930s perhaps the greatest impact of this cross-fertilization was the growing perception that even though each art form is unique, the goals and methods of one have much the same general impact as another. This culminated in the perception that different art forms could and should raise social consciousness and politically galvanize the masses. Thus, the proletarian novel, the murals of Diego Rivera, and even unionizing efforts were seen by many intellectuals on the Left as overlapping greatly. During the 1920s other social and political trends led to the same blending of leftist goals and methods. The flood of European immigrants to the United States, the purported successes of the Soviet experiment, the growth of fascism, the rise of unions and welfarism, and the socially calamitous Depression prompted many intellectuals to believe that socialist principles transcend the disciplines of politics, economics, history, and literary studies, leading to an erosion of the traditional distinctions between them. Writers were beginning to believe that a reorganization of society depended upon changes not only in economic and political structures, but in views of history, art, and philosophy as well. In the early 1930s this realization prompted the further politicization of an already leftist literary culture. Many of the "little" literary magazines started publishing more explicitly political fiction, articles, and editorials, exhibiting increasing theoretical sophistication as the Depression deepened. At the same time political magazines began to publish more prose and poetry. As literary and political magazines became more alike, fiction writers began to speak out on a variety of nonliterary subjects. Burke had long been affiliated with the more important leftist magazines of the era (for instance, *New Republic, Nation, New Masses, Partisan Review*), and in the early 1930s for the first time he began to write about nonliterary matters, without a literary framework.[2]

The penetration of political concerns into aesthetics greatly affected the literary Left. Albert Halper, for example, recounts the excoriation of Diego Rivera by New York's communists on New Year's Day in 1932. Highly regarded as an artist and comrade, Rivera was to speak at the John Reed Club in New York, a communist organization. Halper remembers that there was a "feeling of excitement" in the packed hall and Rivera's entrance was met with a "burst" of applause. After a few remarks by Rivera affirming his solidarity with American communists, a club member shocked the audience by condemning him as "an opportunist who sells his talent to the Rockefellers and other capitalists!"— referring to the fact that Rivera had painted a mural for an automobile company in Detroit and was planning one for Rockefeller Center in New York City.[3] Bill Dunne, the influential communist and editor of the *Daily Worker,* was more extreme, berating Rivera as a "traitor" and a "Trotskyite."[4] At first the crowd was confused. After all, Rivera was one of the great communist artists; his murals were peerless. But the audience quickly caught on and turned mean with "catcalls and further denunciations." This was a situation in which art and politics clashed. Aesthetic sensibilities at first overshadowed the politics of members of the literary Left in the audience. They admired and praised Rivera despite official condemnation. But when the party leadership reminded them of what was politically correct, the writers toed the line.[5] Soon after publishing *Permanence,* Burke suffered a similar experience. While this episode will be treated more fully in the next chapter, a brief description is included here. In

1935 the League of American Writers held its first American Writers' Congress with the intention of establishing communist literature more securely in the United States. Burke presented a short paper, "Revolutionary Symbolism in America," in which he argues that the symbol of "the worker" is not well adapted to American culture and politics but rather is a European symbol that will leave Americans cold. For American literature to be politically effective, Burke felt that it ought to use symbols that were meaningful to Americans; for example, he suggests that "the people" is a better term than "the worker." Burke was not questioning the goals of the communists but merely their tactics. Regardless, he was denounced and viciously attacked. It is true that the denunciations did not come by order of the party, but the attacks had a powerful effect on Burke nonetheless. Later that night, while half awake, he dreamed of excrement on his tongue.[6]

In the 1920s and 1930s many academic intellectuals began reconsidering the relationship between philosophy and society. The problems America faced were not insoluble, they believed. But, they argued, the practical solutions offered for alleviating immediate distresses failed to remedy anything more than symptoms, if they worked at all. The answer to stopgap reform, they believed, would come from better understanding the causes of America's problems. Reworking ideas they had formulated during the previous decade, philosophers and social theorists such as John Dewey, Sidney Hook, Robert Lynd, Lewis Mumford, and Reinhold Niebuhr began to develop sophisticated theories of man in society. They turned to rigorous philosophical analyses to supply new cultural ideals and theoretical frameworks, fearing that traditional views merely duplicated the flaws that led to the problems in the first place. The most interesting philosophers of social reform were involved in some kind of search for community. Southern Agrarians, led by John Crowe Ransom, Allen Tate, and Robert Penn Warren (*I'll Take My Stand,* 1930), suggested that a return to southern values would block the disintegration of society caused by capitalism and urban growth. Lewis Mumford believed that a return to southern values was not enough. In *Technics and Civilization* (1934) he gave southern agrarianism a broader social and economic base, better fit to the kinds of questions that were being asked in the early 1930s. Searching for community in a different way, philosophers and historians such as John Dewey and Charles Beard tried to rework liberalism to be less individualistic. Philosophers such as Sidney Hook (at least the Hook of the early 1930s) argued that Marx's dialectical materialism was the theory and method by which to attain the goals of liberalism. Max Eastman even tried to imbue orthodox Marxism with some element of human inventiveness through which ideas and actions could play a role in social structure.[7] The growing interest in philosophical analysis as the engine of social change shifted the power center of the Left somewhat from political organizers to the intelligentsia. This of course fueled hot debate about the correct methods for social reform (for instance, between Sidney Hook, Michael Gold, Max Eastman, George Soule, Philip Rahv, and William Phillips). It also promoted the integration of aesthetics into the debate, for some of the most astute social criticism and analysis came from leftist writers with keen aesthetic sense (such as Theodore Dreiser, John Dos Passos, Malcolm Cowley, Edmund Wilson, and Van Wyck Brooks).

By the early 1930s the third major trend in the changing intellectual milieu was well established. Psychology in general—and Freud in particular—was stimulating many people in a number of fields. Freud's reconceptualization of the nature and function of the unconscious in its relation to conscious experience and human emotional and social development not only offered a new realm to explore, but served as a new source for the grounding or explanation of a variety of phenomena, including diverse social practices, social institutions, and the appeal or effects of literature. Burke had long been interested in psychology; for example, *Counter-Statement* depended heavily on it to account for literary effect on individuals (in "Psychology and Form" and "The Poetic Process," especially). But Burke's treatment of psychology is very general there.[8] By the time he was writing *Permanence* in 1932–33, he was more informed about psychology and could discuss its concepts with much greater detail and sophistication. For instance, in one section Burke analyzes Ivan Petrovich Pavlov, John B. Watson, Gestalt psychology (*PC*, 11–14), and, in another, Sir Charles Sherrington (*PC*, 247–48). And references to "motives" and "occupational psychoses" pervade *Permanence*. Burke analyzes in some detail Freud (*PC*, 125–29) and theories that modify and apply Freud: William McDougall's psychology of dissociation (*PC*, 129–33); William Marston (*PC*, 34); and William H. R. Rivers's treatment of trauma (*PC*, 136–42).[9] Burke also discusses a large variety of psychological concepts or aspects of human behavior of special interest to psychologists (for instance, "the pleasure principle" [*PC*, 21–23] and dreams [*PC*, 113]). Indeed, psychology pervades the book. Likewise, sociology, though treated generally in *Permanence*, is far less general than it was in *Counter-Statement*. Ideas culled from Thorstein Veblen, John Dewey, and others pervade *Permanence*. Burke also draws from anthropology—for instance in his mention of tribal hunting patterns (*PC*, 38–40), Frazerian analyses of magic (*PC*, 59–65), and Bronislaw Malinowski's study of the myths of the Trobriand Islanders (*PC*, 243).

Interest in aesthetics, politics, philosophy, and psychology in the early part of the Depression came at a time when Burke was going through a period of despair, caused in part by profound social concern and in part by severe personal problems (financial difficulties, divorce, and a near nervous breakdown). In a bitter letter to Cowley, Burke complained, "I sing from morning to night—with trench morale" (Jay, 192). Just three months later, after the publication of *Counter-Statement,* Burke confessed: "Yes, I move toward the end of my nether . . . I all inside me sobbed, and I said I can't conceal it, I am getting frightened. Big taxes on big fortunes—it is so obviously the method of reformation without revolution, I don't see how people can talk of anything else" (Jay, 195). In this despondent period of his life Burke became more political. In October 1931 he wrote to Cowley that he was considering working on three nonliterary pieces: "a pamphlet to be called Invective Against the Republican Party," "a Summons to Poets, and the like," and "a new theory of business cycles" (Jay, 196). Burke also became increasingly interested in the importance of communication and rhetoric in art and politics. In fact, Burke reports that his working title for *Permanence* was "Treatise on Communication." (Fearful that it sounded like a textbook or a "report on telephone or telegraph," an editor suggested that "Permanence and Change" would generate more sales.) Communication, Burke came to realize, is where art, politics, philosophy, and psychology merge. Austin Warren notices another change. An admirer of Burke's skepticism in *Counter-Statement,* he complains that in *Permanence,* Burke was "less confident."[10] In any event, by the time he was writing *Permanence,* Burke says, he was less interested in the "individualistic" bias of his "aestheticist" *Counter-Statement* and "now stressed interdependent, social, or collective aspects of meaning" (*CS,* 214). Even so, the aesthetic tendencies of *Counter-Statement* did not vanish. Writing to Cowley about muckraking journalism, for instance, Burke declared that muckraking "is a dreary thing because it thought that the facts were enough. . . . they are the mere beginning" (Jay, 200). Limited to what in *Counter-Statement* he calls the "psychology of information," he suggested that this form of journalism is simply not aesthetically engaging. Burke lamented that, in the face of muckraking journalism, the public will "be evading, not the depression in society, but the depression in prose" (Jay, 200). As much as Burke turned to communication, his interest was largely theoretical and highly abstract. During the summer of 1933, as he was writing *Permanence,* Burke told Cowley that he was thinking about topics such as "the nature of symbols," "a *conversion* technique," "disputes over the symbols of reference rather than over the objects of reference," "the terminological stressings uppermost at the time" through history, and the relations between religion and poetry, prose, and economic cunning (Jay, 204–5). A year later, with most of *Permanence* probably done, Burke commented that after stressing "first principles" so much he might "go back to straight literary criticism" (Jay, 209).

On the face of it, *Counter-Statement* is about art, literature, and aesthetics. Yet, as has been shown, Burke used the relatively narrow world of art to address broader questions about how to live humanely in a world on the brink of social and economic collapse. By the time he was finishing *Counter-Statement* in 1931,

Burke became increasingly mindful of ideas and values that transcend human differences and that could therefore underpin new perspectives on social, political, and economic relations. Though he may not have put it in these terms, he was thinking about permanence and transitoriness. Believing that art is fundamental to human existence, he framed "Program" with the idea that art is "eternal" because "it deals with the constants of humanity" (that is, "the recurrent emotions, the fundamental attitudes, the typical experiences" [*CS,* 107]). And these constants serve as the basis for his assertions "as to which emotions and attitudes should be stressed, and which slighted, in the aesthetic adjustment to the particular conditions of today" (*CS,* 107). In "Applications of the Terminology" Burke also considers ideas basic to human experience, including hierarchy, "the general bases of critical exhortation," and "'yea-saying' and 'nay-saying.'" With such a wide range of topics, Burke covers a lot. Nevertheless, at some point most of his arguments turn on how misconceptions about the relationship between the permanent and changing aspects of human life affect individual beliefs and institutional policies. For instance, the hollow, deceptive search for a "pure" aesthetic arises out of a misunderstanding of what is truly "permanent" in art. According to Burke, aesthetic "permanence" stems not from some "objective" and "universal" standard of beauty, but from common and enduring emotions (and situations) manifested in a satisfying psychological relationship between artwork, artist, and viewer.

In *Permanence,* Burke's argument for the recovery of the proper "emphases" arises out of concepts and issues basic to psychology, sociology, social psychology, and anthropology, rather than literary aesthetics. These fields of study are alluded to in *Counter-Statement;* but in *Permanence,* Burke more fully embraces the idea that the aesthetic—which now extends to language and meaning more generally—shapes and is shaped by psychological, sociological, and anthropological factors broadly understood. Moreover, his foray into the social sciences, exploiting concepts novel in the 1930s, furthers his cut across disciplinary lines. In *Counter-Statement,* for instance, Burke focuses on the "agrarian-industrial" conflict, overproduction and underconsumption, and unemployment and leisure. In *Permanence* he turns to psychological concepts such as "trained incapacity" and "occupational psychosis." New theories in the blossoming behavioral sciences abounded, and cross-cultural studies convincingly demonstrated to many that there are indeed some universal and stable aspects of human experience. These offered hope to Burke because he was worried that the proliferation of social and political orientations in the 1930s allowed people to find viewpoints that merely justified their already self-serving beliefs and actions. He was worried that a surfeit of views might undermine rational decision making or even prompt people to support merely what was immediately and personally advantageous. Burke feared that a proliferation of orientations might cancel whatever good multiple perspectives may produce. He was worried that the growing complexity of American society was causing or aggravating what he called a "confusion" about "means selection" (the governance of action). The fields of psychology, sociology, and anthropology were then making discoveries, or at least offering the promise of major advances, in precisely these areas. In addition his contemporaries were excited by new ideas in these social sciences.

Though it may not be readily apparent, *Permanence* follows the "Critic's Credo" Burke uses in *Counter-Statement*. In *Counter-Statement,* Burke first "clears the ground" by attacking standard justifications of art (that it is pure, utilitarian, and virtuous). In *Permanence* he instead attacks dominant conceptions of the nature of language, predominantly those that seek a neutral vocabulary, one devoid of connotation and emotion. By attacking Jeremy Bentham's theory of language (and related views), for example, Burke demonstrates that neutral vocabularies are impossible; all terms and systems of terms, he says, have some "weighting" (*PC,* 175–78, 188–94). But even if neutral vocabularies are possible, Burke argues, they would be undesirable for many purposes, especially the most important ones. Consequently "scientism"— the particular, supposedly neutral vocabulary championed in the 1930s (as well as today)—is not the objective, unweighted descriptive tool that champions of science imagine it to be. A comparison of the two apologies shows that by 1932–33 Burke believed that the literary heritage he attacks in *Counter-Statement* is just one manifestation of a more general intellectual problem. Both apologies attack alleged "ideal" forms: pure aesthetics in *Counter-Statement,* "pure language" in *Permanence.* In both cases Burke is not arguing that ideals should be shunned per se, but that there are improper notions of the ideal in matters of human action and community. Flaubert, Pater, and de Gourmont have defective aesthetics precisely because their theories preclude the inevitable effects of social factors on the production and understanding of art. The utilitarian justification of art stems from a transgression of scientific criteria beyond their proper limits. In *Permanence,* Burke argues that science promises "to make a *neutral* vocabulary in the interests of more effective *action*"—another intrusion of science into an area not reducible to scientific criteria (*PC,* 176). In short, Burke clears the ground in both *Counter-Statement* and *Permanence* by criticizing established theories that, in failing to account fully for social factors, end up reducing human activities to scientific factors. Both apologies also hold that this reduction involves misconstruing the nature and role of symbols in human experience: in literary aesthetics in *Counter-Statement,* and language more generally in *Permanence.* It seems that between *Counter-Statement* and *Permanence,* Burke extends the special case of aesthetics to the more general problem of communicating through language.

The rhetorics of *Counter-Statement* and *Permanence* are intended to sharpen critical abilities. We find the rhetoric of *Permanence* in Burke's discussions of "piety" and "perspective by incongruity." Like "rhetorical form" in *Counter-Statement*, "piety" establishes the nature of symbolic appeal on the individual level. Form, the creation and satisfaction of expectations, is at heart a notion of propriety or decorum. A successful expectation–satisfaction curve depends upon an artist understanding the needs of the audience and how the audience will be affected by art. The artist tailors the artwork to both the psychological tenor of people in general and the specific social and aesthetic characteristics of the audience addressed. Form is the foundation of aesthetics in that it makes art fundamentally about how effects are shaped by the audience's psychological disposition. As much as the message affects the audience, the audience affects the message. Thus, there must be some kind of fit between message and audience—in a way, a sense of propriety. In *Permanence*, Burke refers to piety as "loyalty to the sources of our being, . . . [which shows] a marked affinity with childhood experiences . . . [a] deep connection [with] . . . the 'remembrance of things past'" (*PC*, 71, 74). Piety, Burke says, is "a desire to round things out, to fit experiences together into a unified whole. Piety is *the sense of what properly goes with what*" (*PC*, 74). But whereas "Psychology and Form" and "The Poetic Process" deal more with psychological propriety, piety in *Permanence* emphasizes "meaning." "Piety," Burke says, "is a schema of orientation, since it involves the putting together of experiences" (*PC*, 76). The importance of meaning is obvious when realizing that Burke discusses piety in sections on meaning and even begins "The Range of Piety" by saying: "One cannot long discuss the question of meaning, as applied to the field of art, without coming upon the problem of piety" (*PC*, 71). Moreover, the discussion of piety occurs at the start of Burke's discussion of a method for finding meaning, "perspective by incongruity."

The shift of emphasis from psychological satisfaction to meaning tells us something about form that was not quite clear in *Counter-Statement*. "Form," as an inducement of effect, is ambiguous, for "induce" can mean "to cause" or "to lead to." On one level, Burke argues, particular rhetorical forms have a fairly straightforward and immediate impact on an audience—some kind of limited causation. Yet literature also works by leading an audience to a conclusion, the effect gained by the final comprehension of the message after being taken through some "course" of apprehension. This amounts to a leading to a conclusion. Burke found this second sense of inducement so important that he devoted much of the discussion of symbolic appeal in "Lexicon Rhetoricae" to the theory and practice of leading the audience (in particular, "progressive form" and "qualitative form," which involve natural progressions of thought and feeling). Inducement as leading is so important to Burke that throughout his career he paid great attention to how logical progression, telos, and entelechy figure into symbolic appeal.

The shift of emphasis to meaning reveals that by the time Burke was think-ing about piety, his conception of "rhetoric" had become even more distinctly social than it was in *Counter-Statement*. In *Permanence,* for example, Burke sug-gests that criminality—by all indications the utter renouncement of piety—can actually be thought of as pious behavior. "It is *integration,*" he says, "guided by a scrupulous sense of the appropriate which, once we dismiss our personal locus of judgment, would seem to bear the marks of great conscientiousness" (*PC,* 77). The same holds true, Burke argues, for drug addiction.[11] Moreover, Burke concludes his discussion of piety by suggesting that piety involves "inter-action." In the "matter of *interaction,*" he notes, "certain of one's choices become creative in themselves; they drive one into ruts, and these ruts in turn reënforce one's piety" (*PC,* 78). By recognizing integrative and interactional dimensions Burke locates piety and meaning in the textures of lived experience. Later in the book Burke strengthens this connection by arguing that "egoism" and "altruism" are not diametrically opposite terms; "even a simple reference to the self," Burke observes, "involves the organism in a deep concern for things out-side the self " (*PC,* 202–3). It seems clear that Burke recast a psychological notion of form into an epistemological sense of piety because he believed that a pervasive loss of piety was causing or aggravating many of the problems America faced in the 1920s and 1930s. The growth of corporations, industrialism, and sci-ence all created forms of experience that were radically disjointed from basic human needs, and that therefore could not help but corrupt the ways we deter-mined what is meaningful. Economic and intellectual structures had impinged on "meaning" to the point where "meaning" did not mean what it used to.

Perspective by incongruity, the analogue of eloquence, is piety's mecha-nism of symbolic appeal. Whereas in *Counter-Statement* Burke suggests that art is more appealing when it has a proliferation of forms, in *Permanence* he explores how piety is induced by the conjunction of radically disparate per-spectives. Using the grotesque as a convenient motif, Burke argues that what is most needed for developing and refining critical capacities is the ability to see the commonalities and disparities between the most different (not just oppo-site) of perspectives. Perspective by incongruity not only shows us the nature and characteristics of our beliefs and perspectives but, most important, forces upon us a critical view of our own critical capacities. Perspective by incon-gruity, in simple terms, pushes to the limit our ability to generate meaning and make sense of the world through rational, pragmatic means. Perspective by incongruity is a violation of piety for the sake of more firmly asserting the pious. It is a violation of reasonableness to better define "reasonable." Burke opens *Permanence* with a discussion of "All Living Things Are Critics" because, in his view, critical capacities are essential to life, and humans are unique in their ability to criticize their critical capacities. "The human species," he says, is "the only one possessing an equipment for going beyond the criticism of experience to a criticism of criticism" (*PC,* 6).

Finally, both *Counter-Statement* and *Permanence* have programs. In *Counter-Statement,* Burke wants to change political and social emphases. In *Permanence* he is concerned about the way we think about symbols. Eschewing an "informational" view of language, he suggests that we think of language and symbolic appeal as ethical. It is fair to say that *Permanence and Change* is in broad terms a book of ethics, if ethics refers to the general governance of action, covering all that affects the decision to take a course of action (chiefly attitudes, values, and procedures). Burke subsumes traditional concerns about good and bad, making orientation, interpretative methods, and means selection the center of ethics. Burke's view of ethics is thus much broader than traditional views, fully enfranchising psychological, sociological, and anthropological factors. This is not to say that traditional ethical systems ignore such factors but that in them these factors are ancillary. In philosophical ethical systems the definition of "good" is primary; in Christian ethical systems the nature of divine guidance dominates; and in Marxist ethical systems the historical development of economic and class structures is essential (since an analysis of such structures would help emancipate humanity from economic exploitation and class subjugation). Burke upsets the hierarchical relationship between primary and ancillary factors essential to traditional ethical systems because human action, he feels, is too wide-ranging and complex to be accounted for by systems of ethics informed by single hierarchies.

Burke's genius as an ethical theorist lies in his refusal to supplant traditional ethics with another system equally fixed. He offers instead a basic position *toward* ethics, a flexible *attitude* or *approach.* Burke finds the general principles for his ethics in drama and poetry. "At the roots of the ethical," he says, "there is tragedy" (*PC,* 195). He makes this link because tragedy is so much about conceptualizing and manifesting purpose. Although it may not appear so at first glance, focusing on attitudes toward ethics is the beginning of an alternative conception in the fullest sense, for Burke redefines the acceptable limits of ethics. He cautions that going beyond an attitude is to be avoided in order to safeguard against falling into self-serving sureties that intentionally or not abrogate the beliefs, values, and procedures necessary for the collective good. One of Burke's more important contentions is that, in order to adopt the proper attitude toward ethics, we must recognize that language lies at the root of ethics, and therefore we must understand the way language operates in human collectives or organizations. It is this insight that makes *Permanence* an important book. Noting new discoveries in psychology, sociology, and anthropology, Burke came to believe that symbolic capacities fundamentally shape and are shaped by our interior lives, our relations with others in social organizations, and our broader cultural existence. As in his previous book, the program of *Permanence* is a counterstatement to prevailing political dispositions (if we take ethics to be central to the formation, maintenance, and improvement of the polis).

One significant feature of *Permanence* is Burke's shifting politics as the Depression progressed. In *Counter-Statement,* Burke promotes general socialist principles. In *Permanence,* though the argument is more spread out, he quite clearly endorses communism (he often calls it the "communist fiction"). Today's readers of *Permanence* who rely on second or third editions get a very different sense of Burke's attitudes toward communism than readers in 1935 did because Burke made important revisions in 1954. As he was editing the text during the McCarthy era Burke deleted significant discussions of communism out of fear that his audience would misunderstand him and be alienated by his preferences.[12] Commenting about this in 1953 for the second edition of *Counter-Statement,* Burke says: "Unfortunately for the standing of this book in these uneasy times, the family of key words that includes 'communication,' 'communicant,' 'community,' and 'communion' also has a well-known relative now locally in great disgrace—and the experimental author, then contritely eager to think of himself as part of an over-all partnership, had plumped grandly for that word too. Accordingly, statements that concern humanistic integration and cultural reconstruction in general were sometimes localized in terms of this one problematical 'ism'" (*CS,* 215). In the prologue to the second edition of *Permanence,* written the same year, Burke explains that: "Since he [Burke] also subscribed to the notion (and he still does) that communication is grounded in material coöperation, before publication of the [1935] manuscript he augmented it by five or six pages speculating on the form that such material coöperation should take. From the present edition [1954] these pages have been removed. Since, under present conditions, the pages could not possibly be read in the tentative spirit in which they were originally written, the omissions help avoid troublesome issues not necessary to the book as such. There is even a sense in which the omissions could be called a kind of 'restoration,' since they bring the text back closer to its original nature" (*PC,* xlix). Not only did he delete several pages, he also altered the language here and there throughout the text, dropping the word "communism" entirely in favor of allusions such as "productive and distributive patterns of our economy" (*PC* [1954], 66); "a coöperative way of life" (*PC* [1954], 268); and "economic patterns which reduce the coöperative aspects of action to a minimum" (*PC* [1954], 271). In the first edition he is direct: "so far as I can see, the only coherent and organized movement making for the subjection of the technological genius to humane needs is that of Communism, by whatever name it may finally prevail" (*PC* [1935], 93); "a restoration of homogeneity in the means of *communication* is sought in the Marxian emphasis upon one unifying ideology that will inform the Marxian culture" (*PC* [1935], 94); and "Communism is a coöperative rationalization, or perspective, which fulfills the requirements suggested by the poetic metaphor. It is fundamentally humanistic, as poetry is" (*PC* [1935], 344). Burke's praise of communism appears at climactic points in *Permanence*. The longest deleted section is the last two pages of the 1935 version of "On Interpretation," where Burke culminates his psychologically based theory of interpretation by drawing an analogy between individual psychological mechanisms for coping with the world and collective patterns of interpretation (magic, religion, and science). At this point in the second and third editions (*PC*, 65) Burke argues that science's minimization or even elimination of "humanistic or poetic" emphases needs a "corrective rationalization." Burke does not specify what that should be, but careful readers in the 1950s would no doubt have picked up on the allusion, especially if they were familiar with Burke's previous writings. Most readers in the 1950s—at least Burke hoped—would probably not have recognized his communist leanings. By the way, in the first edition Burke also strongly advocates communism at another climactic point, the end.

As much as Burke advocated communism, he was careful not to argue for any particular theory or party. For one thing, Burke had misgivings about the particular ideologies and political organizations then current. This led him to support general principles and goals—indeed, the *promise* of communism—not any specific manifestation of it. Much like his thinking about ethics, he promoted an attitude. In communism he found the ethical values that America needed and the theory of social organization to realize them. But even if he supported one particular brand of communism, he was the sort of thinker who had to treat it on his own terms. As he explained to Cowley in 1932: "I can only welcome Communism by converting it into my own vocabulary. I am, in the deepest sense, a translator. I go on translating, even if I must but translate English into English. [*Permanence*] will have the communist objectives, and the communist tenor, but the approach will be the approach that seems significant to me. Those who cannot recognize a concept, even [if] it is their concept, unless this concept is stated in exactly the words they use to state it, will think my book something else. Having agreed fully with the communists as to objectives, and having even specifically stated in my sinful Program that I considered nationalization of private wealth the fulcrum of the new economy, I diverged solely in my notion of the tactics for arriving at these objectives" (Jay, 202–3). Writers interested in communism faced rapidly shifting power centers and alliances, all vying for the blessings of the Communist Party and even Comintern itself. In such a political environment one could easily be in favor one day and ostracized the next. For free and idiosyncratic thinkers such as Burke, the intellectual orthodoxy endemic to the communist movements surely meant trouble, as it did at the meeting of the American Writers' Congress in 1935.

"The overall background word" of *Permanence*, Burke says in the afterword to the third edition, is "orientation" (*PC*, 305). Burke begins with this word, and all the key ideas in some way relate to it. In a précis added to the second edition he indicates the vital role of orientation to the entire project: "Part I dealt with the 'reading of the signs.' Part II dealt with the intermediate stage between an old and a new way of reading the signs. . . . Part III concerns the 'solution,' insofar as a new fixed way of reading the signs is deemed necessary" (*PC,* 167). The focus on orientation is natural, given the crisis in faith concerning ideologies and institutions during the Depression. But just what does Burke mean by "orientation"? "In a general way," he surmises, "we might say that events take character by a 'linkage of outstanding with outstanding.' . . . The accumulation and interworking of such characters is an orientation" (*PC,* 14). At another point he says, "an orientation is a schema of serviceability" (*PC,* 21). These comments point out that orientation is something like a perspective about how the world operates, stemming from experience. We live in the world and we learn. "Orientation," Burke says, is "a bundle of judgments as to how things were, how they are, and how they may be" (*PC,* 14). Paraphrasing an expression Burke used in 1938, we could say that an orientation is "equipment for living."

This may seem unremarkable. After all, what is profound or even particularly interesting about a "bundle of judgments"? Yet Burke adds two elements that lend some freshness and vitality. First, orientation is not merely a way of looking at the world, a passive function of mind that serves as the basis for processing information; rather, it is an "activity" central to making choices in a complex and often perplexing world. Thus, orientation concerns decisions as varied as choosing between the desirable and the undesirable (for instance, in the discrimination between food and bait [*PC,* 1–2]), between cause and effect (for instance, in the Marxist claim that unemployment results from capitalist economic structures [*PC,* 7]), and between service and disservice (*PC,* 22). Burke's emphasis on decision making becomes even clearer in light of the ideas he associates with "orientation": Veblen's concept of "trained incapacity," Dewey's concept of "occupational psychosis," "means selection," "scapegoating," and "rationalization." All of these have a passive dimension, it is true; but they likewise are mechanisms through which we actively manage daily experience. The second thing that gives Burke's notion of orientation some freshness is the incorporation of aspects of form. In trying to manage our world, Burke says, we deal with the unknown. Orientations help in dealing with contingencies by shaping our anticipation of what will occur. As a linkage of outstanding characters with outstanding characters, orientation "forms the basis of *expectancy*—for character telescopes the past, present, and future" (*PC,* 14). Orientation, Burke says, "affects our choice of means with reference to the future" (*PC,* 18). So put, orientation echoes what Burke is saying about form in *Counter-Statement.* Orientation, like the psychological expectation-satisfaction curve, results from our own experiences and psychological dispositions. But whereas form in *Counter-Statement* is limited to the functioning of an artwork, orientation in *Permanence* applies to all aspects of lived experience.

The relation between form and orientation explains the shifting quality of Burke's analysis. A casual reader of *Permanence* could reasonably ask why Burke so frequently turns to linguistic and literary matters when he is deep into some social, psychological, or political phenomenon (and vice versa). In a discussion of occupational psychosis, for instance, Burke switches from hunting and food gathering as patterns of experience to how "the artist deals largely with the occupational psychosis in its derivative aspects" (*PC,* 39). In a consideration of the impious dimension of reorientation, Burke quickly distinguishes between "necessitous and symbolic labor," which leads to speculations on yellow journalism and poetic symbolism in Hart Crane's work (*PC,* 83). In a discussion of "the ethicizing tendency" Burke analyzes a chapter in Edwin Seaver's novel about American corporate mores, *The Company* (*PC,* 207–9). And in a discussion of perspective by incongruity, Burke comments on how Waldo Frank and Hemingway might use such an idea (*PC,* 110–11) and how Joyce's art and the Oedipus myth involve forms of perspective by incongruity (*PC,* 113–14). The proliferation of literary allusions in *Permanence* could just be examples of social, psychological, and political phenomena, but more is going on. For one thing, psychology is the essence of art; for another, orientation relies on aesthetic and linguistic principles. Put more simply, language underlies the psychological, while at the same time the psychological underlies language. The switching back and forth between the linguistic and the social, psychological, and political reflects the extent to which they all are of a kind. Burke even makes this connection explicit when he argues that "motives" are "distinctly linguistic products" which are "shorthand terms for situations" (*PC,* 35, 29ff.). He observes that we create a terminology of motives "moulded to fit our general orientation as to purposes, instrumentalities, the 'good life,' etc." (*PC,* 29). By conceiving motives this way, Burke has turned a neat trick, for he has altered the idea of motives from its usual conception. A motive is usually thought of as a psychological state—an emotion, desire, physiological need, or similar impulse that incites action. In this usual sense a motive is a purely internal drive which, Burke maintains, is chiefly characterized by a "pleasure principle." Burke dispenses with this typical sense of motives by rejecting the distinction between a pleasure principle and a "reality principle." Both are interpretive psychological responses to the environment. Furthermore, as part of a fundamentally interpretive process, motives are social in that interpretation necessarily is affected by the frameworks, categories, orientations, and habits of practice common to the social group of the interpreter.

What Burke does with motives in *Permanence and Change* is strikingly similar to what he does in *Counter-Statement* with "rhetorical form." Standard conceptions of form see it as a purely internal characteristic of an art object. In *Counter-Statement* form shifts from a characteristic of the art object to the "psychology of the audience." But form is not merely a schematic representation of a psychological state; it is a lived relationship experienced in the interaction between object and audience, a pattern of experience stimulated and individuated by the art object. Rhetorical form cannot exist without an audience observing and interacting with an art object. It is an intermixing of characteristics of the object with factors outside of it. Rhetorical form is a "reality principle," by which Burke means a reflection of the relationship between an object's properties and its environment. Burke shifts motives and form from local, self-contained, *essential* characteristics toward more global and experiential phenomena. As much as *Counter-Statement* broadens art into a psychological sense of form, *Permanence* broadens form further still into the social psychological and even political.

"Perspective by incongruity," like orientation and motives, is a rearticulation of another idea from *Counter-Statement*, eloquence. As previously noted, eloquence provides perspective in that the proliferation of rhetorical forms maximizes the number of ways in which ideas and observations are presented. As Burke points out in *Counter-Statement,* for example, qualitative progressive forms may work through opposition, contradiction, negation, and other such juxtapositions. In sophisticated literature, perspective is gained by juxtaposing fundamentally different viewpoints which organize emotions differently. Eloquence, then, is a specifically literary means for achieving the more general kinds of perspective by incongruity developed in *Permanence*. But the differences run deeper. In the section on the function of metaphor (*PC,* 94–96), for instance, Burke asserts that abstract thinking in general is metaphorical and that "schools of thought" (science in particular) arise out of metaphors writ large. The power of some metaphors to form the bases of perspectives or even worldviews results in part from their richness. Thus, the symbolic component of language is not just one element in a particular perception of the world but functions at the heart of organizing frameworks for perspectives.

One of the more interesting rearticulations in *Permanence* concerns the idea of searching for motives, for it reflects a marked change in Burke's thinking. Whereas in *Counter-Statement* "the search for motives" is engineered principally by negation (a cult of tentativeness, vacillation), in *Permanence* he searches for a more "positive" way in which orientations adjust for intellectual, social, and political pathologies. Indeed, as much as Burke recognizes that we must be wary of simple routines and habits of mind determining our actions, he is far more interested in stimulating the active search for the right "authoritative tests" that lie deeper than our ready conceptualizations. "At times like ours," he warns, "where the entire commercial ethic shaping our contingent demands has brought us to extremities, and where so many patterns of living require us to slight or repress the most rudimentary needs, a 'hand to mouth' conception of duty is not enough" (*PC,* 223). "One must seek" instead, he declares, "definitions of human purpose whereby the whole ailing world of contingent demands can be appraised" (*PC,* 223). Bohemian decadence—even if subtle and telling, as that of Rémy de Gourmont—could not have offered much of a definition of human purpose in a world of dust bowls, bread lines, and Hoovervilles. The basis for Burke's search for motives was not decadence or a cult of vacillation, but the directed and constructive principles championed by Karl Marx. Burke was attracted to Marx precisely because, in his view, "the Marxian perspective is *partially* outside [the accepted circle of contingencies] . . . as regards the basic tenets of capitalistic enterprise" but "inside as regards the belief in the ultimate values of industrialism" (*PC,* 224). Whether or not Burke was correct about the tenets of Marxism, the important point here is that although he was still antinomian, he sought an orientation that in his mind recognized what was good in the status quo and had a complexity that corresponded to the intricacies of the grim 1930s.

"The ethical confusion" is also a rearticulation of the program of *Counter-Statement.* In "Program," Burke affirms a political and social agenda by demonstrating that traditional dichotomies (agrarian-industrial, practical-aesthetic, fascism-democracy, unemployment-leisure, and overproduction-underconsumption) simply do not cast the sociopolitical situation in the proper terms. Burke is not saying that we should reject dichotomization as a way of assessing experience, but that we ought to be wary of clearly false dichotomies and be aware of the deficiencies inherent in all dichotomous thinking. In either event, we should maintain an "indeterminate" attitude toward them. In addition, he seeks to reclaim the artist as the point man of indeterminacy because in his view the artist—by temperament, by the nature of his work, and by his place in society—is inherently antinomian and prepared to consider human problems. Burke contends, for example, that an artist will not blindly accept the agrarian or the industrial viewpoint but will use the dichotomy as a point of departure from which to analyze human experience, the fruits of which ultimately break down this false dichotomy at its root.

The dialectical relationship of "the ethical confusion" to this is most clear in the "egoistic-altruistic merger" (*PC,* 201–4). In this section Burke argues: first, that "egoism" and "altruism" are a dialectical pair; second, that the terms are "functionally merged" ("in a complex universe, even a simple reference to the self involves the organism in a deep concern for things outside the self" [*PC,* 202–3]); and third, that we must be wary of reductions that make one term primary to the other (*PC,* 211). Burke is not arguing that we cannot or should never explain events through a reductionist scheme. We do it all the time, and he even implies that it is inevitable, if not necessary, that we do so.[13] Rather, Burke argues that reductionism is often self-serving myopia. For instance, the reduction of egoism to altruism can result in a materialist "ethicizing of the means of support" such as the Protestant work ethic. And the reduction of altruism to egoism can result in an impulse to explain action through solely subjective, psychological categories (the "pathetic fallacy"). Neither of these, Burke points out, is "incorrect"; they are merely incomplete or slanted views. And since, as he believed, no view is complete or without bias, we must not inflexibly favor one view over another for all circumstances. Reductionism, Burke argues, aggravates "the ethical confusion" by turning what should be a dialectical relationship between ideas into a fixed hierarchy. The ethical confusion in this way obviates what Burke calls the "internal-external merger" (*PC*, 213).

In "The Ethical Confusion," Burke supports a sense of "indeterminacy" similar to what he promotes in "Program." For instance, in *Permanence*'s discussion of Kantian and utilitarian ethical schemes, Burke argues that, regardless of which is adopted, "the same ethical relationship between the individual and his group can be disclosed" (*PC*, 195). Although Burke seeks to justify a general impulse toward indeterminacy in "The Ethical Confusion," he is less concerned with specific cultural alignments and more interested in our general approach to understanding the world. That is, the ethical confusion can be corrected by an adjustment of attitude. In the section concerning "ethicizing of the means of support," for instance, Burke asserts that ethicizing is ubiquitous, mentioning an infant's bottle, Charles Lindbergh's plane, vestal virgins' rites and vows concerning fire, and what might be called "a return to nature" as examples of how we turn objects and activities into goods in themselves (*PC*, 205). By the same token, toward the end of the chapter Burke argues that the pathetic fallacy (the transformation of subjective changes into objective events) "is forever at work molding the qualities of our experience" (*PC*, 215). By linking ethics to general concepts such as "action," "means of support," and "qualities of experience," Burke broadens "ethics" beyond the highly specialized (and academicized) discipline we know today to "humane ways of understanding and living in a complex world."

What are we to make of these rearticulations? What is the significance of Burke's adaptation of his aesthetic theory to broader social and psychological questions? What is the relationship between the merger of aesthetics and social/political concerns in *Counter-Statement* and Burke's call for a readjustment toward the ethical components of symbolic appeal in *Permanence*? Answering these questions in full would require a long monograph, but a preliminary answer is possible here if the role of criticism is considered in both books.

Both *Counter-Statement* and *Permanence* integrate experience-grounded critical principles into aesthetics's basic character. There are differences, however, in the way Burke approaches criticism in the two books. In *Counter-Statement* criticism is treated more as a highly technical method for the analysis of literature. In *Permanence* criticism is conceived from the other direction, as a general orientation or perspective that has something to do with technically complex elements of human society (occupation, magic, religion, science, and psychology, for example). Burke's general sense of criticism in *Permanence* is apparent in his opening conceit, "all living things are critics," which leads to "the criticism of criticism." In a letter to Cowley written in June 1933 Burke said that Cowley was "trying to write an interpretation of certain cultural trends." He explained that, as an alternative, "I am trying to write on the process of interpretation" and that "the *end* of all criticism is the criticism of criticism" (Jay, 206)—or he might just as well have said "orientation on orientation" or "perspective on perspective." Perhaps the best way to understand the difference between criticism in *Counter-Statement* and criticism in *Permanence* is to say that in *Counter-Statement,* Burke is interested in how an individual constructs symbols to deal with social and political structures, whereas in *Permanence,* he is more interested in how our culture constructs social and political institutions (which operate to a great extent through symbols) to deal with what are principally symbolic structures. As Burke said, in *Permanence* he "now stressed interdependent, social, or collective aspects of meaning, in contrast with the individualistic emphasis of his earlier Aestheticist period" (*CS,* 214).

If the 1930s was an era of remarkable politicization of art and a corresponding change in the idiom of aesthetics, why did Burke just then shift away from aesthetics? One clear reason for his shift is that Burke knew quite well that he had failed with aesthetics before. More important, the political turn among literary intellectuals was the wrong sort of change: they had become doctrinaire. Yet how is it that psychology, sociology, and anthropology could supply the impetus Burke sought to push his contemporaries in the direction he desired? These subjects were exciting, provocative, and rapidly developing, and they promised new ways to understand human life and to solve social problems. Developments in evolutionary psychology, experimental psychology, and theoretical and clinical Freudian psychology revolutionized the way the human mind was understood. Freud, in particular, became increasingly popular in the 1930s. Whereas in 1912 in the United States only two of Freud's books were in print in translation and no works about him were available, between 1928 and 1932 nine of his books were in print and four were published about him. Then between 1933 and 1937 eleven were in translation and there were eight studies of his theories. The most exciting area in sociology in the early 1930s was the fairly new field of social psychology, which was shifting from personality analysis to behaviorism. This in part explains Burke's many references to behaviorism and its antecedents. Even anthropology, the most stable of the three fields, was developing in light of new advances elsewhere. Moreover, in the late 1920s and early 1930s the "discoveries" of psychology, sociology, and anthropology were filtering down to the general public. Literature and films with social messages gained popularity, and there was an increase in public interest in psychologically based self-help books (for instance, on child rearing). In one cumulative index the category of "parent and child" shows that three titles were available in 1928, twenty-four from 1928 to 1932, and thirty-seven from 1933 to 1937. As another example, Dale Carnegie's enormously successful *How to Win Friends and Influence People* was first published in 1936.

A brief survey of the topics Burke covers demonstrates how the Depression provided salient social-psychological topics that could grab his audience. Burke opens *Permanence* with a discussion of how environmental factors affect the way we view the world and act within it. These environmental factors are principally labor related but extend well into other areas of life (hence Burke's discussion of behaviorist psychology). It is important not to overlook the fact that Burke frames his discussion of the influence of environmental factors by citing examples in which an individual is *not in control* of his environment. "Trained incapacity," "training," "occupational psychosis," and even concepts such as "means selection" and "scapegoating" can be instances, in Burke's view, of an undue influence of environment. Burke does not use language cavalierly when he draws an "analogy to our human victims" (*PC*, 15). Nor is he careless when he chooses the terms of stimulus-response theory to explain that "motives are shorthand terms for situations," which clearly implies that motives are not purely the fancy of an individual but have some grounding outside the individual (*PC*, 29–36).[14] A look through the rest of *Permanence* reveals discussions of rationalization, piety, perspective, incongruity, and ethics, among other topics. All of these topics suggest that some sort of breach of faith was occurring. It is hard to imagine that in the early 1930s persons concerned about social justice, for themselves or for American society at large, failed to be excited by the close connections Burke drew between situation, motivation, action, and expression.

Burke's audience, the New York intellectuals, would have been especially interested in the kind of argument Burke makes in *Permanence*. After all, the leftist writers produced the proletarian novels, and many of them moved on to progressive reform journalism when proletarian fiction died out. Terry Cooney points out that Jewish intellectuals, a major force in the literary Left of the 1930s, had a special awareness of the sociological and psychological problems of minorities since they lived not only with anti-Semitism but within two harshly disparate cultures.[15] The literary Left was also concerned about the place of blacks in society; several papers about the Negro writer were delivered at the American Writers' Congress in 1935. Academic intellectuals might have been expected to be more open to his ideas since many of them, including Philip Rahv, William Phillips, and the *Partisan Review* circle, had begun to embrace a more literary stance. Yet things did not work out as Burke had hoped. Despite the potential for success, *Permanence and Change* was by and large misunderstood and more harshly criticized than *Counter-Statement*.

Burke again faced the same problem: the ways of thinking that he pointed out as needing changes ultimately proved to be the cause of his rhetorical failure. For instance, in shifting the argument to psychology, sociology, and anthropology Burke questioned the status of science. By charging that science is a "rationalization" on a par with magic and religion, he committed a heresy that the academic intellectuals could not overlook—science was, after all, the epitome of rational analysis. The one passage that seems to have really irritated reviewers is the one in which Burke condemns as torture the use of animals in scientific research. Faith in science—a point that many reviewers argue with Burke—was so strong that an attack on its core (scientific method) was just too much.

As with *Counter-Statement,* the critical responses to *Permanence* show that Burke's message was mostly lost. Edgar Johnson's review, despite its high praise, indicates that he missed Burke's point. Analytically tracing the intellectual lineage of Burke's position on reorientation to T. S. Eliot's "Tradition and the Individual Talent," Johnson says that Burke expands on Eliot's "relationship of interdependence" by "bring[ing] the mechanistic and the poetic interpretations of life into triumphant synthesis."[16] Johnson's interpretation is a serious misreading on two counts. First, Burke does not synthesize mechanistic and poetic interpretations; rather, he keeps them separate and asks for a readjustment of our emphases on them. Second, Eliot, inclined as he was to suffer from what Terry Eagleton calls "extreme right-wing authoritarianism," could hardly have supplied an aesthetic adaptable to Burke's melding of art and politics.[17] Johnson also misunderstood Burke's notion of perspective by incongruity; his description reads: "We break down old conceptions by translating them into an incongruous vocabulary which shows that it was not 'reality' we were describing hitherto, but only a stereotype derived from an arbitrary point of view."[18] His misreading of Burke is serious because it implies that perspective by incongruity is merely a linguistic manipulation of specific concept names, designed to corrupt claims of veridicality. Perspective by incongruity does widen our view, but by yoking disparate viewpoints in a variety of ways. It functions to destabilize a viewpoint not by transforming it but by forcing it head-to-head with other ways of viewing the world. These two misreadings result from the same sort of problem that is betrayed by Johnson's mention of Eliot. Johnson seems to subscribe to a generally Cartesian conception of meaning. His aesthetic follows the search for the singularly foundational and eschews the multiplicity of contingency.

Ernest Sutherland Bates's review of *Permanence* is on the whole harsher and more sophisticated than Johnson's.[19] Bates begins his attack by asserting that Burke's weighted vocabularies are sentimental, as opposed to factual. Bates says, first of all, that Burke's thinking is based on a "nihilistic metaphysics" that rejects the idea of a singular reality and, secondly, that this reality could be accessed by science. Moreover, Bates charges not only that Burke's call for communism is mistakenly populist but that Burke misjudges what is popular. Burke's philosophical skepticism "is one more self-refuting attempt . . . to build a positive system on a negative foundation." *Permanence,* Bates concludes, is "a brilliant essay of ratiocination in behalf of irrationalism."[20] Bates misunderstands Burke in several ways. To begin with, Burke does not fall on the side of sentiment; rather, he argues that the fact/sentiment distinction is illusory. This means not only that fact is sentimental but that *sentiment is factual* (assuming that we accept Bates's claim that Burke adopts a fact/sentiment disjunction in his discussion of weighted vocabularies). Even if we were to agree that Burke favors sentiment, it is inaccurate to say that this stems from a nihilistic metaphysics. Burke does not say that nothing exists or can be known or can be communicated. In fact, he believed quite the opposite: that our problems occur precisely because there are so many things in the world to deal with, because we know about them, and because we communicate about them in very different ways. Burke's attack upon science is not a rejection of the physical or metaphysical; rather, Burke is merely trying to put science in its place. And this is not a theory of irrationalism; rather, he is trying to extend rational thought into an area previously ignored by or thought to be opaque to rational analysis. Furthermore, Bates is mistaken when he claims that Burke was populist. Admittedly, socialism and communism were popular among his audience, but Burke was hardly populist. His endorsement of communism stemmed from his belief that communism was based on stable and perhaps universal human values that were the right correctives for America's social and political malaise. Throughout his career, as much as he often used what was currently interesting, Burke stood outside accepted viewpoints, even in his thoughts on communism in *Permanence.* Bates's differences with Burke could have arisen from Bates's commitment to a traditional rationalism. Bates sought political programs based on and adjudged by secure, foundational principles. Burke also looked for a stable foundation but did not seek one so Cartesian. From his review, Bates seems to have been the sort of foundationalist who could not admit anything other than the absolutes of science. Burke, of course, pointed out the limitations of that worldview.

Writing for the *New York Times,* Henry Hazlitt took a position similar to Johnson's and Bates's. Agreeing with Burke that interpretation is often highly metaphorical, Hazlitt read him as saying that "because we cannot entirely rid ourselves of metaphorical and poetic interpretations of the world we must consciously and always prefer them to 'scientific' interpretations."[21] In fact, Burke says nothing of the sort. He does claim that metaphorical and poetic interpretations are preferable, not because they are always there but because they come closer to accurately reflecting the complexities of social life. Ironically, in the world of politics and human action the poetical achieves the scientific goal of "accuracy" better than science itself does. Of course, "accuracy" is ambiguous; now that the twentieth century has ended, many recognize that scientific accuracy is not the same as poetical accuracy. But in the late 1920s and 1930s the difference was likely not so acute, given the rise of behaviorism and other positive human sciences. Like Johnson and Bates, Hazlitt was an acolyte of scientific method so blinded by the requirement of indubitable and certain knowledge that he could accept neither the limitations of scientific inquiry nor the possibility that other realms of knowledge could best science.

All three reviewers suffered from the same "occupational psychosis" as many of their contemporary intellectuals. The great developments of positive science (and vaguely similar successes in the human sciences), in combination with the profound uncertainties of a chaotic era, prompted an unparalleled confidence in the ability of scientific method to meet human problems and an unparalleled distaste for anything even hinting of contingency or skepticism. The irony, of course, is that Burke's view of science is the one that would prove prescient, as later consensus about science has shown.

Harold Rosenberg in ways makes the same kind of argument as the previous reviewers', but from the other end.[22] He states a belief in a strict separation of science and art and as a disciple of pure poetry expresses a hatred of any suggestion that poetry "works in relation to men's needs and is not an ultimate in itself" (347). Rosenberg complains that although Burke champions poetry as "*the* way of speaking, 'the ultimate metaphor,'" Burke resorts to "more or less rationally organized language" to make his point (348). Rosenberg sees *Permanence* as a "pre-poem," a "philosophic poem" that analyzes "nature, the mind, and the usages of speech, in order to learn their tricks"; and by virtue of that, he sees *Permanence* as tainted by its nonpoetical content. Like modernist poetry, he charges, Burke suffers from "a willed confusion through the obliteration of categories" (349). The reason for this alleged lapse is Burke's supposed belief that in the modern world "words [are] . . . no longer capable of evoking and maintaining collective responses," whereas science can because it "promotes coöperation and thus turns society towards conditions favorable to poetry" (348). By endorsing a perspective by incongruity that allows juxtaposing scientific and social scientific views with artistic ones, Rosenberg asserts that "poetry must cease being poetry in order to be significant" (349). Rosenberg makes all these claims even though he admits that *Permanence* "stands on the fringe of poetic composition."

Rosenberg conveys irritation—perhaps even despair—with modernist poetry, and his criticisms have some justification. Burke does turn to poetry as the basis for the redemption of society, the means to achieve collective ends. And Burke does admit into the picture "science," as Rosenberg conceives it (that is, anything that is "rationally organized" and is not poetry, lumping together philosophy, social science, and hard science). Yet Rosenberg turns Burke inside out. He sees collective society as the redemption of poetry, whereas Burke hopes that aesthetics, broadly understood, will help us through the ethical confusion. By starting with poetry as a problem, Rosenberg betrays a misapplication of Burke's categories. In Rosenberg's view, poetic language differs from scientific language by virtue of something inherent in words themselves, as in his distinction between the language of gesture and the language of definition. While Burke distinguishes between something like gesture and definition in contrasting the psychology of form to the psychology of information, he sees these as *functional* categories. Language, for Burke, is scientific or poetic when it functions as information or form, which depends on the extent to which it creates and satisfies expectations complexly and richly in terms of emotions and human relations. The whole point of treating the languages of science and poetry as metaphorical (and to judge one as superior) is to point out that all language has the same basic qualities. Language is language; the purpose it serves makes the difference. Ultimately, Rosenberg misreads Burke because Rosenberg adopts a strong distinction between science and art and has pure poetry on the one hand and everything else on the other. The "science" he abhors in *Permanence* is hardly science at all. Whereas the champions of science decry Burke's use of the poetic and social psychological for its introduction of irrationality into science, Rosenberg condemns the social psychological and philosophical for its introduction of "rationality" into the "irrational" (poetry). Ironically, Rosenberg buys into the same distinction as does Johnson, Bates, and Hazlitt but chooses the irrational over the rational.

Three more reviews of *Permanence* are of interest because they are the first reviews of Burke to appear outside of literary or political journals. T. D. Eliot, writing for the *American Sociological Review,* does not say much but praises the book highly and states his belief that *Permanence* has great sociological value. Louis Wirth similarly praises Burke in the *American Journal of Sociology* but concentrates on *Permanence*'s value for social psychologists. In the *Quarterly Journal of Speech,* Irving J. Lee adds that *Permanence* contributes to rhetoric as well, especially regarding topoi common in the field of speech communication. These reviews are more descriptive than anything else, a possible symptom of their audiences' lack of familiarity with both Burke and his kind of thinking.[23]

With the failure of *Counter-Statement,* with complaints that it was theoretically vague, Burke rearticulated his message from a new starting point, concentrating on giving his argument a stronger theoretical base. This was a reasonable tactic, for his audience was beginning to see the general kind of argument he was making. But as these reviewers of *Permanence* indicate, they remained blinded by their own perspectives and were still caught up in issues and problems that undermined Burke's message. Burke tried yet again, in *Attitudes.*

4

Attitudes toward History
Conflict in Human Association
━━━━━━━━━━━━━━━━━━━━━━━━━━━━━━━━━━━━■━━━━━

With *Attitudes toward History* (1937), Burke suffered again the disappointments experienced with *Counter-Statement* and *Permanence and Change*. By now a pattern was emerging: each book garnered more attention, but critics were increasingly harsh. At least Burke might have found some consolation in the fact that many of the reviews of *Attitudes* were longer and displayed greater intellectual rigor and sophistication than the reviews of his previous work. Clearly, by the time *Attitudes* was published Burke was being taken more seriously than ever. As seriously as Burke is taken today—*Attitudes* was reissued in a third edition in 1984—the book remains largely neglected. References to it outside of a handful of scholars in English and communication studies is slim indeed, and those scholars who do use *Attitudes* tend to use it piecemeal for their ends instead of his. Perhaps the best way to begin to understand the reception of *Attitudes* then and now is through an unlikely route: by considering a rather curious section of *Attitudes* that has been virtually ignored by scholars today. Though largely forgotten, "The Dictionary of Pivotal Terms" is by Burke's own admission a vital part of *Attitudes*. "The book," he says, "summed up its sociology in a 'Dictionary of Pivotal Terms'" (*CS*, 216). Perhaps the dictionary is ignored today because it does not seem to fit well into *Attitudes*. It is simply different from the rest of the book. Part 1 of *Attitudes*, "Acceptance and Rejection," seems mostly about literary authors and poetic categories. Part 2, "The Curve of History," seems mostly about the historical development of social and political structures. The dictionary, which appears in part 3 ("Analysis of Symbolic Structure"), seems to be a hodgepodge of directionless ruminations about an idiosyncratic collection of concepts that have something to do with something or other. Surely many readers figure that the dictionary must be integrally related to the rest of *Attitudes*, for it is, after all, the third section of the book. Yet just as surely, most readers have trouble figuring out just what the connection is. In a way, the dictionary is indeed something added on. This may not be as apparent to today's reader as it was to readers in the 1930s because first editions (1937) of *Attitudes* are now rare. Virtually all readers of Burke are familiar with the second (1959) and third (1984) editions, which were published as single books, with the dictionary beginning about halfway through the main text. The first edition of *Attitudes* was published as two separate books by the New Republic press. Volume 1 contained "Acceptance and Rejection" and "The Curve of History." Volume 2 contained only the "Analysis of Symbolic Structure," three-fourths of which is the dictionary. Unfortunately, there are no clear indications of why *Attitudes* was published in two volumes.[1]

Scholars today may be ignoring the dictionary because it is so puzzling, even superficially. One glance at the "entries" reveals an odd collection of terms: alienation, clusters, communion, control, cues, discounting, efficiency, essence, forensic, identity, imagery, opportunism, transcendence. Worse still, more than half of the entries are highly idiosyncratic and perplexing:

> Being Driven Into a Corner
> Bridging Device
> Bureaucratization of the Imaginative
> Casuistic Stretching
> "Earning" One's World
> "Good Life"
> "Heads I Win, Tails You Lose"
> Neo-Malthusian Principle
> Perspective by Incongruity
> Problem of Evil
> Repossess the World
> Rituals of Rebirth
> Salvation Device
> Secular Prayer—or, extended: Character-building by Secular Prayer
> Stealing Back and Forth of Symbols
> Symbolic Mergers
> Symbols of Authority

On surveying the table of contents, readers surely must have wondered what he was talking about. Burke's "definitions" are peculiar too. He eschews the short, terse definitions typically found in dictionaries, favoring instead long passages. The thirty-three entries in his dictionary average five to six pages in length and range from one-half page to thirty pages.[2] The long passages are open-ended speculations more suggestive than definitive. For example, even in the shortest entry, "Control," Burke is evocative and allusive: "To control a bad situation, you seek either to eradicate the evil or to channelize the evil. Elimination vs. the 'lightning rod principle,' whereby one protects against lightning not by outlawing lightning but by drawing it into a channel where it does no damage. . . . Pamphleteering. When liberals began to think, not of eliminating war, but of finding 'the moral equivalent for war,' liberalism was nearing the state of maturity" (*ATH,* 236). The longer the entry, the more open-ended and suggestive. An extended analysis of this is beyond the purpose here, but the flavor can be conveyed by an examination of one of them, "Identity, Identification." This section is fairly representative of the longer entries and ties together many themes of *Attitudes.* In fact, Burke begins the entry by noting that "all of the issues with which we have been concerned come to a head in the problem of identity" (*ATH*, 263). If that is so, then *Attitudes* can certainly help us understand *A Rhetoric of Motives* (1950), which centers on the term "identification."

The overall thrust of "Identity, Identification" is that a person's identification with "manifestations beyond himself" is natural and reflects our fundamentally social, political, and historical makeup. Attempts to deny this and "eradicate" identification as a positive concept for understanding human nature are folly and perhaps even dangerous, Burke warns. One example of such an attempt is bourgeois naturalism, which "in its most naive manifestation made a blunt distinction between 'individual' and 'environment'" (*ATH*, 263). This belief was so tenacious that even "when bourgeois psychologists began to discover the falsity of this notion, they still believed in it so thoroughly that they considered all collective aspects of identity under the head of pathology and illusion" (*ATH*, 263). Their attempts at a cure were futile. Other examples are the rejection of identity toward the end of Hellenism and in czarist Russia. They led to Christian evangelism and Marxism, movements that were attractive in part precisely because they embraced identification. Burke asserts what he takes to be an inescapable truth: that "the so-called 'I' is merely a unique combination of partially conflicting 'corporate we's'" (*ATH*, 264). We may substitute one identification for another, but we can never escape the human need for identification. "In fact," Burke comments, "'identification' is hardly other than a name for the *function of sociality*" (*ATH*, 266–67). With this general principle established, Burke turns to the structures of identification so basic to American culture that they are a citizen's "birthright": identification with business corporations and collectivist political structures. However, the identification with financial corporations "is necessarily impaired insofar as the obligations are of a one-way sort" (*ATH*, 265). Attempts by businesses to make identification two-way through insurance plans creates competition between corporations and government for the worker's sense of identification (the government supplies social insurance as well). Since there are many businesses, political parties necessarily have conflicting identifications with various businesses. All of this leads to "confused shufflings of identity" (*ATH*, 265). Making matters more complicated, Burke observes that businesses are not the only entities with which we identify. Family structures, institutions (e.g., an editorial board, church, city, nation, guild, college), and even another person ("love," Burke says, "is shorthand for membership in 'the smallest corporation,' a partnership of two" [*ATH*, 266]) create a myriad of "corporations" in which a person participates.

The rest of "Identity, Identification" (about two-thirds) is a tentacular exploration of various means of identification, how an identification simultaneously promotes and subverts itself, and the negative consequences of such self-promotion. Burke points out that when we engage in "corporate boasting" (praising, even exaggerating, the qualities of the person, group, or organization we identify with), we create conditions that advance our interests and frustrate the interests of others. He describes such self-promotion as "rigging the market" and "cashing in" (*ATH,* 267). Burke also points out that identification, to some extent, centers around aspiration to an ideal. This often involves the creation of symbolic structures that embody the ideal or at least encourage the attempt to attain ideal characteristics. Burke thus explores the role of symbols in what he calls "vicarious sharing": we use literature, he says, to create epic heroes who have divine characteristics we can never acquire. In a "secular" variant of hero worship, "the individual hero is replaced by a collective body" (*ATH,* 268). Burke then points out that identification to some extent involves perspective by incongruity; that is, since identification is never perfect, when we identify, we understand and experience the world from a perspective that we only partially enjoy. Near the end of "Identity, Identification" Burke suggests that "a man 'identifies' the logic of a human purpose with the following *points d'appui*": God, nature, community, utility, history, and "*the self.*" "Or," Burke says, "we might divide the field" into "totemistic identification," "the carrying of the 'family' perspective into the treatment of a vast corporate, latently political organization," "the parliamentary," "historic purpose," and "new co-operative frames" (*ATH,* 271–72). Recognizing several contradictions and paradoxes of identification, he concludes "Identity, Identification" with a proviso. Even communism, the most promising political structure, cannot resolve all the contradictions of identification, for any state is subject to intractable political forces beyond its borders. So, for instance, despite whatever potential Russian society of the 1930s had for minimizing the contradictions of identification, the arming of Germany by Adolf Hitler forced upon Russia new conditions that would lead to conflicts between "corporate we's": "the squandering of vast material resources in purely unproductive ways—that is, the training and equipping of the army," "magical-heroic vessels of authority," and the necessity of peace-minded individuals to "identify themselves with a corporate unit devoted to war" (*ATH,* 272–73). Even so, Burke's final thoughts are in defense of socialism. "Such paradoxes," he claims, "must inevitably distort the logic of a truly socialist development." He hopes that the critics of socialism will "pause long enough to suggest how matters could be handled otherwise" (*ATH,* 273)— though obviously they cannot. Looking at "Identity, Identification" on the whole, two themes emerge powerfully: first, that identity and identification are exceedingly difficult if not impossible to grasp fully, given the many facets, manifestations, and purposes they involve; and second, that these concepts are profoundly social and political in essence and impact.

Entries such as "Identity, Identification" lead readers to wonder what Burke was trying to accomplish with his enigmatic dictionary. Outside of the text itself, there are only a few clues. "My 'glossary' of terms," Burke explains in the 1984 afterword to the third edition of *Attitudes,* "was trying hard to be as mellow as it could at a time when a great nation, with many of the greatest citizens the world has ever known, went mad, and all about us there were such goadings from so many quarters, and they developed from the most trivial of interrelationships" (*ATH,* 422).[3] In a world "gone mad," a world of competing voices that did not listen to one another, Burke was trying to understand the nature and characteristics of conflict in the political community—and to figure out how to get partisans of all sorts to stop rejecting automatically other points of view. Burke felt that the best way to forge a new basis for understanding was "to isolate major moments in the dialectics of allegiance and faction" (*CS,* 216), which was why he called his dictionary a glossary of *pivotal terms.* Each entry concerns some issue or problem that Burke believed was central to allegiance and faction and thus represented a potential hindrance to acceptance, agreement, and social progress.

Burke chose these "pivotal" terms and developed them in his idiosyncratic way because he wanted to create a perspective on perspective taking. He describes the dictionary "as depicting a *comedy* of human relations," with terms "embodying a 'comic frame of acceptance'" (*ATH,* 422). This results in a "methodic view of human antics as a comedy, albeit as a comedy ever on the verge of the most disastrous tragedy" (*ATH,* introduction, n.pag.). The desire to create a frame of acceptance explains why the dictionary is speculative and meandering. Burke believed that the dictionary, as an especially fertile acceptance frame, should incorporate fairly a variety of competing ideas and perspectives (at one point he even refers to the dictionary as a "perspective by incongruity"). In doing this, Burke on the one hand considers enduring and pervasive aspects of perspective taking (terms "which recur quite frequently . . . under various historical conditions" [*ATH,* introduction, n.]). On the other hand, Burke also reflects his specific milieu, especially regarding the particular causes of faction in American society during the Depression and the social, economic, and political changes he deems necessary to improve conditions. "All the terms we consider alphabetically in our fourth section," Burke says, "are of a strongly attitudinal sort. Even when they name a process or a condition, they name it from a meditative, or moralizing, or even hortatory point of view" (*ATH,* introduction, n.pag.). The issues and problems are so complex that Burke felt no single idea or analytical line of development could fairly represent what was going on in the major moments of allegiance and faction. Burke decided instead to investigate the many and varied paths open to those willing to follow the pivotal terms' implications. This "method" stems from the same attitude that drove Burke to use copious footnotes throughout the text of *Attitudes*. "When this book first appeared," Burke remembers in the 1950s, "one reviewer objected to the profusion of footnotes. We grant that they are a blemish. But they were necessary. For the material 'radiated' in various directions, and these 'radiations' could not have been traced in any other way. . . . And, looking again, perhaps we might discover that the last and longest section, on the 'pivotal terms,' is in effect one continuous series of footnotes alphabetized" (*ATH*, introduction, n.).

Although the dictionary is different from the rest of the book in purpose and style, it is integrally related. The dictionary is Burke's way of working out how the general principles concerning poetic categories and historical development apply to sociopolitical organizations. The dictionary also explains key strategies people use to define their place in social structures and maneuver in them.

The relations between *Attitudes* and Burke's previous books reveal a lot about what Burke was trying to do with *Attitudes*. There are, to begin with, important parallels between *Counter-Statement* and *Attitudes*. Near the endings of both are long terminological apparatuses that involve literary themes ("Lexicon Rhetoricae" and "The Dictionary of Pivotal Terms"). More important, literature is vital to both in other ways. The central role of literature in *Counter-Statement* is obvious; Burke conspicuously discusses authors and numerous literary and aesthetic theories. In *Attitudes* the role of literature is more complicated, for the explicit concern is the relationship of attitudes to history. Even so, in half of "Acceptance and Rejection" ("Poetic Categories") Burke discusses the nature, scope, and function of poetic categories; and in the rest of the first part of *Attitudes* he discusses the genesis and destiny of "acceptance frames," which amounts to a treatment of poetic categories.

Another indication of the literary character of *Attitudes* is the opening chapter on "William James, Whitman, and Emerson," in which Burke frames the book by analyzing how the literary life can be an "acceptance frame." It is no mere coincidence that Burke begins both *Counter-Statement* and *Attitudes* with such speculations. "William James, Whitman, and Emerson," like "Three Adepts of 'Pure' Literature," is an analysis of three ways that devotion to a literary life promotes habits of mind and action for dealing with the world. In *Counter-Statement,* Burke rejects the aesthetics of Flaubert, Pater, and de Gourmont because their brands of pure aesthetics divorced the literary life from social concerns. Flaubert's means did not match his ends. According to Burke, whereas Flaubert tried to "make of literature the *verbalization* of experience, the conversion of life into *diction,*" he ended up making "literature the verbalization of *experience,* the conversion of *life* into diction" (*CS,* 7). Pater's aesthetic failed because he used ideas solely to serve aesthetic ends, not to understand social problems and suggest how to address them. As Burke observes: "Ideology in Pater was used for its flavor of beauty, rather than of argument. He treated ideas not for their value as statements, but as . . . any other element of fiction" (*CS,* 14). Burke rejects de Gourmont's aesthetic because, with its essential individualism, it was an *ars gratia artis* conception that supported art regardless of the consequences. These three visions of pure literature are socially and politically bankrupt—something that art, in Burke's view, must never be. By rejecting the aesthetics of three giants of the 1920s and 1930s literary world, Burke is clearly responding negatively to prevailing notions of the artistic life.

In "William James, Whitman, and Emerson," the opening chapter of *Attitudes,* Burke rejects notions of the artistic life but offers a positive alternative. He begins by praising what he calls "perhaps the three most well-rounded . . . frames of acceptance in American literature" for their resistance against explanations (*ATH,* 5). Instead of falling into often self-serving habitual response frames—what Burke in *Counter-Statement* calls "yea-saying" (an acceptance frame) and "nay-saying" (a rejection frame)—James, Whitman, and Emerson each in his own way delved into the ambiguities, enigmas, and profound complexities of human experience and eschewed analytic schemes as means for exploring the richness of poetic forms. Likewise, Burke's reaction against the encroachment of scientist thought into more properly human realms is an attempt not only to break the grip of analytic forms, but to show that their highly touted promise is illusory. And as the three authors do, Burke offers a positive alternative: the emancipation and revitalization of poetic forms.

As one step in the process of emancipating and revitalizing poetic forms, Burke—in what is perhaps his greatest theoretical insight—broadens the idea of "action" well beyond established limits to cover what he calls "symbolic action." But Burke eschewed the simple-minded approach of many who considered themselves "men of action." He began *Attitudes* with the question of acceptance frames in part because of the political situation of the 1930s. For one thing, there were reformers, New Dealers, and other progressives who sought to redress the failures of the Depression by uncritically accepting the government's programs, which many on the Left viewed as merely consolidating the wealth and power of those already rich and powerful. Opposing the reformers were supporters of a variety of socialist political views, the most influential of which was the American Communist Party. As the Depression worsened, the issues grew more divisive, the need for solutions grew more desperate, and the political differences grew sharper. The problem Burke had with many intellectuals on both sides was that they were too easily and uncritically doctrinaire. Put more harshly, they too easily fell into slavish patterns of thought that they mistook for sensitive critical analysis. Desperate times breed desperate thinking. Burke favored James, Whitman, and Emerson because they avoided the simple acceptance frames increasingly common as the Depression progressed. The political mainstream and the Right—including reformers, New Dealers, and progressives of many sorts—proffered various schemes (including reliance on the providence of the market) to restore economic stability, most of which were crassly utilitarian and sometimes even avaricious. In particular, Burke was afraid that utilitarian schemes were especially vulnerable; though they were intended to redress the causes of the Depression, in reality they were only short-term fixes. Burke was not against utilitarian thinking per se, but he did object to *solely* utilitarian modes of thought and to their specific manifestations in the late 1920s and 1930s. Thus, it could be stated that Burke started *Attitudes* in order to use James, Whitman, and Emerson to lay the groundwork for breaking the stranglehold of utilitarian thinking.

The problem of acceptance frames was not merely an academic puzzle to Burke. He believed that conservative politicians had used simplistic acceptance frames to guide their thinking about social and political reform, which had resulted in the repression of dissident voices. Only a generation before, for example, communist intellectuals were routinely harassed, beaten, and even killed in the name of national security. When communists across the nation protested against Tom Mooney's death sentence, the government cracked down on the IWW, arresting 166 members of the union for violations of the Espionage Act. The editorial offices of *Blast,* an anarchist paper, were raided in this crackdown. The Espionage Act of 1917, which supplied the grounds for the indictments, was soon used to prevent mail distribution of the *American Socialist,* the *Jewish Daily Forward, The Masses, Social Revolution,* and the *International Socialist Review.*[4] One particular episode of anti-Left fever culminated in the mass deportation of 249 Left-leaning intellectuals (foreign-born "undesirables") in late 1919, including Emma Goldman. The Espionage Act was not the only grounds for attacking leftist periodicals. The postmaster's office vigilantly and effectively used obscenity laws as excuses to censor. The case of *Broom* is a good example. Like most little magazines, *Broom* faced severe financial difficulties. To survive, the editors printed it in Europe. After several editorial changes Matthew Josephson became the editor, obtained four thousand dollars in funding, and returned the magazine to New York in 1923. Edited by Josephson and Malcolm Cowley, the review lasted only five more issues. The key to its downfall was the post office censor, who had discovered that the November 1923 issue contained a story he found objectionable. He read the next issue after it was printed but before it was mailed. Appearing in that January issue was "Prince Llan," a story by Kenneth Burke in which a "plural breasted woman" appears. The post office censor's interpretation of Section 480 of the postal laws held that the mention of one breast was within the bounds of aesthetic taste, but the mention of two breasts was obscene. The issue was banned from the mail, which was more than the magazine could stand financially.[5]

Though the fear of repression by conservative politicians was still well grounded in the 1930s, members of the Left ultimately had more to fear from within, for the Communist Party was beginning to choke on its own intolerance. As the 1930s progressed, the membership and visibility of the Communist Party grew while its intellectual flexibility deteriorated and the sophistication of its doctrine degenerated. The history of Trotskyism in the United States is a good indication that the American Communist Party became less interested in realizing the ideals of Karl Marx and Friedrich Engels and more interested in simply maintaining the orthodox Soviet party line. Initially supporting Leon Trotsky, the American Communist Party eventually disclaimed him, making his theories taboo. Anyone supporting Trotsky was a traitor to the cause, and failure to denounce Trotskyism was enough to occasion suspicion. This orthodoxy was so strong that many intellectuals, despite the mounting evidence of excesses, failed to denounce Joseph Stalin until his nonaggression pact with Hitler in 1939 spawned profound disillusionment and a mass exodus of intellectuals from the party and its doctrines.[6]

The case of V. F. Calverton, founder (1923) and editor of *Modern Quarterly,* is a good example.[7] He was one of the earliest of the well-known leftist intellectuals to suffer because of the direction the party was going. As early as 1927, wanting to write about Trotsky and Georgy Plekhanov, he was warned by friendly party members to be careful. If his interest in dissent was not enough, his frequent refusals to join the party prompted further suspicion, which was later fueled by the openness of his magazine to discussions of Trotsky. Calverton at that point was not a Trotskyite; he merely thought that Trotsky had something important to say. By 1929 the *Daily Worker* mounted a scathing attack on the *Modern Quarterly,* declaring it Trotskyite and refusing to print Calverton's defense. In late 1932 the Communist Party and the Communist International roundly denounced him as a Fascist. Friends and other writers did little to help him, and regular contributors to his magazine departed. By 1934 Calverton's editorial board, consisting of Max Eastman, Sidney Hook, and Edmund Wilson, had serious misgivings about his editorial judgment. Calverton's influence faded, and he died in 1940 at the age of forty.[8]

Burke too suffered from the intolerance of the party. "Revolutionary Symbolism in America," a paper he delivered at the American Writers' Congress of 1935, was intended to help communist writers in their desire to formulate a truly communist American literature. In this address Burke argued that the symbol of "the worker" was inappropriate for the American situation and that communist literature would be better served if writers used "the people" as a symbol. Burke said later that he made this proposal with "a terrific desire to belong."[9] At the end of the speech there was applause, but Burke was nonetheless attacked afterward during a discussion of the paper. He was even denounced as a heretic (one member of the Writers' Congress, Friedrich Wolf, went so far as to compare Burke to Hitler). The attacks continued, Burke reported, "until I was slain, slaughtered. . . . I felt wretched." The problem of acceptance frames, then, was not a mere intellectual puzzle to Burke. It clearly had dramatic political and personal ramifications, even though soon "all was forgiven."[10]

Because acceptance frames are profoundly symbolic, Burke believed that literature is an especially appropriate starting place for understanding their nature, characteristics, and function in human affairs. In a description of his first intentions for "Acceptance and Rejection," Burke told Cowley that he intended to explore "how thinkers, of either the imaginative or conceptual sort, build vast symbolic bridges to get them across the gaps of conflict," including how "frames of acceptance become irrelevant, and even obstructive" (Jay, 212–13). A glance at some differences between *Attitudes* and his previous books will reveal the extent to which Burke thought that literature figures into acceptance frames. Whereas the center of *Counter-Statement* is literature, *Attitudes* is more explicitly about the forging and breaking of alliances in political communities. "The Curve of History," for instance, considers "productive and mental patterns developed by aggregates" (*ATH*, 11) and certainly has no direct analogue in *Counter-Statement*; and "The Dictionary of Pivotal Terms" is only remotely about literature. The major essays on literary technique in *Counter-Statement* ("The Poetic Process" and "Psychology and Form") have no direct counterparts in *Attitudes*. Perhaps the best way to describe the relationship between *Counter-Statement* and *Attitudes* is to say that *Attitudes* is a grand speculation following the lead of "Program." In a way, *Attitudes* is to *Counter-Statement* as "Program" is to *Counter-Statement;* the difference is a matter of degree. Even so, *Attitudes* is more similar to *Permanence* than *Counter-Statement*. Like *Permanence,* which is a general study of perspective, interpretation, and communication, *Attitudes* attempts to reorder intellectual, social, and political emphases in those realms. In the introduction to the second edition (1959), in a typically general, yet telling comment Burke indicates that "though the tendency is to pronounce the title of this book with the accent on *history,* so far as meaning goes the accent should be on *attitudes*" (*ATH*, n.pag.). His use of the term "attitude" here is much the same as that in *Permanence,* meaning a general disposition (involving thought and action) to respond (by thought and action) in a particular way. Moreover, in *Attitudes,* Burke examines the various ways in which attitudes are influenced, so that people may more effectively cultivate socially beneficial attitudes. But whereas *Permanence* focuses on the anthropological, sociological, and psychological aspects of perspective, interpretation, and communication on the local scale, *Attitudes* draws inspiration from "history," by which Burke means "primarily man's life in political communities" in large-scale formations such as "Christian evangelism," the "medieval synthesis," "naive capitalism," and the sweeping modes of thought described by the poetic categories (*ATH*, introduction, n.pag.). The grand sweep of history in *Attitudes* only distantly affects the small-scale "political" organizations discussed in *Permanence*.

Nonetheless, *Attitudes* and *Permanence* are closer than this difference at first allows. In the largest section of part 1, for instance, Burke analyzes traditional poetic categories such as tragedy, comedy, elegy, and satire. Going beyond what he does in *Counter-Statement*, Burke treats poetic categories in terms of perspective and orientation. He begins "Poetic Categories" by suggesting that "our way of approaching the structures of symbolism might be profitably tested by the examination of various literary categories, as each of the great poetic forms stresses its own peculiar way of building the mental equipment (meanings, attitudes, character) by which one handles the significant factors of his time" (*ATH*, 34). "Our way of approaching the structures of symbolism" refers to the general problem of perspective and adjustment that is treated in both *Counter-Statement* and *Permanence*. In summarizing his thoughts on the poetic category "epic," Burke says that "the epic is designed, . . . under primitive conditions, to make men 'at home in' those conditions" (*ATH*, 35). "At home in" has a strongly psychological connotation (security, comfort, happiness, familiarity, and so on), especially when drawn in the terms of the epic hero and "identification," as Burke does on the pages following this quotation. Burke thus embraces the psychological perspective of *Permanence* but extends the analysis to larger political formations. Burke does much the same thing regarding tragedy, which he says "flowered when the individualistic development of commerce had been strongly superimposed upon the earlier primitive-collectivist structure" (*ATH*, 37). This cultural change "sharpened the awareness of personal ambition as a motive in human acts"; hence tragedy "admonished one to 'resign' himself to a sense of his limitations" (*ATH*, 39). It is in such terms that this poetic category, then, profoundly affected the Greeks' view of their world. Burke makes the same kind of argument for comedy, which "like tragedy . . . warns against the dangers of pride, but its emphasis shifts from *crime* to *stupidity*" (*ATH*, 41). To complete the analysis, epic, tragedy, and comedy, which Burke calls "positive" categories, have "negative" counterparts (elegy, satire, burlesque) that operate similarly. The "transitional" categories (grotesque and didactic) are equally concerned with perspective and orientation, for they supply the materials that allow us to conceive order in a world undergoing change.

The fact that literature occupies an important place in both *Permanence* and *Attitudes* is only a general indication that Burke used *Attitudes* to reiterate ideas developed in *Permanence*. Stronger indications become apparent from the close relationship between *Permanence*'s "On Interpretation" and *Attitudes*'s "Acceptance and Rejection." "On Interpretation" and "Acceptance and Rejection" are most directly related through their focus on the formation of basic attitudes. By using the concepts of "trained incapacity" and "occupational psychosis" in "On Interpretation," Burke points out that the activities we engage in (especially those of great value to us) affect the way we understand the world. Not only do those activities heighten our perceptions by developing our critical capacities, but they limit us by regularizing and normalizing perception and criticism. Motives, in his view, are not purely internal emotions, desires, needs, or similar impulses that incite action, though these do figure into motives; rather, motives are fluid, reflexive mental states that simultaneously reflect situations and order our interpretations of them. Although large-scale collective factors are involved in "On Interpretation," Burke is primarily concerned with individual factors. He could have used a variety of ways to frame his analysis, but he deliberately chose "training" and "occupation" as they affect an individual's social and psychological life. Moreover, in the chapter on motives (*PC*, 19–36) Burke mentions specific situations as an individual might experience them. This emphasis on an individual's interpretation is especially notable on two grounds: the mass unemployment of the Depression, and the special interest that theorists of communism had concerning the impact of labor on an individual's psychological state. It is only in the section on magic, religion, and science (*PC*, 59–66) that Burke begins to discuss large-scale cultural frames more than superficially.

Indeed, Burke begins "Acceptance and Rejection" by discussing individuals' interpretive mechanisms, but he quickly shifts to collective frames. The discussion of James, Whitman, and Emerson focuses on how the three authors interpret, but it is intended more to set up the kind of collective frame that Burke champions. By the time Burke begins to discuss the poetic categories, he is well into "collective" matters such as "the graph of Western culture," "Malthusian limits," the nineteenth century as "the great century of rejection philosophies," and the symbiosis between futurism and fascism. "Poetic Categories" is thus ambivalent. On the one side, it concerns how an individual uses literature to cope with "the significant factors of his time" (*ATH*, 34), such as economic forms and class divisions; on the other side, it concerns literature as a mode of adjustment for an entire culture. The emphasis, though, is certainly on the collective. That is why Burke uses few examples of an individual's responses, speaking of "men" collectively. As the analysis moves to well-rounded frames, Burke becomes even more focused on collective matters. This is especially evident in the discussion of comedy. "Comedy," Burke says, "deals with *man in society*" (*ATH*, 42). As he gets into "The Destiny of Acceptance Frames" (*ATH*, 92–105), Burke speaks almost entirely about a society's general adjustment to conditions.

Whether Burke is talking about an individual's response or a society's form of collective adjustment, the function of interpretive terms is essentially the same. Following the lead of social psychologists of his time, Burke found great value in explaining collective experience through the language and concepts theretofore used to explain the psychology of the individual. While both "On Interpretation" and "Acceptance and Rejection" analyze how attitudes are instantiated in literary forms, "On Interpretation" approaches this from the perspective of style ("In its simplest manifestation, style is ingratiation" [*PC,* 50]). Style is a mechanism for navigating through the social and political world. For the tumultuous 1930s Burke felt that a "scrupulously critical vocabulary" of definition was most needed (*PC,* 55)—hence his disparagement of the trespass of the "technological psychosis" (Burke believed that the premium on *description* made science and technology inherently anticritical, "non-human," and inhumane). Style, in this view, becomes the most sophisticated medium for scrupulously critical exegesis. Thus, Dante and Joyce are for Burke examples of attitudes that function as "correctives" to disorders of the communicative medium. In "Acceptance and Rejection" attitudes find their instantiation in structural relations inherent in the various poetic categories. Rather than emphasizing the creation of literature as an individual's response, Burke focuses on the widespread ability of a poetic form to capture or inform a general collective response to current conditions. So Burke argues that epic forms were "successful" because they met the needs of people living "under primitive, noncommercial conditions." Tragedy, he argues, is successful when capitalistic relations gain prominence while collectivist structures are still dominant. The didactic category is successful when a society, synthesizing various viewpoints, demands antisynthetic frameworks to retain a coherent center. These are examples of attitudes in poetic categories.

Permanence and *Attitudes* are also similar regarding the function of interpretive terms in Burke's discussion of how orientations are self-limiting. Trained incapacities and occupational psychoses, he points out in *Permanence,* are habitual ways of viewing and responding to the environment. They develop because of uniform exigencies that are successfully met by the same response over and again until that response becomes routine. But, Burke points out, as much as our routines allow for successful living, they limit or incapacitate us because their channeling of our perceptions reduces the chance that we may see and embrace alternative perceptions and actions. The frames discussed in "Acceptance and Rejection" are similarly self-limiting. No acceptance frame is all-accepting. To accept one thing, Burke says, is to reject another—which is inherently limiting. As a frame prepares us to cope effectively with our environment, it conditions us to accept some things and reject others: "the materials incorporated within the frame are never broad enough to encompass all the necessary attitudes. . . . As regards *all* the necessities, the very glories of the frame become its menace" (*ATH*, 40). This is why Burke urges the adoption of "well-rounded frames," by which he means perspectives that are least limited in terms of the richness of human relations. For instance, in Burke's view behaviorism is not well rounded because it treats questions of human will in terms of mechanistic motion. Although well-rounded frames still put blinders on us, as all frames must, they limit us to a lesser degree than other frames. Moreover, well-rounded frames have built-in capacities to transcend their own limitations. For example, Burke suggests that the comic frame is especially suited for treating human relations because it contains both material and spiritual elements. Finally, *Permanence* and *Attitudes* are similar in that they both suggest that orientations tend to be self-perpetuating. Burke argues that orientations, attitudes, and motives, to the extent that they are successful, interfere with their own revision by disallowing alternative points of view. In "Acceptance and Rejection," for example, Burke charts how a poetic category, once well fitted for the culture it served, becomes ill-suited when it remains dominant in a society whose cultural forms have changed.

The similarities between *Permanence* and *Attitudes* extend to the problems collective groupings have in dealing with transitional states. In *Permanence,* Burke addresses change in orientations and frames mostly in "Perspective by Incongruity," which develops principles for formulating and effecting change in a world of pious relations. Our lives, Burke argues, are profoundly structured by our previous experiences (both individual and collective). As conditions change, our pieties may not support the best perspectives and actions needed for the new conditions or even for transitional states. Burke believed that the best course is to promote a perspective that is inherently structured to make apparent the virtues and limitations of our pieties by juxtaposing them with other perspectives. The more different the juxtaposed perspectives, the more we learn about our pieties. From seeing other ways, we may see that there are better ways—hence, perspective by incongruity. In *Attitudes,* Burke discusses transitional states explicitly in "Acceptance and Rejection" and implicitly in "The Curve of History." In "Acceptance and Rejection" poetic categories deal specifically with incongruity. Humor, for instance, "specializes in incongruities" but prompts us to accept difficult situations by undermining the importance or stature of the problem (*ATH*, 58). Humor uses incongruity to support the status quo in nontransitional states. On the other hand, the grotesque, "the cult of incongruity *without* the laughter," more properly applies to transitional states (*ATH*, 58). It "comes to the fore when confusion in the forensic pattern gives more prominence to the subjective elements of imagery than to the objective, or public, elements" (*ATH*, 59–60).

This confusion occurs, Burke says, because of a breakdown or destabilization of objective or public structures. It is precisely this confusion that is one of the grotesque's limitations. The very repair of the limitations inherent in sub-jective elements, Burke argues, itself requires stable public structures. The sec-ond limitation is that the grotesque is a "passive" corrective. It offers little positive direction for change and even tends to avoid the realities of daily liv-ing (the grotesque, in its purest form, reduces "the richness of life" to opera-tions of the subconscious). Burke makes this quite apparent through his analysis of "monasticism," the institutional analogue of (and "improvement" upon) the grotesque. Monasticism, Burke suggests, is a form of thought that "fixes the transitional" by normalizing incompatibilities (*ATH*, 70). It makes crisis per-petual by transforming "spiritual" problems into "'material' organization" (*ATH*, 74). In so doing, monastic thought promotes a "gang morality" that "converts the old negatives into new positives" which justify their deviations (*ATH*, 73). Hence, in Burke's view monastic thought is limited because it vio-lates our pieties, supplanting them with new structures that institutionalize the dif-ferences essential to the transitional state. Incongruity, in monastic thought, serves only to fix the transitional rather than transcend it. This is just the problem Burke has with Marxism. In "The Curve of History," Burke implicitly addresses the prob-lem of transitional states. On the surface it appears as if the chapter does just the opposite—analyzes stable historical phases. Each great phase Burke covers repre-sents a solid set of intellectual ideas and social and political structures. Yet the assumptions underlying the chapter indicate the important role of transitional states in Burke's thinking about historical development.

The critical responses to *Attitudes* were similar to those to *Counter-Statement* and *Permanence*. Reviewers tended to read the book with a set of intellectual blinders on, exaggerating some features to the detriment of others. Yet *Attitudes* not only received more responses than the other books, criticism of the book was more sophisticated and searing.

Groff Conklin, writing for *New Masses*, begins "The Science of Symbology" with a discussion of the importance of the study of symbols to public relations, advertising, and political propaganda. Advances in "symbology," he tells us, are most needed in the political realm. *Attitudes* can help there, and Burke, he writes, will "be surprised to learn that its value is largely in the field of practical agitation."[11] Overall, Conklin emphasizes "The Dictionary of Pivotal Terms" because of the potential value of the dictionary in general and because of Burke's ideas about "symbols of authority" in particular. At one point he comments that the first three-fourths of *Attitudes* is made up of notes for the dictionary. As pointed out earlier, far too many readers of Burke dis-count the dictionary. Although one could sympathize with Conklin's attempt to redress this lapse, he is wrong to overemphasize it and its value for political agitation. Conklin exaggerates the dictionary because he fails to recognize

Burke's integrative thinking and instead separates literature from social experience. Conklin asserts that "in producing an apparatus for the use of social scientists, [Burke] has had to take the literary symbol, inject psychological significances into it (where . . . they are of relatively small social importance), and then 'transcend' (his own word) this concept into the psychological study of public symbols" (26). Missing Burke's point that literature is a particularly fertile form of expression that helps us understand fundamental aspects of social life, Conklin laments that Burke merely lays social and psychological factors upon literature. Perhaps the ultimate source of this misreading is indicated by his title. By calling symbology a "science," Conklin, like many other students of culture in the 1920s and 1930s, sought to infuse the principles and goals of science into humanistic disciplines. Conklin thus betrays a framework for reading Burke that runs counter to the very point Burke is making.

Crane Brinton used his review of *Attitudes* in the *Saturday Review of Literature* as an occasion to attack contemporary approaches to history. The "Old Guard," he wrote, was interested in "past politics" and applied well-developed scientific methods to its study. He felt that history had moved away from the older ideas and methods and merged with sociology. In his review Brinton argues that Burke, like contemporary historians, has a "wider and looser" sense of "history" than the "Old Guard": "History seems to mean to him the sum of all things. . . . [It] can explain everything that can be explained."[12] In his opinion, Burke, like other new "philosophers of history," offers his own "beat of the rhythm" of historical development.[13] But the attempt to find a single principle that guides historical development, Brinton suggests, has caused the study of history to lose much of its rigor. Burke and other contemporary historians, Brinton laments, fail on three grounds: first, that to explain historical development, they must abandon "the hard-won gains of their predecessors in the field of . . . scientific method"; second, that they are misdirected because there is in fact no "key to the riddle of the universe"; and third, that their search is misbegotten because they should learn what scientists have already begun to suspect— namely, that "there is no riddle" (11). Obviously Brinton ignored the bulk of *Attitudes*. Most of what he says concerns "The Curve of History." "Acceptance and Rejection" and "The Analysis of Symbolic Structure" seem to be used only for general comments. Brinton's slant reads the book as if Burke merely intended to develop another historical engine. Brinton could not of course have benefited from Burke's comments in the introduction to the second edition (1959), but what Burke says there is indeed implicit in the first edition. *Attitudes*, he says, is not about history as much as it is about attitudes. Burke uses history not only as a grand illustration, but as a convenient way of setting up a more basic problem, namely the workings of symbols in the collective sphere.

Margaret Schlaugh, in her review of *Attitudes* in *Science and Society*, takes

Brinton's mistake one step further. Instead of focusing on one major part of the book, she spends one-third of her review attacking a single, restricted issue, a statement Burke makes in passing about phonetic relations operating when we use "cues."[14] To compound things, Schlaugh's criticism of the phonetic argument adds nothing to her more visceral, but less specific, criticisms of *Attitudes*. For instance, she questions Burke's use of the terms "acceptance" and "rejection" because they seem to be used as intransitive verbs (they "appear, not as natural reactions to historical objects, but as mysterious separate forces").[15] However, as was earlier noted, Burke uses "acceptance" and "rejection" ambivalently, referring to habitual reactions to particular, local experiences (for example, in James, Whitman, and Emerson) *and* to generalized worldviews (for instance, Aquinas's acceptance of class structure "as punishment for the fall of man" or the "collective poems" discussed in "The Curve of History": Christian evangelism, medieval synthesis, etc.).[16] Schlaugh's most important criticism of *Attitudes* is that the "emphasis is frequently placed upon psychological (rather: psychoanalytical) relationships at the expense of others" (130). By "others" she seems to be thinking mostly about economic factors (132). This criticism betrays her unwillingness to accept Burke's contention that the future of socialist theorizing and reform lies in moving away from models of economic determinism. She will not even discuss the possibility that socialism might have to accept that there is a "coordination of various poetic-psychological forms with history" (132).

Arthur E. DuBois has the distinction of twice reviewing *Attitudes*. His first review appeared in the *Sewanee Review* and analyzed only "Acceptance and Rejection" as it appeared in the *Southern Review* before inclusion as part 1 of *Attitudes*.[17] In this review DuBois on the whole focuses on what he considers to be Burke's major goal in "Acceptance and Rejection," a reconciliation of classical and romantic literary values. His most basic criticism challenges Burke's contention that classical forms of poetry (e.g., comedy, tragedy) disappeared during the romantic era. But, more important, he criticizes what he considers to be a "confusion" or "contradiction" that is "fairly wide-reaching in the middle part of 'Acceptance and Rejection'" (349). Referring to "Poetic Categories," DuBois seems to argue that Burke misstates the nature of the accepting-rejecting function of literary forms. Burke, he suggests, ties specific forms of acceptance and rejection to specific classical literary forms. But acceptance and rejection, DuBois says, are actually analytically separate from, and wider-reaching than, their manifestation in literary forms (the accepting-rejecting function, he says, sometimes does not even produce literary forms). Hence particular functions of acceptance and rejection are not dedicated to specific literary forms and may even imbue them all. In sum, DuBois says that Burke "seems to be talking about literary forms whereas he is actually discussing only the accepting-rejection function which characterizes all literature, which distinguishes some of the forms, and which never lapsed" (349).

This criticism arises out of what DuBois considers an even deeper confusion in Burke's essay. On the one hand, he says, Burke claims that poetry is a highly individual mode of "either living or equipment for living" (346).Yet, he says, Burke also claims that literary forms are large-scale, cultural frames. In light of Burke's attempt to "revivify" classical forms that lapsed during the romantic era, DuBois argues that "the only purpose of re-distinguishing the literary forms would be to 'reject' by means of an escape into an exclusive formalism" (347). Such a move into formalism, DuBois suggests, carries a significant cost: "the distinguished personality of the author [is] sacrificed for the more accountable literary forms of tradition" (348). This sacrifice, DuBois contends, contradicts the idea that poetry is an individual mechanism for coping with the world. In short, DuBois sees in the discussion of acceptance and rejection the old rift between subjectivity and objectivity.[18]

Burke offers much to suggest that DuBois's reading is off the mark. A careful reading of "Acceptance and Rejection" makes it clear that Burke intends no rift between subjectivity and objectivity. The section on James, Whitman, and Emerson demonstrates how subjectivity and objectivity intermingle (or, better, how the subjective/objective distinction leads to misrepresentations of how literature is experienced). Even if the point was not clear in the essay, it should have been apparent from Burke's two previous books. For instance, Burke's extended comments about form in *Counter-Statement* clearly cut across the distinction between objectivity and subjectivity. If anything, Burke posits "psychological form" in *Counter-Statement* in order to show how subjectivity and objectivity intermingle. Even the oxymoronic term "psychological form" conveys this. "Psychology" might as well be "subjectivity," and "form" could be "objectivity." Given that DuBois was familiar with the world of little magazines and even knew about Burke, he should have been familiar with *Counter-Statement* and should have seen that Burke, far from being confused about a rift between subjectivity and objectivity, was addressing the distinction in an attempt to transcend it.[19] Moreover, Burke makes a similar point in *Permanence*. "Trained incapacity" and "occupational psychosis," for example, show that Burke does not sacrifice personality for formal structures. If anything, formal structures arise in part from what DuBois referred to as one's "distinguished personality." In sum, Burke's position on the relationship between subjectivity and objectivity is clear: he says that individual/subjective frames and cultural/objective frames are manifestations of roughly similar coping mechanisms. He also says that it is wrong to think of subjectivity and objectivity as two mutually exclusive worlds.

Because DuBois's misreading is typical of the sort Burke suffered then and today, it could be valuable to take a closer look at why, given all the evidence to the contrary, DuBois read "Acceptance and Rejection" as he did. One cause of DuBois's misreading was that he so strongly subscribed to a split between subjectivity and objectivity that he could not see the distinction Burke was transcending. Moreover, Burke's treatment of subjective frames and poetic categories in *Attitudes* could easily lead to the view that frames and categories are distinct from one another—the two discussions chiefly occur in different chapters, and Burke is notorious for detailed analysis that confounds the broad view. In addition, in the 1930s (and today) there were profound reservations concerning the applicability of findings about the psychological and sociological lives of individuals to larger social contexts (and vice versa). The extension of the analysis of individuals' lives ("William James, Whitman, and Emerson") to larger social frames (poetic categories) could well have been missed or judged improper.

In a general way DuBois's misreading may stem more from his "trained incapacity" as a literary critic. There is not much written about DuBois, but clearly he was involved in the literary world of the 1930s, principally with magazines interested in modernist poetry and poetics. His poems were published in *Alentour* and *Chameleon,* and his criticism in *Avenue,* the *Sewanee Review,* and the *Southwest Review.* For a time he edited *Avenue.*[20] The review of "Acceptance and Rejection" betrays how his interests and training affected the way he read the essay. A good part of the review discusses Burke's definitions of literary forms (DuBois calls it Burke's "discussion of terms") and the question of whether or not classical literary forms lapsed during the romantic era. DuBois thinks that, with such criticisms, he strikes at the heart of Burke's analysis. In fact, he is quite off the mark. He may be right in demonstrating that certain forms do not promote the acceptance or rejection functions precisely as Burke suggests; but Burke's overall idea that the acceptance/rejection function is closely related to literary form (and is a good way to understand it) remains sound. DuBois's questions are interesting, but not nearly central; given the social and political importance of *Attitudes,* they end up as quibbles about the definitions of literary forms.

There is yet another, more serious problem. DuBois, it is clear, misunderstands the general tenor of the article. He makes "Acceptance and Rejection" far more literary than it really is. DuBois is simply wrong when he contends that "Acceptance and Rejection" is nothing but an attempt to reconcile classical and romantic literary forms. Even without the benefit of the rest of *Attitudes* (which was unavailable to DuBois when he wrote this review), "Acceptance and Rejection" clearly investigates how lived experience informs the symbolic components of human experience. The world of literature, as it is used in "Acceptance and Rejection," is principally a means for sustaining this investigation. "William James, Whitman, and Emerson" and "Poetic Categories" do have a literary cast, but they also display broader concerns that are more important to the essay. Moreover, the final sections, "The Destiny of Acceptance Frames" and "Conclusion," are more about life and history than about literature per se. DuBois does call the conclusion of the essay "the best part," but he does not have much to say about it.[21] Overall, DuBois reads into the main theme of the essay what he wants to see, not what Burke talks about. And what DuBois wants to see stems primarily from his occupation as a man of letters.

Particularly in Burke's time, literary aesthetics and social responsibility were often viewed as separate realms, if not antithetical. As early as in "The Status of Art," for instance, Burke points quite clearly to the tension between the *ars gratia artis* view and the pragmatic demand that art should be useful. Literary aesthetics, when tied to pragmatic ends, typically loses much of its vigor (the proletarian novel, as it grew into a slavish, hack formula, is an example of the difficulties confronting rapprochement). Burke, it is clear, is trying in "Acceptance and Rejection" to follow the lead of "The Status of Art" and his other essays by transcending the bifurcation of literature and life. In his review, however, DuBois is still entirely immersed in the kind of thinking Burke is trying to leave behind.

DuBois's review of the entire book is more sophisticated than his review of "Acceptance and Rejection." Now DuBois discusses the central issues more than he did before. More than any other review of *Attitudes,* it draws a strong connection between *Attitudes* and *Permanence:* "The method of *Attitudes toward History,*" DuBois says in the first sentence, "is mainly 'perspective by incongruity.'"[22] Although DuBois does not directly develop the connection, it is in the background; and he gets back to it in the end, where he comments on the relationship between perspective by incongruity and the comic attitude (especially 230–31). DuBois strikes at what might be an important weakness in Burke's championing of the comic attitude. The comic attitude, DuBois suggests, has overtones of the "humanist attitude." He protests that unfortunately the comic attitude and the humanist attitude (and especially a comic attitude flavored by a humanist attitude) are not "finally creative. Both are reconcilers, not proposers or, very often, actors. They are tonics, not foods or poisons" (227). "Comedy," DuBois later suggests, "solves no problem and is only critical, not creative" (230). DuBois thus challenges Burke at the core. He recognizes the essentially *critical* character of Burke's perspective and questions whether or not criticism offers enough to redress contemporary problems.

This question gets at what could be considered one of the most difficult problems Burke faced. Phrasing it another way, the question becomes (as it did for many of his contemporaries): Was Burke a conservative or a liberal (or, even, a radical)? Given an answer to that question, the next question might be, Of what brand? At heart, DuBois is saying that Burke's criticism cannot induce real social change because criticism is essentially conservative. It does not offer enough positive change and ends up hollow compared to political action. To use DuBois's terms, criticism is "avocation" rather than "vocation." The comic attitude, he suggests, is better as a way of understanding action than as a source of action. "Laughter," he says, "is like oil on a gear" (231). Yet DuBois's question is inappropriate. He assumes a relatively simple division between being conservative and being liberal. In many cases a simple division may exist. But Burke, who cut along the bias, was both liberal *and* conservative simultaneously. He was liberal in the sense that he truly wanted to make significant changes that would make America a better place and that would upset the structures of American society in the 1930s. "Program" points this out better than anything else Burke had written up through *Attitudes,* if not after. Yet at the same time Burke realized that there was much good in contemporary society. He never, for instance, seriously called for the sort of revolution that many communists of the 1930s demanded. Social, political, and intellectual structures arise, he believed, because they are useful. Situations might change so that certain structures are not so useful anymore, but they nonetheless often exist because they serve some purpose still.

Burke's cut across the conservative/liberal distinction is why, in part, *Permanence* is about *permanence* and *change.* Burke seeks what might seem in a variety of ways enigmatic if not paradoxical: preservation through change, change through preservation, and preservation through change *coextensive with* change through preservation. Thus, in *Permanence* he considers three "orders of rationalization." Sir James George Frazer believes that magic, religion, and science are merely adaptations of the same impulse to different situations, which amounts to preservation through change. In *Attitudes* the same holds true for the progression from "Christian evangelism" to "emergent collectivism." Change is the engine of preservation. Yet, as much as these are examples of preservation through change, they are also examples of change through preservation. When seeking to change social, political, and intellectual structures to meet new needs, the preservation of these structures becomes the mechanism to meet new situations. This becomes quite clear when we understand that "change," in Burke's idiom, is not the chance occurrence of something different. Burke is most interested in change that is generally directed or teleological in a non-Hegelian sense. The "curve" of history, what Burke calls the five acts of "the historic drama," clearly shows that for Burke change is often channeled by the past. The curve of history is a continuous line of development, neither punctuated nor truncated. In short, Burke offers a theory of historical mutation or evolution, not revolution.

Oddly, evolutionary change is often more difficult to conceive of than revolutionary change. At first glance this may not seem so. People often feel that it is easier to make minor adjustments to living conditions than it is to upset the entire social order. For instance, someone dissatisfied with capitalist structures of dominance in American society might propose that we somehow dissolve capitalism and supplant it with communism. One manifestation of this might be to have a communist revolution that dissolves the existing government, institutes a communist political order, and nationalizes businesses and vast accumulations of personal wealth. Most Americans would say that such steps are ridiculous, that they comprise a simplistic, knee-jerk reaction to a complex problem. It is more realistic, most believe, to make small corrections to the current system. For instance, we have written antitrust legislation and have legalized unions and unionizing activities; and we might legislate against or change the way we regulate junk-bond trading, greenmail, leveraged buyouts, and corporate takeovers. But such changes are not truly evolutionary, for there is no significant alteration of the structures of capitalist dominance. The changes just make capitalist domination more palatable. The really hard conception involves somehow mutating capitalism so that it still maintains many of its essential features, yet does not dominate. To use another example, true evolution has occurred in Brazil's *Candomblé* versions of Catholicism, which combine African and Christian religious beliefs and practices. Burke makes clear a case for the complexity and difficulty of evolutionary change in his discussion of the various stages in the development of the curve of history.

Readers of Burke may find his cut across the bias of the distinction between liberal and conservative difficult to accept because such a distinction does not make sense in Burke's evolutionary position. If we force the distinction on Burke, we must say that he is *both* liberal and conservative. People such as DuBois—indeed many of Burke's contemporaries of the 1930s—had much trouble understanding him because, in a world of easy distinctions, Burke did not easily fit in. There was always some significant element in his thinking that was objectionable because it necessarily contained elements that a partisan deplored. So Burke was criticized by liberals and revolutionaries because he was too conservative, and he was criticized by conservatives because he was too liberal or revolutionary.

Henry Bamford Parkes's review of *Attitudes* in the *Southern Review* is similar to the reviews by DuBois. He finds the same contradiction and identifies the same source for it as does DuBois. But Parkes departs from DuBois in two significant ways. First, he protests that Burke fails to stress the role of rational choice in historical development. Burke, he asserts, is a "Spenglerian." Second, he protests that Burke cannot justify his humanistic values or his belief that they should undergird particular social and political structures. Both of these protestations stem from the demand for a foundation upon which truth, human choice, and human destiny can be resolutely based. Parkes finds in *Attitudes* a contradiction between subjectivity and objectivity. Although Parkes hardly uses the terms "subjective" and "objective," he clearly makes the same kind of distinction as DuBois when he draws a distinction between individual freedom and life in a collective (including the rule of the state and historic destiny). Parkes argues that Burke champions both subjectivity and objectivity, which results in a fundamental, irreconcilable contradiction. He accuses Burke of suffering from a "split personality."[23] Parkes likely perceives this contradiction because he identifies in Burke what DuBois sees: a progression through *Attitudes* in which Burke shifts from individual freedom to submission to the collective. Whereas *Counter-Statement* encouraged "individual freedom," Parkes says, *Permanence* "showed that the evaluations of individuals were relative to their interests and therefore devoid of objective validity" (695). *Attitudes* goes further, he says, because it "examines—and approves of—the methods by which individuals achieve conformity with a social system" (695). Following this line to its logical end, Parkes argues that *Attitudes* never fully transcends the individualism of *Counter-Statement*. Burke, he says, must "ascribe the adoption of a new 'frame of acceptance' on the part of an individual to an act of will" (701). Such an ascription, according to Parkes, contradicts the Spenglerian and communist components in *Attitudes*. Like DuBois, Parkes takes this to be an irreconcilable contradiction that invalidates Burke's argument.

Though there are similarities in DuBois's and Parkes's thinking on Burke, there are also marked differences. Whereas DuBois decries the poverty of criticism in a world that demands action, Parkes recognizes its value. Even so, he charges that in analyzing frames Burke "fails . . . to lay any stress upon the element of rational choice in human affairs" (698). Burke's failure, Parkes argues, stems from two factors. First, he says, Burke adheres to a pragmatism that is epistemologically relativist. Burke's pragmatism and relativism, Parkes says, "must necessarily lead to a denial of human freedom and to resignation to historic destiny" (699). Second, he charges in no uncertain terms that Burke is a "Spenglerian" who, appallingly, petitions historic destiny as the source for the growth and diminution of acceptance and rejection frames (700). Moreover, Parkes locates the problem of rational choice at the center of a contradiction between leftist practices and their rationale: "The revolutionary movement may often profess a belief in determinism, yet actually it is a struggle not to guide history along a predestined path but to divert it in new directions; and its participants may emphasize the primacy of the economic factor, yet actually they are fighting not only for the satisfaction of economic needs but also for noneconomic values, for freedom and human dignity" (705). Parkes is correct. Yet, ironically, we might as well have read the same words in *Attitudes*. He states rather nicely precisely what Burke is trying to get at in "Acceptance and

Rejection" and "The Curve of History." How can Parkes so misread Burke as to use one of Burke's main points against him? The answer to this question, which also relates to other reviews of Burke's work, is: Reading Burke from within the intellectual or political confines of a standard frame of reference, the reviewer cannot see beyond the perspective that Burke is trying to transcend. As much as Parkes goes beyond DuBois to make what might be, if better developed, an important point, he nonetheless traces the problem to incorrect assumptions about *Attitudes*.

As critical as DuBois and Parkes are, they certainly did not have the impact of Sidney Hook. Frequently cited because it is a severe attack by a highly regarded philosopher, Hook's review is important for several reasons. First, it was at the time the harshest criticism of Burke to appear in print; in addition, it appeared in the premiere issue of the revamped, well-regarded, and highly influential *Partisan Review*.[24] Second, referred to by Burke as a "hatchetman job" and a "stinko," it is the one review Burke saw fit to "beg" William Rueckert to include in *Critical Responses to Kenneth Burke* thirty-five years later.[25] Third, it occasioned a short dialogue between Burke and Hook concerning *Attitudes* (the next issue of *Partisan Review* published Burke's response and Hook's rejoinder).[26] Burke seldom replied in print to reviews, but Hook provoked a long response.[27] Fourth, the dialogue between Burke and Hook shows precisely how political factors profoundly affected the reception of Burke's ideas.

Hook makes three basic charges against Burke. First, he argues that Burke's criticism fails because Burke does not think a problem through, is unclear, and writes "by suggestion." "The result," Hook says, "is that there is neither beginning nor end to his argument. Its course meanders into all fields of knowledge where . . . its force is weakened by a lore more quaint than precise" (57). Second, Hook charges that Burke's analysis is impoverished by a "home-baked objective relativism," which falls prey to both of the "fundamental errors" of relativism: the inability to judge the validity of one perspective in relation to another; and the tendency to reduce all competing perspectives to special cases of the relativist's favored point of view (58). Third, Hook argues that Burke is nothing more than a blatant Stalinist: "His own function consists in being an apologist, not after the fact, but *before* the fact, of the latest piece of Stalinist brutality" (61).

To today's reader, this third criticism seems thoroughly vituperative and out of line with the other two, which are analytical in nature and epistemological in content. To us, Hook's charge of Stalinism simply does not display the sophistication and presence of mind of his other criticisms (ad hominem criticism is neither the matter nor instrument of exemplary philosophy). Yet Hook's charges follow a logic quite in keeping with the actual rhetoric of leftist criticism of the 1930s. Often torn between nonpolitical intellectual commitments and sympathies, on the one hand, and "proper" political allegiance and pretensions, on the other hand, a critic of the Left frequently came to incongruous conclusions. Some critics ended up taking political stands obviously incompatible with their nonpolitical judgments. Such contradictions are easily recognized and readily explained. Other critics recognized these contradictions for what they were and either stifled politically unfavorable nonpolitical thoughts or offered tortured rationales of consistency. Hook represents a potentially more menacing permutation. He has something important to say, both philosophically and politically. Unfortunately, his politics are the true source of his intellectual and critical convictions. Even though he makes some valid philosophical claims, he could be accused of casuistically generating philosophical arguments to support his political beliefs. In order to understand the manner in which this disingenuous reasoning distorts in obscure ways otherwise incisive philosophical and political reasoning, the relationship between the charge of Stalinism and the two epistemological arguments needs examination.

Many of Hook's contemporaries undoubtedly understood his ad hominem attack for what it was. However, they probably also saw it as a natural and coherent outgrowth of the epistemological argument, an impression enhanced by Hook's argumentative technique. Hook was well known in the 1930s for rigorous and penetrating philosophical analysis. His *Towards the Understanding of Karl Marx* (1933) was considered sophisticated and an important contribution to the study of Marx. Given Hook's philosophical stance, he might have been expected to criticize any position with a hint of relativism—and to attack stronger relativist arguments scathingly. Other critics have chided Burke for relativism, but their criticisms are generally shallow. Parkes, for instance, treats the question of relativism by tracing Burke's position on frames to a pragmatist cosmology with relativist overtones: "Interests and 'frames of acceptance' determine each other, and there is no appeal to any factor outside the circle. The only escape from the circle would be by the assertion of some kind of absolute truth" (699). Burke, he says, rejects absolutes. Parkes frames the discussion of relativism chiefly with the question of whether or not human choice exists. The role of historic destiny and Burke's putative inability reasonably to account for how frames change are ancillary matters. As the previous discussion of Parkes's review makes clear, he misses the point that Burke very much allows human choice into his equation. Parkes's sally into relativism thus never gets to the better question: Given that Burke does indeed allow for human choice in his attitude toward history, what justifies or legitimates the principles, norms, guidelines, and criteria, for example, that inform human choice?

Hook's analysis is keener, more solidly grasping something problematical and even disturbing about Burke's position. In contrast to Parkes, Hook realizes that Burke does allow for human choice, but he questions the ability of relativism in general and Burke's relativism in particular to supply satisfactory answers to questions of justification and legitimation. Hook's argument develops thus: Burke has "a position which can be used as a 'justification' for taking any position" (57). This raises the problem of how to judge the validity of one perspective relative to another (58). Burke solves this problem by privileging one perspective over all others, reducing competing perspectives to special cases of the particular one he favors (thus turning "subjectivism" into "absolutism"). Authority, for Burke, ultimately rests in this privilege. Yet his relativist principles forbid any such foundation or absolute authority. And even if it were theoretically possible in relativism to privilege one perspective over another, Burke cannot offer unconditional or even good justification for the privileging of any one perspective. Hook has thus made a predictable foray against relativism. At this point Hook takes a penetrating yet deceptive turn. He argues that the perspective-driven skepticism of relativism, in its typical implementation and in Burke's, is misdirected because it appeals to "the equal validity of all points of view *in the abstract*" in order to undermine a perspective as it applies in specific circumstances (59). Abstract theoretical conundrums, he says, function in a realm different than that of "immanent" judgment and thus cannot subvert it. To prove his point, Hook sets the analysis within an orbit of Stalinism, the Moscow trials, Dreyfus, Sacco-Vanzetti, and the Tom Mooney arrest. These famous cases are used to make a relatively simple point: that it is wrong to use psychological evidence, as Burke does, to argue that the defendants in the Moscow trials could possibly be guilty—because when psychological evidence is used, decontextualized possibilities become the bases for definite judgments about contingent matters. Just as validity in the abstract cannot be a criterion that applies to specific circumstances, psychological evidence in the abstract fails as evidence for the possibility of guilt in a concrete situation.

In referring to Stalinism and the other famous cases, Hook makes a much stronger point. By using these examples, Hook subtly invokes a new argument: that regardless of the soundness of relativism's critique of absolutism and foundationalism, there comes a point when such a theory leads to consequences that are categorically unacceptable. If relativism in any way gives standing to totalitarianism and thus opens us to its consequences, whence comes moral authority and the limits of moral acceptability? The excesses of totalitarianism, says Hook, should stir us not only to distrust, but to shun relativism. Hook's implicit charge is clear: these cases are proof enough that relativism is morally bankrupt and is therefore unacceptable. By locating the crux of relativism in the question of moral authority and the limits of moral acceptability, Hook strikes more directly than Parkes at a central problem in Burke's thinking.

This is a clever turn, for it assumes that epistemological argumentation is the germ of moral argumentation, that the two are somehow organically related, and that one feeds the other. Moreover, Hook now assumes that the specific contingencies he mentions are the proper referents for ascertaining the role of moral authority and the limits of moral acceptability in Burke's theories. By framing the issues as he does, Hook constructs an impression of seamless reasoning. But as clever as he might be, he is nonetheless quite misleading. A careful examination of the dialogue between Burke and Hook shows that something else is going on. Relativism is not the major player Hook pretends it to be, and the question of moral authority and moral acceptability does not derive from his analysis of relativism. Politics is the real point of difference between Burke and Hook. Burke's response—titled "Is Mr. Hook a Socialist?"—forgoes a point-by-point refutation of the review because Burke believed that Hook, by misreading, by taking ideas out of their context, and by misplaced emphases, attacked not *Attitudes* but "a work generated in Hook's not very inventive fancy" (40). Burke offers instead, as the heart of his response, a lengthy quotation from "Bureaucratization of the Imaginative" in order, he says, "to convey the general tenor of my concerns" (40). Burke ends his response with the charge that Hook, were he a socialist, ought to have appreciated how *Attitudes* "might be used . . . for anti-capitalist diagnosis and exhortation" (43). Instead, Burke laments, Hook attends to minor points, neglecting the potentials of *Attitudes* for cultivating socialism. Burke's complaint is not just that Hook misreads him, but that Hook's judgment is impaired. "If the attack itself is not Leftist in perspective, if it loses all interest in the analysis of capitalist dilemmas and the ways of surmounting them," Burke admonishes, "the attacker thereby incidentally adopts a position that 'places' him decidedly elsewhere" (44).

Hook's rejoinder—titled "Is Mr. Burke Serious?"—focuses on three issues raised in Burke's response: Burke's claim that Hook misreads *Attitudes;* the criticism of relativism; and Hook's political affiliation. In the rejoinder, unlike Hook's initial review, the problem of political affiliation is more emphatic than the other points. In particular, he lays out his specific objections to Burke's political "intentions and allegiance." Hook at first says, "I cannot give Burke credit for his socialist intentions . . . *until I know what kind of socialism he believes in!*" (47). This is a credible complaint, since Burke does indeed favor a generalized socialism independent of particular brands (as was pointed out earlier); and there are serious questions whether such a stance is good, practicable, meaningful, or even theoretically possible. But as in Hook's initial review, the complaint is misleading, for in further developing the point Hook uses images and issues clearly drawn from the turmoil over Stalin's rule. By mentioning "judicial and extra-judicial frame-ups," "the Moscow trials," "the literary pogroms of the Communist Party," "the apotheosis of Stalin," and other references, Hook clearly implies that Burke endorses Stalinism (47). In a letter written to Benjamin De Mott in 1963, Burke explained that the phrase "bureaucratization of the imaginative" got him into trouble. He said that in the 1930s the term "bureaucracy" was used by Trotsky to attack Stalin. But if one were to say, as Burke does, that bureaucracy is everywhere, then that concept could not be used to attack Stalin. Hence, positing that bureaucracy is universal was taken by Hook and other anti-Stalinists as a de facto (if not surreptitious) defense of totalitarianism in general and Stalinism in particular.[28] Reading Hook's rejoinder points out that the wider orbit of terms mentioned in the initial review dilutes the real culprit: alleged Stalinist sympathies. It is one thing to question Burke because he gives standing to totalitarianism and cannot provide moral checks against tyranny's inevitable excesses. It is quite another thing simply to charge "Stalinist!" As much as Hook was notorious for acidic political assault, the pointed analytical and epistemological argument—by sheer weight, some dissembling, and a hint of verity—obfuscates the way in which Hook's political enmity informs his judgment and thus deflects attention from the real source of his animosity. That is one reason Burke wrote his odd response. Recognizing that there was no effective way to argue against the charge of Stalinism, Burke told De Mott that he chose simply to redefine and justify the broader application of his criminal "bureaucratization of the imaginative."

The same sort of rhetorical problems faced Burke with *Attitudes* as faced him with *Counter-Statement* and *Permanence*. Critics, blinded by their own intellectual and political interests, were prone to misreadings and were unable to treat Burke on his own terms.

5

The Philosophy of Literary Form
Literature as Equipment for Living

———————————————————————■————————

Demarcating a lifetime of scholarly writing into periods is a dangerous business: lines can be drawn in a number of ways, and differences between periods might be overemphasized while similarities are diminished. Despite such hazards, it is important to note that *The Philosophy of Literary Form* is a critical juncture in the development of Burke's thought, a moment that simultaneously marks the culmination of one phase and the inception of another. Therein lies the difficulty in understanding what Burke accomplished with this book: when two "traditions" coalesce in a transitional moment, the reader may easily fail to grasp the relationship between, or even the presence of, both phases. Seldom do we have a foot planted solidly on each bank of the river. In the case of Burke, this problem is aggravated by the preeminence of dramatism (the nucleus of the second phase), which many consider to be Burke's major contribution in a long and distinguished career. Because *Literary Form* anticipates dramatism more than Burke's earlier books do, many readers naturally tend to highlight the germ of dramatism in it. They emphasize the new phase and minimize the old. This bias interferes with understanding *The Philosophy of Literary Form* for what it is—a complex work that is simultaneously a rearticulation of Burke's previous work and an extension of it.

Published in 1941, *The Philosophy of Literary Form* is a thick and wide-ranging collection of essays, book reviews, and miscellaneous pieces, most of which Burke published between 1937 and 1939 in a variety of literary periodicals, social and political magazines, and academic journals (the *Southern Review,* the *Kenyon Review,* the *Nation,* the *New Republic, New Masses, Hound and Horn, Poetry,* and the *American Journal of Sociology,* among others). Burke divided *Literary Form* into four sections. Section 1, roughly one-third of the book (137 pages), contains just one essay, "The Philosophy of Literary Form." Widely recognized as a masterwork of literary criticism and the set piece of the collection, "The Philosophy of Literary Form" is the only item Burke wrote specifically for this volume. Section 2, another third of the book, contains six "Longer Articles": "Semantic and Poetic Meaning," "The Virtues and Limitations of Debunking," "The Rhetoric of Hitler's 'Battle,'" "The Calling of the Tune," "War, Response, and Contradiction," and "Freud—and the Analysis of Poetry." Sections 3 and 4 constitute the remaining third of *Literary Form.* Section 3 includes nine "Shorter Articles," some of which are short essays and others book reviews. One item is Burke's rejoinder to Margaret Schlaugh's review of *Attitudes toward*

History. Burke included this, no doubt, because he thought *Attitudes* had been misunderstood. "Literature as Equipment for Living," the lead article in section 3, is one of the most cited essays in Burke's entire corpus. Section 4 is an appendix containing twenty-two brief pieces, mostly book reviews.

A recurring pattern emerges in how this book is typically used by readers: heavy emphases on the titular essay and smatterings from "The Rhetoric of Hitler's 'Battle,'" "Semantic and Poetic Meaning," "Freud—and the Analysis of Poetry," and "Literature as Equipment for Living." The rest of the book is hardly mentioned except in a quotation here and there. Moreover, in most of the writings that analyze or use *Literary Form,* "The Philosophy of Literary Form" dominates the discussion even if it is not mentioned often. It sets the conceptual framework in which the other essays are interpreted. Readers familiar with secondary sources should notice, too, that most scholars tend to refer repeatedly to the same few pages or small sections of the book. Clearly, a relatively small portion of *The Philosophy of Literary Form* has captured readers' imaginations.

Just what makes this small portion so compelling? Of course, contained within it are fascinating observations about the nature and function of language and criticism, in particular Burke's distinction between poetic and semantic meaning and his idea of "symbolic action." More generally, readers have been taken by Burke's techniques for analyzing literature as rhetoric and his casting of this in terms of "sociological criticism." Yet on the whole readers have been attracted to the general theoretical statements and critical methods that roughly follow the procedures of traditional forms of literary criticism.[1]

This small portion is just as attractive for what it does *not* include as for what it does. One important lacuna is the criticism in *Literary Form.* Burke's analyses of Clifford Odets's *Golden Boy* and Samuel Taylor Coleridge's "The Rime of the Ancient Mariner" have gotten some notice, as have the Hitler piece and "Antony on Behalf of the Play"; but rarely are there citations to the more than twenty pieces in sections 3 and 4, in which Burke takes on particular writers and books. He analyzes works by Erskine Caldwell, Samuel Taylor Coleridge, George Herbert Mead, John Dewey, Otto Neurath, Stuart Chase, Karl Mannheim, William Empson, Thomas Mann, Clifford Odets, and other writers. He also reviews a painting by Peter Blume. (The same omission holds true for the longer articles, many of which contain extended criticism of particular authors and works.) Some of the works and writers Burke analyzes have largely been forgotten since his reviews first appeared more than half a century ago. Yet there is another, more important reason that his criticism in sections 3 and 4 has been ignored. Most of the reviews simply do not do what readers want them to do. The books Burke analyzes include very little literature; they contain mostly philosophy, sociology, political science, and some literary criticism. And in these subjects Burke ends up talking more about social and political perspectives than he works to extend explicitly the theoretical statements he develops in "The Philosophy of Literary Form" and the longer articles. In fact, in sections 3 and 4 Burke often quite explicitly uses particular works to address the relation of language to the social or political world.

For example, in the review of Lord Raglan's *The Hero: A Study in Tradition, Myth, and Drama* ("A Recipe for Worship" [*PLF,* 411–13]) Burke argues that myths, even if they are "merely" dramatic rituals, as Raglan claims, are not just spectacles of a life that ordinary people do not live; rather, Burke says, "the dramas could retain their hold only in so far as the spectators were 'glued' to them—and one is glued to a work of art only when that work is reliving for him some basic pattern of his own experience, with its appropriate 'medicine'" (*PLF,* 413). Burke suggests that the dramatic rituals of a culture, even when most rarefied, serve important social functions for their viewers. While it is true that many readers of Burke accept his idea that "literature is equipment for living," they run with the idea and ignore what Burke means by it as demonstrated in his criticism. At a basic level it does not seem to matter whether Burke is talking about a work of philosophy or sociology, a novel, a poem, or a play. All contribute to the same general point. Perhaps many readers of Burke ignore the reviews precisely because of the sociological and political content; after all, just a glance at the authors reveals Burke's general nonliterary concerns. If readers intentionally ignore what Burke treats explicitly, they could hardly be expected to embrace fully the more subtle presence infusing his literary criticism. This is the most serious gap in the reading of *Literary Form.* Readers tend to see Burke's literary criticism simply as an articulation of how the aesthetics of a piece of literature operates. They miss the fact that Burke's critical methods are as much social and political statements as are the specific social and political programs he endorses.

One recent example of a literary bias in reading *Literary Form* can be seen in René Wellek's multivolume history of literary criticism.[2] In a harsh assessment of Burke, about half of Wellek's citations to *Literary Form* are to "The Philosophy of Literary Form"; most of the rest are to "Freud—and the Analysis of Poetry."[3] This pattern is common in writings about *Literary Form;* an author tends to cite mostly "The Philosophy of Literary Form" and just one other essay, the one that explores that critic's particular perspective, interest, or concern. In this case, Wellek sees Burke as a Freudian. "His basic approach to literature," Wellek says, "has been psychoanalytical and has become more exclusively so in his recent practice" (247). So, naturally, Wellek focuses on the essay that is most explicitly psychoanalytical, ignoring the social and political elements of the book. Wellek had long disliked Burke for not being a formalist critic who looked only at the text. When Burke does focus on "internality," Wellek excoriates him for the importation of psychoanalytic concepts and methods because they are to some degree extratextual. In a reply to Wellek, "As I Was Saying," Burke complains of Wellek's "piecemeal, hit-and-run mode of reporting" (11), lamenting that Wellek failed to consider his other work.[4] All in all, readers who rely on the small portion of *Literary Form* that has gained wide circuit are like theatergoers who, stuck in the cheap seats, roll up a playbill into a makeshift telescope only to gain a view that is a cheat, for the focus elides breadth and the magnification is an illusion.

Understanding how the essays in sections 1 and 2 touch on some of Burke's social and political concerns will lend a sense of what Burke is saying in the part that has piqued many readers' interest. Hardly a writer on Burke explores the longer articles in detail. Typically, the longer articles are used for quotations to support some point about Burke's views on literary theory, often a point from "The Philosophy of Literary Form."

"The Philosophy of Literary Form" is a long and complex essay in which Burke mixes literary criticism, biography, linguistics, philology, phonetics, psychology, philosophy, sociology, political science, anthropology—and more. To what end? Burke covers a wide range of topics, but they all gravitate around one problem, which he explains in the 1953 postscript to *Counter-Statement.* "The Philosophy of Literary Form," he says, "aims both to give a summarization of the author's notions about the symbolic function of literary forms and to sketch a technique for the analysis of a work in its nature as a structure of organically interrelated terms. Whereas the stress in *Counter-Statement* had been rhetorical . . . the stress now was upon the work in its internality" (*CS,* 217). A simple enough statement but one that masks Burke's tantalizingly effervescent imagination. A glance at the titles of the fifteen subsections of "The Philosophy of Literary Form" hints at the range and variety of issues Burke addresses. Some of the more intriguing ones for a book ostensibly about literature are: Situations and Strategies, Magic and Religion, Aspects of the Scapegoat in Reidentification, The Sacrifice and the Kill, Ritual Drama as "Hub," and Electioneering in Psychoanalysis. Readers familiar with *Permanence* will recognize its influence, for many of the fifteen titles echo themes central there. They also remind us of the provocative entries Burke created for "The Dictionary of Pivotal Terms" and foreshadow subsections in *A Grammar of Motives* and *A Rhetoric of Motives.*

If one concept is key to "The Philosophy of Literary Form," it is "symbolic action." Burke reveals a lot about symbolic action, in "The Philosophy of Literary Form" and elsewhere, but he does not supply a concise and detailed definition, opting instead for metaphors and broad statements about how language is used. Burke opens "The Philosophy of Literary Form" with a discussion of "Situations and Strategies," arguing that "critical and imaginative works are answers to questions posed by the situation in which they arose" (*PLF,* 1). He goes on to say that proverbs reflect attitudes that have become stable because those attitudes promote successful responses to recurring situations. Even the act of naming, Burke suggests, reflects a "sizing up" of a situation. In what might be his most cited quotation, Burke declares that "the symbolic act is the *dancing of an attitude*" (*PLF,* 9). That description is highly suggestive but hardly definitive. Unfortunately, glosses on the metaphor have not helped much. Perhaps the best angle is Burke's own: he compares *practical* acts to *symbolic* acts. We do things sometimes with our hands, he says, and sometimes with our words. Burke does tell us that there are different levels of symbolic action: "the bodily or biological level," "the personal, intimate, familiar, familistic level," and "the abstract level" (*PLF,* 36–37). William Rueckert gives one of the best explanations of the idea of symbolic action, though he emphasizes too much the "hidden" or private element as a defining feature of the symbolic act.[5]

The lack of a clear definition of symbolic action in "The Philosophy of Literary Form" is not the weakness some might imagine it to be, for the idea of symbolic action is just a beginning point. Burke is simply distinguishing between broad classes of human experience, with the intention of confining his discussion to the dimension of action in language. Burke is more interested in *how* we craft language into a "strategic" or "stylized answer" (that is, in how symbolic action works) than in defining symbolic action in the first place. He discusses symbolic action not for metaphysical definition, but to explain his ontological assumptions. Burke makes this quite clear in the section titled "On Methodology," where he draws a distinction between two kinds of critical questions: "what to look for, and why"; and "how, when, and where to look for it" (*PLF,* 68). The discussion of symbolic action (a relatively small part of the essay) answers the first kind of question, which Burke calls "ontological." Much of the rest of "The Philosophy of Literary Form" is Burke's answer to the methodological question. The distinction between practical and symbolic action serves much the same purpose as the distinction between the "psychology of information" and the "psychology of form" in *Counter-Statement,* and between action and motion in *Permanence.*

Burke's analysis of symbolic action centers on the idea of "clusters" or "equations" (that is, on concepts and structural features that through a variety of associational linkages create significant units of meaning in a poetic work. A poetic work will have several key clusters. (This is similar to what he says in *Counter-Statement* about eloquence. On the whole, works that are rhetorically effective, that are eloquent, have a proliferation of rhetorical form. Likewise, a poetic work that is aesthetically effective will have several associational clusters.) From time to time in "The Philosophy of Literary Form," Burke distinguishes between musical chords and arpeggios. This distinction points clearly to what Burke is trying to get at in the essay overall. Literature, by its very nature, is linear, despite whatever attempts an author makes to undermine that essential characteristic; however, the emotional world the writer speaks of, and attempts to influence, is a temporal jumble. Past, present, and future swirl together, despite our pretensions otherwise. The recognition of clusters is Burke's attempt to find synchrony in diachrony. When Burke hit upon the distinction between chords and arpeggios as a way of understanding how literature functions, he was quite excited. In perhaps his first formulation of this idea, in a July 1939 letter to J. S. Watson, Burke mentions that a chord combines polar opposites. In discussing thesis and antithesis as an example, Burke comments that the chord is a synthesis whereas the arpeggio is a "historical" pattern that has thesis or antithesis dominating in different historical eras. Clearly, Burke was influenced heavily by his thinking in *Permanence* and *Attitudes*. In this early formulation he not only casts the distinction in terms of psychology, but imbues that with a temporally developmental flavor. He says the chord-arpeggio distinction reflects the psychological process of "reversal" whereby the natural order of one emotional state leading to another is reversed, with what would normally be the consequent leading to the antecedent. Yet in *Literary Form* the distinction between chord and arpeggio has lost much of the narrowness of this first formulation. Clusters combine virtually any elements, not just bipolar opposites; and Burke does not cast matters in terms of developmental history or psychological development of the narrow sort just mentioned.

The problem for the literary critic, Burke suggests, is to come up with a method that reconstitutes the synchrony underlying the diachronic distillate. Burke's answer to that problem is, at one level, disarmingly simple: by figuring out "what goes with what" in a poetic work, one will understand the motivations of the artist, the meaning of the text, and how the text works on readers. According to Burke, "The work of every writer contains a set of implicit equations. He uses 'associational clusters.' And you may, by examining his work, find 'what goes with what' in these clusters—what kinds of acts and images and personalities and situations go with his notions of heroism, villainy, consolation, despair, etc. . . . The motivation out of which he writes is synonymous with the structural way in which he puts events and values together" (*PLF,* 20).

Burke bases his method for analyzing associations on three fundamental concepts: "dream," "prayer," and "chart." Each refers to what Burke calls a "subdivision" of the analysis of poetic works. Dream, he says, is "the unconscious or subconscious factors in a poem." Prayer concerns "the communicative functions of a poem," which Burke takes to mean primarily its hortatory functions. Chart refers to "the realistic sizing-up of situations that is sometimes explicit, sometimes implicit, in poetic strategies" (*PLF,* 5–6). Dream, prayer, and chart are central functions of symbolic acts and are observable in literature. Much of "The Philosophy of Literary Form" is Burke's description of how one might analyze poetic works, using his notions of symbolic action, clusters or equations, chord and arpeggio, and dream, prayer, and chart. Although Burke analyzes many works, he focuses on Clifford Odets's *Golden Boy* and Samuel Taylor Coleridge's "The Rime of the Ancient Mariner."

"The Philosophy of Literary Form" concludes with one of Burke's most peculiar detours: "Electioneering in Psychoanalysia." He calls it a "burlesque" of democratic elections that serves two main purposes: first, as in the section "Recalcitrance" that appears toward the end of *Permanence,* as a reminder that practicalities obtain regardless of our analytical schemes; second, with that in mind, as a warning of the dangers of improperly charting the political realities of 1940s capitalist America. One need only look at the beginning and end of "The Philosophy of Literary Form" to discover the impulse underlying Burke's intentions. He begins the essay arguing that strategic communications are informed by social and political situations, and that we can discover much about our circumstances by looking carefully at our rhetoric. He concludes with a warning that rhetoric, if it is to work toward appropriate social, political, and ethical goals, has to be grounded in a realistic assessment of our circumstances.

Section 2, the middle third of the book, contains six "Longer Articles" that build on themes from "The Philosophy of Literary Form." Burke describes the first essay, "Semantic and Poetic Meaning," as a "rhetorical defense of rhetoric." Much as he argued before in *Permanence,* Burke condemns the impulse to adopt a purely neutral vocabulary (now referred to as "semantic meaning") because it "attempts to make a totality out of a fragment" (*PLF,* 138). Semantic meaning, Burke suggests, is perfectly adequate for some purposes but fails as an ideal conception of language because it fosters "the notion that one may comprehensively discuss human and social events in a nonmoral vocabulary" (*PLF,* 164). Human action, he says, is inherently moral and ought to be addressed in a vocabulary rich in "poetic meaning."

In "The Virtues and Limitations of Debunking," Burke uses Thurman W. Arnold's *The Folklore of Capitalism* to explore debunking as a form of liberal critique; in particular, he is interested in the humanitarian motives of the typical debunker who does something such as deflating an overinflated reputation by exposing "low" motives. The problem with debunking, Burke argues, is that it is inconsistent, violating its own reasoning. The debunker, Burke tells us, "discerns an evil" and wishes to "eradicate" it. "In order to be sure that he is *thorough enough*" about his business, Burke charges, "he becomes *too thorough*" (*PLF,* 171). According to Burke, although the debunker assiduously applies his principles to a politician or program, he is unwilling to apply them to himself, either at all or with the dedication mustered against his typical victim. Moreover, when the debunker reaches "a point at which he too must advocate something or other," Burke observes, "he *covertly* restores important ingredients of thought that he has *overtly* annihilated" (*PLF,* 171). Burke points out several ways Arnold does this. Perhaps the most important is that Arnold focuses too much on the "irrational" factors of ritual and ceremony as the motivation behind many people's pronouncements, ignoring their interests. This problem suggests to Burke his most telling criticism—that debunking is faulty because it has a "humanitarian ideal of truth" that, in the end, separates "exposition" from "exhortation," only to then import human interests as an afterthought, as a corrective. Burke admonishes us to embrace "social truths" in the first place, so that the "humanitarian afterthought" is not needed.[6] This criticism is not new for Burke. It is pretty much a clear implication of the difference between the psychology of information and the psychology of form (that is, when scientism works as intended, the humane is exorcised, only to be restored after the "pure" methods have resulted in untainted knowledge). Moreover, Burke makes much the same point in distinguishing between semantic and poetic meaning.

"The Rhetoric of Hitler's 'Battle,'" the third essay in section 2, is probably the most cited essay in Burke's extraordinarily prolific career. It is also probably his most accessible. Troubled by critics who, incensed by Hitler's creed, spurned his blueprint out of hand, Burke suggests that we must read *Mein Kampf* carefully so that we can expose his rhetoric: "let us try also to discover what kind of 'medicine' this medicine-man has concocted, that we may know, with greater accuracy, exactly what to guard against, if we are to forestall the concocting of similar medicine in America. . . . Hitler found a panacea, a 'cure for what ails you,' a 'snakeoil.' . . . And he was helpful enough to put his cards face up on the table, that we might examine his hands. Let us, then, for God's sake, examine them. This book is the well of Nazi magic; crude magic, but effective. A people trained in pragmatism should want to inspect this magic" (*PLF,* 191–92). Burke determines that Hitler worked his "magic" by creating a unifying device—an essentialized enemy, an international "devil": the Jew as scapegoat. This unification device, he says, was made all the more powerful by setting it within a secularized Christian framework that promoted "categorical dignity" by virtue of Aryan racial and national supremacy. The scapegoat, as a "projection device," resulted in "purification by dissociation," which led to a "symbolic rebirth" for the German people. The bulk of the essay examines the nature and characteristics of the symbols Hitler used to manifest these ideas.

In "The Calling of the Tune," his first publication of many in the *Kenyon Review,* Burke analyzes arguments that art should be free of social, political, and economic constraints (in particular, those imposed by systems of art patronage). Burke points out Grace Overmyer's contention, in *Government and the Arts,* that "the state should pay the piper, but should not call the tune." He also cites the argument of anti-authoritarian Herbert Read in *Poetry and Anarchism* for a radical rejection of any external influence on art, positing "poetry as the opposite of authority." Read, Burke laments, views the problem "divisively, with artists and patrons as conflicting classes" (*PLF,* 225). Burke rejects both views, calling for a more sophisticated understanding of "this vacillating relationship between the artist's freedom and the society's commands" (*PLF,* 221). He insists that the artist's "work derives its strength as much from the structure of authority as from his modes of resistance" (*PLF,* 232). He states his belief in an intermediary position that makes "the interests of piper and tune-caller identical, hence allowing the poet simultaneously to 'be himself' and to act as public spokesman for his patrons, or customers" (*PLF,* 225). Unfortunately, Burke does not specifically describe this intermediary position. He calls it a "Whitmanesque strategy" that "focuses attention upon the 'human element' in our patterns of sociality" (*PLF,* 224).

"War, Response, and Contradiction" is the earliest of the longer articles, having been published in *Symposium* in 1933. Here, Burke uses a disagreement that arose between Archibald MacLeish and Malcolm Cowley over *The First World War* (edited by Laurence Stallings) as an occasion to explore rationalist biases in criticism. MacLeish criticized Stallings on the ground that Stallings "omits the heroic and adventurous aspects" of World War I and includes only the horror (*PLF,* 236). MacLeish argued that one should admit the noble aspects of the war and understand that humanizing the war allows the true horror to emerge. Cowley, in opposition, responded that Stallings's book is not so much about World War I as it is a poetic statement about a future war; hence, it does not need to be objectively valid. In observing this argument, Burke comments that "MacLeish seems mainly concerned with the poet's response to experience, and Cowley with the public's response to the poet" (*PLF,* 235). Burke recognized that these authors were working at "cross-purposes," yet both points of view, he tells us, are instructive concerning the nature of art as "a means of communication . . . designed to elicit a 'response' of some sort" (*PLF,* 235–36). Burke's analysis is complex; however, in essence, he argues that life is full of contradictions (especially in a capitalist society) and that fully "poetic" or "ethical" works of art can reasonably be expected to manifest the contradictions of the world. A "'complete' response to a contradictory society," Burke asserts, "should be contradictory" (*PLF,* 250). In the end, Burke warns of the dangers of a rationalist bias in criticizing literature. Such a bias, he says, stems from an encroachment of the methods and goals of science into ethical affairs.

"Freud—and the Analysis of Poetry," the last of the longer articles, was solicited by the *American Journal of Sociology.* Burke was asked "to consider the bearing of Freud's theories upon literary criticism" (*PLF,* 261). In response, Burke suggests that literary criticism and Freud's psychological theories have important "analogous features" (*PLF,* 258): "The acts of the neurotic are symbolic acts. Hence in so far as both the neurotic act and the poetic act share this property in common, they may share a terminological chart in common. But in so far as they deviate, terminology likewise must deviate. And this deviation is a fact that literary criticism must explicitly consider" (*PLF,* 261). One area of overlap identified by Burke is method. Looking at Freud's methods as they developed over the years, Burke distinguishes "proportional" strategies from "essentializing" strategies. Freud's early work, Burke tells us, was based on free association and sought to define clusters of associated images. Later in his career Freud came to depend upon making one concept essential, the root from which all others stem. "The important matter for our purposes," Burke says, "is to suggest that the examination of a poetic work's internal organization would bring us nearer to a variant of the typically Freudian free-association method than to the purely symbolic method toward which he subsequently gravitated" (*PLF,* 266–67). Burke goes on to highlight ways in which Freudian analysis can aid understanding of literary works. He analyzes concepts such as the unconscious, infantile regression, childhood development, wish fulfillment, Oedipus complex, patriarchy, condensation, displacement, and others—all according to Burke's own concepts of dream, prayer, and chart. Ultimately, Burke suggests that in comparison to Freudian analysis, literary criticism should have a greater emphasis on proportional strategies, matriarchal symbolizations, and literature as prayer and chart.

A brief description of "The Philosophy of Literary Form" and the six longer articles cannot, of course, convey the richness and complexity of Burke's writing. However, even this quick summary should make clear to those familiar with the secondary literature that many writers on Burke, including current students of him who typically refer to a few parts of *Literary Form,* approach him piecemeal. On the whole, Burke's critics in the early 1940s focused on three essays—"The Philosophy of Literary Form," "Semantic and Poetic Meaning," and "The Rhetoric of Hitler's 'Battle'"—giving the book a literary flavor. Of ten reviews examined, only two depart from this formula. William S. Knickerbocker and Harry Slochower cast *Literary Form* in a wider context, analyzing at length its relations to Burke's earlier books (especially *Attitudes*).[7] Perhaps these two reviewers were given more space in which to concentrate on more sophisticated questions.

Perhaps the literary bias in the reading of *Literary Form* has a simple explanation. To most readers of Burke in 1941 there was apparently little new in *Literary Form.* Almost two-thirds of the book had been published previously, mainly in 1937, 1938, and 1939; moreover, Burke makes many of the same points in the essays and reviews that he makes in his earlier books and in "The Philosophy of Literary Form." Readers could reach the conclusion that the title essay is the most original and stimulating of the lot, but "The Philosophy of Literary Form" constitutes only one-third of the book. What is gained from the other two-thirds? The longer articles serve many purposes, one of which is exploring the nature and function of language. For example, in "Semantic and Poetic Meaning," Burke clearly defines the meaning of symbolic action and how it works. In "The Rhetoric of Hitler's 'Battle'" he explores in detail how symbols function, especially when the rhetor takes advantage of his audience's impulse to scapegoat. In "Freud—and the Analysis of Poetry," Burke explains how the similarities and differences between literary criticism and poetry can help us better understand how symbols work. Yet in each of these essays there is an underlying social concern that infuses Burke's literary judgments. In "Semantic and Poetic Meaning," Burke does more than just talk about some abstract issue relating to language; he criticizes a cultural vector. He is making the same point he made in *Counter-Statement, Permanence,* and *Attitudes,* which is that science is encroaching on ethical or moral realms of experience. In "The Rhetoric of Hitler's 'Battle,'" Burke offers his clearest political warning: we must defend ourselves against the arsenal of symbols used by tyrannical "medicine men."

Burke does not simply use Hitler as one example of a medicine man, even though Hitler is the perfect archetype, given the virulence of his message, the effectiveness of his rhetoric, and the heinousness of his crimes; rather, Burke uses Hitler in part to demonstrate the role literature and literary criticism can play in helping us understand how social and political discourse affect the public's thoughts and actions. Burke makes this point in "Freud—and the Analysis of Poetry" when he attacks, among other things, the "patriarchal symbolizations" in psychoanalysis in particular and in culture in general. In "The Calling of the Tune," Burke argues for a politics in which a patron of the arts (be it a government, philanthropic institution, commercial organization, or wealthy individual) and the artist can be seen as working toward mutual goals. The same point is made in the shorter articles, notably in "The Nature of Art under Capitalism" and "Reading While You Run," in which Burke laments the impact of journalistic writing on the way we criticize the political world. "My purpose," he says, is "to show how thoroughly the merest commonplaces of language serve to confuse the criticism of capitalist methods"—a result of the fact that "capitalist propaganda is so ingrained in our speech that it is as natural as breathing" (*PLF,* 323).

In the foreword to the first edition Burke hints about how to read portions of *Literary Form:* "I am more concerned with the *general problems* of internal structure and act-scene relationships—and I introduce reference to particular poems, novels, or dramas as illustrative material rather than as central theme" (*PLF,* xvii). No doubt this is true, but illustration works in different ways. Sometimes it simply shows how a clear and precise principle applies—as numbers might be plugged into an equation, or premises and conclusion into a deductive syllogism. Readers of *Literary Form* often understand the illustrative material in this way, ignoring much of the book because they believe that many sections simply give examples of what Burke is saying in "The Philosophy of Literary Form." However, when a principle is vague or may be interpreted in a variety of ways, illustrations—as embodiments of that principle—can actually be more telling than the principle itself; that is, the meaning of the idea may reside more in the illustrations than in the principle. Burke often thought and wrote in this way. He established a rather vague or multifaceted principle and then defined it through applications. We see this in *Counter-Statement* with the "Lexicon Rhetoricae"—in Burke's words, "Being a Codification, Amplification, and Correction of the Two Essays, 'Psychology and Form' and 'The Poetic Process.'"[8] *Permanence* is replete with this—for example, in Burke's explanation of what he means by "motives" (*PC,* 19–36). In *Attitudes* the entire "Dictionary of Pivotal Terms" is a series of such illustrations. By the time Burke wrote *A Grammar of Motives* he recognized the need to make readers aware of this style. "If you ask why," he states in the introduction, "with a whole world of terms to choose from, we select these rather than some others as basic, our book itself is offered as the answer. For, to explain our position, we shall show how it can be applied" (*GM,* xv). Burke's references to particular poems, novels, and dramas throughout *Literary Form* and much of the criticism in sections 3 and 4 are illustrations of this second sort. They are more than examples; they add to the theoretical foundation in "The Philosophy of Literary Form."[9]

Myopic reading of *Literary Form* has occurred because of the problem that bedeviled Burke in his earlier books: his audience failed to understand or accept his scrambling of categories and rejected his specific social, political, and aesthetic programs. Readers tend to latch onto what they understand and accept, which unfortunately overemphasizes the literary and linguistic elements. This was precisely Wellek's problem. He read *Literary Form* simply as a book of psychoanalytical literary criticism, failing to recognize, much less embrace, Burke's social and political arguments. This is seen especially in that Wellek ultimately derides Burke for an epistemological relativism and mushiness that, he says, undermines the integrity of viewing a piece of literature as an artwork. Wellek charges that in Burke's theory, "literature becomes absorbed into a scheme of linguistic action or rhetoric so all-embracing and all-absorbing that poetry as an art is lost sight of and the work of art is spun into a network of allusions, puns, and clusters of images without any regard for its wholeness or unity. . . . He moves in a self-created verbal universe where everything may mean everything else" (255–56). In a world of strict and pure category definitions, where sociological, political, and rhetorical interests dare not step on the toes of literary criticism, Wellek's criticism may well be justified. Even in a formalist climate that is more forgiving, Wellek could be making a good point. Yet he condemns Burke for adopting methods that do precisely what Burke wanted to do, which was to tease out possible connections between literary structure and nonliterary aspects of literature. Wellek ignores the fundamental goal and methodology of Burke's literary criticism: to create not a new universe where everything can mean everything, but a new universe that unites what Wellek would call the rhetorical and the aesthetic. Burke does not spin out a work into allusions, puns, and clusters of images; rather, he uses such devices as a way into the rhetoric of the work. Burke is not engaging in some hermeneutic magic whereby, through shifty linguistic alchemy, meaning is transmuted. But he does use resources of language to push the limits of interpretation so that we may better understand the core of an aesthetic expression and how it serves individual and collective rhetorical functions in our lives. Put another way, Wellek is a strict formalist, and Burke is not. Burke proposes to study the internality of literary texts, thereby violating Wellek's turf. The important point is that Wellek refuses to accept the boundary that Burke sets up: to speak of literature as symbolic action, to see how the internal and external interpenetrate. Wellek simply does not accept this cut across traditional ways of talking about literature. If Wellek were to speak of the epistemological and methodological difficulties of doing what Burke sought to do, he would be on better ground. In response to Wellek, Burke maintains that he is not a formalist critic. In fact, he says, "there seem to be some humanistic speculations that I consider important with regard to literary texts but that the nature of Wellek's project requires him to slight."[10]

Another example of literary bias in a contemporary reading of *Literary Form* occurs in Frank Lentricchia's *Criticism and Social Change*. Lentricchia has a better feeling than most authors for the general thrust of what Burke was trying to say, and he embraces potential social and political implications of Burke's ideas. Despite this sympathy, Lentricchia by and large characterizes the literary criticism of "The Philosophy of Literary Form" as he does the *Grammar*—the flowering of a critical method that has "the classical austerity of the structuralist ideal."[11] Lentricchia goes so far as to say that Burke has created a "high-flying Platonic structuralism" (69). This assessment is bewildering. It is true, as Lentricchia points out, that Burke focuses on the internal structure of literary works and uses binary coordinates to analyze literature, notably Clifford Odets's *Golden Boy*. Yet structuralism has no patent on the idea of structure, on binary coordinates, or on the combination of the two in literary analysis. Speaking about literary structure in terms of polar opposites does not make one a structuralist. Moreover, Burke's use of binary coordinates in analyzing *Golden Boy* is not at all representative of his method in general. Burke uses *Golden Boy* because its equations neatly and clearly explain a simple form of "associational cluster." *Golden Boy* is the first of many extended applications of Burke's method to literary works. The binary coordinates are not an essential feature of his method, but an integral characteristic of Odets's play. When we look at Burke's criticism in the rest of the essay and in the book, we see a complex of relationships far richer than binary coordination.

Lentricchia and others who have looked to Burke as a structuralist are misled because they failed to see his method in context. Burke's criticism in *Literary Form* is heavily influenced by his notion of perspective by incongruity, first explored in depth in *Permanence*. There, in a method in which Burke has "extremes meet," the coordination of bipolar opposites makes none of the ontological and metaphysical claims that such oppositions hold in structuralist methodology. Indeed, structuralism operates under metaphysical and ontological assumptions inimical to Burke's positions. If all this is not enough to make us question the idea that Burke is structuralist, structuralism in the latter half of the twentieth century has had political overtones that have been markedly different from the politics of Burke's aesthetics in the late 1930s and early 1940s. One explanation is that Lentricchia sees different strands at work in Burke. It certainly is the case that Lentricchia's book is against deconstruction, especially the ethical bankruptcy of Paul de Man. Burke is the antidote. At the same time Burke's methods are a separate strand (which is why, to Lentricchia, Burke is both structuralist and antistructuralist). Lentricchia does not recognize that in Burke the rhetoric and the program are not separate. The great challenge that Burke offers is to see the internality of the text as a manifestation of the external. In a way, this is similar to what Wellek missed. The implications of Lentricchia's statement extend beyond whether or not Burke is indeed a structuralist. In assessing Burke's literary theories as Lentricchia ultimately does, it is easy to distort Burke's brand of criticism, making him in some ways more than he is, in other ways less. Equally important is what Lentricchia does with Burke, assuming him to be correct. *Criticism and Social Change* seems to be a remarkably insightful and heartfelt plea for critics today to change their bearing. However, there does not seem to be much Burke in it, apart from the sort of inspiration that critics from any number of perspectives can find in Burke's penetrating insights about language and human relations.

Misinterpretations in contemporary readings of *Literary Form* are due in part to the fact that in this book Burke is more indirect than ever about his social and political concerns, especially in "The Philosophy of Literary Form." He has achieved better than before what he sought in previous books: a blending of what he calls aesthetic and social "integers." Hence, when Burke gets into literary aesthetics, albeit in an idiom freshly steeped in the terms and concepts of linguistics, he is simultaneously addressing literature and the social-political world. While not diminishing the literary achievement of "The Philosophy of Literary Form" or the book overall, nor imposing upon either an unwarranted sociological or political interpretation, it is important to point out that Burke's literary "theory" must be understood as part of a larger set of social and political concerns that had occupied his heart and mind since the early 1920s. The only way to gauge this aspect of Burke's literary criticism accurately is to recognize that *Literary Form* represents a rearticulation and development of ideas similar to those he went through from *Counter-Statement* through *Attitudes*.

To understand what Burke was trying to accomplish with *Literary Form,* it is necessary to look more closely at his intentions after *Attitudes.* Having finished *Attitudes* in the late 1930s, Burke was still disturbed by old social and political problems he believed had never been solved. Writing to Malcolm Cowley on 24 December 1939, Burke recognized that efforts were being made to improve American society. Nonetheless, he deemed them inadequate: "I share your feeling that there is another cultural recombination (or dispersion?) taking place now. Yet I can see no great hopefulness. For the most we could conceivably hope for would be some surprise whereby men were found capable of running their factories without having a factory model of the state. Even if this were got, we'd have the barren norms of bookkeeping, machinery, and journalism necessarily taking up far too large a segment of our cultural frame" (Jay, 227). Social instability, factory conditions, the industrial state, and what Burke referred to as a "technological emphasis" are key issues he addressed in the late 1920s and early 1930s. Indeed, the feeling that such problems remained unresolved would haunt Burke for many years. More than a decade later Burke again complained to Cowley, lamenting that "the muddle I discussed . . . [in 'Program'] is still quite with us" (Jay, 312). Despite his discouragement in 1939, Burke remained optimistic. A year later, analyzing Cowley's plans for a memoir, Burke complained about the growing number of new accounts of the aesthetic-political world of the 1930s intellectual Left. The faddish histories, he wrote, had a "red-baitingish quality" that unfairly condemned the Communist Party. Burke had no great love for the Communist Party of the 1930s, but he felt that it had served some good. In his reproach of the revisionist historians, Burke reveals his hope that a way could still be found to address contemporary problems effectively: "I simply feel a slight distaste for this whole business of copy-making out of the welching act. . . . Whatever reservations there are to be made about the whole alliance between art and politics, one should make these at a time, and in a spirit, when they can be made for purposes of *enlightenment,* and not when the writing of such stuff is just one last final bit of the same sort of tactics, angling for position, etc." (Jay, 232–33).

How was Burke to do this? *Counter-Statement, Permanence,* and *Attitudes*—three attempts at enlightenment in three different intellectual idioms—had been largely misunderstood, had received increasingly severe criticism, and ultimately had little impact. Ever self-reflective, Burke began to reevaluate the path taken so far. On Christmas Eve of 1939, after being awakened late at night by his crying child, Burke lay sleepless in bed surveying his career: "I lay awake for a long time, with my customary Christmas-cheer gloom, plotting curves of development over the years, and wondering just what were better dropped, what better recovered" (Jay, 227).

Perhaps at that moment Burke felt that he ought to recover literary criticism. In the four years after *Attitudes* he had published a few poems, a dozen essays, and almost thirty reviews. On the whole, these publications resemble more what he was doing in *Counter-Statement* than anything he had done since then. "Semantic and Poetic Meaning" (Winter 1938) and "The Philosophy of Literary Form," for instance, are much closer to "Psychology and Form" (1924) and "The Poetic Process" (1924) than to *Permanence* and *Attitudes*.[12] Semantic meaning is similar to "psychology of information," and poetic meaning is similar to "psychology of form," though in both cases the concepts from *Literary Form* are broader. In both "The Poetic Process" and "The Philosophy of Literary Form," Burke describes how an artist fashions symbols; however, in the latter, Burke is concerned more with the hortatory and strategic functions of symbols than he is with their expressive functions. The similarities between *Literary Form* and *Counter-Statement* are also evident in "War, Response, and Contradiction" (1933), "The Virtues and Limitations of Debunking" (1938), "The Calling of the Tune" (1939), and "The Nature of Art under Capitalism" (1933). Like "Program" (1931) and "Applications of the Terminology" (1931), they set forth the principles underlying Burke's call for social and political change. Despite his unremitting interest in sociological and psychological matters, Burke in fact now discusses literature more directly than he has for some time.

An examination of Burke's intentions for "The Philosophy of Literary Form" can be helpful in understanding the relations between *Literary Form* and Burke's previous books. In the 1953 postscript to *Counter-Statement,* Burke explains that "The Philosophy of Literary Form" summarizes his notions about the symbolic function of literary forms and offers a method for analyzing the internal structure of a literary work. However, the problem of internality, for Burke, does not exist in vacuo. This is indicated by his telegraphic description of the goal of the book, which occurs in a comparison of *Literary Form* to *Permanence* and *Attitudes: Literary Form* "had another sort of problem to solve. . . . Problem of circumstantiality in critical analysis. There was the old school, immured in the text. There were the leftists, strong on talk of relations between literature and society, but weak on internal analysis. Tried to bridge this gap. To this end, the theory of 'clusters,' 'equations.' To find out *what goes with what* in a book, so that one's analysis is internal; yet to note the social relevance of such 'equations'" (Jay, 291–92). Again he writes of "internality" and "externality," or, in other words, literary theory and sociological analysis. It is important to remember that Burke's chief goal was to *bridge* the difference between them. This explains why Burke included "The Calling of the Tune," "War, Response, and Contradiction," "The Nature of Art under Capitalism," and "Reading While You Run" in the collection—essays more political than literary, more external than internal. It also explains the presence of "Electioneering in Psychoanalysia," a political lampoon. These parts of *Literary Form* do not easily fit into a conception of the book as pure literary criticism; perhaps that is why they are hardly mentioned in most analyses of *Literary Form*. In other essays Burke more obviously mixes internal and external elements (for instance, in "The Rhetoric of Hitler's 'Battle,'" "Semantic and Poetic Meaning," and "Literature as Equipment for Living"). But even when considering these essays, most scholars simply ignore the political and social arguments, focusing instead on aspects of "internal" analysis. Despite how scholars have approached *Literary Form,* it is clear that Burke fully intended to bridge the gap between literary criticism and sociological analysis.

The real achievement of *Literary Form* is that Burke finally achieves this synthesis, a union he gropes for in his earlier books. Even so, *Literary Form* is an adaptation to his milieu. The sorts of questions Burke now asks about literature have changed. In a letter mentioned earlier Burke comments that "Psychology and Form" and "The Poetic Process" are but two parts of a projected trilogy that was never finished because he "ran into *The Meaning of Meaning,* and was so knocked over that [he] was unable to write the third essay." Burke adds that "it was not until the 'Philosophy of Literary Form' item . . . that I was able to treat of the material for that third essay, though it is there in a much altered state, affected by all that has intervened.[13] The questions Burke asks about literature in *Literary Form* are quite different than the questions he asks in *Counter-Statement* because *Literary Form* was informed by the psychological and sociological researches of *Permanence* and *Attitudes.* In fact, one typescript draft of "The Philosophy of Literary Form" is titled "The Psychology of Literary Form." "The Philosophy of Literary Form" approaches the poetic process with greater psychological sophistication and a more sociological point of view than *Counter-Statement.* In the earlier book Burke uses psychology in a general way, distinguishing, for instance, between the "psychology of information" and the "psychology of form." In "The Poetic Process" he explores how a symbol or other artistic conceit is a response to the artist's feelings, an externalization of mood that stimulates a desired emotional response in an audience. "We have the original emotion," Burke explains, "which is channelized into a symbol. This symbol becomes a generative force, a relationship to be repeated in varying details" (*CS,* 61). A fairly simple psychology is operating here, and the literary criticism based upon this is likewise psychologically simple.

In *Literary Form,* Burke's psychology is more complex. Instead of simply assuming that creative works result from a largely undifferentiated welling up

of the creator's emotions, he posits what he calls the symbolic action of "associational clusters." Burke is not so much interested in the fact that the symbol
is a manifestation of an author's emotions as he is concerned with how that
knowledge allows us to see more clearly the relationship between an artwork's
structure and its rhetorical effect. As Burke makes clear in his analysis of
Coleridge's "The Rime of the Ancient Mariner," the relationship between the
public and the private is closer than ever before ("the private and public areas
of a symbolic act at once overlap and diverge," he says [*PLF,* 25]). What the
symbol does for the author, Burke acknowledges, is not what it does for us
(*PLF,* 73). This is why, in a tantalizing homology, Burke equates the terms "symbolic" and "statistical" (*PLF,* 18, 25).[14] There are many other ways in which
Burke's psychology developed from 1931 to 1941. By introducing Paget's theory of gesture speech (*PLF,* 12), ablaut punning (*PLF,* 52 ff., 369–78), and a
variety of other concepts from philology and phonetics, Burke creates a psychology of meaning, albeit primitive and questionable (even in the 1940s Burke
was roundly criticized for linguistic excess). But that does not diminish the fact
that Burke was trying to establish a psychology of literary style that combines
phonetic, biological, social, and cognitive structures.[15] This is certainly a more
sophisticated vision than Burke displays in *Counter-Statement, Permanence,* or
Attitudes. Burke's developing psychology is also present in his discussion of
dream, prayer, and chart. It is to Burke's credit that he avoids falling into the sur-
realist trap of the percolating subconscious; instead dream, prayer, and chart are
alternative modes of psychological orientation, literary form, and rhetorical effect.
And each of these elements mutually informs the others, giving his psychology a
texture that begins to capture more fully the complexity of literary appeal.

This brings us to perhaps the most important sense in which Burke's psychology has developed. In *Literary Form* in general, and even in "The
Philosophy of Literary Form," Burke moves toward a more fully rhetorical
sense of the psychological. Such an observation may sound odd, since Burke
said that with *Literary Form* he shifted from the rhetorical to the linguistic (from
the external to the internal); yet Burke also tells us that a main concern of his
in "The Philosophy of Literary Form" is how "critical and imaginative works
are answers to questions posed by the situation in which they arose. . . . [how]
they are *strategic* answers, *stylized* answers" (*PLF,* 1). Despite a focus on the internal workings of literature, Burke still sees literary effect as fundamentally
rhetorical. The distinction here is one of emphasis. In "The Philosophy of
Literary Form," Burke simply wants to talk more about matters of literary form
than he had for some time. The discussion of Coleridge, for example, indicates
how Burke's literary and linguistic concerns serve the rhetorical even better
than before. Burke expends great effort to explain that the analysis of
Coleridge's personal problems (in particular, drug addiction and marital difficulties) is not simply an explanation of the welling up of private emotions into

a public symbol; rather, they help us understand the internal structure of the work, a "road in" to how "The Rime of the Ancient Mariner" is Coleridge's strategic and stylized response to a situation. "If we try to discover what the poem is doing for the poet," Burke advises, "we may discover a set of generalizations as to what poems do for everybody" (*PLF,* 73).

The rhetorical flavor of Burke's psychology is evident too in the first article of the appendix (section 4), a review of the published lectures of George Herbert Mead (*PLF,* 379–82). It was hardly accidental that Burke placed this at the beginning of the appendix. Mead's philosophy of the act, Burke tells us, "substitutes for the notion of an Absolute Self the notion of mind as a social product, stressing the sociality of action and reflection, and viewing thought as the internalization of objective relationships" (*PLF,* 379–80). This is about as clear a statement of Burke's perspective as can be found. Burke and Mead certainly differ in several regards, as Burke points out in the review, but Mead at least establishes a sort of rhetorically flavored psychology sympathetic to Burke's perspective. The presence of rhetorical elements in Burke's psychology is especially notable in his discussion of Freud, and Burke's admiration of Freud's earlier work is particularly relevant. More than just a matter of methodological coherence and elucidation, the favoring of Freud's proportional strategies over essentializing strategies represents a great rhetorical turn for Burke. It could be argued that it is, in principle, a preference for Cicero over Plato.[16] The rejection of essentialism in literary criticism, when combined with Burke's focus on exhortation and strategy, can be viewed as an attempt to focus on the problem of contingent knowledge and its place in rhetorical effect. This explains why prayer and chart play such an important role in the critical methods of *Literary Form.* Burke rejects the dialectical and deductive methods central to the epistemology of essentializing strategies; proportional strategies, being fundamentally hortatory and rhetorical, demand methods that can effectively analyze these dimensions of symbolic acts. Whether or not one agrees with Burke's psychological preferences, his emphasis on association and prayer and chart indicate a marked advance over the relatively primitive psychology of *Counter-Statement.*

Burke's developing psychology is not the only way in which his return to literary criticism echoes, albeit in a more complex way, his work in *Counter-Statement.* A variety of essays, including "Literature as Equipment for Living," "War, Response, and Contradiction," "The Nature of Art under Capitalism," "Semantic and Poetic Meaning," and several of the reviews in the appendix do for *Literary Form* what "Program" and "Applications of the Terminology" do for *Counter-Statement.* They chart out how the theoretical analysis of poetic effect might apply to the criticism of social structures. Instead of developing a situationally based "antinomian consciousness" through exhorting what effects the writer should generate, as he does in *Counter-Statement,* he now examines how literary criticism shades into "sociological criticism." This marks a further shift from the study of literature as a specialized field of poetic effect to the study of literature as the criticism of strategies of social action.

"The Rhetoric of Hitler's 'Battle,'" perhaps Burke's most popular essay, is an especially good example of how *Literary Form* marks Burke's return to the analysis of literature. In an incidental comment in a review of *Counter-Statement*, Malcolm Cowley remarks that Burke "has provided us with many brilliant examples of the [literary] critic's art; and yet the most brilliant of all the examples is possibly his essay on *Mein Kampf*."[17] On reading this review, Burke lamented that Cowley was "tragically wrong about the Hitler piece," suggesting that his "pieces on *Julius Caesar, Othello,* and *Faust* are all better" (Jay, 319).[18] This raises an important question. How can Cowley and so many others, from Burke's point of view, be so off the mark? It could be that they disagree because they are actually talking about different things. Burke, thinking of his criticism overall, looks to how well his critical method elucidates literary aesthetics; this is indicated when he says, "For, when one is equal to it, the method does better by a better book" (Jay, 319). The more artful the literature, the more the method explains—and the more the method is elucidated. This is one reason, for instance, that Burke spends so much time in "The Philosophy of Literary Form" and other essays discussing "The Rime of the Ancient Mariner" and other works by Coleridge. Coleridge's writings nicely illustrate how Burke's method works. Cowley, curiously truer to Burke's overall concerns in *Literary Form,* is speaking of how well Burke's criticism elucidates the social rhetoric of *Mein Kampf.* Looking at this difference of opinion in another way, Burke and Cowley are talking about different kinds of social influence. The sledgehammer rhetoric of Hitler, as important and influential as this kind is, simply is not as complex and pervasive as the kind of social influence Burke observes in literature.

Literary Form marks a significant shift in Burke's approach to literature that has largely remained unnoticed. In the period between *Permanence* and *Attitudes,* Burke became convinced that the focus of the study of literature and other symbolic creations should not be on pure literary aesthetics or entreaty, but on how literature functions as "symbolic action." Burke also came to realize that much of what he had been writing about in two decades of criticism could be crystallized in that idea. In short, Burke began to broaden what he meant by "criticism"—in particular, he developed critical techniques better adapted to nonliterary forms. Unfortunately, "symbolic action" remained ill-defined; hence, by the late 1930s and early 1940s Burke returned to literature—what he knew best—to begin addressing this new critical problem. In the foreword to the first edition of *Literary Form,* Burke says that his "interest is in speculation on the nature of linguistic, or symbolic, or literary action—and in a search for more precise ways of locating or defining such action" (*PLF,* xvii). Hoping to avoid the "excesses" of "environment-alist" and "structure-alist" literary schools, Burke focuses on the general problem of internal structure and its relation to what has usually been considered extraliterary matters. His criticism of particular literary works, he says, functions "as illustrative material rather than as central theme" (*PLF,* xvii). Analyses of internal structure and act-scene relationships, though generally implicit (and at times explicit) in Burke's first three books of criticism, are now the explicit emphases in his work.

Although Burke might have set out to make his point with a book-length monograph, as he did in *Permanence* and *Attitudes,* his publication of a collection of more or less self-contained essays makes sense. In the late 1920s and early 1930s, when charting a new field that combined aesthetics and politics, Burke chose to make his first major statement by collecting essays into one volume of criticism. Now, intent upon finding out "what goes with what in a book," a collection of individual critical studies seems appropriate. Moreover, Burke's approach to the problem addressed in *Literary Form* lends itself to separate essays. "The method was somewhat phenomenological in aim," Burke says, "seeking to get at the psychological depth of a work through the sheer comparison of its surfaces. The method was illustrated by reference to various works" (*CS,* 217). Burke may also have soured to the idea of writing another singular, book-length treatment. *Counter-Statement,* a collection, was better received than *Permanence* and *Attitudes.* In addition, Burke was finally learning that book-length monographs committed him to writing within an idiom that compromised the chances that his readers would appreciate his corruption of traditional intellectual categories. In a letter to Cowley dated 22 October 1937 Burke indicates his dissatisfaction with the very real tension between his desire to cut across the bias and the pragmatic necessity for articulating his thoughts along the bias: "The main interest in my stuff seems to come from sociologists—which is beginning to lead me to think that what I once called 'metabiology' is pure and simple sociology-without-portfolio. Tactical problem: How [to] proceed with one's attempt to scramble the categories of specialization, when only by specialization can one assemble the kind of curriculum vitae necessary for a job?" (Jay, 221). Burke understood that the rhetorical strategy of giving *Permanence* a sociological cast, despite its strengths, was a weakness. The sociological turn promoted neglect by literary critics and co-optation by sociologists.

Despite the differences between *Literary Form* and Burke's earlier writings, one important element remains constant: he follows the basic strategy of his "Critic's Credo"—an apology, a rhetoric, and a program. As Burke evolves intellectually, his credo becomes more obscure, though vital nonetheless. In *Counter-Statement* the apology clears the ground by arguing against common aesthetic theories (pure aesthetics, utilitarian theories of art, and virtue as a gauge of art). In *Permanence* he attacks conceptions of language, predominantly those that seek a neutral vocabulary devoid of connotation and emotion. In *Counter-Statement,* Burke's rhetoric describes the means for realizing critical capacities (rhetorical form, eloquence, and the critical "machine" of "Lexicon Rhetoricae").[19] In *Permanence* the rhetoric occurs in Burke's discussions of "piety" and "perspective by incongruity."[20] In all his books the program is more diffuse than the apology and the rhetoric, though there are usually key touchstones. In *Counter-Statement,* Burke suggests a modification of political and social "emphases." In *Permanence* he calls for a move away from the informational and toward the "ethical" components of symbolic appeal. In Burke's view, "ethics" refers to the general governance of action, covering all that affects how we decide to take a course of action—chiefly attitudes, values, and procedure. With *Attitudes* the credo is modified. The apology is an encomium on the aesthetics of William James, Whitman, and Emerson, three writers who were not merely "adepts" at pure literature. The rhetoric appears in his discussion of poetic categories and acceptance frames and in his survey of the curve of history. The program appears in his "Analysis of Symbolic Structure," especially in the brilliant "Dictionary of Pivotal Terms."

In *Literary Form* the credo is even less distinct. This is key to understanding Burke's achievement in the book. After a decade and a half of grappling with the relations between literary analysis and the relationship between literature and society, Burke finally integrated the two. It is ironic, then, that most readers of *Literary Form* focus almost entirely on "The Philosophy of Literary Form" and read it merely as literary analysis. In *Literary Form* the apology takes two forms. On the one hand, there are parts that clearly discredit certain views. In "Semantic and Poetic Meaning," for instance, Burke argues against the idea of a neutral vocabulary (the "semantic ideal"), thereby offering a "rhetorical defense of rhetoric" (*PLF,* 138). In "The Virtues and Limitations of Debunking," Burke argues that debunkers fall prey to what he elsewhere calls "the bureaucratization of the imaginative." Burke discredits what he calls "a purely *quantitative* mode of propaganda" (*PLF,* 175). In "Freud—and the Analysis of Poetry," Burke "discredits" psychoanalytic criticism by marking its limits. On the other hand, Burke makes an apology by crediting a certain view of literary analysis. This is seen most clearly in "The Philosophy of Literary Form" but is apparent in other essays (for instance, in the celebration of the "poetic ideal" in "Semantic and Poetic Meaning"). The rhetoric, like the apology, is more spread out than in Burke's earlier books. Many writers have recognized in "The Philosophy of Literary Form" Burke's analysis of the processes that make a work of art effective. Some have noticed Burke's attention to distinctly psychological or even psychoanalytic concepts, for instance in "Freud—and the Analysis of Poetry," "The Rhetoric of Hitler's 'Battle,'" "Antony in Behalf of the Play," and other shorter articles and appendixes.

A consideration of the program in *Literary Form* shows how complex Burke's achievement is. Some of the articles have a distinctly programlike cast. "The Calling of the Tune," with Burke's discussion of art's integration with the "national life" and the relationship between a "structure of authority" and "modes of resistance," somewhat echoes "Program" in *Counter-Statement*. In "War, Response, and Contradiction" and "The Nature of Art under Capitalism," Burke discusses the relationship between art and society, and how that relationship affects the "ethical" life. Burke's call for a countermorality is not much different than the positions he takes in the other programs (an antinomian consciousness, a communist corrective, an attitude *toward* history). Calls such as these motivate some of the observations in Burke's reviews within the last quarter of *Literary Form*. But there is a more important question: How do the programlike concerns manifest themselves in the essays that are predominantly part of the credo's rhetoric, especially "The Philosophy of Literary Form"? The key here is his "theory" of "clusters" and "equations." Burke develops a kind of associationalism based on synecdoche. In the discussion of "statistical analysis" Burke points out that an author's motives are apparent in the structure of the work itself (*PLF,* 18–25)—that is, internal analysis of a work is coextensive with analysis of the author's situation and motivation. However, this approach to an author's motivation is *not* the sort of psychoanalytic dimension many readers of Burke take it to be. Burke forsakes traditional psychoanalytic concerns and instead focuses on how the text functions for the reader. This is seen in Burke's comments on Coleridge: "I am *not* saying that we need know of Coleridge's marital troubles and sufferings from drug addiction in order to appreciate 'The Ancient Mariner.' . . . I am saying that, in trying to understand the psychology of the poetic act, we may introduce such knowledge, where it is available, to give us material necessary for discussing the full nature of this act. Many of the things that a poet's work does for *him* are not things that the same work does for *us*. . . . If we try to discover what the poem is doing for the poet, we may discover a set of generalizations as to what poems do for everybody" (*PLF,* 73). Burke later points out that the main goal of the structural analysis of literature is pragmatic. "A poem's structure," he says, "is to be described most accurately by thinking always of the poem's function"—by understanding that a "poem is designed to 'do something' for the poet and his readers" (*PLF,* 89). Burke calls this kind of analysis "'sociological,' in that it can usefully employ coördinates bearing upon social acts in general" (*PLF,* 102).

In "Ritual Drama as Hub" the sociological and political elements of the literary analysis of "The Philosophy of Literary Form" become apparent. In discussing the relation between drama and dialectic, Burke points out that an author's encompassing of a situation in a poem is directly related to "a social structure of meanings by which the individual forms himself"—a "collective revelation" (*PLF,* 108). "Charts of meaning" in a work, Burke says, "are relative *approximations* to the truth." And this amounts to a "perspective for the analysis of history" (*PLF,* 109). Burke continues by discussing the American Constitution, the Crown, mercantilist paternalism, private and class structure, the consequences of a social scientific point of view, the "charting of life," Bentham as debunker, Marx's debunking of bourgeois motives, and other such attempts of authors suggesting "proper emphases."

These aspects of "The Philosophy of Literary Form" are too frequently ignored by commentators on Burke, who instead favor merely the technical aspects of Burke's literary "theory." These social and political concerns—and their more developed statements throughout the entire text of *Literary Form*—are as much a part of "literary analysis" as Burke's more traditional statements about method are. Burke points out that he seeks to make internal analysis socially relevant. To understand *The Philosophy of Literary Form* and its title essay as Burke intended, we must fully enfranchise his interest in the relations between literature and society.

PART III

The Tactics of Motivation

In the 1940s Kenneth Burke must have been a man of remarkable hopefulness. For more than twenty years he had pleaded for a move "towards a better life," hoping to steer people away from what he believed were pathological cultural trends and toward ways of thinking that would guide them to a more humane and ethical life. At the least, he hoped to forestall the increasingly severe damage resulting from economic, political, social, and intellectual differences. In *Counter-Statement* he uses aesthetic criticism as an occasion to argue that a better life will result from a new understanding of the relationship between art and politics, but only if people adopt new political ideals. In *Permanence and Change* he explores the nature of interpretation, communication, and cooperation, suggesting that a more ethical life will result if we adopt "cooperative correctives" to our unbalanced social structure.[1] In *Attitudes toward History,* Burke turns his attention to the relations between culture in general and political organizations in particular. He argues that because cooperation is always affected by the means chosen to enact goals, we should understand the complex impact of interpretation and communication on our cooperative efforts. Yet Burke was harshly criticized from many corners, and to him it seemed that no one used his ideas. As the Great Depression deepened, he felt a greater sense of urgency about the problems faced and the need for new ways to address them. When the worst of the Depression was over, Burke's commitment remained unabated, if not heightened, for he felt that people had merely muddled through that great crisis. Making matters worse still, in the late 1930s and early 1940s, as fascism spread through Europe and war commenced and widened, Burke saw the very cultural formations he for so long warned against become increasingly potent. In 1942 Burke wrote Cowley of his discouragement about the current state of affairs. "I am gloomy not only about our own country, but about the whole damned human race," he lamented (Jay, 249). These new crises not only made Burke's mission all the more urgent, but they began to focus his attention on human motivation as the area within which change could be made: "Meanwhile, all I know is, so far or so long as I am able, to go on trying to increase our awareness (my own and others') of the ways in which motives move us and deceive us, and what kind of knowledge the nature of motives demands of us, if we are not to goad one another endlessly to the cult of powers that can bring no genuine humaneness to the world" (Jay, 249).

In addition to being a man of tremendous hope, Burke must also have been a man of tremendous will; despite harsh criticism against him and the little influence his writing had, in the 1940s he was fully immersed in an enormous decade-long attempt to treat more systematically the questions that had occupied him for his entire scholarly life. He called this his *Motivorum* project. Originally begun as "On Human Relations," an extension of *Permanence* and *Attitudes,* it evolved into a whole new venture intended to comprise three volumes; however, Burke published only two: *A Grammar of Motives* (1945) and *A Rhetoric of Motives* (1950).[2] Given the reception of his previous books, it is no wonder that, when he was finishing up the *Grammar* in 1945, Burke was not optimistic about how it would be received or what impact he would have: "we can look forward to the usual reception: i.e., my noble colleagues will pilfer bits here and there, and scrupulously give credit to dead Frenchmen or half-dead Harvard professors. A tiny pooplet of a succès d'estime, carefully bitched by dumps like the *Nation* and the Fartisan, reviewed in the *New Republic* by somebody who talks about some other book. . . . For I got infloonce [*sic*]" (Jay, 266).[3] Indeed, almost thirty years after the publication of the *Grammar,* in a series of lectures at Clark University, Burke commented on the disappointing reception of the *Grammar:* "In going over reviews that appeared when the *Grammar* was first published, I was struck by the fact that no reviewer, to my knowledge, discussed the section on 'The Dialectic of Constitutions.' Yet several reviewers raised objections that would have been irrelevant had this portion of the book been systematically considered."[4] As he was working on the *Motivorum* books, Burke was not entirely pessimistic. Writing to Cowley in 1940, at the start of the *Motivorum* project, he said, "I think that this might prove to be as fertile an essay for me personally as my 'Psychology and Form' one was" (Jay, 233). Two years later he told Cowley that "it would be silly to think" that books could solve the world's problems, but he described his *Motivorum* project as "one of the steps in the right direction" (Jay, 249). Well into *A Rhetoric of Motives,* still not expecting to have much impact, he nonetheless hoped that he might. "I guess what I am most interested in doing," he told Cowley in 1947, "is to write a trilogy into which one could immerse himself, in case there should ever be a time again in which people wanted to immerse themselves in protracted contemplation generally and in the protracted contemplation of the Logos particularly" (Jay, 277).

For readers not familiar with the *Motivorum* project, a brief description will help clarify things. The heart of the *Motivorum* project is the analytical method Burke called "dramatism," five terms (act, scene, agent, agency, purpose) drawn from drama and used to analyze the motivational assumptions inherent in all sorts of arguments, political doctrines, social theories, and even philosophic schools. The goal of dramatism—indeed of the *Motivorum* project generally—is to study human relations by examining the relationships among groups of concepts that are essential to various ways of accounting for human motivation. For instance, Darwin's theory of evolution purports to explain the natural world in terms of the scene out of which it arises. The dramatistic critic would analyze the way "scene" defines or is the ground for act, agent, agency, and purpose in Darwin's thinking. In the end, dramatistic analyses of Darwin's theories would open up a complex set of conceptual interrelations in his thinking, thereby helping clarify the intricate way in which Darwin's theory of natural evolution amounts to a theory of human motivation. As with most of Burke's theorizing, the *Motivorum* project makes the most out of "act," for Burke believed that "action" is a uniquely human enterprise that defines what it means to be human. In the Clark University lectures Burke commented, "If I were to rewrite the [*Grammar*] . . . I would now present it as a 'Cycle of Terms Implicit in the idea of an "Act,"' based upon my anti-Behaviorist equation, 'Things move, persons act.'"[5] Without doubt, Burke is most widely known for dramatism, and hardly an analysis or application of his work fails to use it implicitly, if not explicitly.

In a cruel irony, dramatism is also Burke's nemesis, for many readers of Burke interpret dramatism apart from his earlier work, thereby finding in dramatism a superficial kind of semantics that misses entirely the social and political purposes that dramatism was intended to serve; worse yet, in so doing, they imbue dramatism with a systematicity so rigid that it actually undermines dramatism's largely heuristic and suggestive nature. To understand what Burke was trying to get at with the *Motivorum* project—to understand what the motives project was an entreaty for and what Burke hoped to achieve with dramatism—an examination of the *Grammar* and the *Rhetoric* is necessary, as is a brief description of the milieu to which Burke responded.

In 1943 the *Partisan Review* published a series of articles appearing under the title "The New Failure of Nerve," the first three of which ("Part I") were written by Sidney Hook, John Dewey, and the logical empiricist Ernest Nagel.[6] These luminaries of American intellectual life argue that modern civilization is in a state of crisis because of a loss of faith in science and a widespread "flight from responsibility" into "obscurantism" and mysticism. The articles range over a variety of topics, including social theory, truth, authority, the nature of scientific method, theology, Christianity, faith, materialism, political economy, and values. Hook, Dewey, and Nagel express their wish to expunge the world of what they take to be irrational hopes, beliefs, and faiths; at the same time, to quote Dewey, they want people to "employ courageously, patiently, persistently and with wholehearted devotion all the *natural* resources that are now potentially at our command" (39). Of course, by "natural resources," Dewey meant the methods of science and natural philosophy. One overall thrust of "The New Failure of Nerve: Part I" is that philosophic naturalism and scientific method are the only sound bases for knowledge—and that all other purported grounds for knowledge (especially religion) are not just false, but lead to ways of thinking that are positively harmful. According to Hook, assaults against scientific method open "gateways to intellectual and moral irresponsibility" (5) ultimately capable of "infecting" us with an "intellectual hysteria" (8). The authors reject categorically any distinction between different kinds of truth, going so far as to repudiate all limits on the applicability of deductive reasoning to human problems. In fact, Hook, Dewey, and Nagel hold that the vocabulary of science, which they take to be systematic and unprejudiced, is superior to the murky languages of literature and religion. "Those who disparage the application of scientific methods to the evaluation of human goods," declares Nagel, are "well on the road to identifying the sheer vividness and the emotional overtones of ideas with their validity" (57). As an alternative, the three philosophers promote scientific method as the proper recourse for solving social problems. "The chief causes of our maladjustments," Hook states, "are to be found precisely in these areas of social life *in which the rationale of scientific method has not been employed*" (9). The search for common ground to solve problems—and, indeed, for democracy itself—they say, is not to be based on "the Hebraic-Christian tradition" or on any transcendental faith, but on reason as defined by philosophical naturalism and manifested in scientific method.

Although Burke is never mentioned in these articles and there is no evidence that the authors had him in mind, they in fact attacked principles central to Burke's theories of the previous twenty years. On the one hand, they were supporting the idea of a "neutral vocabulary." Readers of Burke's earlier works will remember that he argued against the idea of a neutral vocabulary in his discussion of Bentham in *Permanence and Change,* in "The Dictionary of Pivotal Terms" in *Attitudes toward History,* and in "Semantic and Poetic Meaning" in *The Philosophy of Literary Form*. Burke held that the search for a neutral vocabulary was destined to fail because there are different kinds of meaning appropriate to different realms of human experience: "semantic meaning," the language of science, is perfectly appropriate for the study of natural phenomena; "poetic meaning" is appropriate for the study of human action and values. Moreover, he demonstrated that careful attempts to create neutral vocabularies had been dismal failures. Hook, Dewey, and Nagel also promote what Burke would take to be "inhuman" means for the solution of human problems—inhuman because these means, in Burke's view, are the result of the transgression of scientific norms into realms of human experience not amenable to the methods of science. Without a doubt, Burke could easily have been the spark of these attacks and condemnations.

It would be interesting to know Burke's thoughts as he read "The New Failure of Nerve: Part I." Not only did it issue forth from the *Partisan Review*—

the journal Burke most despised—the point man of the assault was his old enemy, Sidney Hook. Burke was probably disheartened to see these luminaries of American intellectual life continue to promote ideas that he had long labored to counter. Worse yet, these apocalyptic essays, coming deep into World War II and certainly taken by many to be the most advanced statements on the matter, presaged the entrenchment of the very ways of thinking that Burke had so assiduously labored against. It would also be interesting to know how Burke felt when the editors of a short-lived journal titled *The Chimera* asked him to join with literary critic Philip Wheelwright, the Catholic philosopher Jacques Maritain, and the poet W. H. Auden in writing responses to the essays by Hook, Dewey, and Nagel. Burke's response, "The Tactics of Motivation" (also published in 1943), turned out to be a remarkably clear and succinct summary of ideas basic to the *Motivorum* project generally and to dramatism in particular.[7] In fact, some portions of "Tactics" appear in the *Grammar* verbatim. (Since "Tactics" was written before Burke finished the *Grammar,* much of what he says in the *Rhetoric* is missing.) If the essay is any indication of his emotional reaction to "The New Failure of Nerve: Part I," Burke was concerned and level-headed. His tone in "Tactics" is moderate, not at all apocalyptic and polemical, as are the *Partisan Review* essays.

If Burke was a man of hope, just what did he hope for? What was this project on motives about? Burke provides several descriptions of his goals. In the *Grammar* he says, "We sought to formulate the basic stratagems which people employ, in endless variations, and consciously or unconsciously, for the outwitting or cajoling of one another" (*GM,* xvii). That sounds similar to what he was doing in "The Dictionary of Pivotal Terms," although in that part of *Attitudes* he focused on stratagems fundamental to organization and bureaucracy. There is another difference too. In the *Motivorum* books Burke is more analytically systematic than he was before, seeking a method that is more defined and rationalized than the almost frenetic "Dictionary" but still flexible enough to account for the richness of human problems: "Our work must be synoptic . . . in the sense that it offers a system of placement, and should enable us, by the systematic manipulation of the terms, to 'generate,' or 'anticipate' the various classes of motivational theory. And a treatment in these terms, we hope to show, reduces the subject synoptically while still permitting us to appreciate its scope and complexity" (*GM,* xxii–xxiii). Burke makes a clear distinction between his method and that of Hook, Dewey, and Nagel. He looks to the resources of language as a way into understanding human motivation, whereas his opponents think that language fogs the lens of scientific method (again, they search for a neutral vocabulary). His method is superior, Burke says, because "the discussion of human motives cannot with accuracy be reduced to the level of the physical or sheerly biological" ("Tactics," 30).

Another difference between Burke's perspective and that of Hook, Dewey, and Nagel concerns the purpose of analysis. According to Burke, the philosophers—good foundationalists that they are—seek to "disprove" competing philosophies. (In Burke's mind, a philosophy has much in common with a theory of motivation because an explanation of the grounds for action is implicit in any philosophy.) Philosophical naturalism is superior to all other methods, they say, because it is free of emotion and bias. The cold rationality of deduction, when used properly, will not be led astray. Yet according to Burke, no method can be neutral. Hence, the purpose of method ought not be to "disprove" competing "philosophies," but to "anticipate" possible motivational accounts in any situation ("Tactics," 41). In the *Grammar*, Burke argues that this kind of method should be combined with an "attitude": "The attitude itself would be grounded in the systematic development of the method. The method would involve the explicit study of language as the 'critical moment' at which human motives take form, since a linguistic factor at every point in human experience complicates and to some extent transcends the purely biological aspects of motivation. The attitude would be mildly that of 'hypochondriasis,' a kind of 'cultural valetudinarianism,' which recognizes that the school of ideas is divisible into both a gymnastic of ideas and a clinic of ideas, and which would assist health by aiming always at the first without forgetting the claims of the second" (*GM*, 318). This attitude is at heart a skepticism training the critical eye on certain features of statements about motives. But it is neither a form of relativism nor a form of eclecticism. Burke posits that his method "should enable one to 'anticipate' the specific linguistic choices and manoeuvres" of people who, by nature, construct motivational schemes around the concepts of act, scene, agent, agency, and purpose. Dramatism "would thus serve a 'synoptic' end, rather than a purely 'eclectic' one" ("Tactics," 43). Some critics of Burke have charged that dramatistic analysis is just wordplay, fancy linguistic tricks that have little to do with reality. In defense of such a charge, Burke claims that dramatism is not locked into a world of language. It uses language as a window onto human problems: "The whole project aims to round out an analysis of language [that] . . . seeks for observations that, while central to the study of any given expression in its internality, also have reference to human quandaries and human foibles generally" (*CS*, 218–19). Thus, Burke did not believe that dramatism is merely a superficial form of semantics. Moreover, he did not believe that the *Motivorum* project is about the personal psychology of an individual, although personal factors do figure in. Rather, it is about motivation as a public phenomenon. In "Tactics," Burke is concerned about how "theories" of motivation end up affecting policies and actions; in other words, he is interested in the relationship between forms of reasoning and the public statements we make about why we act as we do or think we ought to act as we should.

(Thus, it comes as no surprise that toward the end of the *Grammar,* Burke focuses on dialectic in general and "the dialectic of Constitutions" in particular.) In this way he is in line with Hook, Dewey, and Nagel. However, his attitude toward analysis is quite contrary to what the philosophers were up to. There is one point, however, on which both Burke and the *Partisan Review* essayists agree: that speculations about the grounds for knowledge and methods of analysis are all the more urgent because of the war. As he begins the second part of "Tactics," Burke asks, "Just what, indeed, would be the philosophy . . . most appropriate to a world in which the 'global' war was followed by some kind of global peace, or at least global pacification?" ("Tactics," 37).

The *Motivorum* project is Burke's answer to this question. The most appropriate "philosophy"—the one he develops in the *Grammar* and the *Rhetoric*—begins with speculations about human motivation in order to find alternatives to hand-to-hand combat, rifle fire, and aerial bombardment. As such, Burke's "philosophy" is an attempt to find better ways to establish common ground between people with differing interests and views of the world. Given his focus on sets of related concepts and terms, and his view toward the verbal stratagems we use to cajole and outwit each other (including "social strategies and diplomatic devices"), it is no wonder that at heart the *Motivorum* project is an inquiry into the grounds of disagreement and agreement. Yet it is not a mere intellectual exercise. Readers of Burke's earlier works will remember that, as he argued so well in *Literary Form,* "literature"—fiction, prose, criticism—is "equipment for living." "The Rhetoric of Hitler's 'Battle,'" for instance, was intended to equip us should we encounter another evil "medicine man." Likewise, dramatism is intended to help prevent disagreement and difference from escalating into violence. In a haunting epigraph to the *Grammar,* a phrase that captures the essence of the entire *Motivorum* project, Burke dedicates the book to *ad bellum purificandum* (toward the purification of war). Near the end of the *Grammar* he explains the overall thrust of his *Motivorum* project:

> All told, in this project directed "towards the purification of war," the *Grammar* should assist to this end through encouraging tolerance by speculation. For it deals with a level of motivation which even wholly rival doctrines of motives must share in common; hence it may be addressed to a speculative portion of the mind which men of many different situations may have in common. The *Rhetoric,* which would study the "competitive use of the coöperative," would be designed to help us take delight in the Human Barnyard, with its addiction to the Scramble, an area that would cause us great unhappiness could we not transcend it by appreciation, classifying and tracing back to their beginnings in Edenic simplicity those linguistic modes of suasion that often seem little better than malice and the lie. And the Symbolic, studying the implicit equations which have so much to do with the shaping of our acts, should enable

us to see our own lives as a kind of rough first draft that lends itself at least somewhat to revision, as we may hope at least to temper the extreme rawness of our
ambitions, once we become aware of the ways in which we are the victims of
our own and one another's magic. (*GM*, 442)

Pentad

purpose
(why)

scene
(where)

Act
(what)

agent
(who)

agency
(how)

6

A Grammar of Motives
Ad Bellum Purificandum through "Dialectic"

<hr>

If Burke has one outstanding intellectual achievement, it is "dramatism." Its prominence is no doubt why it is the subject of the only reference piece Burke wrote about his own work, an entry for the *International Encyclopedia of the Social Sciences*.[1] Dramatism has caught the eye of rhetorical theorists, literary critics, philosophers, sociologists, political scientists, anthropologists, psychologists, historians, and others because it is a relatively simple method that brings to the foreground assumptions about human motivation that may not be apparent in a wide range of texts, many of which may not be thought relevant in the first place. Burke develops dramatism in a variety of places, including *A Rhetoric of Motives, Language as Symbolic Action, Dramatism and Development,* and several uncollected essays. But with the major statement of it occurring in *A Grammar of Motives* (1945), dramatism and the *Grammar* have become inextricably bound, making the *Grammar* Burke's best-known book.

The *Grammar* so dominates Burke's corpus that for many readers it is the first and only Burke work they read. That makes him somewhat daunting for the initiate, since the *Grammar* is complex and its staggering array of concepts, theories, and figures from nearly all the liberal arts and sciences can obscure Burke's intentions. More important, reading the *Grammar* without the benefit of his earlier work leads to distortions that seriously compromise what Burke was trying to get at with dramatism. One distortion is a semantic bias, a separation of dramatism's linguistic methods from the social and political critique. Reading the *Grammar* in the context of the earlier work makes it readily apparent that dramatism is an extension of his previous theories, which themselves are analyses of different aspects of social and political problems. Yet in reading the *Grammar* alone, many readers seem to miss or ignore the social and political aspects of Burke's thinking. A second distortion is a kind of rigid systematicity that readers impose on dramatism, which turns it into a simplistic formulaism. This examination of *A Grammar of Motives* will focus on explicating Burke's thinking in relation to his earlier work, for the most part following the text chronologically.

At heart terminological, dramatism uses the concepts "act," "scene," "agent," "agency," and "purpose" as points of reference for inquiring into the extent to which an idea, message, theory, doctrine—indeed any product of the intellect—touches on motivation (Burke calls these five concepts the "pentad").

In particular, the dramatistic critic employs the concepts in examining how "clusters" of key terms work together. According to Burke, "dramatism is a method of analysis and a corresponding critique of terminology designed to show that the most direct route to the study of human relations and human motives is *via* a methodological inquiry into cycles or clusters of terms and their functions."[2]

A good example of how dramatism involves clusters of terms occurs in "The Tactics of Motivation," when Burke discusses Sidney Hook's association of two ideas in the phrase "faith in intelligence." Readers of "The New Failure of Nerve: Part I" will notice that this association is basic not only to Hook's argument, but to Dewey's and Nagel's as well.[3] In applying the pentad to the idea of faith in intelligence, Burke suggests that philosophical naturalism and scientific method, which may be effective at, say, determining the parts of a literary work, cannot supply the "synthesis" that ideas such as "'imagination,' 'vision,' 'revelation,' etc." provide. And works of art demand it. Without such a synthesis, naturalism and science are limited in what they can reveal about human choice and conduct. Burke also uses dramatistic methods to show that the idea of faith in intelligence has several interpretations, none of which takes precedence over the others. His reasoning is that for Hook, "faith in intelligence" is much the same as "faith in knowledge." Coordinating faith and knowledge, according to Burke, amounts to an alignment of the concepts "act and scene," for faith is a "practical or imaginative act" and knowledge is "of the scenic conditions in which that act could be enacted." As such, Hook's "cluster" of faith and intelligence "obliterates the [traditional] distinction between 'faith' and 'knowledge.'" Yet this is only one possible conclusion generated by dramatistic analysis. By reference to another pair of concepts, the "expression, 'faith in knowledge,' could similarly be classed as an *attitude of the agent* directed towards *agency;* for 'intelligence,' like 'scientific method,' can be interpreted as a *means* rather than a *substance*" ("Tactics," 26). There is no way, Burke says, by which either of these conclusions could be demonstrated scientifically. We can accept one or the other (or both!), but that is a matter of faith, not scientific proof. Readers familiar with "The Philosophy of Literary Form" will notice that in the *Grammar,* Burke develops the idea of association that figures so prominently in that earlier essay. In addition, echoing the distinction between "semantic meaning" and "poetic meaning" he makes in "Semantic and Poetic Meaning," Burke contends that the dramatistic terms draw us into the realm of human action, not inanimate motion (as do the methods of science).[4] Therefore, in Burke's view, dramatism promotes inquiry about human choice and morality in ways that the logico-deductive methods of science and naturalistic philosophy cannot. Ultimately, in the case of Hook's faith in intelligence, dramatistic analysis demonstrates the limited usefulness of faith in intelligence as a criterion for analyzing motives.

Although Burke describes dramatism as "methodical" and "systematic," it is really more heuristic than definitive. Dramatism does not seek positive knowledge in the scientific sense; rather it is intended as a guide to understanding accounts of human motivation. Burke describes this through an analogy: "In an exhibit of photographic murals . . . there was an aerial photograph of two launches, proceeding side by side on a tranquil sea. Their wakes crossed and recrossed each other in almost an infinity of lines. Yet despite the intricateness of this tracery, the picture gave an impression of great simplicity, because one could quickly perceive the generating principle of its design. Such, ideally, is the case with our pentad of terms, used as generating principle. It should provide a kind of simplicity that can be developed into considerable complexity, and yet can be discovered beneath its elaborations" (*GM,* xvi). Thus, dramatism is relatively simple, but not simplistic. In a way, it is akin to what Burke was trying to do in "The Dictionary of Pivotal Terms" in *Attitudes.* There, Burke creates a brief taxonomy of modern topoi or argumentative strategies used in the brokering for position in bureaucratic and political organizations. "Heads I Win, Tails You Lose," for instance, is a "device whereby, if things turn out one way, your system accounts for them—and if they turn out the opposite way, your system also accounts for them" (*ATH,* 260). Burke collects strategies such as this to build a set of tools for the analysis of entreaty within organizations. The "Dictionary" is not intended to be a complete system; rather, it is a set of commonplaces by which the analysis of organizational rhetoric may commence and proceed. Likewise for the dramatistic pentad, although the five concepts are more systematic and apply to far more than bureaucratic and political organizations.

Just what Burke intends dramatism to apply to is central to understanding its purpose. For one thing, the *Grammar* covers nearly all the liberal arts and sciences, and Burke even says that the pentad is universal in application. Yet readers quickly realize that philosophy garners much of Burke's attention in the *Grammar.* In fact, the middle section of the *Grammar*—nearly half the book— is a study of "the philosophic schools," broad categories of philosophical theory such as materialism, idealism, and realism. One point that Burke makes in this part of the *Grammar* is that each philosophical school grounds its explanatory system in the pentadic elements: materialism falls under scene; idealism, under agent; realism, under act; and pragmatism, under agency and purpose. Burke admits that he has trouble maintaining the consistency of his pigeonholing, yet he maintains that it is accurate and telling nonetheless. His emphasis on philosophy and use of the pentad as an organizing scheme makes sense biographically. As Burke notes in several places, the pentad grew out of his creation of a typology of philosophical theories for students at Bennington College. Yet that does not explain why philosophy plays such an important role in his account of human relations and why the pentad ultimately becomes the center of dramatism and his grammar of motives.

Burke believed that to move "towards a better life," one must be ready to question assumptions about human nature, especially when a system of thought purports to give a final answer to why we act as we do. If anything, philosophy on the whole is a collection of accounts of human action, each purporting to be correct and discounting competing explanations. You either accept, for example, the materialism of Hobbes *or* the idealism of Berkeley *or* the pragmatism of Dewey, or you do not. Even if you cobble together elements of different theories, you either accept the result or not. Whatever the case, with few exceptions, one system of thought excludes all others. Even among closely allied philosophical theories, exclusivity reigns. For example, atomistic and global epistemologies are incommensurate. In Burke's view, all philosophies are partial, each explaining some aspects of human relations but none ever accounting for everything. Moreover, the history of philosophy demonstrates that philosophers have trouble maintaining the consistency of their accounts; and when the inconsistencies become too significant, other philosophers posit new philosophies that obviate the inconsistencies, giving birth to new schools. These two features of philosophical thought suggest why Burke was drawn often to mystical and religious thought. They are systems that come closest to being "complete" explanations of human relations, in that they excel at explaining away inconsistency. In any event, Burke believed that each philosophy is a "casuistry," a strategic rationalization that serves the purposes of the proponent of that philosophical doctrine.[5] If we are to move toward a better life in a world that seeks sureties, Burke says, we must understand how philosophies are casuistries and just where that can lead us. In this sense, dramatism is a kind of skepticism that does not reject outright. It is a frame of acceptance based on skeptical heuristics. Instead of rejecting "opposing" positions, dramatism questions sureties by exploring philosophical possibilities: "'Dramatistically,' one would act rather to 'anticipate' the various philosophies, actual or possible, by analyzing the interrelationships that prevail among the five master terms and then noting how the exploitation of the possibilities contained in these interrelationships can lead to one or another of the philosophic strategies. . . . One can engage this part of the mind even in cases where he already has a fixed philosophy, provided only that he is capable of meditating upon the resources and embarrassments indigenous to the systematic use of language" ("Tactics," 41–42).

Some of Burke's critics have complained that dramatism is just verbal gymnastics that appear profound but turn out to be nothing more than wordplay (Nagel, for instance, accused him of mistaking the vividness and emotionality of language for the validity of ideas). Burke may at times give such an impression. After all, his interest in exploring "the purely internal relationships which the five terms bear to one another" leads to a lot of verbal manipulation and many cognitive leaps (*GM*, xvi). And in "Tactics," "anticipating" possible philosophies and "meditation upon the resources and embarrassments" of language might seem to invite exactly the kind of wordplay his critics deplore. Yet we should recognize that Burke's heuristics lead somewhere. For one thing, the *Grammar* leads to the conviction that a philosophical theory is never as coherent as its creator might imagine. A good example is Darwin's theory of evolution, as it appears in *The Origin of Species*. (Burke uses the term "philosophy" to include a wide range of theories, virtually any system of thought that bears upon human relations. The discussion of Darwin appears in *GM*, 152–58.) Burke points out that Darwin's theory of evolution is thoroughly materialistic (physical mechanisms—the "scene"—are the ground for explaining the nature and characteristics of all aspects of the world, including human actions). The point is that Darwin has trouble maintaining the materialist stress, his "scenic" logic. Burke offers several examples of how he falters: First, terms such as "adaptation," "competition," "struggle for life," "natural selection," and "survival of the fittest" violate the materialist philosophy by introducing a "personalizing of impersonal events" (*GM*, 153). Second, Darwin goes so far as to explain natural selection in terms of "purpose," such as when he says that flowers have colors *in order to* attract insects. Of course, purpose cannot be part of the mechanical world. Third, the organization of organisms into families assumes that there are generic characteristics that are largely responsible for an individual's character. In this way, Burke says, Darwin introduces "agent" into his scenic theory. Burke sums up his analysis of Darwin: "All told, what is our point? We are trying to specify the exact nature of a great biologist's Grammar, when the nature of the experimental sciences in general calls for a *scenic* stress, yet the study of lineal descent almost inevitably shifts the stress to the motivational functions covered by our term *agent*. Or we might put it this way: In reducing all phenomena to terms of motion, biology is as unambiguously scenic as physics. But as soon as it encounters the subject of *self*-movement, it makes claims upon the areas covered by our term *agent*" (*GM*, 157). Of course, Darwin's situation does not prove much about philosophy in general. But Burke applies dramatism to dozens of philosophical doctrines, making a strong case that all systems of thought that bear on human motives fail to maintain their logic because precluded pentadic elements appear nevertheless, albeit often in disguise. In the end, we arrive at the conviction that philosophy usually starts out straightforwardly enough but that eventually philosophers have to muscle things into order to maintain coherence.

Burke's heuristic *Grammar* also leads to the conviction that human experience and relations are so complex that life does not easily fit into the mold of a philosophy. Philosophers have to strain to make their explanatory systems work. As early as *Permanence,* Burke argues that "motives are shorthand terms for situations" (*PC,* 29 ff.). The term "shorthand" is important, for if motives cannot fully encompass a situation, how could something as rarefied as a theory? In the *Grammar* he still maintains that accounts of motivation arise out of situations, but the emphasis here is on how systems of thought and language have a logic which always at some point becomes a force of its own that requires rationalizations to account for recalcitrant situations, experiences, and ideas. Burke makes this clear in his survey of the philosophical schools and in a fascinating discussion of the nature and characteristics of definition. Definitions regarding human experience, he shows us, are always partial. Burke is quick to note too that agreement and disagreement sometimes arise out of differences in the logics of competing motivational accounts. In fact, one key role of dramatism is to provide a means for mapping the logic of one account upon that of another in order to reveal points of agreement and disagreement. For instance, one account (based on "scene-act") and another (based on "act-scene") may not be as different from each other as the proponent of each believes them to be; at the least, dramatism locates a commonality that can serve as the basis for addressing differences. In the end, dramatism is heuristic because Burke provides new ways to talk about the ways we talk about experience.

In the first third of the *Grammar,* the introduction and "Ways of Placement," Burke makes two major points: first, that inquiry into human relations necessarily draws one deep into the realm of persuasion and rhetoric; second, that the underlying principles of dramatism are sound bases for inquiry into human relations, especially as questions about persuasion and rhetoric bear upon it. Dealing with human relations, Burke says, is largely a matter of dealing with *accounts* of human motivation (be they, for example, psychological theories, religious doctrines, or philosophical systems). Accounts of human motivation, he further contends, ultimately amount to definitions. When we say that such and such is the case, or that Smith did "A" for reason "B," or propose a theory that has implications for understanding human motivation, we are creating a "vocabulary," a set of related terms and concepts. Broadly speaking, that vocabulary says what something is. Still countering the belief in a "neutral" language that Bentham, Hook, and many others held as the ideal, Burke suggests that, despite our hopes and pretensions, all definitions are partial: "Men seek for vocabularies that will be faithful *reflections* of reality. To this end, they must develop vocabularies that are *selections* of reality. And any selection of reality must, in certain circumstances, function as a *deflection* of reality" (*GM,* 59). Because definitions are partial, they are partisan, with no definition in principle privileged over another: "One could think of . . . the various philosophies as *casuistries* which apply these [grammatical] principles to temporal situations. . . . And whereas a statement about the grammatical principles of motivation might lay claim to a universal validity, or complete certainty, the choice of any one philosophic idiom embodying these principles is much more open to question. Even before we know what act is to be discussed, we can say with confidence that a rounded discussion of its motives must contain a reference to *some kind of* background. But since each philosophic idiom will characterize this background differently, there will remain the question as to which characterization is 'right' or 'more nearly right'" (*GM,* xvi–xvii). Accounts of human motivation are fundamentally persuasive and rhetorical because talk about human relations is subject to the necessarily partisan nature of language, naming, definition, and meaning.

Throughout the introduction and "Ways of Placement," Burke contends that dramatism is an appropriate (and often superior) method for the analysis of human relations. He argues that only a vocabulary that at its core is oriented toward action can form an adequate basis for the investigation of human relations. Echoing arguments he makes in *Permanence* and elsewhere, Burke maintains that the scientific idiom, which is based on motion, is hopelessly inadequate for investigating human relations beyond narrowly defined limits. "Our speculations," Burke comments, "should show that the subject of motivation is a philosophic one, not ultimately to be solved in terms of empirical science" (*GM,* xxiii). Since drama is profoundly action oriented, he suggests that we borrow its essential elements in order to create a method for the study of human relations. Hence, Burke offers the concepts "act," "scene," "agent," "agency," and "purpose" as the basis for dramatism. "The titular word for our own method is 'dramatism,'" Burke notes, "since it invites one to consider the matter of motives in a perspective that, being developed from the analysis of drama, treats language and thought primarily as modes of action" (*GM,* xxii). Since action is purposeful, the study of it necessarily draws us into matters of entreaty, persuasion, and rhetoric. The proof for all this, he says, is *A Grammar of Motives.*

In "Ways of Placement," Burke introduces the major themes of the *Grammar.* One theme concerns the nature of meaning. Burke suggests that things, concepts, actions—perhaps all aspects of experience—become meaningful in part because we "place" them in relation to other things, concepts, or actions that have meaning to us. The relationships that exist in the cluster are the source of meaning. A second theme is that, despite the almost infinite variety of relationships that might exist, there are some "ways of placement" that pervade human experience. The simple act of naming something, Burke suggests, is one such way of placement. To give something a name is sometimes to state an essence or to demarcate it from other things. Defining something is another way of placing it. When we say "X" is "Y," or define "X" by its context, or define it as part of a family of related items, or engage in any number of other kinds of defining, we are creating meaning. Some of the most thoroughgoing ways of placement are doctrines that bear on human relations, be they philosophies, theologies, scientific theories, or political theories. A third theme is that the pentad characterizes the nature or essence of, for instance, philosophy or theology. As an example, the belief that human actions stem from the environment (the "scene") is implicit in Darwin's theory of evolution (a doctrine that Burke suggests makes assumptions about the nature of human motivation). As another example, in Henrik Ibsen's *An Enemy of the People*, a "middle-class drama" that arises out of the "typical middle-class setting," the action is caused by the scene from which it arises. A fourth theme is that the history of thought about human relations shows us that no way of placement takes precedence over the others. All points of view, Burke maintains, are partial. Burke points out that even if that were not the case, human experience usually can be understood from a variety of perspectives, with each one focusing on some aspect of experience that the others ignore or underplay. We might say that acts are caused by the scenes in which they arise, or that acts are caused by the will of the agents who enact them, or that the heart of it all is a scene affecting an agent. According to Burke, human experience is so rich that no one can "prove" that any one way of placement is absolutely right. This raises a problem: if something is defined relative to something else, it is defined by that which it is not. Burke calls this a "paradox of substance," an "unresolvable ambiguity" in which the "intrinsic and extrinsic can change places." A fifth theme in "Ways of Placement" is that the paradox of substance is central to the study of human motivation. If we are to understand the "way of placement" implicit in some account of human motivation, Burke says, we are caught in a fluctuant realm in which any number of "extrinsic" factors can be imputed as the essence of human motivation. Hence, accounting for human relations draws us into a "dialectic" of competing perspectives, which necessarily draws one into the realm of persuasion and rhetoric.

By virtue of these speculations on the nature, characteristics, and consequences of placements, definition, and meaning Burke establishes a defining perspective of his own for the study of human relations, his own "way of placement": drama as a "representative anecdote."[6] Burke contends that by basing his perspective on principles of drama, he ensures "a selection in the realm of *action*, as against scientific reduction to sheer *motion*" (*GM*, 61).[7] In what is widely taken to be the hallmark of dramatism, Burke devises a universal topical scheme, a heuristic, for analyzing the many ways human motivation is expressed. The scheme is based on five concepts borrowed from drama, the pentad. Burke argues that any "rounded" investigation of motives (that is, one that captures the complexity of human action and motivation) will ultimately bring you to questions about what happened, in what context it occurred, who did it, through what means it was done, and for what goal.[8] He contends that these questions apply universally.

The real action in dramatism, Burke demonstrates, begins with understanding how one concept, as key to a basic organizing perspective, serves as the ground for conceiving another concept. Burke calls such a relationship a "ratio." (For instance, when actions are caused by the scene in which they arise, that is a "scene-act ratio"; when an action is said to be caused by the agent performing the action, that is an "agent-act ratio." All the permutations obtain.) A ratio is not merely a determination of which term is basic; it is a recognition of a relationship—for instance, that purpose is understood here as some way informed by the nature of, say, acts. A ratio, however telling it might be in some way about motivation or rhetorical strategy, is fairly useless on its own as a *dramatistic* tool. Identifying a ratio does not tell us much per se, but it becomes a useful dramatistic tool in two ways. First, it is useful when various ratios within a perspective are analyzed. There are few perspectives that are purely and solely of one ratio. So, for instance, in the predominately scene-act perspective of Darwin, Burke examines ratios based on purpose, agent, and act.[9] Second, ratios become a dramatistic tool when ratios from competing philosophies or theories are compared in order to find common ground. For example, when a scene-act ratio is compared to a purpose-act ratio, we discover that competing schemes differ in how they account for the genesis of human acts. Once that is established, there may be a clearer understanding of how the two perspectives differ. This aspect of dramatism is a modern form of rhetorical invention analogous to stasis theory in Greek and Roman rhetoric.[10]

As an example, in discussing G. W. F. Hegel and Karl Marx, Burke at one point says that he is "trying to show how certain key terms might be used to 'call the plays' in any and all philosophies" (*GM*, 201). Burke begins by noting that Hegel supposes "a superagent (Spirit) manifesting itself in progressively changing historical conditions (scenes of narrowed circumference)," whereas Marx "deriv[ed] the character of human consciousness in different historical periods from the character of the material conditions prevailing at the time" (*GM*, 200). At one level the difference between Hegel and Marx, he says, is "a simple shift from agent to scene as point of origin" (*GM*, 200). Yet dramatistic analysis does not stop there. Burke suggests that dialectical materialism contains an element of idealism, in that, arising out of the idealism of Hegel, "there must be some quality of agenthood permeating the scene itself " (*GM*, 201). He uses Lenin's *Materialism and Empirio-Criticism* for support. Moreover, Burke argues that "dialectical materialism, in its constant call upon human agents, and above all its futuristic stress upon kinds of social *unification,* is intensely idealistic" (*GM*, 201). Of course, we may disagree with Burke about all this, but that is not the point; he conducts his dramatistic analysis on these assumptions. Seeking to understand better the relationship between ideas and conditions in Marxism, Burke engages in a complicated analysis of various ways in which the universal scene in Marxism contains elements of the ideal, especially when we realize that Marxist theory cannot be divorced from the propagandistic purposes its political documents serve. As he sums it up: "So far as our dramatistic terminology is concerned, the Marxist philosophy began by grounding *agent* in *scene,* but by reason of its poignant concern with the ethical, it requires the systematic featuring of *act.* On the Symbolic level, it does feature act implicitly but intensely, in having so dramatic a pattern. On the Rhetorical level, its scientist and anti-scholastic vocabulary is needed for purposes of political dynamism" (*GM,* 210). Although the sections on Marx and Hegel are principally about Marxism, Burke uses the ratios to tease out the extent to which there is common ground uniting both theorists.

Dramatism identifies not only which ratios obtain, but *how* they obtain. For instance, the *Grammar* shows a variety of ways in which act may be based on scene. The pentadic terms, as a *grammar,* can be thought of as the bases for a *syntax,* the ratios.[11] All of this is implied in what is perhaps the most quoted phrase in the *Grammar:* "what we want is *not terms that avoid ambiguity,* but *terms that clearly reveal the strategic spots at which ambiguities necessarily arise*" (*GM,* xviii). Writing to Malcolm Cowley in 1945, Burke explained that the pentad does not form a neat typology: "My five terms are the undistributedest bastards you ever saw. When you see the whole venture, I think you'll realize that that's the point. Every one of them merges into the others" (Jay, 264–65). In a later letter to Cowley, Burke summarized the role of the pentad in the entire work: "*Grammar* tries to show how these terms can serve to elucidate basic methods of placement and expression in different literary orders: (treated as aspects of 'symbolic action') drama, poetry, theology, metaphysics, law, etc. Aims to show the transformations needed for turning them upon different kinds of subject matter (transformations needed to keep the analysis from being a mere analogizing, as were one to treat *all* forms purely and simply as 'drama')" (Jay, 292).

In part 2 of *A Grammar of Motives,* "The Philosophic Schools," Burke examines the broad sweep of motivational assumptions in more than two dozen seminal figures and theories in philosophy—as various as Plato and John Dewey, and mysticism and rationalism—to explore the adequacy of the pentad as a critical tool by studying some strategic points at which important ambiguities necessarily arise. In doing so, he provides detailed examples of dramatism in practice. Part 2 is organized into sections titled "Scene," "Agent in General," "Act," and "Agency and Purpose." Burke contends that many philosophic schools cluster around one element of the pentad or another, using that term as the ground for explaining all sorts of questions about how humans think and live. For example, under the heading "agent" Burke examines how the philosophies of George Berkeley, David Hume, Gottfried Leibniz, Immanuel Kant, Marx, Hegel, and George Santayana promote the human agent as a motive force, and how such a featuring of agent informs the understanding of other concepts—especially action, agency, purpose, and scene—when conceived within those philosophical systems. On the one hand, Burke shows that various ratios are implicit to these doctrines. But more to the point, he demonstrates that various ratios can occur precisely because of ambiguities that necessarily arise when using concepts such as act, scene, agent, agency, and purpose. Going on to chart huge tracts of philosophic terrain, Burke then categorizes whole philosophic schools under the various terms of the pentad: materialism features scene, idealism features agent, pragmatism features agency, mysticism features purpose, and realism features act. Some critics have complained that this typology is dubious. Burke admits that it has several problems: first, the whole idea of featuring a term is questionable because one term leads inevitably to the others; second, there is terminological cross-fertilization between the philosophic schools; third, some schools, notably nominalism and rationalism, do not fit well into the classifications (in fact, he says, all the terms of the pentad apply to them);[12] and fourth, in applying philosophical concepts and solving philosophical problems generated by those concepts, the philosopher is often led away from his original conception (*GM,* 128–30). Nonetheless, Burke staunchly espouses his pentad as a scheme for organizing philosophical thought: "with the pentad as a generating principle, we may extricate ourselves from these intricacies, by discovering the kinds of *assertion* which the different schools would exemplify in a hypothetical state of purity. Once this approach is established, problems are much less likely to conceal the underlying design of assertion, or may even serve to assist in the characterizing of a given philosophic work" (*GM,* 131). Thus, Burke intends the pentad, at least in this application, to be a heuristic tool for beginning a conversation—not the end itself of critical technique. The parts of "The Philosophic Schools" that treat individual philosophers demonstrate how one pentadic element is central to that philosophy, how ratios may be used to understand the complexities and ambiguities inherent in complex motivational schemes, and how dramatistic analysis might be used to understand various philosophies as "ways of placement." Ultimately, as mentioned earlier, the point is that philosophical doctrines end up being casuistries, doctrines that are self-fulfilling in their interpretative imprimatur.

The section titled "Scene" conveys a sense of the kind of analysis in which Burke engages. Burke here points out that philosophies that feature scene tend toward materialism and reduce action to motion. For instance, Thomas Hobbes in the *Leviathan* treats "reason," "the passions," personal motivations, and to some degree "will" in "terms of a scene mechanically determined" (*GM,* 135). Burke contends that even when Hobbes considers "action" and "acts," his conception is "quite close to the metaphysics of modern behaviorist psychology" (*GM,* 136). Benedict de Spinoza, with his emphasis on "God as the ground of all possibility" and his equating of God and nature, also reduces action to motion. Burke describes this as a "narrowing of the circumference from a scene comprising both creation and creator to a scene comprising creation alone" (*GM,* 138). Burke argues that even within the idealism that penetrates the latter parts of Spinoza's *Ethics,* the scenic imprint remains. Although in Hobbes act, agent, agency, and purpose occur, they are effectively subsumed under scene. In Spinoza we find "a scenic philosopher more ambiguously placed [than Hobbes] because of the action-motion equation underlying the God-Nature equation" (*GM,* 153). Burke buttresses this argument by analyzing Darwin and Hellenic materialism. In any event, according to Burke, all these views are "arbitrary" in the sense that each theorist has selected one term as the "substance" of the others, no principle exists to justify this privilege, and each philosophical doctrine must engage in rationalization to maintain the logic of that initial choice. Certainly, dramatistic analysis is not necessary to come to these conclusions, but no method in the liberal arts has a patent on creating knowledge. Dramatism makes coming to this judgment more likely, however. In the works of the philosophers and in the philosophies Burke discusses, dramatism pinpoints fundamental relationships clearly and efficiently. This reveals the extent to which philosophy must wrestle to maintain its motivational theory.

The fact that all philosophies are arbitrary in these ways is not just an abstract problem of philosophy or, by analogy, of theology, science, law, and so on. Burke suggests that the same situation occurs in communities, polities, and societies. Hence, for the remainder of the book, part 3, Burke turns that realm in which "prior" selections most obviously figure into the creation and maintenance of communities, the political constitution. In "On Dialectic," Burke frames the discussion of constitutions with the idea that dialectical processes figure into the management of human motivational processes. ("By dialectics in the most general sense," he says, "we mean the employment of the possibilities of linguistic transformation" [*GM,* 402.]) In the first and larger section of "On Dialectic," "The Dialectic of Constitutions," Burke analyzes in detail the nature and characteristics of political documents, using political constitutions as the representative anecdote. He uses the Constitution of the United States to focus on how constitutions are interpreted and the role they play in the dialectical symbiosis of legal and legislative institutions. Burke examines constitutions in part because the process of creating a constitution is "*summational* in character, . . . *wherein human relations grandly converge*" (*GM,* 324). The process of creating a constitution, he says, is dialectical and exhibits many of the characteristics of motivation, agreement, and disagreement that are the subjects of his book. "The Dialectic of Constitutions" is hard to summarize because much of it is about complex political and economic relations. For instance, in a section on religious and secular futurism Burke points out that if the market for long-term investments of private capital dwindles, the futuristic idiom will seem less natural because "in proportion as financial futurism weakens . . . we may expect a corresponding weakness of futuristic imaginings in the wider, cultural circle" (*GM,* 335).

"The Dialectic of Constitutions" opens with Burke explaining why he decided to use constitutions to conclude *A Grammar of Motives.* Much of the opening discussion involves reasoning through the strengths and weaknesses of a variety of alternative representative anecdotes. Rejecting reductive, admonitory, and hortatory anecdotes, Burke favors one that focuses on substance and is practical rather than idealistic. Satisfied that political constitutions fit his bill of particulars, Burke goes on to analyze at length two books which, "by propounding 'constitutions' in the name of freedom," demonstrate the complex ambiguities inherent in establishing a constitution (*GM,* 360). Herbert Read in *Poetry and Anarchism,* Burke tells us, suggests that anarchism should not be rejected as impractical because practicality is not the proper test of a political "vision." According to Burke, the problem with Read's book begins when Read goes "on to propose the kind of social and political organization by which this ideal could be embodied . . . 'anarcho-*syndicalism*'" (*GM,* 345). Anarchism, Burke allows, is "an *ideal* term." Unfortunately, "syndicalism" is "a *practical* term" and thus conceptually at odds with anarchism. This is "particularly relevant to the tactics of Constitutions" because, although constitutions establish principles that are conceptually harmonious, in practical applications they often conflict. Courts subsequently adjudge that the constitution has conflicting clauses. According to Burke, a problem analogous to Read's occurs in Henry Bamford Parkes's attack against Marxism and defense of laissez-faire, *Marxism: An Autopsy* (*GM,* 349–55).

After demonstrating these tensions, Burke turns to other characteristics basic to constitutions. He reminds us that although constitutions are *addressed* by agents to agents, they also establish a scene in which future acts take place. However, the scene is necessarily incomplete, for no human document can account for all possibilities—whereupon instead of appealing to "the social, natural, or supernatural environment in general," the institution of "'positive' law has tried to uphold the fiction that the Constitutional enactment itself is the criterion for judicial interpretations of motive" (*GM,* 362). Burke warns us that devices such as positive law may support institutions inimical to the general good.[13] With such concerns in mind, Burke briefly explains how, when circumstances change, interpreters of constitutions may abandon those whose rights were originally represented. For instance, in feudal thought, "the rights that had been enunciated as *group rights, belonging to 'the people' as a class in dialectical opposition to the crown and the crown's administrators as a class,* became the rights of men as *individuals, in dialectical opposition to men as a group*" (*GM,* 364). If new situations arise that compel interpreters to move to a sufficient level of generalization, new interpretations may attain the status of universal principles. Burke recognizes that even though constitutional provisions may become universal, they have limits. For instance, rights guaranteed by a constitution may be rescinded in the future or in other ways disappear. Moreover, whatever ideals the framers of a constitution may have, those ideals cannot perfectly represent the wishes of the entire citizenry; even if that were possible, a public document could not perfectly embody those ideals; and even if *that* were possible, Burke argues, the different kinds of principles inherent in a constitution make for inconsistency and conflict among constitutional edicts themselves. Given conflict among principles, courts often must appeal to principles outside the constitution to resolve the conflict. In sum, given these limitations, Burke suggests that "Constitutions are of primary importance in suggesting what coordinates one will think by. . . . but Constitutions are important in singling out certain directives for special attention, and thus in bringing them more clearly to men's consciousness" (*GM,* 367). This is reminiscent of what Burke says in "The Philosophic Schools." Philosophies, like constitutions, start out well enough in an attempt to account thoroughly for varieties of human experience and motivation. However, at some point they are incomplete because no "well-rounded" system can account fully for the complexity of human relations; and at some point, having aggregated numerous principles in an attempt to be complete, the philosophy necessarily will contain motivational schisms. Burke is not interested in arguing that philosophies are defective because they contain contradictory principles; rather, he simply indicates that we must not expect too much of philosophy. This gets at the fundamental problem analytical and systematic philosophers have with Burke. Thinkers such as Hook and Nagel express their beliefs wholeheartedly that philosophy can do just that. They deplore the "extra-philosophical" factors—for instance, emotive language, rhetoric, social scientific principles—that Burke relies on for filling out philosophy.

Much of the rest of "The Dialectic of Constitutions" concerns various "extra-constitutional" factors that we appeal to in order to make constitutions work. Burke begins this discussion by offering an interpretative framework for resolving constitutional conflict that he believes is superior to the two standard approaches (strict constructionism and broad constructionism). As alternatives, he suggests "essentializing" and "proportional" strategies, which, he says, cut across the bias of strict and broad constructionism. In *Literary Form,* Burke makes much of essentializing and proportional strategies, particularly as they relate to Freud and the interpretation of poetry.[14] "The essentializing strategy," Burke says, "select[s] some one clause or other in the Constitution, and judg[es] a measure by reference to it. The proportional strategy . . . would test the measure by reference to *all* the wishes in the Constitution. . . . The aim would be to state explicitly a doctrine of *proportions*" (*GM*, 380). Burke points out various benefits of essentializing strategies and notes that Justice Marshall's decision establishing the Supreme Court's right of judicial review was an essentializing strategy that soon proved deficient because he judged constitutional principles more essential than legislative laws, which did not help in deciding which of several competing constitutional principles were preferable when they came into conflict. This eventually prompted the Court to adopt proportional strategies when necessary, such as when "undefined private rights" conflict with "undefined public powers" (*GM*, 387).

Burke concludes "The Dialectic of Constitutions" by briefly considering more overtly political factors that not only affect how constitutions work but were particularly relevant to American politics in the late 1930s and early 1940s. He notes that, given the political diversity of our nation, "the whole party structure developed outside the provisions of the Constitution" (*GM*, 390). The president of the United States, he observes, must evoke unity while maintaining political diversity. Political rhetoric itself introduces ironies into the political scene (for instance, Franklin Delano Roosevelt's "'collectivism' made its most important contribution to individualism, in that he drew upon the government credit . . . to underwrite the traditional modes of private investment" [*GM*, 394]). Burke argues that in wartime, America needs collectivist political structures and a concomitant reconceptualization of wealth.

In the final section of the *Grammar*, "Dialectic in General," Burke returns to more abstract theoretical issues, focusing on the nature of dialectic to bring the *Grammar* back to themes with which it began. Burke first notes that dialectic concerns "the employment of the possibilities of linguistic transformation" (*GM*, 402). He then discusses three categories of concepts that have figured prominently in dialectic: the merging and dividing of ideas; major dialectical pairs (action-passion, mind-body, being-nothing); and the idea of transcendence. Using Kant, mathematics, Christian Atonement, Hitler, Otto Neurath, Bergson's *Creative Evolution,* Coleridge, card tricks, and other topics, Burke argues that in the dialectic between merger and division a new principle is generated that is a transformation of one of the original concepts. The major dialectical pairs, he says, "generalize the first major steps usually taken towards the localizing of identity"; that is, they are standard ways one might "'idealize' his own cause while 'materializing' that of his opponents" (*GM*, 418–19). Transcendence takes many forms, the most important of which for Burke's concerns is "the temporizing of essence" (the transformation of logical priority into temporal priority and vice versa). As the *Grammar* concludes, Burke comes full circle because, he points out, "dialectic is concerned with different levels of *grounding*" (*GM*, 440); it is an essential part of the process of defining and the attribution of motives. This process, he asserts, is itself grounded in a complex scene that lies beyond. Therefore, Burke argues, dramatism is grounded in the "non-dramatist" and leads to its own dissolution. Burke completes the *Grammar* with an appeal to a "neo-liberal ideal" neither "local" nor "imperialistic": "Surely, all works of goodwill written in the next decades must aim somehow to avoid these two extremes, seeking a neo-liberal, speculative attitude. To an extent, perhaps, it will be like an attitude of hypochondriasis: the attitude of a patient who makes peace with his symptoms by becoming interested in them. Yes, on the negative side, the 'Neo-Stoicism' we advocate would be an attitude of hypochondriasis. But on the positive side it would be an attitude of appreciation. And as regards our particular project, it would seek delight in meditating upon some of the many ingenuities of speech. Linguistic skepticism, in being quizzical, supplies the surest ground for the discernment and appreciation of linguistic resources" (*GM*, 443).

In previous chapters the "Critic's Credo" was used to explain the basic moves in Burke's books; it is equally helpful with the *Grammar*. In *Counter-Statement* the credo is discrete, with different essays pretty much serving as either apology, rhetoric, or program. In his other books different sections often serve two or even all of these functions.[15] The *Grammar*'s three major sections fall roughly into the pattern of apology ("Ways of Placement"), rhetoric ("The Philosophic Schools"), and program ("On Dialectic"), although each section serves the other functions to some extent.

As Burke's career progressed, his apologies changed; he less often attacked competing theories and more often championed views he considered superior. In *Attitudes*, Burke commends the aesthetic theories of William James, Walt Whitman, and Ralph Waldo Emerson. In *Literary Form* he apologizes to some extent by attacking certain views of language and criticism, but more by explaining and justifying his theory of literary association. As much as the apologies are similar in that they are positive, we must not ignore the unique qualities of the *Grammar*'s apology, especially in questioning what he is apologizing for. The answer to that question tells us a lot about what Burke was up to in this *Motivorum* project.

On one level, in the earlier apologies Burke directly or by implication condemns the encroachment of science, technology, and positivism on a variety of human endeavors.[16] In the *Grammar* he continues the attack against positivism by making brief and scattered direct remarks; however, positivism and its pathologies have, overall, receded into the background. Burke is more concerned about various self-serving reductionisms, about which he makes many explicit arguments. One of the most prominent forms of reductionist thinking that he targets is capitalism. But even on this topic he is less forceful than he was in *Permanence*. On the whole, Burke tempers his apology, offering more seasoned reasoning and fewer histrionics. The main mechanism of the apology is a robust argument for the principles underlying dramatism and the benefits of dramatistic analysis. To counter reductive thinking, Burke focuses on a few themes. First, he crafts the entire project around doctrines of motives, which draws one into so many aspects of human relations (ethics, theology, law, biology, psychology, for example) that only the most stubborn could be reductive. Second, by making the nature and characteristics of transformation a major concern, Burke problematizes reductionism. Third, he also does this by encouraging what he calls an attitude of speculation, by which he means imagining possibilities. The pentad, though thought to be reductive by some critics, is actually a mechanism for imagining all sorts of possibilities: "It is important that we try to see around the edges of our customary perspective, if we would understand the part that motivational assumptions play in implicitly and explicitly substantiating human decisions, hence in shaping human relations" (*GM,* 335). Fourth, speculation is enhanced by a robust skepticism. Reductionism thrives most in our basic beliefs. Burke demonstrates masterfully that there are complex contradictions in what we take to be plain and simple beliefs.

An important feature of the *Grammar* is the linguistic and philosophical turn that Burke makes. This may be what has confused those who read the *Grammar* independently of Burke's earlier books (and, indeed, many who have read them). On its own, especially because Burke opens and ends with general philosophical and linguistic concerns, readers have largely missed the strong social and political purposes to which these concerns are directed. In fact, as he is developing the book Burke sees the *Grammar* as a direct outgrowth of the explicitly social and political books that preceded it. In a letter to Cowley, Burke described the close relations: "Had originally intended to write a third volume to P&C and ATH. It was to be called On Human Relations. Had been taking notes (social strategies, diplomatic devices, ways of outwitting others and oneself, etc.). Began to write these up. Found that they needed a general theoretical introduction. Thought a few thousand words would do the job. But the project grew into the *Grammar*. The five terms with which the work now begins were settled upon toward the end of the first version, and the book was turned around accordingly" (Jay, 292). Put another way, Burke saw no need to make the same arguments in the same way again. He realized that there are dimensions of his overall concerns that are slighted in his previous works, and he wrote the *Grammar* to address them. But foremost in Burke's mind was that his thoughts might be put to social and political use. While revising the *Grammar* for publication Burke wrote to Cowley that he had been working on material for the *Grammar* since the middle 1930s and retained some of the attitudes he had then: "Meanwhile, all I know is, so far or so long as I am able, to go on trying to increase our awareness (my own and others') of the ways in which motives move us and deceive us, and what kind of knowledge the nature of motives demands of us, if we are not to goad one another endlessly to the cult of powers that can bring no genuine humaneness to the world. It would be silly to think that any book, or even a whole library of books, could solve such difficulties. But such books are, I know, one of the steps in the right direction. Until the steamrollers flatten out all" (Jay, 249).

The rhetoric of the *Grammar*, where Burke shows us how the system works, occurs to a large extent in "The Philosophic Schools," though its basic principles are set forth in "Ways of Placement." Careful readers of Burke's writings will see that dramatism is, at heart, an extension of the rhetoric of *Permanence*, "perspective by incongruity." But whereas the rhetoric of *Permanence* is diffuse and somewhat simple (its basic operating principle is yoking opposites—perhaps a reflection of the times in which it was written), the rhetoric of the *Grammar* is more sophisticated and methodical. The philosophical and linguistic turn that Burke made was due in large part to the desire to craft better methods for analyzing human relations, especially as linguistic dimensions are fully enfranchised. Burke pointed this out to Cowley: "The study of linguistic action is still in the stage of the maps that Columbus had. . . . The middle section, analyzing philosophies as languages, is what the semantics gents have been trying to do, without exception bungingly (since their terms were too inaccurate and inapposite)" (Jay, 260, 270). Burke came to realize that any method he proposed was inherently limited by its own character. So in much of the discussion of method in the *Grammar*, Burke is explicitly concerned with what his instrument leads one to say. "Terms are interrelated," he wrote to Cowley. "Once you select a few," he said, "you are no longer free simply to apply them like labels to external situations, but must also follow through all sorts of internal battles, as the terms bring up obligations with relation to one another" (Jay, 237). In "The Philosophic Schools," Burke uses philosophy as subject matter to demonstrate how one might use dramatism to study motivational schemes. Of course, he wanted to make a statement about the particular philosophies he treated. But that should not diminish the fact that the middle section of the book is in large part an exploration of the "internal battles" and a grand exemplar of dramatism in practice. In any case, the section on the philosophical schools, which came later in the writing of the book, clearly has a tone of demonstrating the method in practice.

The program of the *Grammar*, where Burke shows how the theory should be applied, occurs chiefly in "On Dialectic." In one way this is the most practical of Burke's programs. Even though the program of *Counter-Statement* deals with such practical matters as unemployment, leisure, welfare, and overconsumption and underconsumption, it nonetheless is directed toward large-scale social forces. The calls for communist correctives in *Permanence* are likewise rather broad. The "Dictionary of Pivotal Terms" in *Attitudes*, though often particular regarding specific social and political problems, is too idiosyncratic and systematically undeveloped to be of much use in practical politics (a reader could surely gain a better understanding of bureaucracy, and perhaps a person's criticisms of government might be stimulated by some of Burke's observations, but there is little that would help organized grassroots politics). "The Dialectic of Constitutions," on the other hand, seems largely directed to specific practical judgments about constitutional and juridical matters. It also marks the first time Burke conceives the enactor of his program to be a conservative institution. Previously, programmatical change came from outside—leftist artists, communists, the people; now, Burke shows us how, within the language and principles of the courts, his desired social thought can be attained.

The critical response to *A Grammar of Motives* is especially instructive about the problems of reading Burke. Outside of Sidney Hook's vicious attack, few criticisms of Burke are as cutting as those that the *Grammar* garnered from philosophers. Max Black, writing for the *Philosophical Review,* clearly understands many of Burke's intentions. His description of Burke's basic assumptions is sound. Several aspects of the review are noteworthy. First, he suggests that Burke is "formulating a system of related categories."[17] Second, he questions the "inevitability" of the paradox of substance and the "universality" of the system. Third, he dismisses Burke's use of biographical material as "unhelpful." Fourth, he argues that Burke offers no evidence for the claim that reductionism is misleading. Ultimately, Black charges that Burke's "vast rambling edifice of quasi-sociological and quasi-psychoanalytical speculation seems to rest on nothing more solid than a set of unexamined and uncriticized metaphysical assumptions" (490). Abraham Kaplan is more forgiving. Although he states that "Burke's treatment shares the obvious weakness of any such schematization," he allows that "it does at many points provide a fresh and illuminating perspective."[18] Kaplan says that "the rationale of his method" is "more important than his specific findings." In addition, he points out that the failures of Watsonian behaviorism do not justify Burke's claim that empirical science is inadequate for studying human motivation. On the topic of internal analysis, Kaplan argues that "the so-called internal transformations traced by Burke in motivational discourse are not strictly logical, but socio- and psycho-logical" (234). Ultimately, Kaplan's strongest criticism is that "Burke explicitly declares his concern to be with the analysis of language, not 'reality'" (233). This leads him to complain that "it is dialectics with a vengeance to localise our problem in [linguistic] changes rather than in the personal and social patterns of which the vocabulary of motive is the instrument and expression" (234).

It is striking how similar these reviews are to the criticisms of Hook, Nagel, and Dewey in "The Failure of Nerve." Like the others, Black and Kaplan key in on systematicity, universality, extraphilosophical factors, and the difference between language and reality. In each case they hold Burke to the standards of analytical philosophy, as if there can be only one way to approach the question. Burke's statements about the systematicity and universality of dramatism can be likened to the claims that Freud and Marx made about their theories being "sciences." From the vantage point of the quantum physicist, dialectical materialism looks nothing like a science. But within the world of nineteenth-century political economy it is indeed fairly scientific. Likewise, compared to rhetorical theories of generations past, Burke's dramatism seems universal and systematic. Of course, Burke never intended his claims to be taken so strongly, but that does not matter to the systematic philosophers. Regarding extraphilosophical factors, it should not be surprising that the systematic philosophers discount anything other than philosophical principles; but how could one talk about human motivation without appealing to the social and psychological aspects of human life? Perhaps another way to say this is that the systematic philosophers approach *A Grammar of Motives* as if it is a philosophical work rather than a work about the principles underlying what amounts to a broad theory of rhetoric. Perhaps this is why neither Black nor Kaplan mentions "The Dialectic of Constitutions" in any detail. Why should they when they see a clear breach between language and "reality"? Of course, Burke believed that the nature and characteristics of language very much affect the way we view and respond to "reality." He believed that it is nonsensical to talk about reality apart from the influence of language and social structure and politics. The philosophers omit mention of "The Dialectic of Constitutions" because discussion of that section would move them away from acceptable "underlying principles" to those which their vision of philosophy does not allow. While Black and Kaplan make good points from within the world of systematic philosophy, they do not take Burke on his own terms. This kind of intellectual rift would haunt Burke throughout his career.

A Rhetoric of Motives
Communication, Hierarchy, and Formal Appeal

───────────────■───────────────

Kenneth Burke wrote most of *A Grammar of Motives* during World War II. He wrote most of *A Rhetoric of Motives* during the early years of the cold war. Perhaps the cold war was a form of "ad bellum purificandum," but if the *Rhetoric* is any indication, Burke did not believe so. Still haunted by the specter of what individuals are capable of doing—and far more by what organizations of humans can do in the name of abstract principles such as honor, race, and justice—Burke felt the need even more to make an entreaty for better ways to move "toward a better life." In the *Grammar* he approached the matter in terms of the casuistic nature of philosophical doctrines and political constitutions. With the *Rhetoric*, Burke turned to the casuistic nature of appeal in social hierarchies. As he did with *Counter-Statement, Permanence and Change, Attitudes toward History,* and *The Philosophy of Literary Form,* Burke continued to suggest that better ways to understand human relations will arise from a better understanding of rhetoric and persuasion. Much as he did in "The Dictionary of Pivotal Terms" in *Attitudes,* Burke in the *Rhetoric* offers the reader a variety of strategies humans use to place themselves in social organizations.

In each of his books of criticism Burke explored facets of questions he raised previously. *A Rhetoric of Motives* is particularly interesting because it is simultaneously part of the *Motivorum* project begun in *A Grammar of Motives* and a development of themes from his earlier books. Burke provides some summaries that help us understand the *Rhetoric* in context and on its own: the *Grammar,* he says, "deals with a level of motivation which even wholly rival doctrines of motives must share in common; hence it [is] addressed to a speculative portion of the mind which men of many different situations . . . have in common" (*GM,* 442). *Rhetoric,* in contrast, studies "the competitive use of the coöperative" in an effort to transcend enmity by "classifying and tracing back to their beginnings in Edenic simplicity those linguistic modes of suasion that often seem little better than malice and the lie" (*GM,* 442). Moreover, in the appendix to *Counter-Statement* he indicates that "the *Rhetoric* returns to the problems of bureaucracy, but now considers them in terms of 'hierarchy' and its 'mysteries,' antitheses of association and dissociation thus being modified by a concern with the 'pyramidal' nature of social orders, as these affect consciousness and expression" (*CS,* 218). Thus, whereas the *Grammar* is more concerned with the relations between competing doctrines of motives, the *Rhetoric* emphasizes the various linguistic or rhetorical tactics we use to establish, maintain, and alter our place in social structures. Ideas such as social class, difference, hierarchy, mystery, persuasion, rhetoric, and identification recur throughout the *Rhetoric* and form the foundation from which Burke's analysis radiates. That hub embraces a lot indeed. It is important to keep in mind that Burke's catholic scope derives in part from the fact that "the characteristic invitation to rhetoric" occurs at that moment when the difference between community and separateness is murky; "since identification implies division," Burke notes, "we found rhetoric involving us in matters of socialization and faction" (*RM,* 45). Moreover, we have to recognize an aspect of Burke's thinking that commentators by and large ignore: much of the *Rhetoric* explores and elucidates "that fluctuant realm midway between ideas and images," with Burke locating ideology as a key point where the line between ideas and images is indistinct (*RM,* 150). With this focus on social class, hierarchy, ideology, etc., Burke obtained a mature synthesis of themes that occupied his mind from the late 1910s.

In the 340 packed pages of *A Rhetoric of Motives,* Burke ranges far in exploring the role of rhetoric in human relations. As in the *Grammar,* he has a broad conception, which is that rhetoric has something to do with virtually all of the innumerable ways in which persons communicate. This ranges as far as clothing fashions, which, though not verbal, clearly have communicative functions. Burke applies rhetoric to fictional characters, literary genres, biblical stories, political theories, economic doctrines, philosophy, and a variety of political situations. In this sweeping collection Burke finds what he calls "rhetorical ingredients" in so many realms theretofore thought immune to rhetorical analysis that he risks what some may take to be a fatal attenuation of the concept of rhetoric. Burke asserts some fundamental principles for his view of rhetoric, but he does not offer a systematic theory—a virtue unless one demands otherwise. Certainly, the *Rhetoric* is more rigorous conceptually than Burke's early work, yet the book is still more suggestive than systematic. Burke is intent on suggesting a variety of attitudes toward language and rhetoric intended to reveal rhetorical functions operating where we do not expect them and to open paths to accurately gauge their implications. This suggestiveness regarding a broadened conception of rhetoric is justified, if Burke's thinking is accepted, by the assumption that rhetoric is fundamentally a study of how language, through its aesthetic and social functions, contributes to the formation of ethical communities—that is, that the study of rhetoric is about the movement "towards a better life."

As with *A Grammar of Motives,* Burke divides *A Rhetoric of Motives* into three main sections. The first, "The Range of Rhetoric," comprises about one-eighth of the book and has twenty subsections with intriguing titles typical of Burke (for instance, "Qualifying the Suicidal Motive," "The Identifying Nature of Property," and "Rhetoric and Primitive Magic"). Though relatively short in length, it is seminal to *A Rhetoric of Motives,* for here Burke sets out his general point of view, major concerns, and basic concepts. Burke's strategy in "The Range of Rhetoric" mimics his approach in the opening sections of *A Grammar of Motives:* he surveys a field to show its scope and to find commonalities among a variety of views. In the second section of the *Rhetoric,* "Traditional Principles of Rhetoric," Burke surveys several definitions of rhetoric, demonstrating that there are many subtle and complex differences between them. Despite the wide range of meanings and some profound differences, Burke argues that the various views of rhetoric have two features in common: all concern symbolic activity that is "addressed"; and all involve "identification." "Traditional Principles of Rhetoric," which comprises almost half of the book, ostensibly is an analysis of the way the term "rhetoric" has been conceptualized in the West since its first systematic treatments in ancient Greece. But there is much more to it. As Hugh Dalziel Duncan, a sociologist influenced heavily by Burke, puts it, "Burke considers various conditions of symbolic appeals such as those going on between sexes, age groups, persons, status groups, classes, political, religious and aesthetic groups, in terms of how such social placement affects the use of language and other symbols."[1] Burke also considers how the use of language and other symbols affects social placement. The third and final section of the *Rhetoric,* "Order," which comprises a little less than half of the book, is a description of tensions and ambiguities in social hierarchies that make for rhetorical processes as the mechanisms for staking a place in social organizations.

"The Range of Rhetoric." This section opens with striking images of suicide and murder. In Matthew Arnold's poem "Empedocles on Etna," Empedocles casts himself into a volcano, seeking release through self-immolation. In Milton's dramatic poem *Samson Agonistes,* Samson tugs and shakes "those two massy pillars" to smite his enemies (as Milton puts it, "At once both to destroy and be destroy'd"). In Arnold's "Sohrab and Rustum," Rustum battles a man whom he does not know is his father. When Rustum hears his father's name and realizes the true identity of his mortal enemy, he becomes paralyzed—and suffers a fatal wound. What do suicide and murder—real or imaginary—have to do with rhetoric? Burke explains by comparing Milton's poem *Samson Agonistes* to Milton's speech on freedom of the press, the *Areopagitica.* Milton's address to the English Parliament, Burke observes, was "literature for *use,*" not *ars gratia artis.* Of course, the distinction between pure art and utilitarian art was one of the most important themes in Burke's early thinking, as seen especially in *Counter-Statement.* At that time Burke attacked conceptions of pure art on two grounds: (1) that the *ars gratia artis* justification of art, which arose in the middle of the nineteenth century, was a response to then new cultural formations that by the

1920s were moribund; and (2) that, in any event, the criterion of effectiveness does not apply to art because "no categorical distinction can possibly be made between 'effective' and 'ineffective' art" (*CS,* 90). In the late 1940s, by contrast, Burke was responding principally to the "New Critics," who construed poetry and literature purely "as a structure of internally related parts," with no regard for use, however conceived (*RM,* 4).[2] Reaffirming the view of literature that he had championed in essays such as "Applications of the Terminology" and "Literature as Equipment for Living," Burke contends that Milton's poem "is no mere evidence of a virtuoso's craftsmanship." Rather, Burke says, Milton used the poem to commit suicide symbolically and to make a statement about the political struggles between the Royalists and the Puritans (the poem incorporates imagery that mimics their conflict). Thus, *Samson Agonistes* "is almost a kind of witchcraft, a wonder-working spell by a cantankerous old fighter-priest who would slay the enemy in effigy, and whose very translation of political controversy to high theologic terms helps, by such magnification, to sanction the ill-tempered obstinacy of his resistance. . . . This is moralistic prophecy, and is thus also a kind of 'literature for use,' use at one remove, though of a sort that the technologically-minded would consider the very opposite of use, since it is wholly in the order of ritual and magic" (*RM,* 5). Arnold's poems were literature for use too, for they were mechanisms by which the author identified symbolically with his father. Yet to Burke, "use" is far more than just psychological palliation and political symbology. He opens the *Rhetoric* with the poetry of murder and suicide because these themes clearly suggest that there is much at stake in poetry—and therefore, by implication, that literature on the whole has rhetorical dimensions usually assumed to occur solely in the realm of political, judicial, and ceremonial speech making. As in his earlier books, Burke is making an apology for the importance of aesthetic expression according to the beliefs and concerns of his readers.

In addition, Burke uses this imagery to point out that, when accounting for motivation, it is all too easy to be simplistic. "Empedocles at Etna" showcases a suicide. "Sohrab and Rustum" is more complicated; although there is a killing, it has elements which suggest that Rustum's death was to some extent a suicide—after all, his death was due to a "fatal admiration" for his father. This is a literary manifestation of a theme that occupied Burke for a long time: "faulty means selection." For instance, in *Counter-Statement* he speaks of this in terms of antitheses, such as agrarian-industrial, bourgeois-bohemian, unemployment-leisure. And in *Permanence* he talks of "trained incapacity," "occupational psychosis," and "ethical confusion." The idea of choosing the wrong means figures prominently in the *Motivorum* books in that casuistic doctrines ultimately lead to social policy. The current debates over welfare and "workfare" are perfect examples of this. In any event, Burke goes on to show that it is easy to be simplistic about motivation by using the example of *Samson Agonistes,* which is more clearly ambiguous than the other poems, for Samson explicitly sought *his own* destruction *and* that of his enemies. According to Burke, "Looking back at the poem by Milton, we find there, united in one poem, what Arnold has divided between two poems: the suicide and the warlike death are united in the same image" (*RM,* 9). Burke is careful to note that this is not a matter of *dual* motivations; rather, it is an "order of motivation" that *transcends* the categories of suicide and murder. The same holds true, Burke says, for the story of Cain and Abel in the Book of Genesis. Though Cain's murderous blow is not usually thought of as a *suicide,* Burke follows Coleridge in suggesting that there is "a point at which murder and suicide can become convertible, each in its way an image for the same motive":

> . . . in His vast family no Cain
> Injures uninjured (in her best-aimed blow
> Victorious Murder a blind Suicide).
>
> (*RM,* 10)

In the opening pages of "The Range of Rhetoric," by tracing images of murder and suicide, Burke shows that tracking down motivations in texts is no easy business, that accounting for motivation leads quickly into complex matters that admit of essentialization only at great cost: "The dramatic terms provide a rich context that greatly modifies whatever modicum of suicide may be present in the motivational formula as a whole. But all such important modifications, or qualifications, are dropped when we reduce the complexity to one essential strand, slant, or 'gist,' isolating this one reflexive element as the implicitly dominant motive, an all-pervasive generating principle" (*RM,* 5).

The choice of images of murder and suicide is particularly significant because, to Burke, not all images are equally important. Images of life, death, birth, and killing are particularly rich and salient to our interests, he says (*RM,* 12). By using imagery such as this, Burke is indicating that he wants to apply his methods to complex human experiences. In the *Grammar* this desire led to the fertile section on the dialectic of constitutions. In the *Rhetoric* this led Burke to discuss a variety of ways in which rhetorical elements pervade the way we navigate in social hierarchies (including, for instance, the "administrative rhetoric" of Niccolo Machiavelli, the use of manners as symbolic appeal in the sixteenth century Italian court, and "theological elements" in status systems in bourgeois society). Burke approached his task differently than did some analytical philosophers of the 1930s and 1940s and some 1950s philosophers of language, who left complex human experiences to implications drawn from their analyses of the most far-reaching abstractions. As Hannah Arendt did later in the 1950s and 1960s, Burke engaged complicated social structures from the start. It is not surprising that both were attacked; directly criticizing communism or portraying Adolf Eichmann as the embodiment of the banality of evil did not confer upon Burke or Arendt the immunity attendant to logical abstractions and hypothetical situations. Certainly, though, Burke uses rarefied abstractions as a beginning and endpoint of many discussions. For instance, in *A Grammar of Motives* he uses "ultimate" terms to uncover what in the *Rhetoric* he calls a "dramatic equivalent for an 'entelechial' pattern of thought" (*RM,* 19).[3] Murder and suicide are indeed ultimate conceptions, for what in the realm of human experience, other than the translation of the soul, could be more ultimate than slaying? But in a very real way he is saying also that the abstractions we derive from literary forms can reveal much about motives operating in the dearest of human experiences.

Another way to think about this imagery is that Burke begins the *Grammar* by using ultimate terms as a way into the *logic* of transformation; in the *Rhetoric* he invokes images of slaying as a way into the logic of the *rhetoric* of transformation. "The imagery of slaying," Burke tells us, "is a special case of transformation" (*RM,* 20); in addition, "a poet's identification with imagery of murder or suicide . . . is, from the 'neutral' point of view, merely a concern with *terms for transformation in general*" (*RM,* 11). Thus, murder and suicide are ultimate examples of the transformations among symbols occurring in human activities, expressions, and institutions that serve social and political needs.

Echoing what he argues in the *Grammar,* Burke notes that a transformation is usually "a development *from* one order of motives *to* another" (*RM,* 11). Of course, in the *Grammar* he discusses transformations among terms basic to the philosophic schools, whereas in the *Rhetoric* he discusses principles basic to social and political hierarchies. Accusations have been made that all the turns Burke wends through in discussing transformation and in developing and applying his analytical methods for understanding it are merely language games, even verbal tricks. Those who agree should consider that the transformations Burke speaks of are serious and sometimes even grave. In the opening pages of the *Rhetoric* he points to instances of transformations that benefited the psychological health of authors and possibly some readers. Much later in the *Rhetoric,* Burke's discussion of Baldassare Castiglione's *Book of the Courtier* points out that courtship was a rhetoric of transformation vital to the maintenance of a large-scale sociopolitical structure. As important as these two examples are, Burke shows how chillingly far matters of transformation take the critic who is willing to note its darker reaches: "The Nazis, locating the *transformandum* in the whole Jewish people as their chosen vessel, gave us a 'scientific' variant: genocide" (*RM,* 13). Of course, Burke makes a similar point in "The Rhetoric of Hitler's 'Battle,'" though in that essay he is interested primarily in the psychological mechanism of scapegoating and how such a psychology can be used for rhetorical ends. In the early pages of the *Rhetoric* he is more interested in establishing the rhetoric of transformation's scope regarding different orders of motivation.

identification + slaughter = 2 keys for rhetoric

Burke indicates that transformations—particularly among orders of motivation—are often matters of *transcendence* among ideas essential to social and political structures. Although transcendence is not the only kind of transformation Burke analyzes in the *Rhetoric*, it dominates because one of the most common forms of transformation is the creation of a transcendent category to dissolve a dialectical pair. Burke was interested in this kind of transcendence early on (for instance, in *Permanence* and the "Dictionary of Pivotal Terms"), and it takes a prominent place in the *Grammar*. In the *Rhetoric* he makes the same point early on by referring to *Samson Agonistes*. Transcendence is central to the *Rhetoric* because it is central to how we create social and political structures and how we use rhetoric to stake a place in that hierarchy. Murder and suicide in literary masterworks are certainly far afield from social advancement of the sort championed by Castiglione; yet, in Burke's view, they are but extreme or ultimate examples of transformation and transcendence, the study of which he presumes will help us better understand social estrangement.

Burke begins the *Grammar* with what he calls a "representative anecdote" (drama), an image, story, or situation that captures the essence of a realm of experience and can be used to form the basis of an analytical method (dramatism). Despite the fact that he hardly mentions representative anecdotes in the *Rhetoric*, slaughter serves that function, "because invective, eristic, polemic, and logomachy are so pronounced an aspect of rhetoric" (*RM*, 20). Some scholars have criticized Burke's view of rhetoric as too aggressive and uncooperative.[4] Unfortunately, they misconstrue how Burke thinks. Familiarity with Burke's early writings makes clear that he often uses the method of "perspective by incongruity" that he argues forcefully for in *Permanence and Change*. The key term of the *Rhetoric*, Burke tells us, is identification; yet the representative anecdote is slaughter—a seeming contradiction. Burke wants to demonstrate that there is identification in activities that might initially be taken to be far from identification. In "The Range of Rhetoric," Burke says that "to begin with 'identification' is, . . . though roundabout, to confront the implications of *division*. . . . Identification is compensatory to division" (*RM*, 22). An analogous problem arises in the interpretation of drama as a representative anecdote of dramatism. Some scholars interested in dramaturgical theory believe that dramatism is just one example of a group of critical theories that hold that human social behavior is best understood as theatrical performance. An irony of Burke's thinking—stemming from his perspective by incongruity—is that he uses drama (action and doing) to explain philosophical systems (thinking). In any event, just as Burke argues for the "dissolution of drama" in the *Grammar*, he argues in the *Rhetoric* that his interests extend well beyond slaying. Shifting to a higher level of generalization, he explains, "enables us to transcend the narrower implications of this imagery, even while keeping them clearly in view" (*RM*, 20).

One purpose of these opening pages of the *Rhetoric* is to establish the representative anecdote. Another is to introduce us to "identification," a concept which, to many admirers of Burke, competes with dramatism as his great contribution. Many readers focus on the idea that identification is a matter of bridging gaps, of finding some common ground between persons who differ on some issue. Although that certainly is one element of identification as Burke conceives it, he introduces the concept because it raises a problem fundamental to life in social hierarchies: whenever we say we identify with an idea, a principle, a philosophy, a person, or a group, we are necessarily saying that we are divided from something else. Identification implies division. Likewise, division implies identification. This is the rhetorical counterpart of the "alchemic moment" that Burke speaks of in the *Grammar*.

The idea of identification, in various forms, pervades Burke's entire corpus, though in his early works it occupies a relatively minor place and is more prototypical than archetypal. It is tempting to say that in the early works Burke gropes for an idea that comes to fruition in the later works. To some extent that is so; however, a more accurate description would be that in the early works Burke more clearly differentiates social and political factors from literary aesthetics. If he was groping for anything, it was the synthesis of the literary and sociopolitical. By the time he was writing *The Philosophy of Literary Form,* the synthesis had matured. By the late 1940s and 1950s, when he was writing the *Grammar* and the *Rhetoric,* the synthesis was as singular as Burke would ever make it.

As his career progressed from his essays of the 1920s, Burke analyzed various social, political, and aesthetic concerns as if they were matters of identification, although he did not use the term. By 1937 he had begun to use the term in a few of his published writings, the longest and most significant of which is "Identity, Identification," a section of "The Dictionary of Pivotal Terms" in *Attitudes toward History.* There, Burke argues that identity involves a person establishing relations or connections to a variety of "manifestations beyond himself " (*ATH,* 263). Burke is not clear on exactly what a "relation" or "connection" is, though *Attitudes* in its entirety showcases dozens of them. (This method of explanation occurs elsewhere in Burke's writing, notably in the *Grammar;* in regard to why he chose act, scene, agent, agency, and purpose for the pentad, Burke comments that the *Grammar* "itself is offered as the answer.") In *Attitudes,* Burke suggests that identity is formed in relation to environment—not sui generis, disconnected from the world. Although Burke was not particularly interested in defining identity and identification or exploring their theoretical implications, he was keen to discuss how these concepts figure into the way the particular social, political, and economic environment of 1930s affected the way Americans saw themselves. To begin with, he says in *Attitudes,* "the so-called 'I' is merely a unique combination of partially conflicting 'corporate we's'" (*ATH,* 264). He suggests that businesses so pervade our lives that they have become some of the most significant bodies conditioning our identifications. Burke goes on to examine a variety of ways in which various identifications we make conflict with one another and how we resolve those contradictions by creating new identifications. In this early statement about identification Burke is interested in how large-scale social structures can pervert our sense of self, distort our values and goals, and impair the means we have developed to resolve the problems we face.

Identification is even more prominent in *The Philosophy of Literary Form,* most tellingly in "The Rhetoric of Hitler's 'Battle'" (1939) and "The Philosophy of Literary Form" (1941). Although Burke hardly uses the terms "identity" and "identification" in "Hitler's 'Battle,'" the whole point of the essay is to show how one medicine man performed his identification "magic" at a particular historical moment. Burke again indicates that identification is a matter of drawing connections or relations; however, he seems to be more concerned with identification as a mechanism for the creation and cohesion of a social body. At one point Burke goes so far as to describe this cohesion as a "sense of 'community'" (*PLF,* 217). For Germany in the 1930s, Burke asserts, one mechanism for the animation and propagation of nationalistic unity was the cultivation of identifications through propaganda based on a "bastardization of fundamentally religious patterns of thought" (*PLF,* 219). In "The Philosophy of Literary Form," Burke turns to an examination of the way a poet, as a manipulator of language, cultivates identifications. In fact, he uses the term "medicine man" again, this time in reference to the poet (*PLF,* 64). Evidently, in Burke's view the "magic" of a poet is not so different from that of a Hitler. In "The Philosophy of Literary Form," Burke argues that art is effective as symbolic action when a text prompts the reader to relive experiences. This reliving of experiences occurs in part because the reader and author participate in social structures of meaning that have elements in common. In Burke's view, the reliving of experience is a form of identification. Since Burke argues that the structure of meaning is objectively present in the structure of the text, "The Philosophy of Literary Form" is largely a study of how literature is a medium for effecting identification.

In "The Range of Rhetoric," Burke uses identification the same way he does in his earlier books—as a general orienting concept to be fleshed out in the analysis of literature, politics, and human motives. He goes on to explore some theoretical aspects of the concept in the middle section of the book, "Traditional Principles of Rhetoric," but in the early pages of the *Rhetoric* he is more concerned about focusing readers' attention on his overall perspective and the kinds of problems he wants to address. In the subsection "Identification," Burke first argues that the images of killing cited previously were examples of identification (slaying is a "special case" of identification). He concludes the section by explaining "what difference it makes" to conflate slaying and identification (*RM*, 20). In fact, it makes *quite* a difference: "We need never deny the presence of strife, enmity, faction as a characteristic motive of rhetorical expression. . . . Yet we can at the same time always look beyond this order, to the principle of identification in general, a terministic choice justified by the fact that the identifications in the order of love are also characteristic of rhetorical expression" (*RM*, 20).

Through most of the rest of "The Range of Rhetoric," Burke elaborates on what he means by identification. In "Identification and 'Consubstantiality,'" for example, he makes it clear that in the realm of rhetoric, identification is the counterpart of "substance." As was pointed out earlier, the "paradox of substance" was part of the conceptual foundation of dramatism (the *Grammar,* Burke says, "dealt with the universal paradoxes of substance"); likewise, a paradox of identification is foundational to the rhetoric of motives, for identification is closely aligned with division (to base a rhetoric on identification is "to confront the implications of *division*"). "If men were wholly and truly of one substance," Burke observes, "absolute communication would be of man's very essence . . . not an ideal" (*RM*, 22). Burke also indicates that the paradox of identification is its animation: "In pure identification there would be no strife. Likewise, there would be no strife in absolute separateness, since opponents can join battle only through a mediatory ground that makes their communication possible, thus providing the first condition necessary for their interchange of blows. But put identification and division ambiguously together, so that you cannot know for certain just where one ends and the other begins, and you have the characteristic invitation to rhetoric" (*RM*, 25). Thus, like substance, identification implies that X is simultaneously X and not-X. At one point Burke says that identification and division are compensatory; at another he says that they are ironic counterparts. I tend to think that they are but different modes of presentation of a single idea.[5]

Burke's insight here is significant, for at the core of his view of rhetoric he sets up a conceptual distinction that once again cuts across the bias of traditional categories. Some recent critics of Burke charge that his rhetoric is purely about the divisions that necessarily ensue in hierarchy, and that his rhetorical theory is hopelessly flawed and misdirected because he assumes that hierarchy and division are essential elements of rhetoric.[6] Eschewing such ontological assumptions, these critics believe that a better rhetorical theory would be based on concepts of cooperation and equality. Perhaps these critics have not carefully read Burke. In *Permanence and Change,* Burke says he champions a communist corrective in part because of the particular social and economic conditions prevailing in the late 1920s and early 1930s. Moreover, he says, under different conditions he could easily champion the interests of big business that here he pointedly derides. The same holds true for the *Rhetoric*. Burke would have fashioned a very different rhetoric had other social and economic conditions existed. But even so, as he says in *Attitudes,* "in a sense, all perspectives are 'perspectives by incongruity'" (*ATH,* 269). To the Burkean mind, one idea draws a person into others. One can approach division through identification or identification through division. This is not a singular view of rhetoric, but one adaptable to different social, political, economic, philosophical, and aesthetic conditions—with an end goal of "a better life."

Several subsections that follow "Identification" and "Identification and 'Consubstantiality'" have been largely ignored in analyses of Burke's work and even in discussions of identification. That is unfortunate, for in these sections Burke further indicates how identification is to be used. In "The Identifying Nature of Property," Burke attends to the role of identification in economic matters. This is no coincidence, for Burke frequently follows a conceptual discussion with a discussion of the economic or political significance of that concept. He begins by observing: "Metaphysically, a thing is identified by its *properties.* In the realm of Rhetoric, such identification is frequently by property in the most materialistic sense of the term, economic property" (*RM,* 23–24). As examples of this materialistic sense of identification Burke discusses the "turmoil and discord" that result when economic and noneconomic identifications clash in "man's moral growth," the rhetoric of identification in postwar diplomatic posturing over American aid, and the support of science in postwar military imperialism. Ultimately, his point is that property is one of a class of identifications that evoke feelings of stability because of the singularity or purity of the association (status, reputation, citizenship, and political affiliation are in the same orbit). Associations such as those, Burke points out, lead us to underemphasize other identifications, creating fertile rhetorical opportunities.

If we do indeed have many identifications, Burke next wonders to what extent intellectual activity can be independent of social, political, and economic concerns from which identifications arise. In "Identification and the 'Autonomous'" he argues that identification cannot be reduced to a single factor: "the fact that an activity is capable of reduction to intrinsic, autonomous principles does not argue that it is free from identification with other orders of motivation extrinsic to it" (*RM,* 27). The extrinsic factors Burke mentions are social and economic: "we are clearly in the region of rhetoric when considering the identifications whereby a specialized activity makes one a participant in some social or economic class" (*RM,* 27–28). Burke claims that in this intellectual climate the critic who supports the autonomy of literature is indeed a political conservative.

The possibility of purely autonomous activities is an important concern, for their existence would limit severely the role of identification and the range of rhetoric. If purely autonomous activities exist, then rhetoric becomes a "Neo-Cartesian" influence through emotion, which presupposes subjectivities that remain intact even after "persuasion" has been successful. Burke was responding to a line of thinking that flowered in the twentieth century, half a millennium after its inception in the elevation of logic—at the expense of rhetoric—by Petrus Ramus.[7] In that long line of foundationalist thinking, the discovery of purportedly indubitable foundations of knowledge is taken to be cause for constraining all "true" knowledge to claims that, by application of appropriate methods, are deduced from those foundations. In the early twentieth century the scientific foundationalism of Pavlov and Watson was a great threat to the province of rhetoric—if "true" knowledge is derived from scientific methods, then rhetoric ought to be consigned to the realm of misdirection and deception. A parallel strain of foundationalism occurred in analytical philosophy. In fact, much of the criticism that Burke received, especially from philosophers, centered on the existence of autonomous activities. Even today some critics still debate the universality of dramatism. In contrast, as will be discussed below, Burke categorically declares that rhetoric is based on a kind of truth that is distinct from scientific truth. In any event, much of the discussion after "Identification" concerns whether or not autonomy exists. In "Identification and 'Consubstantiality,'" "The Identifying Nature of Property," and "Identification and the 'Autonomous,'" Burke makes brief arguments against purported autonomous activities. He reserved the next several subsections for the treatment of the most important area purported to be autonomous: science.

In "The 'Autonomy' of Science," Burke claims that the belief that science is autonomous of other activities is often accompanied by the belief that science is an "*absolute* . . . an intrinsically *good* power" (*RM,* 30). At one point Burke call this "a theological function . . . smuggled into a term on its face wholly secular" (*RM,* 30). His argument against the autonomy of science arises out of specific concerns regarding the basis of knowledge. Autonomists, he says, look to "authorities and their precepts"; Burke instead looks to "the nature of things," which he asserts compels one to recognize the extrinsic identifications associated with an activity. In this case, "science takes on the moral qualities of the political or social movements with which it becomes identified" (*RM,* 31). This is no small point. In "'Redemption' in Post-Christian Science," Burke notes the terrible course science can take. "With a culture formed about the idea of redemption by the sacrifice of a Crucified Christ," Burke asks, "just what does happen in an era of post-Christian science, when the ways of socialization have been secularized?" (*RM,* 31). The answer is frightening: genocide. Of course, the twentieth century was a century of genocide—a problem no less relevant as the century drew to a close with nationalism on the upswing worldwide and no reason to believe that Burke was out-of-date in declaring that "there is a high percentage of Fascist motivation in our own society" (*RM*, 35). In "Dual Possibilities of Science," Burke recognizes that science does not necessarily "take on such malign identifications." Even in a Fascist state, he says, there can be good science. However, a "perverted" science is likely to develop when conditions are right—for instance, when the growth of atomic weaponry is paired with messianic obsessions over national security. Burke was responding to political conditions prevalent right after World War II, but was his admonition any less relevant when the Reagan administration was building arsenals and funding billions of dollars for Star Wars technology in order to keep the Soviet "evil empire" in check? Burke admonishes us that despite whatever good intentions scientists and others might have, science is tainted when justified by "war potential." He charges that ultimately the ideology of the autonomy of science is so powerful that even if its adherents admit that "a faulty political structure" results in "a correspondingly perverted science," they would "be outraged if you follow out the implications of their own premises" (*RM*, 29–30). The point overall is that even in the best case for an autonomous activity, extrinsic identifications are part of the nature of the activity and provide a rhetorical context for the promulgation of the alleged autonomy.

In the last four subsections of "The Range of Rhetoric," Burke continues to delineate issues to which his rhetoric of motives should apply. In "Ingenious and Cunning Identifications," by briefly citing examples from psychological theory, politics, and literature, Burke indicates that identification may be unconscious or unintentional. "One can systematically extend the range of rhetoric," he notes, "if one studies ... terms which may not be directly imposed upon us from without by some skillful speaker, but which we impose upon ourselves, in varying degrees of deliberateness and unawareness" (*RM*, 35). The idea that *identification* extends to the unconscious is not particularly remarkable; however, Burke is talking about rhetorical discourse in general. Since rhetoric is traditionally grounded in explicit reasoning and overt argumentation, the positing of unconscious identification is an important expansion of rhetoric beyond its traditional bounds. Though identification is central to the rhetoric of motives, Burke devotes only this two-page section to the expansion of rhetoric beyond reason. There are three reasons for this. First, as stated before, the discussion of identification is more a conceptual prolegomenon than a theoretical end in itself. Second, much of "The Range of Rhetoric" covers some of that ground anyway, albeit unsystematically. Third, in this subsection Burke seems more interested in pointing out that the structures of feeling and meaning the listener brings to a text subconsciously are important parts of identification. When at times Burke called his *Motivorum* project a "sociology of knowledge," he was saying that sociology cannot ignore the subconscious aspects of communicative behavior. As in much of "The Range of Rhetoric," Burke simply was not concerned about creating a systematic foundation for his rhetoric.

As Burke moves toward concluding "The Range of Rhetoric" ("Rhetoric of 'Address' [to the Individual Soul]" and "Rhetoric and Primitive Magic"), he pushes the limits of rhetoric by positing that various mental activities—for example, reflections about morals, self-aggrandizing rationalizations, Freudian dream work, the tangle of id/ego/superego, hysteria, the neurotic dance seizures of the Tanala of Madagascar, and Navaho witchcraft—are rhetorical in that each is "addressed" to an "audience." On moral choices, he claims that when we ponder a moral choice, our internal reflection is tantamount to "a parliamentary wrangle" in which many voices argue until a course of action is decided upon. On the subconscious, Burke asks, "What could be more profoundly rhetorical than Freud's notion of a dream that attains expression by stylistic subterfuges designed to evade the inhibitions of a moralistic censor?" (*RM*, 37). On magic, which is introduced also to continue the analysis of science, Burke analyzes the view of language in Ernst Cassirer's *Myth of the State.* Cassirer holds that primitive magic is not only a defective form of science, but antithetical to it. "In this scheme," Burke says, "'rhetoric' has no systematic location" (*RM*, 41). Cassirer's "dialectic of simple antithesis," Burke charges, cannot account for political discourse or any kind of rhetoric: "Now, the basic function of rhetoric, the use of words by human agents to form attitudes or to induce actions in other human agents, is certainly not 'magical.' If you are in trouble, and call for help, you are no practitioner of primitive magic. You are using the primary resource of human speech in a thoroughly realistic way. Nor, on the other hand, is your utterance 'science,' in the strict meaning of science today, as a 'semantic' or 'descriptive' terminology for charting the conditions of nature from an 'impersonal' point of view, regardless of one's wishes or preferences. A call for help is quite 'prejudiced'; it is the most arrant kind of 'wishful thinking'; it is not merely descriptive, it is *hortatory*" (*RM*, 41). In Cassirer's view, Burke says, the best one could do is say that political discourse is a modern version of primitive magic and therefore is inferior to scientific discourse. Burke argues that this simple antithesis is wrong and that political discourse "should be handled in its own terms"—as rhetoric, an "art." Moreover, he contends that Cassirer's apology for a science devoid of rhetoric "is really about nothing more nor less than a most characteristic concern of rhetoric: the manipulation of men's beliefs for political ends" (*RM*, 41). "Such considerations," Burke notes, "make us alert to the ingredient of rhetoric in all *socialization,* considered as a *moralizing* process. The individual person, striving to form himself in accordance with the communicative norms that match the cooperative ways of his society, is by the same token concerned with the rhetoric of identification" (*RM*, 39). While pushing rhetoric beyond its traditional bounds into the subconscious and perhaps even the irrational, Burke is quite clear to maintain that rhetoric is *addressed*. This is an important point that is sometimes forgotten by scholars, especially those who think that Burke's "new rhetoric" is a quantum advance beyond classical and even modern conceptions of rhetoric. As much as identification expands rhetoric into new areas, Burke circumscribes the role of rhetoric with traditional principles. In other words, Burke supposes that there are many more instances of *address* than previously imagined, and therefore we must understand better how address works. Debates about the limits of Burke's thinking, such as appear in the communication journals, typically focus on identification and its dimensions, diminishing the element of address. Those who might make much of identification would do well to recognize the dual nature of rhetoric in Burke's approach, for parts 2 and 3 are as much about address as they are about identification.

Burke ends "The Range of Rhetoric" with the "Realistic Function of Rhetoric." Much as he does in "Recalcitrance" at the end of *Permanence and Change,* he reminds us that, despite his sometimes far-flung abstractions and suggestions, rhetoric is about experience, that there is a rhetorical element in many realms of experience heretofore not thought to be rhetorical, and that the various academic disciplines that have developed to explain them overlap in that they all in part explain this rhetorical element. "The term rhetoric," Burke says, "designates a *function* which is present in the areas variously covered by" terms such as "'magic,' 'witchcraft,' 'socialization,' 'communication,' and so on" (*RM,* 44). The positing of a rhetorical function, whatever that might be, is noteworthy. It is difficult, if not impossible, to name a rhetorical theorist before Burke who conceived of rhetoric quite this way. Burke goes on to reassert that the rhetorical function is not subject to the standards of truth used in science. However, he reminds the reader that all knowledge and action are not reducible to rhetoric—that rhetoric concerns "the *persuasive* aspects of language, the function of language as *addressed,* as direct or roundabout appeal to real or ideal audiences, without or within" (*RM,* 43–44). Rhetoric "falls in an area of deliberation that itself draws upon the resources of rhetoric; it is itself a subject matter belonging to an art that can 'prove opposites' . . . [on] a wavering line between peace and conflict" (*RM,* 44–45).

Having ended his review of several areas not usually thought to be rhetorical, Burke turns to classic conceptions of rhetoric. However, he quickly introduces theorists whose works are typically not deemed part of the canon of rhetorical theory.

"Traditional Principles of Rhetoric." In the middle section of the *Rhetoric*—almost half the book—Burke turns his attention to "varying views of rhetoric that have already prevailed," beginning with an examination of some of the ways rhetoric has been conceptualized in the West since its first formulations in ancient Greece

(*RM,* 46). He then goes well beyond the classic statements to texts which, though not in the rhetorical canon, he assumes are relevant to understanding a rhetoric of motives. These texts bear upon rhetoric because they demonstrate a variety of ways in which ideas are formed and ideology is conceptualized, defended, and propagated. In surveying these traditional and nontraditional texts, Burke demonstrates that various conceptions of rhetoric are reflections of the social, economic, political, and intellectual conditions under which they arise. He shows, too, that a view of rhetoric ripples through social, economic, political, and philosophical thought. Throughout much of "Traditional Principles of Rhetoric," Burke is especially concerned about how social and class differences shape the way we think and act (hence, his focus on ideology). Still stretching the limits of rhetoric, he even finds rhetorical elements in mystical thought and spirituality, arguing ultimately that nature "*contain[s] the principle of speech*" (*RM,* 180). By the end of "Traditional Principles of Rhetoric" it is clear that, for Burke, rhetoric is profoundly one with our thoughts and deeds. It is important to keep in mind that Burke does not just provide an analysis of the concept of rhetoric; he also analyzes the many kinds of rhetorical tactics people use in an effort to manage identification and division.

Although parts of the middle section of the *Rhetoric* are roughly chronological, Burke does not hesitate to jump from one era to another in order to tease out an idea. In doing so, he introduces an astonishing array of thinkers, including ancient and modern philosophers, social theorists, scientists, political economists, psychologists, politicians, novelists, and more. He reveals an overall sense of evolution in rhetorical theory but also that the basic situations giving rise to rhetoric as a way to manage social hierarchies occur in new manifestations under new historical conditions.

By turning to the rhetorical canon Burke initially appears less exotic than he seems in "The Range of Rhetoric." Even when he examines in detail several authors who are not generally taken to have much to say about rhetoric (Bentham; Marx; Veblen; de Gourmont; Denis Diderot; François, Duc de La Rochefoucauld; and Blaise Pascal, to name some), he still remains closer to traditional conceptions of rhetoric than when considering the rhetoric of slaying. He nonetheless departs markedly from the traditional views. Whereas Plato, Aristotle, Cicero, Quintilian, and other classical rhetoricians explain how to be persuasive (with persuasion conceived narrowly), Bentham, Marx, de Gourmont, and the other unexpected entrants into the rhetorical orbit explain how ideas and representations are reflections of the social and political circumstances under which they arise (and, conversely, how the circumstances are reflections of ideas). Even more, they focus on how ideas form the bases of ideology. In fact, much of "Traditional Principles of Rhetoric" is a study of ideology and mystification—the process by which certain ideas are held to be universally valid by those who benefit from their espousal—with special emphasis on the rhetorical tactics people use to promote ideas that mystify. In the first two-thirds or so of "Traditional Principles of Rhetoric," Burke for the most part examines the relationship between ideas, ideology, and identification. In the last third he turns to division. (It is important to keep in mind, however, that since identification and division are counterparts, the discussion of one inevitably is a discussion of the other. As the *Rhetoric* proceeds, the differences between identification and division become increasingly indistinct.) With Burke's focus on the relationships between rhetoric, ideology, mystification, and identification and division, his expansion of the traditional principles of rhetoric brings him ever closer to social and political analysis.

In the first half of "Traditional Principles of Rhetoric," Burke suggests that ideology and mystification result from "a 'mystifying condition' in social inequality" (*RM,* 123). To demonstrate that social mystery is pervasive, he analyzes the markedly different views of ideology of Karl Marx and Thomas Carlyle (Marx condemned ideology as illusion; Carlyle celebrated it as a reflection of a divine order in human experience). Despite this difference, Burke contends that the theories of Marx and Carlyle were responses to "the kind of hierarchy that arose in the world with the division of labor" (*RM,* 118–19). Burke introduces other writers who had something to say about ideology, and ultimately this parade of theorists suggests that ideology may be formulated, attacked, and defended in an astonishing variety of ways, perhaps in as many as there are social situations. Accounting for this great variety completely is, of course, an impossible task. Notwithstanding the hopes of those who find in Burke a universal and complete "system," Burke makes it clear that one theory could hardly explain all the situations out of which ideology can arise.

In directing his attention to ideas and ideology, Burke still locates the functions of rhetoric in "identification," "consubstantiality," and "address." Indeed, early on in "Traditional Principles of Rhetoric" he even includes *another* subsection titled "Identification." This second treatment is notably different from the first, for here Burke begins to reveal a remarkable perspective on rhetoric, one largely ignored by those who champion Burke's "new rhetoric": style as the unification of identification and address, and therefore the essence of rhetoric itself.

In the early subsections of "Traditional Principles of Rhetoric," Burke surveys a range of ancient theories of rhetoric in order to determine the essence of traditional conceptions. According to Burke, the rhetorics of Aristotle, Isocrates, Cicero, Quintilian, Saint Augustine, and other classical theorists centered on the concept of persuasion, by which they meant an "inducement to action." Despite this similarity, each author gave rhetoric his own connotation, some of which are: eloquence, the faculty of discovering the persuasive means in a given case, the craftsman of persuasion, the science of speaking well, moving, bending, the art of cheating, power, the art or science that identifies right doing with right speaking, the source of most good things, the outward image of a good and faithful soul, oratory, the "counterpart" of dialectic, ingratiation, and delight. After demonstrating that even subtle differences have significant implications for rhetoric and noting that ancient rhetorics were largely adversarial (they "prove opposites"), Burke suggests that the essential characteristics of rhetoric in these ancient views derive from the fact that "the competitive and public ingredient in persuasion makes it particularly urgent that the rhetoric work at the level of opinion" as opposed to truth (*RM*, 54).

Burke suggests that rhetoric as he conceives it—based on identification—concerns a different kind of opinion: "The kind of opinion with which rhetoric deals, in its role of inducement to action, is not opinion *as contrasted with truth*. There is the invitation to look at the matter thus antithetically, once we have put the two terms (opinion and truth) together as a dialectical pair. But actually, many of the 'opinions' upon which persuasion relies fall outside the test of truth in the strictly scientific, T-F, yes-or-no sense. Thus, if a given audience has a strong opinion that a certain kind of conduct is admirable, the orator can commend a person by using signs that identify him with such conduct. 'Opinion' in this ethical sense clearly falls on the bias across the matter of 'truth' in the strictly scientific sense. . . . Here the important factor is opinion (opinion in the moral order of *action,* rather than in the 'scenic' order of truth)" (*RM*, 54–55).[8] In this view, opinions are derived ultimately not from facts and scientific method, but from the sort of "proof" generated by identification—hence the second subsection on identification, in which he uses Aristotle's ideas about rhetoric to clarify the relations between rhetoric, opinion, truth, and style. The turn to Aristotle makes sense, despite epistemological differences between him and Burke, because Burke found in Aristotle elements quite agreeable to identification. "You persuade a man," Burke says of Aristotle, "only insofar as you can talk his language by speech, gesture, tonality, order, image, attitude, idea, *identifying* your ways with his" (*RM*, 55). Burke points out that in the Aristotelian conception, identification arises out of topical invention (the use of commonplaces) and the employment of tropes and figures of speech (for example, repetition, climax, successive antitheses). Burke makes an important distinction between Aristotle's "common topics" and other discussions of topoi in Aristotle's *Rhetoric* (i.e., the special topics and pathos in II.2 ff.). The common topics lead to persuasion "got by the manipulation of tactical procedures, by following certain rules of thumb for inventing, developing, or transforming an expression, by pun-logic, even by specious and sophistical arguments" (*RM*, 57).[9] Aristotle's other discussions of topoi, Burke says, concern opinions, beliefs, attitudes, states of mind, etc., that can be sources for the invention of persuasive arguments. Thus, the common topics reflect argumentative strategies arising from the structural or logical relations among ideas, whereas the other topoi reflect widely held beliefs or attitudes about humans and our experiences.

The distinction Burke notes is relevant to the purposes here because figurative language, as he explains it, operates much like the common topics. Moreover, like the common topics, tropes and figures are content free—a conventional, archetypal manipulation of ideas or words. Of course, a figure or trope does not mean much out of context, but that is exactly Burke's point. Figures and tropes, Burke tells us, are "*functional,* and not mere 'embellishments'" (*RM,* 57). Using the idea of "form" that he first proposed in "Psychology and Form" twenty-five years earlier, Burke contends that figurative language involves some sort of psychological connection between audience, message, and speaker. "Could we not say," Burke suggests, that "the audience is exalted by the assertion because it has the feel of collaborating in the assertion?" (*RM,* 58). Collaboration is the key to style as the engine of identification.

Unfortunately, Burke does not explain just what he means by collaboration or the psychology operating here; in fact, he basically leaves it as an assertion. Most likely his failure to elaborate had several causes. First, this was to be a book about the rhetoric of motives, not the theoretical bases of it. (Indeed, the *Grammar* served the latter purpose, albeit through an examination of logical and philosophical bases.) Second, by the 1950s Burke had largely abandoned the psychological studies that captivated his attention in the early part of his career. Third, he had made the case before in *Counter-Statement* and *The Philosophy of Literary Form.* Fourth, and perhaps most important, the point he was trying to make about style would be either patently clear to some readers or, to the skeptical, amenable to proof only by an exhaustive case, if at all. This is similar to the stance Wayne Booth takes in *Modern Dogma and the Rhetoric of Assent* for his anti-Cartesian "rhetoric of assent." Booth contends that it is practically impossible to convince a hardcore "scientismist" or "irrationalist" that his position is untenable. Besides holding positions that are impossible to falsify, proponents of these views hold them as matters of faith. Booth laments that the best you can do is make your case and hope that those amenable to change will alter their views. Using a similar psychological basis of style, Burke, like Booth, makes an exhaustive case through many examples of psychological aspects of identification. Burke even argues that symbol use and language are defining features of the human mind.[10]

The idea that style is central to rhetorical invention is an important distinction, for it contravenes the way we view style generally and scholarship about Burke. Most people today continue to think of style as either mere aesthetic embellishment or as an aesthetic element that imbues communication with a kind of magical propagandistic power—in both cases, part of an emotional realm distinct from reason and opposed to it. Writers on Burke by and large seem to think that identification is either a state of affairs in which values are shared or the actual process of sharing values. According to Burke's use of the term, these are indeed aspects of identification. Yet Burke is saying much more. By aligning style with identification and topical invention, Burke is contending that it is a form of "proof" (πίστις, *pistis,* a means of persuasion, an argument). As such, persuasion arises in large part out of style, not because style makes thought generated independent of it more palatable or effective, but because style is at one with the thought basic to a persuasive message. Even Burke was not fully clear on this when writing the *Grammar* and the *Rhetoric.* In an addendum to the *Grammar,* Burke notes that he has "found one modification [of the pentad] useful for certain kinds of analysis," the addition of the term "attitude" (*GM,* 443). Burke describes "attitude" as the "manner" or "how" of an act. The term "inflection" might apply. For example, a perky "yes" is worlds apart from a sullen "yes"; the somber attitude of General Eisenhower in his terse "mission accomplished" note to F.D.R. was as much a part of his meaning as was the explicit information transmitted. Because "attitude" can mean many things, and Burke did not elaborate on precisely which kinds of analysis the addition of attitude is useful to, readers must be careful not to assume too much. Yet attitude can be seen as playing a major role in all of Burke's works, since he exerted significant effort trying to capture how attitude affects meaning—and style is central to attitude.

The idea that identification and style are part of proof offers Burke's characteristic challenge to be wary of any explanatory system. Style has been part of rhetorical theory for two thousand years. Yet much of what we have learned about it amounts to competing taxonomies. Style is the least satisfactorily explained of the five canons because it is ineffable. We really do not have a clear idea of how style works other than saying of a particular stylistic choice that "it works." Burke has the most sophisticated explanation of style (in "Psychology and Form" and "Lexicon Rhetoricae"), but he still relies much on the unsubstantiated assertion that there is some kind of psychological disposition to respond to certain forms of language in certain ways. For instance, regarding "qualitative form," he says: "We are prepared less to demand a certain qualitative progression than to recognize its rightness after the event. We are put into a state of mind which another state of mind can appropriately follow" (*CS,* 125). Although Burke often mentions mystical thought because mysticism occupies an extreme end of the rationality-irrationality dualism, he seems to have been attracted to mystical thought as a form—whatever its dubiousness— because it explicitly questions an explanatory system. If identification and style are central to invention, and there is this ineffable quality about them, what are we to make of purportedly complete explanatory systems? A good example of this is the *Grammar.* The overall point of the book is that each of the great philosophic schools has just one take on accounting for motives. Even dramatism, by Burke's own admission in "Dissolution of Drama," is not comprehensive. If identification and style are taken seriously, noting Burke's copious analyses of identification and style, it becomes clear that a rhetoric of human motives must be open.

Regarding Burke's thoughts on truth, he tries to clarify this still murky notion of opinion by turning to two traditional literary concepts, image and imagination (by image, Burke means images in poems, literature, speeches, and other forms of symbolic communication). Although image and imagination are not the same, much of what Burke has to say about one applies to the other. There are several reasons why they are relevant to opinion and rhetoric. First, image and imagination have competed with persuasion as the wellspring of rhetoric. Second, image and imagination lie at the nexus of science, poetry, and psychology and therefore have the flavor of opinion about them. According to Burke, "Theories of imagination as a kind of *knowledge,* work best in those areas where poetic and scientistic thought overlap" (*RM,* 78). Third, image and imagination are categories under which "today any representation of passions, emotions, actions, and even mood and personality" are likely to fall (*RM,* 81). The most interesting reason that image and imagination are relevant to opinion is that—according to thinkers such as Longinus, Francis Bacon, and William Hazlitt—imagination has rhetorical functions. Longinus suggests that the "'best use of imagination' in *rhetoric* is to convince the audience of the 'reality and truth' of the speaker's assertions" (*RM,* 79). Bacon defines "rhetoric" as an ability "to apply Reason to Imagination for the better moving of the Will." But for both these thinkers imagination is still subordinate to reason. On the other hand, according to Burke, Hazlitt "prepares the way for [imagination's] modern emancipation from reason when he says that imagination itself 'must be the immediate spring and guide of action'" (*RM,* 83). The point is that imagination can be construed as a place where sensation and reason meet and, therefore, as a basis for judgment and a grounding for motivation. By virtue of this role, imagination is a proper element of "truth."

Burke introduces imagination and image in part because they are an intermediary step to a main concern of the *Rhetoric,* one that will occupy most of "Traditional Principles of Rhetoric": the relationship between rhetoric and ideas. Since at least the sixteenth century, when Petrus Ramus fully divorced logic and rhetoric, dominant strains of thought have held that literary devices and other symbolic representations have little to do with ideas other than being mediums that transmits them. Burke contends that images are not free-floating entities dialectically opposed to ideas (as Kant believed); rather, because images in a poetic work are purposefully ordered, ideas are essential to them. "Behind productive *poetic* imagery, as contrasted with the reproductive imagery of raw sensation," Burke argues, "there are *organizational principles*" that could "be named in terms of *ideas.* . . . An idea can be treated as the *principle* behind the systematic development of an image" (*RM*, 86, 88). Burke is quite clear that images and ideas are not the same; but if we take them to be two separate worlds, with images inferior to ideas, he asks us to recognize that ideas and images have elements in common. One of the goals of the *Rhetoric* is to redeem image and imagination by destroying the hierarchy and consigning idea, image, and imagination to the realm of reason. This is one way in which style has argumentative value. If images and the imagination have a rational component, they can be said to have some argumentative force beyond emotional contrivance, albeit a force not quite the same as that of logic in traditional conceptions. Rhetorical theorists who today promote the "rhetoric of inquiry" and the "rhetoric of science" could benefit from Burke on this matter. They typically reduce a discipline (the sciences and philosophy, in particular) to just a matter of rhetorical argumentation. Since all knowledge is produced through arguments, some say, all knowledge stems from rhetoric. They invert the hierarchy. All academic disciplines, no doubt, are conducted in argument communities. But the reduction of any to just arguers arguing is simply unfair. Instead of inverting the hierarchy, Burke would transcend it. He recognizes that each discipline has particular metaphysical, ontological, epistemological, and methodological assumptions that make it different from other disciplines. And that is just the point—one must understand the assumptions of a discipline and the implications of holding them. Burke uses deep intension as a way to begin to understand extension.

Having established that image, imagination, and rhetoric are grounded in the rational, Burke turns his attention to how imagery promotes ideology. Burke uses Jeremy Bentham, Karl Marx, Oliver Cromwell, Thomas Carlyle, William Empson, Thorstein Veblen, and others as examples of authors who reveal much about ideology. Each supposes a different sense of the relationship between ideas and the material world, and therefore of the role rhetoric plays in establishing, maintaining, and modifying ideology. But in all cases ideology and rhetoric are linked closely. His treatment of ideology commences with Bentham and Marx, two thinkers who condemned ideology as a deception that undermines truth and morality. Then Burke turns to writers who saw some good in ideology.

Burke begins his analysis of ideology with Bentham's views of language and motivation (as seen in *Theory of Fictions, Book of Fallacies,* and *Table of the Springs of Action*). Prior to the *Rhetoric,* Burke cautioned that the ideology of science and the search for a neutral language should not extend beyond certain realms of inquiry (*PC,* 175–78; and "Semantic and Poetic Meaning," *PLF,* 138–67). In particular, he used Bentham as an example to attack the transgression of scientific ideals into nonscientific realms ("Secular Mysticism in Bentham," *PC,* 188–94). What Burke has to say about Bentham in the *Rhetoric* is similar to his comments in *Permanence and Change,* but there are differences that stem from the direction he takes in the *Rhetoric.*

In *Permanence,* Burke criticizes Bentham harshly, deriding his "patient labor of hate" as a radical point of view that borders on the mystical (*PC,* 191). Of course, although Burke accuses Bentham of radicalism, Burke in *Permanence* offers the radical prescription of a "coöperative emphasis," a turn toward a communism, albeit loosely conceived.[11] At the nadir of the Depression, when America was desperate for practicable solutions to grimly visible despair, the charge of mysticism was undoubtedly quite a condemnation. In the *Rhetoric,* Burke is not as interested in attacking Bentham. He certainly is no less skeptical of either the transgression of scientific norms or of the belief that there can be a neutral vocabulary; yet he does not make much of this. He is more interested in explaining how Bentham's theories function ideologically.

In both books Burke concentrates on the implications of Bentham's belief that all language has a metaphorical quality, focusing on the similarities between the scientific views of Bentham and certain aspects of capitalism. In *Permanence,* Burke notes that Bentham hoped to create a method through which we could guard against the metaphors lurking in language. But, Burke observed, "even while guarding against the misguidance of metaphor on one level," Bentham is "simply forcing the covert operation of metaphorical thought to a deeper level" (*PC,* 194). This metaphorical thought, Burke says, "makes moral assumptions without revealing to uncritical listeners the fact that it does so" (*PC,* 189). In particular, Burke notices that Bentham's neutral vocabulary is analogous to money: "Bentham's own entire philosophy of *values* seems to have been framed within the metaphor of *price.* He wanted to perfect a 'moral arithmetic'" (*PC,* 194). In the *Rhetoric,* Burke develops these monetary implications. In a "productive and distributive system" such as ours, Burke says, a neutral terminology "can function as rhetorical inducement to action insofar as it can in any way be used for monetary advantage" (*RM,* 96).

Burke interprets Bentham somewhat differently on another matter. Whereas he previously focused on how Bentham sought a neutral vocabulary designed to reveal and purge assumptions, he now suggests that for Bentham, the analysis of language was a means to promote morally desirable ends. Bentham posited "a systematic withdrawal from the world of appearances . . . after which there may be a return" in which "eulogistic and dyslogistic have changed places, with a *neutral period of transition* between them" (*RM,* 95). This new view of Bentham reflects the evolution of Burke's idea of perspective by incongruity, first treated at length in *Permanence.* In that book perspective by incongruity is largely a matter of contrast—the butting up of one idea against another. In the *Rhetoric,* having gone through *A Grammar of Motives,* Burke has a specific direction that incongruity takes. This does not mean that all perspective by incongruity operates like this, but rather that in the *Rhetoric*, Burke frequently uses this form of perspective by incongruity. The reason for this is that this form of perspective by incongruity is well suited for the analysis of transformation in fluctuant realms such as that between ideas and images. As such, this form of perspective by incongruity can help us better understand how ideology works.

Whether or not Burke's new reading of Bentham is correct is not the concern here; rather, it is that his attention is now directed to examining the role of rhetoric in the maintenance of ideas and ideology. Burke is pointing out that even this extreme version of scientific, anti-ideological thinking is highly ideological in both practice and implication. With this in mind, Burke turns to Karl Marx, who, despite his strongly ideological position, condemned ideology and mystification.

In "Marx on 'Mystification,'" Burke continues with some of the issues he raised in "Rhetorical Analysis in Bentham" but turns to how universal ideas (ultimate terms) can be used for ideological advantage. As was pointed out earlier, universal ideas are concepts that serve as the foundation for a system of ideas, beliefs, values, attitudes, actions, and institutions, serving especially as organizing principles for hierarchicalization. Concepts such as honor, truth, loyalty, rights, liberty, equality, fraternity, duty, and consciousness are universal ideas. In Marx's view, as defining elements of ideologies, universal ideas mask reality: "'ideology' is equatable with illusion, mystification, discussion of human relations in terms like absolute consciousness, honor, loyalty, justice, freedom, substance, essence of man—in short, that 'inversion' whereby material history is derived from 'spirit'" (*RM,* 110). Bentham and Marx differed in what they took to be the ground of ideology. "Where Bentham had looked into extraverbal, situational factors behind rhetorical expressions," Burke says, "Marx imposingly formalized such 'conditional' thinking by linking it with his revisions of the Hegelian dialectic" (*RM,* 103). Despite this difference, both condemn ideology. Marx maintained that property, the division of labor, and their resultant creation of class structure lead to enduring "ruling ideas" that serve the purposes of the ruling classes. Burke points out that in Marxist political economy the analysis of motives is influenced by the assumption that ideas and ideology derive from class conflict: "the Marxist analysis would apparently begin with a principle of division. . . . It admonishes us to look for 'mystification' at any point where the social divisiveness caused by property and the division of labor is obscured by unitary terms" (*RM,* 108). Although both Bentham and Marx condemned ideology as misleading, and both sought to purify speech of ideological influences, Marx's theories were far more complex than Bentham's. By positing that ruling ideas stem from class conflicts, Marx introduced a level of mediation that suggests a more sophisticated sense of how ideology operates and makes Marxism more mystifying than Bentham's theories. "Whatever may be the claims of Marxism as a 'science," Burke says, "its terminology is not a neutral 'preparation for action' but 'inducement to action.' In this sense, it is unsleepingly rhetorical, though much of its persuasiveness has derived from insistence that it is purely a science, with 'rhetoric' confined to the deliberate or unconscious deceptions of non-Marxist apologetics" (*RM,* 101).

When trying to account for the relationship between ideology and human motivation, we have to realize that some theorists applauded ideology. Thomas Carlyle (*Sartor Resartus*) believed that class structures reflected a divine social order rich in class mystery. For him, ideology was good, and the social distinctions that clothing promotes were to be celebrated. So Burke used Carlyle to show another side of the relation between ideas and rhetoric. Yet Burke also used him to expand the notion of class to other forms of social difference. Marx said that universal ideas stemmed from the class distinctions that arose out of the ownership of property and the division of labor. In "Carlyle on 'Mystery,'" Burke suggests that differences not unlike class distinctions result from "*any* pronounced social distinctions, as between nobility and commoners, courtiers and king, leader and people, rich and poor, judge and prisoner at the bar, 'superior race' and underprivileged 'races' or minorities" (*RM,* 115). Social distinctions, he says, are based on "social *principles,*" and each principle "calls for a corresponding rhetoric." It would be too much, of course, to expect Burke to outline all social distinctions and to map upon each its corresponding rhetoric. It is doubtful that such a project, if intended to create a rhetorical calculus, was what Burke hoped for his rhetoric of motives. He sought not to create a taxonomy, but to suggest a heuristic openness regarding the deep and often subtle role of rhetoric in human relations. And this openness allows us to learn as much from Carlyle as from Marx.

"Carlyle on 'Mystery'" is a turning point in "Traditional Principles of Rhetoric," although since Burke does so much at the same time, this is more a matter of emphasis than outright change. Up to this point Burke had examined the meaning of rhetoric and the general sphere to which rhetoric applies— extending the range of rhetoric to a point where it becomes central to that fluctuant realm of image, imagination, idea, and ideology. Now he began to examine a variety of texts in order to provide a sense of the wide range of strategies that are possible when trying to account for motives. Thus, in the rest of "Traditional Principles of Rhetoric," Burke turns to topics such as pastoral identification in Empson, pecuniary motivation in Veblen, obsequiousness in Diderot, the rhetoric of dissociation in de Gourmont, casuistry in Pascal, the "administrative" rhetoric of Machiavelli, and the language of "infancy" in Dante—each author using different rhetorical strategies to account for human motivation. In treating these writers Burke does not abandon his examination of the range of rhetoric, for the study of rhetorical strategy is also a study of the meaning of rhetoric.

As odd as it might seem at first, Carlyle's thoughts on clothing are relevant to rhetoric because he believed that we use clothing rhetorically to move within a social structure. According to Burke, Carlyle uses "clothes as a surrogate for the symbolic in general," a symbolic primarily of class and social distinctions (*RM,* 118). Burke previously focused on the elimination of class distinctions and social hierarchy. With Carlyle, he turned to a different kind of relationship, one sometimes more positive than what Marx supposed: "courtship" between social classes that are "typically masculine" and "typically feminine." Whatever differences exist between classes, in this scheme all classes are thought to benefit by being in the hierarchy—those below cultivate the class above, and those above benefit by having a stable class underneath (*RM,* 115).[12] The idea of courtship between classes led Burke to wonder what sexual imagery can tell us about motives. Courtship, he says, often takes a "form quite analogous to sexual expression: for the relations between classes are like the ways of courtship, rape, seduction, jilting, prostitution, promiscuity, with variants of sadistic torture or masochistic invitation to mistreatment" (*RM,* 115). Likewise, sexual imagery can sometimes be manifestations of these kinds of class relations. Burke finds examples of this in the sonnets of Shakespeare, Oscar Wilde's *The Soul of Man under Socialism,* and Henry James's *The Turn of the Screw.* Regarding *The Turn of the Screw,* for example, Burke argues: "The governess' struggle with the ghosts of her predecessors for the possession of the children is not sexual, as judged by literal tests of sexual appetite. But it is ambiguously sexual, a sexuality surrounded at every point by *mystification*—and we believe that this mystification can be largely explained if seen in terms of one class struggling to possess the soul of another class" (*RM,* 117). Burke is not intent merely on indicating that sexual imagery can represent class distinctions, social mystery, and social courtship. The point is that the situation, plot, and action in literature such as this reveal different ploys, tactics, and strategies (for example) used by one class to achieve its ends in relation to another class.

Having established that a certain kind of imagery can function as a form of courtship between classes, Burke goes on to posit that an entire literary genre can be considered a form of courtship too. Burke uses the pastoral genre as an example, relying on William Empson's seminal analysis in *English Pastoral Poetry.* According to Burke, Empson "is profoundly concerned with the rhetoric of courtship between contrasted social classes. For pastoral, as a literary *genre,* was, in its essence, 'felt to imply a beautiful relation between rich and poor'" (*RM,* 123). Pastoral literature, Burke tells us, offers "a stylistic transcending of conflict" (*RM,* 124). Using pastoral is a way of managing social differences that, unlike the antagonism of Marx or the fawning acceptance of Carlyle, is a rhetoric of politeness, humility, respect, and irony. Burke suggests that this stance allows acceptance of social inequality. The kind of rhetoric that results from this attitude functions to stabilize potentially unstable social formations by giving a reason for social compromise. Whatever tangible results might accrue from making such compromises, Burke observes, the real appeal arises out of the principle of hierarchy that the pastoral manifests: "we are led to feel that the impulse behind such compromises is not merely an underling's fear of a superior, but rather the magic of the hierarchic order itself, which imposes itself upon superior and inferior both, and leads them both to aim at a dialectic transcending their discordancy of status" (*RM,* 124). Put another way, politeness, humility, respect, and irony, among others, are mechanisms through which division can result in identification—an instance of the paradox of identification mentioned earlier.

"The magic of the hierarchic order itself" deserves clarification. In the next three subsections, in his inimitable way, Burke provides that. Beginning with Thorstein Veblen's *Theory of the Leisure Class* as a foil, Burke examines the "dialectical" nature of money and pecuniary motivation to suggest that first principles, as part of a hierarchical order, have a kind of persuasive pull by virtue of their place in that order. As did Thorstein Veblen, Burke recognized that money has an appeal beyond its power to purchase goods and services. But Burke believed that Veblen oversimplified pecuniary motivations. He suggests that if we are truly to understand the power of money as a symbolic order, we must go beyond the associationalism of Veblen's pecuniary emulation to the richer area of dialectic. Ultimately, Burke's dialectical understanding of money is a critique of capitalism and cuts across the ideological principles that distinguish Bentham, Marx, Carlyle, and Veblen.

Burke was particularly interested in the language Veblen used to portray pecuniary motives, arguing that it reveals relationships that cripple the explanatory power of Veblen's theory. According to Burke, the root of the difficulty is that Veblen puts "invidious," "competition," and "pecuniary" in the same orbit, suggesting that pecuniary relations are fundamentally predatory in nature. Burke contends that such a view is an oversimplification that masks "a profounder rhetoric." "There is nothing essentially 'predatory' in the symbolic nature of money," Burke declares; "its nature is in its *dialectical* or *linguistic* function as a 'spiritual' entity, a purely symbolic thing, a mode of abstraction that 'transcends' the materially real" (*RM,* 127). Suggesting that pecuniary emulation and competition are really special cases of imitation, Burke suggests that his own reduction infuses pecuniary motives with more meaning than Veblen's does. This is because the terms "pecuniary," "competition," and "invidious" are conceived by Veblen as scientific terms, whereas "imitation" is conceived by Burke as a dramatistic term (thereby drawing a person into identifications precluded by Veblen's scientism). In contrast to Veblen's stress upon a reductionist scientific vocabulary, Burke addresses "social display itself, rather than the malaise behind it . . . is taken as a basic motive" (*RM,* 129). Burke points out that "men can either crudely imitate one another's actions as revealed on the surface, or subtly imitate the *underlying principles* of such actions" (*RM,* 131).

As a cultural form, money had long interested Burke, and his treatment of it in the *Rhetoric* reflects his evolving interests. Early on, Burke warned of the corrosive effects of the profit motive, in particular as they occur in an industrial, capitalist economy. In *Counter-Statement,* for example, Burke argues for the redistribution of wealth: "technological unemployment must be . . . subsidized from . . . the appropriation of excess profits" (*CS,* 116). And in *Attitudes* he cautions that "money is *per se* an alienating device, leading to impersonality and individualism . . . making drudgery tolerable" (*ATH,* 316). Yet even from these early writings Burke maintained an ambivalent attitude about money and profit, for he believed that the problems resulting from the profit motive occur under specific cultural conditions that are neither necessary nor universal.[13] Whereas the tone of his early work is largely antiprofit and anticapitalist, by the 1940s, when he was writing the *Grammar,* Burke was concerned less with attacking capitalism and more with understanding the role of monetary motives in sociopolitical thought. Technology and money, he argues in the *Grammar,* create a materialist and reductionist "second nature" that serves "so dominant a role in the rationalization of motives" (*GM,* 115, 116). Burke even went so far as to suggest that "capitalism, Fascism, and Communism may all three be variants of the 'monetary psychosis' insofar as all three are grounded in the occupational diversity . . . of technology" (*GM,* 116). Of course, this is quite a departure from the communist corrective he champions in *Permanence* and *Attitudes.* In the *Rhetoric,* Burke explores fundamental rhetorical aspects of money, arguing that the pecuniary motive "should be analyzed as a special case of the linguistic motive," which "involves kinds of persuasion guided not by appeal to any one local audience, but by the *logic of appeal in general*" (*RM,* 129). Readers may wonder just what the relationship is, in Burke's mind, between money and imagery. Indeed, in the *Rhetoric,* Burke is more interested in imagistic elements of money: "money itself is symbolic of general dialectical processes themselves not monetary. It is an aspect of reductive, abstractive, and substitutive resources inborn to symbolism. There is its nature as an imagery interwoven with other images" (*RM,* 135). Perhaps this shift is partially a result of the turn he took in *The Philosophy of Literary Form,* adapted to his new interests in the *Grammar* and the *Rhetoric.*

Having examined a number of ways in which identification can form the basis of ideology, Burke turned to how division can do it. As an intermediary step ("Priority of the 'Idea'" and "A Metaphorical View of Hierarchy"), Burke establishes the conceptual basis that unites identification and division: they meet in entelechial first principles. As complex as this is in itself, Burke's analysis is even more complicated because he is simultaneously working toward three other goals: First, he suggests that the positions of the ideologist and the anti-ideologist are not mutually exclusive: "Would it then be possible to make a distinction that allowed for 'ideology' within limits? That is, could we consider the Marxist critique as usefully limiting the application of the ideological, but not as wholly discrediting it? . . . We are not merely trying to strike a compromise between irreconcilable opponents, or treating the two positions as ideal opposites, with the truth somewhere between. Rather, we are assigning a definite function to each of the positions—and we are saying that, insofar as each performs its function, they are no more at odds than the stomach and liver of a healthy organism" (*RM,* 136–37). Second, he suggests that ideology can be better understood when we recognize that ideas can function entelechially— that is, echoing Spengler, a fundamental idea "participates" in second-order principles that derive from it or are in other ways related to it. He explains this by considering three ways in which first- and second-order principles can be related to organize thought. The most basic is simple association. A "more organic" relationship occurs, he says, through analogical relationships—an "'imaginative' transference of principles from one field to another" (*RM,* 133). John Dewey's notion of "occupational psychosis," which Burke discusses in *Permanence,* is an example of this (see *PC,* 37–49). An even more complicated relationship involves "distinct, specialized expressions, *all derived from the same generating principle, hence all embodying it, without the need of direct 'interactive' borrowing*" (*RM,* 135). Referring to Marxian social evolution, he says: "The hierarchic principle is not complete in the social realm, for instance, in the mere arrangement whereby each rank is overlord to its underlings and underling to its overlords. It is complete only when each rank accepts the *principle of gradation itself,* and in thus 'universalizing' the principle, makes a spiritual *reversal* of the ranks just as meaningful as their actual material arrangement" (*RM,* 138). In this entelechial view, the principle of hierarchy or order is as much a part of ideology as the ideas themselves. This is what Burke meant earlier by the logic of appeal in general.

Burke's third goal for "Priority of the 'Idea'" and "A Metaphorical View of Hierarchy" was to clarify just what he meant about the dialectical nature of money. He used the three levels of analysis just mentioned to explain this. At the accidental level, one can desire something simply because of the status it conveys. This is what Veblen meant in his famous essay on pecuniary emulation. At the level of analogy, Burke returns to Veblen's predation metaphor, which is an analogy distinct from the level of accident: "The 'predatory' instinct which Veblen imputed as the basic motive of the 'leisure class' would seem to be . . . grounded in the natural constitution, but inured through 'education, habit, and accident.' 'Accident,' of course, would refer to linkages of the first sort, the almost automatic response to signs. . . . But the notion of a natural trait, selected, developed, and trained by the conditions of living, implies rather a central core or principle from which all sorts of expressions could radiate" (*RM,* 134). By going to the third level, the entelechial sense in which a fundamental idea participates at once in an entire order of ideas, Burke is offering a critique of capitalism quite at odds with classic Marxism.

One example of an ideology based on division is the "enigmatic" divisiveness which pervades Denis Diderot's *Neveu de Rameau* (first published in 1805 in a German translation by Johann Goethe). "Favoring the movement from royalism towards bourgeois liberty" when such ideas were dangerous, Diderot employed a courtly rhetoric that expressed taboo ideas safely in the king's court. For instance, Diderot represented the antiroyalist views in the character "Him" while putting the royalist ideas in the character "Me" (*RM* 142). "Him," Burke observes, "was a point of convergence that represented both the 'royal' *cause* . . . and its demoralizing *effects*" that culminated in a courtly obsequiousness designed to respond to a state of division (*RM,* 144). Another rhetoric of division occurs in the *Maxims* of François, Duc de La Rochefoucauld (1665). The differences between identification and division become clearer when we compare the rhetoric of the pastoral to the *Maxims.* Both are rhetorics of humility. But whereas the pastoral seeks what Burke describes as a stylistic transcendence of conflict (*RM,* 124), La Rochefoucauld crafted a rhetoric that uses "humility as a ruse, a false submissiveness designed to make others submissive, a self-abasement used for self-exaltation, the 'first stratagem' of pride" (*RM,* 146). According to Burke, La Rochefoucauld has constructed a rhetoric that, while based on individual interests conceived divisively, is expressed in the social terms of a "courtly rhetoric" of "self-love."

A more explicit rhetoric of division appears in Rémy de Gourmont's essay "La Dissociation des Idées" (1899). "Indeed, if we were allowed but one text to illustrate how identification operates in language," Burke notes wryly, "we would select this essay, which is almost sadistically concerned with the breaking of identifications" (*RM,* 150). Burke was attracted to de Gourmont because the idea of dissociation is similar to perspective by incongruity. Burke had reservations about de Gourmont because, as Burke noted along with many other writers, de Gourmont "smuggles in new linkage[s]" that contravene the very purpose of his method to begin with. Nonetheless, Burke saw great value in de Gourmont because his essay demonstrates a variety of ways to reason about abstract ideas in relation to rhetorical invention: "We need not try to persuade ourselves that dissociation is the ultimate in intellectual prowess. . . . But we can make out a strong case for it as a method for helping the initiate experimentally to break free of all topical assumptions, and thereby to cease being the victim of his own naïve rhetoric" (*RM,* 153).

In the *Grammar* and the *Rhetoric,* Burke raises the point that identification and division are counterparts—one implies the other. Near the end of "Traditional Principles of Rhetoric" he begins to explore more fully the implications of this idea. Burke notes that, as thorough a rhetoric of advantage as *The*

Prince is, Machiavelli's theories straddle the line between division and identification. Even though Machiavelli "starts from the principle that men are *universally at odds with one another*" and develops a set of norms by which the ruler can secure and maintain his power in a treacherous and uncooperative world, ultimately "the interests of a feudal ruler will be *nationalistically* identified, thought to represent one state *as opposed to* other states" (*RM*, 165). In the last chapter of *The Prince*, in which the ruler is cast as the salvation of the nation—a people and a state—"by such identification of ruler and ruled, Machiavelli offers the ruler precisely the rhetorical opportunity to present privately acquisitive motives publicly in sacrificial terms" (*RM*, 166). This is division cast in terms of identification. This might be thought of as a lie (or "political expediency"); yet Burke points out that it is a political rhetoric arising out of an "ambiguity of nationalism itself, which to some extent does fit with the ends of universal cooperation, and to some extent is conspiratorial" (*RM*, 166).

The Prince helped Burke return to the problem of action. Machiavelli created an "administrative rhetoric," a rhetoric that "is a mixture of symbolism and definite empirical operations" that can be powerfully symbolic themselves (*RM*, 161). Action-as-rhetoric also figures in medicine, which both in medieval practice and in the twentieth century used traditional persuasive technique, empirical operations, and the mere existence of artifacts to "convince" the patient. "We could observe," Burke notes, "that even the medical equipment of a doctor's office is not to be judged purely for its diagnostic usefulness, but also has a function in the *rhetoric* of medicine" (*RM*, 171). Apparently, in the fluctuant realm between ideas and images, if we are to have a rounded rhetoric of motives, we have to account for nonverbal elements such as the white lab coat or a flotilla steaming toward the Falklands. One implication of the idea of an "administrative rhetoric," which Burke does not address, is how the verbal is affected by the nonverbal.

Burke concludes "Traditional Principles of Rhetoric" with a summation of the major themes in the section. In this middle third of the *Rhetoric,* Burke uses the themes to explore several cuts across the bias of traditional categories (reason/action, idea/thing, idea/image, identification/division, for instance). Burke indeed began the *Rhetoric* with the idea of identification and employed it throughout "Traditional Principles of Rhetoric." Despite what systematizers of Burke assume, the section overall demonstrates that the wide range of rhetorical tactics we employ in accounting for human relations resists systematization—for there is always another relationship between ideas and motives lurking around the corner.

"Order." The third and last section of the main text of the *Rhetoric* comprises almost half the book. Rather than containing major advances on what preceded, much of "Order" goes over ground already covered. Even so, Burke is not simply being repetitive; he focuses on the concept of hierarchy, exploring the extent to which we can push this principle as a central element of rhetoric. Reading this part of the book, we are students in a master class observing the virtuoso. I recall a film of Pablo Casals teaching at a university. Casals critiqued student performances and played the cello. One student played her piece repeatedly, for after each performance Casals said it was not quite right and that she should do it again. He told her that she was playing the cello as if it were merely a cello. Try to make it sing, he urged. It worked. In this final part of the *Rhetoric,* I wonder if Burke is asking of us, as observers of hierarchy in literature and the rhetoric of human motives, to watch him sing. Since much of the material of "Order" was covered earlier by Burke, it is enough to comment on only the aspects that are otherwise noteworthy:

(1) Despite the featuring of difference, division, partisanship, etc., throughout the *Rhetoric,* and even in the opening anecdote of slaying, the overall "paradigm" of rhetoric is courtship between social classes—variously manifested in Carlyle, the pastoral genre, or (as seen in "Order") Shakespeare in *Venus and Adonis* (*RM,* 208–12, 212–21) and Baldassare Castiglione in *Book of the Courtier* (*RM,* 221–33). In analyzing Shakespeare's poem, Burke recommends a "socioanagogic" interpretation: "one should view this poem in terms of the hierarchic motive, or more specifically, in terms of the *social order*" (*RM,* 216). This form of interpretation searches for "implicit identifications" with status and social mystery. Thus, in "Order," Burke reinforces the emphasis on identification and hierarchy—and ultimately suggests that the criticism of human motives ought to focus on social distinctions and the social order that arises out of them. Burke suggests that the analysis of identification and division is limited if we do not ask about identification or division *in terms of what?* And Burke maintains that treating identification in terms of hierarchy and social order leads to a better understanding of the nature of motivation and human relations.

(2) This critical perspective is not just a matter of saying that understanding human motivation has something to do with social hierarchy and order. In fact, Burke is again suggesting a cut across the bias—that rhetoric and social hierarchy mutually inform one another.

(3) In "Order," Burke continues his analysis of motives largely through literary criticism. This perspective arises out of the idea that literature is "equipment for living" that Burke argues for in *Counter-Statement* and *The Philosophy of Literary Form.* Yet, by the time Burke was writing the *Rhetoric,* he had for the most part abandoned the psychoanalytical tone he adopted in "The Philosophy of Literary Form." He more fully reincorporated social and political elements, which characterizes his methods in *Counter-Statement, Permanence and Change,* and *Attitudes toward History.* The general social and political issues remain largely the same, yet now he emphasizes the dialectical nature of sociality, not specific political programs.

(4) In "Pure Persuasion" (*RM*, 267–94)—the final subsection before appended critical pieces—Burke argues that the ideal of pure persuasion can never be obtained. In fact, he says, not only has no method for pure persuasion been discovered that is free of "impure" elements (that is, ideological partisanship), but the idea of rhetoric and persuasion assumes difference. Nonetheless, as an element of analysis the ideal of pure persuasion is extremely helpful to the critic, for it can "supply a principle of interference which, whatever its origin, often has a high ethical value" (*RM*, 271).

(5) However roundabout, Burke sees his rhetoric of motives still within the realm of ethics which early on he understood his theories to be part of. In *A Rhetoric of Motives*, Burke expresses long-standing concerns in new ways.

In sum, Burke in the *Rhetoric* provides all sorts of strategies for living in hierarchies. In so doing, he demonstrates not only that persuasion takes on many complex forms but also that it is marked deeply by tensions and ambiguities arising out of the interpenetration of identification and division. One major way of solving tensions and ambiguities is to appeal to some transcendental—even mystical—conception, for not only does the transcendental embrace elements that are at odds, it satisfies our impulse toward perfection. The reduction to essences and transcendentals forms the basis for whole doctrines of human motivation, which themselves gradually move away from their initial integrative purpose and become fixed as principles of division. Hence, in order to overcome division and strife and work "toward a better life," we must approach the reductive philosophies with an ironic detachment that exults in the way we act symbolically and rhetorically. The study of rhetoric, conceived in this way, is the study of human relations.

The stakes are great. Burke's general concerns in the late 1940s about language, rhetoric, and their relation to social life are no less relevant today. When American culture was settling into the sureties of postwar growth, he was exploring ambiguities, vagaries, and the contingent, cautioning that it is all too easy, in ascribing motives, to be seduced by the obvious and self-serving. Today's problems may not be the same ones Burke was concerned about in 1950, but there are similarities. As the welfare system on which so much is dependent seems poised to collapse, the demonizing of the welfare recipient escalates. Regardless of whether or not a person supports public welfare (either in principle or concerning any particular program), he or she should be troubled by the simplistic rhetoric sweeping the country. As citizens increasingly fear crime—and feel helpless to do anything about it—the characterization of criminals as animals becomes harsher. It is possible to be hard on crime without dehumanizing the criminal. In these two examples we find elections being won by hard-line, reactionary candidates espousing simplistic notions of why persons act the way they do. Spokesmen preened in Washington think tanks (virtually all of which today are extremely conservative and funded by multi-national corporations to promote self-serving ideas and policies) dominate the national news media, attenuating motives to what Burke in *Attitudes toward History* calls "heads I win, tails you lose" (*ATH*, 260–63). In particularly worri-some cases, simplistic notions are masked by seemingly sophisticated language. In California, for example, "balancing the budget" is offered as the problem, whereas the rights and privileges of illegal immigrants are the real issues. Nationwide in the affirmative action debates, the meanings of "discrimination" and "equality" are contested hotly when the issue is really the shrinking pie.[14] "School choice" is promoted when the issues are really the collapse of public school systems, a growing anti-intellectualism in America, and closer alignments between the government, business, and education. In all these examples propo-nents purport to make their cases one way, but other motives lurk behind.

This is not to suggest that Burke was a debunker, for he was not particu-larly happy with the debunker's view of the world (see "The Virtues and Limitations of Debunking" in *The Philosophy of Literary Form*). Nor was he a deconstructionist. Rather, he believed that our documents and institutions con-tain clues to our motivations, that motivations occur in complex "motivational schemes," and that the methods of rhetoric can tell us a lot about motives. Moreover, as a man who for a lifetime pondered the many ways we can account for our positions—and resisted all explanatory schemes as partial at best, including those of the great philosophers—Burke believed that we should exult in the many ways language is used and that we should study and understand language in all its richness. To that end, the *Rhetoric* is as much a compilation of tactics or topoi as it is an analysis of rhetoric in general or of particular social issues.

Working out the application of Burke's ideas to our problems today would not only help us better understand our situation, it would demonstrate how Burke meant his ideas to be used beyond what is widely taken to be the purpose of Burkean criticism—either the identification of the pentadic term key to a speech, or the setting forth of a metaphysical, ontological, and epistemological relativism, or a theory of rhetorical deconstruction. But such a task would be an exercise in criticism, not in the analysis of the development of Burke's thought. Thus, in this chapter, while some of these applications are pointed out, their development is left to the reader, who can look to the *Rhetoric* for hints on how such criticism might proceed. Burke provides many examples to emulate.

8

The Rhetoric of Religion and Language as Symbolic Action
Burke in the 1950s and 1960s

▬▬▬▬▬▬▬▬▬▬▬▬▬▬▬▬▬▬▬▬▬▬ ■ ▬▬▬▬▬

Burke's career—the various forces in his life, his intellectual and political predilections, and his strengths and weaknesses overall—showed remarkable consistency from the 1920s through the publication of *A Rhetoric of Motives* in 1950. It is true that his career fell into phases driven by different concerns. The early aestheticist period of *Counter-Statement* gave way to the "united front" period that came to fruition in *Attitudes toward History*. Then *The Philosophy of Literary Form,* which returned to literature, ushered in Burke's monumental study of human relations in *A Grammar of Motives* and *A Rhetoric of Motives*. Yet throughout, Burke kept returning to basic concerns that almost bordered on obsession: a suspicion of science and technology, a favoring of action over motion, a love of literature and the mysteries of language, the belief that language defines human experience, a terminological approach to studying ideas and words, preoccupations with "tracking down implications" and "association," the use of ultimate terms and teleological arguments, a scrambling of intellectual categories, and a penchant for suggestion at the expense of systematic exposition. Perhaps most important was his passion for ameliorating human problems through creating what he took to be more ethical and effective approaches to understanding language and human relations—from the start and throughout, a profoundly social and political sensibility that was sometimes disguised by other concerns. Despite personal turmoil and changes over the decades, Burke was remarkably consistent on a personal level. An insomniac, he wrote obsessively. He almost desperately wanted to be heard, be accepted, and gain a following. Reading his letters to his mentor and confidant, James Sibley Watson Jr., reveals two Burkes: one is sure of his ideas, almost arrogant; the other Burke is plagued by doubt, uncertain about whether he is right and how he will be received. (While a fellow at the Center for Advanced Study in the Behavioral Sciences at Stanford in 1957, he kept quiet most of the time for fear that he would make a fool of himself.) After all, throughout his career, this man who lacked academic credentials relished standing on the fringe. Consistent too was his critical reception. His books were often misunderstood, his ideas used piecemeal or for purposes not Burke's. Given all this, Burke was remarkably consistent in that for a period of thirty years he basically tried to make the same point again and again. His genius lay in his ability to use new methods to explore new aspects of the aesthetic, rhetorical, social, and political issues that drove him from the start.

After 1950, in a way not much changed. Burke's great undertaking was his study of human relations, the *Motivorum* project, and the bulk of his career in criticism after the *Grammar* and the *Rhetoric* was spent filling it out by returning to literary criticism that included theoretical essays and analyses of specific texts and authors. Burke had intended to complete his trilogy on human relations with "A Symbolic of Motives," but it never appeared in print. At one point he even reported to Malcolm Cowley that he was finishing up this work and taking notes on a fourth volume, having decided that a trilogy was not enough. We can only guess as to what a published "Symbolic of Motives" would have been like and what direction he would have taken had he continued on after that. Perhaps the completed work would have been followed by extensions of his ideas into new subject matter. In any event, in the 1950s and 1960s Burke focused his attention on exploring how language operates generally by analyzing the ways words and symbols function in specific literary texts—and what a focus it was. As much as Burke thought in many of the same ways as he had before the *Rhetoric,* there is a sense that the 1950s and 1960s were almost a frenzy of activity. Burke toiled over a number of projects, often at the same time, producing volumes of words (some of which got published, some not). In 1959 he complained to Watson about his own "obsessive note taking" when working on Freud. In a brief survey of Burke's career for the *New York Times Book Review,* Richard Kostelanetz credits him with "a mind that cannot stop exploding."[1] Soon after *A Rhetoric of Motives,* Burke began in one way or another working on his "Symbolic of Motives," a major work on poetics that never appeared in grand form, verbal action in Saint Augustine's *Confessions,* and the first three chapters of Genesis. These works evolved over a period of years and were reworked again and again.

After *A Rhetoric of Motives,* Burke published two major works of criticism: *The Rhetoric of Religion: Studies in Logology* (1961); and *Language as Symbolic Action: Essays on Life, Literature, and Method* (1966). *The Rhetoric of Religion* had a long gestation. For a few years in the 1950s Burke worked up ideas on Saint Augustine and, initially as a separate project, Genesis. Eventually he realized that both pieces fit together well and presented them in a series of lectures at Drew University in 1957 and 1958. He then worked these into essay form and at various points considered publishing them in different journals and putting together various combinations of these and other essays into a book or two. In 1957 the *Nation* was interested in publishing his work on Genesis, as was John Crowe Ransom (though not for the *Kenyon Review*). In 1958 the *Hudson Review* was interested in his work on poetics (again, so was Ransom). In addition several press editors wanted to put something out. The earliest reference to what we now know as *The Rhetoric of Religion* was in June 1957, when Burke indicated to Watson his intentions for the book.

In *The Rhetoric of Religion,* Burke considers the extent to which "theological principles can be shown to have usable secular analogues that throw light upon the nature of language" (*RR,* 2). Burke uses common theological concepts such as order, guilt, sacrifice, the Fall, and Redemption—and how these form "cycles of terms"—to analyze the relationship between rational thought and narrative expression (a distinction, he says, between the "logical" and the "temporal"). This ultimately ends up being a large-scale investigation of the subtleties of the idea of order. Burke demonstrates that religious texts, which sometimes are as thoroughgoing expressions of order as can be, nonetheless contain ambiguities which arise when logical relationships are expressed in narrative sequences. Whereas some contemporary critical theorists would see these ambiguities, especially when contradictions, as undermining the meaning of a text, Burke suggests that they are subtle rhetorical resources that are exploited for powerful rhetorical effect. Of course, since he is drawing analogies between religious and secular language, Burke is suggesting that the rhetorical resources found in theology exist in language generally. Some readers have taken this to mean that all language is fundamentally theological. Burke means nothing of the sort. Analogies operate in two directions. Calling theology "words about God" and logology "words about words" (*RR,* 1), Burke says that "the relation between theology and logology should not be conceived simply as proceeding in one direction" (*RR,* 36). Just as theological language can reveal something about language in general, secular language is a window into theology. Readers of Burke's earlier books will remember that the ambiguities of order figure highly in the *Grammar,* in the general sense that he is looking for "terms that clearly reveal the strategic spots at which ambiguities necessarily arise" and more specifically in the dialectic of constitutions. It is also important to remember that Burke uses the last third of *A Rhetoric of Motives* to explore the ways language is used to navigate in social hierarchies (which themselves manifest order in a variety of ways). The second major book that Burke published after the *Rhetoric* is *Language as Symbolic Action,* largely a collection of articles that appeared in academic journals and literary magazines in the 1950s and 1960s. In this anthology Burke combines theoretical essays on the nature of language and critical analyses of particular works and authors, such as Shakespeare, Goethe, and Coleridge. Developing ideas from "The Philosophy of Literary Form" in light of dramatism, Burke considers how the temporal linearity of narration and the atemporal "circularity" of logic shade into one another in literature and drama rather than in religious texts. *Language as Symbolic Action* marks Burke's return to relatively straightforward literary criticism, such as he produced for *Counter-Statement* and *The Philosophy of Literary Form.* In *The Rhetoric of Religion,* Burke treats Saint Augustine's *Confessions* and the first three chapters of Genesis from a literary standpoint, albeit one somewhat interested in the theological doctrine involved.

It might seem that upon completing the *Grammar* and the *Rhetoric,* Burke would have gotten right on his "Symbolic of Motives." Indeed he did. Yet he always seemed about to finish it if he just had the time. Over a period of years he often told Watson that he just needed a few more months. A question may be asked why a writer so prolific had so much trouble completing a book that he was so eminently qualified to write. One answer is that in the 1950s and 1960s Burke was quite busy, even overwhelmed, by a variety of obligations. He taught and lectured at universities and colleges nationwide and participated in several eminent scholarly institutes; he repeatedly complained to Watson about the toll these activities were taking on his writing. (In fact, over the years Burke rejected many teaching opportunities, full-time and part-time, for fear of the effect on his writing.) He prepared new editions of all his books, from *Counter-Statement* to the *Rhetoric,* including his novel (*Towards a Better Life*), and expanded editions of his short fiction (*The Complete White Oxen*) and poetry (*Collected Poems, 1915–1954*). With all that going on, he managed to write *The Rhetoric of Religion,* collect essays into *Language as Symbolic Action,* and produce essays, book reviews, unpublished manuscripts, and more. As middle age began to wane, Burke had some health problems and seemed to slow down a bit, but he was nonetheless more productive than most scholars half his age.

Despite all this, it seems that Burke's failure to produce a "Symbolic of Motives" stems more from the nature of the project and, paradoxically, the acuteness of his prodigious critical talents. For one thing, as much as the "Symbolic of Motives" would be a step forward, and in ways a narrowing of the project from broad philosophical and rhetorical concerns, it would draw Burke into a labyrinth of authors, texts, and "poetic effects." His profound critical acumen, driven by a penchant for "tracking down" the philosophical, aesthetic, social, and political implications of terms singly and in clusters, propelled Burke into an exploration for which there was no end. Critics such as René Wellek and R. P. Blackmur mention this, complaining that Burke never gets anywhere; Blackmur also disparagingly says that Burke can apply "with equal fruitfulness" any kind of literature.[2] In a way they are right if "getting anywhere" means precisely what they mean, dismissing where Burke wants to go. It would be easy to get lost in the philosophical speculations of the sort found in the *Grammar* and the *Rhetoric,* but Burke was at heart a literary critic who used philosophy to help make his case about language and human relations. Whereas for Burke there was a point at which his philosophical speculations were enough, the world of literary effects for him was boundless and led always to another variation or association. In this sense Burke truly had a mind that could not stop exploding. Perhaps Burke's failure to produce the "Symbolic of Motives" stems from the fact that in the 1950s and 1960s Burke did not have a clear idea of how this work would differ in principle from the aesthetic theorizing and criticism he had done throughout his career, except for the general intellectual and political sentiments that motivated him at any particular time. Perhaps it would be more systematic. In any event, the major goal of his work after *A Rhetoric of Motives* was to demonstrate the complex ways in which words and symbols function in texts. As Burke continued writing literary criticism, he produced what probably amounts to a "Symbolic of Motives" anyway. These articles are collected in *Language as Symbolic Action*.

The *Rhetoric of Religion* complicates an understanding of what Burke was up to after *A Rhetoric of Motives*. For one thing, although religion is mentioned fairly frequently in Burke's essays and books, he had not devoted an entire work to it. Moreover, in *The Rhetoric of Religion*, Burke offers a "theory" called "logology." However, the term "theory" is deceptive here. Like all of Burke's "theories," it is more a loose set of intellectual predilections, commonplaces, and techniques than a full-blown theoretical system. In fact, much of what undergirds logology is precisely the sentiments that occupied Burke's mind for his entire career. Logology departs from his earlier work in that Burke develops certain commonplaces and perhaps techniques that apply specifically to theological texts. Logology is as much a theory as, say, the particular commonplaces and analytical techniques Burke applies to bureaucratic and political organizations in *Attitudes* constitute a theory. In other words, logology is an application of Burke's earlier work to a specific subject matter. The relationship between logology and the dramatism that Burke spent much of his career after *A Rhetoric of Motives* filling out is exceedingly close. Many of the terms and basic concepts of dramatism are fundamental to logology. (And much of what Burke establishes in dramatism has its roots, explicitly and implicitly, in his earlier work.) In *The Rhetoric of Religion*, Burke is quite clear on the debt logology owes to dramatism—so clear that his discussions of the relationship suggest less difference in the two theories than some readers of Burke today suggest. Much contemporary thinking about Burke has been heavily influenced by works that interpret dramatism through the filter of logology, such as William H. Rueckert's *Kenneth Burke and the Drama of Human Relations*. For instance, Rueckert goes so far as to say that *The Rhetoric of Religion* "is a wonderfully creative action by Burke in which he derives his own last or ultimate terminology from the most ultimate terminological and motivational ground he knows . . . theology."[3] Rueckert goes on to say, essentially, that Burke's theories culminate in logology (242). Robert Wess suggests that logology is a "reorientation" that "was destined to upstage *GM*'s dramatism."[4] Judgments such as these stem in part from desire to find in Burke a system of thought. Also, both Rueckert and Wess virtually ignore "Verbal Action in St. Augustine's *Confessions*," which is more like traditional criticism and makes up 40 percent of the book. These are grounds for skepticism regarding the claim that logology supersedes dramatism and what preceded it.

One of the major challenges to understanding what Burke was doing after *A Rhetoric of Motives* is recognizing how the intellectual currents of the 1950s and 1960s affected both the way Burke presented his material and how his audience read him. Throughout his career Burke used terms such as "method," "machine," and "system" to describe his theories; he also made wide-sweeping claims, even at times calling his principles and methods universal. Such statements brought harsh criticism from some quarters, especially from systematic philosophers such as Sidney Hook and Max Black (Burke called him "blackmax"). Even so, in an era in which scholars of all fields conceived the pinnacle of success to be the creation of universal systems of thought, Burke's predilection for sweeping statements led to interpretations of his work that defined his thinking for a generation and are largely influential still. Of course, such interpretations began in the 1940s, after the publication of the *Grammar,* but they became more prevalent and powerful in the 1960s after *The Rhetoric of Religion.* The drive for finding systematicity is powerful. Robert Garlitz, in "The Sacrificial Word in Kenneth Burke's Logology," one of the best studies of *The Rhetoric of Religion,* argues that *The Rhetoric of Religion* falls prey to such thinking.[5] There are two reasons why readers of *The Rhetoric of Religion* do this. First, Burke sometimes explicitly states that "logology" is a systematic method. Yet these statements are more a rhetorical accommodation to the intellectual climate than a serious belief in logology's systematicity, for Burke belies his own words. Not much is systematic about *The Rhetoric of Religion* other than the fact that Burke throws together a bunch of related terms and techniques. Put another way, of course logology is systematic, but only at an extremely high degree of generality. (After all, even statements such as "either you see the bottle half full or half empty" are systems of thought in an exceedingly general way.) Second, major concepts in *The Rhetoric of Religion*—guilt, Redemption, the Fall, etc.—have been taken by many readers to constitute a "secular Christianity," with all the attendant connotations of completeness, coherence, and explanatory power of that particular religious doctrine. But even if Burke indeed presents some sort of "system" for understanding the rhetoric of theological thought, it is another thing altogether to claim that the peculiarities of religious thought capture the essence of human relations overall and therefore are the basis for understanding language and rhetorical appeal on the whole. The possible existence of a theological "system" in the guilt, sacrifice, etc., cluster does not suggest a parallel system in language generally. Drawing too strong a parallel is not too different from believing that language in general is essentially the "system" of terms Burke finds in "The Rime of the Ancient Mariner."

What, then, was Burke up to after *A Rhetoric of Motives*? How does his work from the 1950s and 1960s fill out the human relations project? In both *The Rhetoric of Religion* and *Language as Symbolic Action,* Burke focuses on tracking down the "implications" of terms. He looks for the ways one idea or word leads to another in literary texts, especially when they form cycles or clusters.

In particular, he focuses on terms that involve the idea of order. This is no surprise. Much of his work since the 1920s involves order in one way or another, given that social structure and politics are inherently about order. Of course, his motivations for discussing order, and therefore the direction his analyses took, varied over the years. In the 1920s and 1930s Burke was driven by immediate and local sociopolitical factors, even if he was sensitive to the theoretical and philosophical issues they raised. In the 1940s, with *Literary Form* and the *Grammar,* Burke increasingly shifted the balance toward the theoretical and philosophical, even though he was still interested in immediate factors. The *Grammar* is particularly interesting in this regard, since philosophical aspects of order play an important part in the first two-thirds and the end, with the local ("The Dialectic of Constitutions") appearing in between. In the *Rhetoric,* Burke more evenly balances these coordinate interests, though the section "Order" is highly abstract. It seems that in the 1950s and 1960s Burke was still pulled in these two directions. Wanting "to treat of further problems that have to do with the intrinsic analysis of texts," he approached this microscopically sometimes and abstractly and macroscopically other times (*CS,* 218).

The fullest expression of the theoretical aspect of order appears in two ways. First, Burke suggests that there is a "cycle of terms implicit in the idea of 'Order.'" He discusses, on the one hand, terms implicit in the idea of a covenant and, on the other hand, in order in general. The second way in which Burke is most theoretical is revealed in his continual return to the differences between logical structure and narrative expression. It seems as if Burke finally settled on the reconciliation of ideas and words—as it reflects and creates order—as the central "problem" of communication, rhetoric, and human relations.

Any attempt to summarize *The Rhetoric of Religion* will be hopelessly inadequate. For one thing, it is too complicated for brevity. More significantly, although it has a strong theoretical element, the book overall is a demonstration of how words operate in Saint Augustine's *Confessions* and in Genesis. All the nuances and complex relationships Burke identifies can hardly be summarized, especially because, as Joseph Frank observes about the essay on Saint Augustine, "the reader is hard put to find any general thesis emerging from the welter of detail."[6] Some of the more important theoretical and critical observations Burke makes in the book overall can be highlighted. The first two sections, "Introduction: On *Theology* and *Logology*" and "On Words and The Word," explain Burke's basic perspective and define his terms and methods. He defines logology as "words about words," suggesting that the point of the book is to show that religious language can reveal a lot about the nature of language in general. For instance, since theology is "words about God," Burke is drawn early on to the word "God." He says that the "unitary concept of God" has analogues in "the nature of any name or title" that "sums up a manifold of particulars under a single head" (*RR*, 2). Burke suggests that there are six major analogies between theology and language in general. The first is "between 'words' (lower case) and 'The Word' (in capitals)" (*RR*, 11). According to Burke, words function in four realms: (1) "words for the natural . . . for things, for material operations, physiological conditions, animality, and the like"; (2) "words for the socio-political realm," including "social relations, laws, right, wrong, rule and the like"; (3) "words about words . . . the realm of dictionaries, grammar, etymology, philology, literary criticism, rhetoric, poetics, dialectics"; and (4) "words for the 'supernatural'" (*RR*, 14–15). The first three realms "cover the world of everyday experience," whereas the fourth "is by definition the realm of the 'ineffable'" (*RR*, 14, 15). The distinction between the fourth realm and the others was important to Burke because, he says, our words for the supernatural "are necessarily borrowed from our words for the sorts of things we can talk about literally" (*RR*, 15). This interpenetration of the natural and supernatural in language is one of the reasons why Burke finds the relation between theology and secular language so fertile. As Garlitz points out, the supernatural adds a "new dimension" to the empirical, and vice versa (35). This first analogy (with its four realms) is the most important to the book. The others are: "words are to the non-verbal things they name as Spirit is to Matter" (*RR*, 16); both theology and language in general come "to a head in a theory of the negative"; a "drive towards a Title of Titles"; "'Time' is to 'eternity' as the particulars in the unfolding of a sentence are to the sentence's unitary meaning" (*RR*, 33); and "the relation between the name and the thing named is like the relations of the persons in the Trinity" (*RR*, 34). Burke offers these analogies as a response to the limitations of "a mode of thought that is now quite prevalent"—that is, "critics who like to approach secular literature in terms of 'myth'" and the "simple historical development from the 'sacred' to the 'profane'" (*RR*, 34, 35). Burke also reminds the reader that logology arises out of two "contrasts" he has long discussed and made basic to dramatism: "'Dramatism' against 'Scientism'" and action against motion (*RR*, 38–40).

After these introductory remarks Burke turns to "Verbal Action in St. Augustine's Confessions," an essay that evolved over a period of years. Burke began it well before he delivered it at Drew University in the middle 1950s and then revised it significantly for inclusion in *The Rhetoric of Religion*. It is a complicated essay, alternating between detailed close reading and speculations concerning highly abstract theological and literary relationships. There is a general sense that much of the secondary literature ignores "Verbal Action," except for those few writers specifically interested in Augustine or the theological questions that Burke addresses. Burke provides an outline of his observations (43–49), but the overall thrust is that there is a profound shift in the way Augustine discusses his conversion. The first nine sections of the *Confessions* are fairly standard narrative autobiography based on temporal progression, the unfolding of events. The rest (beginning with "Memory"), in which Augustine discusses knowledge of God, become "logical" or atemporal. This shift from the narrative to the logical is important because the overlap between the two realms is an "alchemic moment" when biography, faith, spirit, doctrine, and confession coalesce.[7] At this moment perversity, violation, crisis, opening up, seeking, and other concepts flutter in the ineffable realm of religious conversion. *Confessions* is a powerful literary and rhetorical document precisely because of the complexity and beauty of the way Augustine creates a cluster of associations that, seemingly temporal in nature, end up yielding to a "logical" moment of transformation "in principle," thereby demonstrating that the divine was present in the secular all along. Given that, Burke is not saying that the secular in general is really sacred; rather, *in this text* it is so.

Studies of Burke more frequently focus on the next section, "The First Three Chapters of Genesis," probably because it is more accessible and clearer theoretically. It could also be said that it fits better into the ways of thinking and intellectual agendas of his audience. The essay centers on the idea that logic and narrative are different modes of thought, each with its own virtues and limitations. In particular, Burke is interested in how these two modes shade into one another. Genesis is especially apt for demonstrating this because it is a *narrative* that can "be interpreted as dealing with *principles* (with *logical* 'firsts,' rather than sheerly *temporal* ones)" (*RR,* 180). Two of the most basic ideas in Genesis are the Creation and the Covenant, which "implicate" concepts such as sacrifice, Redemption, the Fall, justice, mercy, and guilt, making biblical Creation and Covenant "principles of governance." Put another way, both ideas have secular "equivalents" in the concept "order." Drawing a parallel to the realms of the word from "Verbal Action," Burke offers three models of order (verbal, social, supernatural) that are not entirely distinct. "The term 'Order' is ambiguous," he says, "since it can be applied to two quite different areas, either to such natural regularities as tides and seasons, or to socio-political structures in which people can give or receive orders, in which orders can be obeyed or disobeyed, in which offices are said to pyramid in an orderly arrangement of powers and responsibilities" (*RR,* 181). This is especially important because this ambiguity allows an "alchemic moment" in which different conceptions of the world can transform into or otherwise influence one another: "consider the strategic ambiguity whereby . . . our ideas of the natural order can become secretly infused by our ideas of the socio-political order" (and vice versa) (*RR,* 183). Readers familiar with dramatism will recognize a close similarity to what Burke argues in the *Grammar.* The dynamics of order apply on the small scale (personally and socially) or, as Burke ominously points out, globally. "Today we must doubly fear the cyclical compulsions of empire," he warns, "as two mighty world orders, each homicidally armed to the point of suicide, confront each other" (*RR*, 236). Although such comments are few, they are reminders that Burke is still working *ad bellum purificandum*.

Burke's argument is that the biblical conception of order involves clusters of terms. He wants to "ask how the narrative, or 'rectilinear,' style of Genesis compares with the 'cycle of terms' we have found to revolve 'endlessly' about the idea of 'Order'" (*RR*, 183). He locates in the Bible different notions of order. The first chapter, he says, revolves around creation by decree and the "principle of governance" that arises out of that form of authority. The second chapter involves order stemming from the Edenic covenant, which introduces the ideas of the negative and the Fall. With Noah, the covenant comes to involve the idea of sacrifice. And the Abrahamic covenant takes on shades of personal victimage. Overall, the term "covenant" involves concepts such as faith, obedience, transgression, sin, mortification, sacrifice, and redemption; the particular set of associations and their nuances depends upon which sort of covenant is involved. By extension, this applies to the other biblical covenants that Burke does not analyze. The secular cycle of associations includes, for example, concepts such as command, obey, pride, act, free will, imagination, reason, faith, and natural law. Of course, since the sacred and secular cycles are analogous, they overlap; put another way, humans develop different sets of associations to capture certain general experiences (in this case the experience of order). In both cases Burke makes much of the fact that "disorder" and "disobedience" are implicit in the idea of order. In drawing analogies between the sacred and the secular, one problem is the difference between narrative and logic. Narrative involves conceptual progressions, whereas in logic the terms mix. The cycle of terms in order, he says, "follows no one sequence. . . . However, when such terministic interrelationships are embodied in the narrative style (involving acts, images and personalities) an irreversibility of the sequence can become of major importance" (*RR*, 182). This is similar to the ambiguity in "form" that is relevant to *Permanence and Change*. Form (as an inducement of effect) is ambiguous because "induce" can mean "to cause" or "to lead." The logical sense of order is largely "causal," whereas theological order in a complicated way "leads" the reader. On the whole, Burke aims in *The Rhetoric of Religion* to show the reader the complex ways in which these two modes of thought relate to each other, both in theory and in the effect on readers. Regarding the latter, Burke observes that "when we turn from the consideration of a terministic cycle in which the various terms mutually imply one another, to the consideration of the narrative terminology in these opening chapters of Genesis, we note that the narrative terms allow the idea of Order to be 'processed'" (*RR*, 215–16). This processing function in part arises out of the ability of theological discourse to lead the reader. Even so, Burke is not suggesting (as some commentators put it) that religious discourse is superior to secular. For one thing, they are just different modes of thought and expression; for another, theology is just one form of narrative.

Garlitz's summary of *The Rhetoric of Religion* is quite good for its detail, accuracy, and clarity. Garlitz is especially adept at putting complex material in perspective. More than other commentators on *The Rhetoric of Religion,* he fully recognizes the centrality of the analogy at the heart of the book, embracing the logic-narrative problem that Burke contemplates. Yet there is room for disagreement over two aspects of his position. First, Garlitz makes sacrifice central to logology. In discussing the four realms of the word, he says logology "reads the supernatural realm allegorically," the "chief 'lesson'" being "the necessity of the sacrificial principle to all forms of order" (36). Garlitz also says that "while the sacrificial principle is intrinsic to Order, as it is embodied in the Cycle, *Leviathan,* and Genesis, and as it constitutes the universal motivational scene in which man acts, it also stands at the center of the relation between the cyclical and linear forms of language" (39–40). There may be good reason for believing this, since Burke's statements can be read that way, especially in Burke's comment that "the sacrificial motive is intrinsic to Order" (*RR,* 173; quoted by Garlitz). Yet Burke is not arguing that the specific forms of order in theology—or even its essence—are at the center of logology, but that the principles of theological order have analogues in secular patterns of order. It may well be that there are conceptions of secular order that are essentially sacrificial; at the same time there are conceptions of order that are not. At best, Burke's comments about sacrifice are not declarations of essences in language in general, but allusions regarding tendencies in language. Garlitz may also see Burke's creation of a logical order of ideas as making a statement that such an order is "real," and that texts manifest that order because it is natural and right and better than other orders. This is the same mistake made by some other readers of *The Rhetoric of Religion.* Instead, Burke suggests that order is exploited rhetorically. In sum, logology is a "method" for comparing systems of thought, not identifying the "universal motivational scene" manifested in secular language. Sacrifice may be essential to theology, but not to logology, for logology merely *accounts* for sacrifice in religious texts and asks if there happens to be an analogue for it more generally. The second key element of Garlitz's analysis that raises misgivings is the tendency, in overemphasizing sacrifice, to get drawn into the linearly progressive cycle of terms in theological narratives of sacrifice (e.g., the covenant "No" leads to temptation, which leads to sin, which leads to guilt, which leads to mortification, which leads to victimage, and so on). When Garlitz makes sacrifice the central conceit of all language, language perforce gets entrapped in the sacrifice cycle. Thus, Garlitz is led to say that "using language at all as our locus of origins and principles is simply a way of shifting the blame from man to language" (42).

The possible disagreements with these two aspects of Garlitz's thinking stem from the same problem that has haunted Burke for years, the attempt to systematize his thought. As well as Garlitz seems to understand the complexities of *The Rhetoric of Religion,* by trying to make Burke systematic he ends up making more of sacrifice than is warranted, in the process creating a theoretical edifice that makes stronger claims than Burke intended. The tendency to systematize is demonstrated in Garlitz's remark that "only after having worked out Dramatism has Burke been fully able to name the culminating rationale—the Logos—of his search" (42). And sacrifice is the linchpin. One theme underlying his analysis is the idea that Burke's "discovery" of sacrifice is an improvement upon earlier, similar conceptions. "The chord-arpeggio and the Temporizing of Essence permit too simple a relation . . . in suggesting a narrative solution to the logical problem," he notes (41). Garlitz is quite right about that. However, creating a new system based on sacrifice may not be the improvement; rather, the improvement arises out of Burke's critical perceptiveness. A comment that Daniel Hughes makes concerning *Language as Symbolic Action* applies well to *The Rhetoric of Religion:* "We should stop looking for fugal consistencies in his work. . . . I think the only 'systems' in the literary study of our time have come from *beyond* literature, in those unspoken dogmas—religious, social, political—from which the critic was operating the better to pursue his 'autotelic' endeavor. . . . These have been system-built, but not the visionary books, and not truly the work of Kenneth Burke whose movement from a theory of symbolic action to 'dramatism' is a creative method, not a system."[8] Noting that Burke's argumentative style in *Language as Symbolic Action* is at times almost poetic, Hughes suggests that Burke's not-very-systematic essays "[use] everything they can" in order "that the wordy tabernacle swing open to show us just what out 'symbolicity' is" (253). As Denis Donoghue, a particularly astute reader of Burke, says, "Burke has never put himself into the position of treating language as the privileged form of ultimacy: beyond or beneath the words, he has always posited a ground of action, a realm of motives which are mediated by words and symbols."[9]

If *The Rhetoric of Religion* complicates our understanding of what Burke was up to after *A Rhetoric of Motives,* oddly enough so does *Language as Symbolic Action,* particularly because of the way it is used by scholars. Burke wrote many of the essays in a different style than his earlier work, making them clearer, simpler, and more revealing about what he was thinking as he argued. He even added lengthy explanatory notes at the ends of essays for further clarity. In the 1960s Burke may have still felt that his message was not getting through, so he set about again making his case. Indeed, in the late 1950s and 1960s, as his ideas gained notice, Burke was repeatedly asked to write and lecture about his theories. For these reasons *Language as Symbolic Action* focuses on some of the basic concerns that had occupied Burke's mind from the early 1920s. This time, though, he does not go into a new field of inquiry, but largely chooses to restate his positions and do more literary criticism. In fact, at times he is rather reductive about his basic tenets, offering fairly simplistic versions of ideas that he took a lifetime to elaborate. The prime example of this is "Definition of Man," which is one of the most cited of Burke's essays overall, especially in works that cover *Language as Symbolic Action.* "Definition of Man" captures some of Burke's basic assumptions about language and human relations in slogan form with short explanations. But twenty pages of that can hardly capture complexities of symbol use, as in, for instance, the analysis of negation in *The Rhetoric of Religion.* "Terministic Screens," the second most cited essay in the collection, borrows heavily from dramatism and suggests that the words we use color our perceptions of things. These are good essays, but they have garnered the attention of readers of Burke for two reasons. First, they are accessible summations of Burke's ideas. The chief problem with their influence, though, is not reductivism per se but what Burke leaves out in simplifying his ideas. Lost are the explicit connections with the social and political issues that infuse his work overall. I recall as an undergraduate encountering Burke's statements that man is "rotten with perfection" and "goaded by a spirit of hierarchy." I had no way, on the basis of "Definition of Man," of recognizing the profound ways in which bureaucratization of the imaginative, dialectic, the Human Barnyard, and *ad bellum purificandum* were part of being goaded by hierarchy. Worse yet, I could not infer the profoundly ethical stance Burke takes and the particular ethics he champions. The second reason a small part of *Language as Symbolic Action* is so popular is no different than the reason for the emphasis on the theoretical sections of *The Rhetoric of Religion* at the expense of "Verbal Action in St. Augustine's *Confessions.*" The complex literary criticism that Burke conducted in this part of his career simply does not easily fit into the interests in theory and systematization (of dramatism or logology) that many commentators on Burke favor. It is true that *Language as Symbolic Action* has many theoretical essays. Yet most of them tend to repeat what Burke said before or expand on themes specifically about dramatism without saying much that is new. In the scholarly literature "A Dramatistic View of the Origins of Language" is one of the more cited essays in the collection, largely because it refines his views somewhat further than the other essays do, especially regarding the idea that "the negative" is a fundamentally linguistic entity that characterizes symbolic expression. For instance, in Wess's final chapter *Language as Symbolic Action* is not mentioned to nearly the degree that *The Rhetoric of Religion* is, though the chapter is largely about the latter, and whereas there are only scattered references to the other essays, "A Dramatistic View of the Origins of Language" gets several pages. Rueckert too underplays *Language as Symbolic Action.* In other words, the dramatistic and logological elements of *Language as Symbolic Action* are emphasized at the expense of Burke's literary criticism.

Language as Symbolic Action is divided into three parts. Burke begins with "Five Summarizing Essays" that together "best convey the gist of the collection as a whole" (*LASA*, 2). Part 2 contains fairly traditional literary criticism covering Shakespeare, Goethe, Emerson, Coleridge, Theodore Roethke, and William Carlos Williams. Part 3 returns to symbolism in general, where Burke focuses on the relation of rhetoric and poetics, motion and action, naming, and the negative.

Regarding the five summarizing essays, there are a few points to make. First, in "Poetics in Particular, Language in General," Burke uses Edgar Allan Poe to discuss the special characteristics of poetical language, as distinct from language more generally. "What we might say about the poem specifically *as a poem*," Burke says, "might not adequately cover the wider motivational problem of what we might say about the poem . . . as aspects of *language in general*" (*LASA*, 27). Poetics, he says, "is but one of the four primary linguistic dimensions"; the others are logic, rhetoric, and hortatory usage (*LASA*, 28). Poetics is marked by its "sheer exercise of 'symbolicity' . . . for its own sake" (*LASA*, 29). When approaching poetics, "one should try ideally to work out explanations in terms of the poem as poem," even though that might require "a wider range of derivations" (*LASA*, 29–30). Ultimately Burke argues a fairly simple point, which is that the realm of poetics is separate from the other primary linguistic dimensions. A reasonable next step is to ask what happens if "theology" is substituted for "poetics." It certainly is the case that theological discourse is not one of the primary dimensions. Yet if language in general should not be confused with the other primary dimensions, then surely something like theology should not either. Readers of this essay should be even more suspicious of the attempts to essentialize religious discourse.

"*Coriolanus*—and the Delights of Faction" garnered some notice by reviewers of *Language as Symbolic Action* when it was published. This essay is particularly interesting because, like a good deal of Burke's literary criticism, it involves social hierarchies. In discussing this essay Wess virtually ignores this aspect, favoring instead what can be surmised about subjectivity on the basis of Burke's analysis. That is to be expected, since he places Burke in the contemporary critical debates about subjectivity.[10] Yet that ignores the importance of social division. "Fundamentally, then," Burke states, "the play [*Coriolanus*] exploits to the ends of dramatic entertainment, with corresponding catharsis, the tension intrinsic to a kind of social division, or divisiveness, particularly characteristic of complex societies, but present to some degree in even the simplest modes of living" (*LASA*, 88). *Language as Symbolic Action* was published in 1966, and Burke notes that "an ironic turn of history has endowed this play with a new kind of 'timely topic,' owing to the vagaries of current dictatorships"; but he goes on to reject such an interpretation "because the frankness of [Coriolanus's] dislike for the common people would make him wholly incompetent as a rabble-rouser" (*LASA*, 89). Burke also observes a "motivational split" in the play, with "four overlapping loci: nation, class, family, individual" (*LASA*, 90). The point of the essay overall is to explain why the sacrifice of Coriolanus is satisfying to the audience. Burke suggests that it is because social factors (family, class, nation) "come to a focus" in the individual, and that Coriolanus's trials are therefore cathartic of the audience's social dissatisfactions. While an essay such as this might provide some sort of theoretical statement about individual psychology or even about language in general, it seems that Burke is clearly attempting again to account for ways in which "literature is equipment for living." Readers of *Language as Symbolic Action* may have noticed that the five summarizing essays begin with a "definition of man" and end with a reminder of the social functions of literature, especially regarding the divisiveness of social class. Too much can be made of that, but it does not seem to be a coincidence.

In the second part of *Language as Symbolic Action*, "Particular Works and Authors," Burke builds on the social functions of literature. In "Shakespearean Persuasion" he argues that underneath the more obviously entertaining elements of Shakespeare are subtle persuasive appeals based on social experiences of the audience (for instance, in his use of eunuchs and parent–child relationships). It is important not to overstate that case, because Burke discusses a variety of persuasive elements. Yet most of them revolve around an individual's place in the social world, either regarding specific relations or a more general sense of things. In "Form and Persecution in the *Oresteia,*" Burke explains that he is "generally concerned with stylistic resources whereby the important social relations involving superiority and inferiority could be translated into a set of 'mythic' equivalents" (*LASA*, 126). Suggesting that this essay builds on the concept of form from *Counter-Statement,* Burke says that form in that work can be understood as a "network of expectancies and fulfillments" that function "*dramatically* in such terms as Law, Right, Fate, Justice, Necessity" (*LASA*, 127). And in tragedy, he points out, these motives become "cosmologized." Burke goes on to suggest many ways in which this happens, even going so far as to say that "in the Athenian *polis* there was an unresolved civic guilt with regard to women" and that in *Prometheus Bound,* when the Chorus of Women enter after the deity is tortured, "the terror is not merely felt by the audience as witnesses; rather it is ingrained in the very behavior of the drama. . . . That is, the drama does not merely make us afraid; rather it itself *is* afraid" (*LASA*, 130). In other essays in part 2 Burke embarks on more standard criticism of imagery and symbol use. But even so, the overall tenor of part 2 is strongly flavored by the sort of general social and political concerns that Burke displayed throughout his career, even in his more traditional literary criticism.

Burke spent much of his time after *A Rhetoric of Motives* applying his ideas to theological and literary texts. As Rueckert says about *Language as Symbolic*

Action—which relative to dramatism could hold true for *The Rhetoric of Religion* too—"there is very little that is new in this book. . . . Much of it is a summing up, and all of it is *refining* rather than *defining*" (267).[11] While recognizing that this is the case, it is important to note that a great part of that refining involves what Burke had in mind for his "Symbolic of Motives": a detailed examination of the generally social and political uses of symbols. In particular, he is concerned with the virtues and limitations of various modes of discourse—narrative, logic, poetics, myth, tragedy, theology, and language in general. This detailed examination largely occurs in fairly traditional literary critical ways, albeit with Burke's unique intellectual stamp.

What, then, can be made of Burke's contribution overall? As his career progressed he became increasingly interested in the abstract, the theoretical, the philosophical—especially concerning the nature and characteristics of language, though throughout he never abandoned the concrete specifics of literary texts. Despite his great speculativeness at times, from the start Burke was profoundly concerned about the social and political dimensions of language, communication, and rhetoric. Much that has been said about Burke was influenced heavily by his later works, in which his social and political concerns are somewhat disguised; at least they are easily passed over in a quest to systematize Burke and fit him into some intellectual tradition not his own. One strong tendency to be resisted is to make Burke more systematic than warranted. Many of his most insightful critics, even his detractors, recognized the suggestiveness and undisciplined elements in his scholarship. And they were right, though it is questionable whether being more heuristic than systematic is good or bad. Another tendency to resist is passing over his criticism and sociopolitical arguments. In the current theory-driven intellectual climate, where the self and subjectivity reign, where the abject rejection of the political is mistaken for engaging politics (or at least political sentiments are rarefied beyond recognition), it is important to recognize that on the whole Burke addresses tangible *collective* matters, especially as they figure into ethics. That is why his theories are largely *rhetorical* and why essays such as "Program," or the explicitly political arguments in *Permanence and Change* and *Attitudes toward History,* or the delights of faction in *Coriolanus* should not be ignored.

Burke suggests that his early ideas capture well the gist of his thinking overall. Everything after that was a rearticulation and extension of those seminal ideas in new subject matters. Thus, to do justice to Burke one must read his early work carefully. At the same time it is important not to make Burke into something he is not. Throughout his career various groups tried to call him their own. Communists, general semanticists, New Critics, and now deconstructionists and postmodernists all find in Burke a forebear or fellow traveler. Yet Burke always resisted co-optation, and his writings bear him out.

From the start Burke was an outsider. Without academic credentials, he stood on the other side of the fence, peering at intellectuals in many disciplines and saying, "But don't forget . . ." and "Yet, if you think about it this way . . ." and even "Wait a minute!" He was interdisciplinary—or perhaps better, multidisciplinary; or better still, antidisciplinary. A self-proclaimed "antinomian," he believed that it is easy to praise Greece in Athens. But underlying it all was some remarkable consistency. For half a century and more he kept returning to the same themes, among them the importance of action over motion, a suspicion of "scientism," and the belief that the study of language and literature is the best way to understand human relations. To do justice to the great legacy of Kenneth Burke, our attitude toward him must be one of caution. For the moment we call him one of our own, or become too sure of his theories, or systematize him, or pigeonhole him, there he is saying "Wait a minute!" Wayne Booth, one of Burke's great admirers, fell prey to this from the other end when he sympathetically tried to "take Burke on his own terms," defending him by saying that Burke's pluralism vitiates Wellek's criticisms. In response, Burke was "dancing with tears in my eyes" and went on to refute Booth point by point. Many commentators on Burke, friends and foes alike, suggested that he was idiosyncratic, that his subject was his own thoughts and fancies. Some even called it "Burkology." No doubt, there is some truth to this. But such judgments miss the point. Burke stands on the fringe largely because he refused to reduce his subject matters—life, literature, method, and above all language in human relations—to the limited, convenient, and often self-serving conceptual systems of the academic disciplines. Language and human relations are just too complex and wonderful and mysterious for that. Whenever we think we understand things, just wait to be turned upside down.

So, what then is Burke's legacy? I suggest that three themes emerge from his prolific career: first, Be awed by the mystery of language; second, Listen well; and third, Have a heart.

Appendix

This appendix supplies the major passages from the first edition of *Permanence and Change* that were deleted from the second and third editions. Pagination of the original is indicated by the insertion of bracketed page numbers. Bibliographic information on the three editions may be found in the bibliography.

1) In the second and third editions, "The Three Orders of Rationalization" (part 1, chapter 5) ends on page 65 with "the magic lure of progress as a slogan is ended." The 1935 edition ends the last paragraph of the section with:

> [91] And the great danger of Fascism, in contrast with Communism, is that, whereas both seek to establish the integration of industry and politics which is the ultimate requirement of the scientific rationalization, and hence, both stimulate precisely the same desire to stabilize a *status quo,* Fascism may undermine the prestige of progress as a slogan too soon, thereby crystallizing a structure which still admits too wide a range of inequalities.

2) In the second and third editions, "A Humanistic, or Poetic, Rationalization" (part 1, chapter 5) ends on page 66 with "but an art in its wider aspects, an *art of living.*" In the 1935 edition it reads "Communism a Humanistic, or Poetic, Rationalization" (91) and continues with:

> [93] So far as I can see, the only coherent and organized movement making for the subjection of the technological genius to humane ends is that of Communism, by whatever name it may finally prevail. For though Communism is generally put forward on a purely technological basis, in accordance with the strategy of recommendation advisable in a scientific era, we must realize the highly humanistic or poetic nature of its fundamental criteria. The very word suggests its latent affinities with the religious or pre-technological rationalization, which perfected the attitude of inducement that flowers in man's maximum capacities for the coöperative (a coöperative ability which, as Marx points out, greatly fitted it for preëmption by a privileged class, who could so apply it that a submerged class did most of the coöperating). Indeed, precisely as science, with its emphasis upon the impersonal, has even tended in its speculations to abandon the notion of the personality (the essentially humane concept) and to be concerned with a general stream of consciousness instead, it was under the earlier coöperative rationalization that the concept of the personality arose—having first designated the mask worn by an actor, then the part played by the actor, then the analogous role in life, and finally the character playing this role. The very name Communism [94] suggests echoes of the word "communicant," perhaps the key term about which the entire religious rationalization of the West was constructed.

We do not mean that Communism is a reversion, though some adherents of the capitalist structure have condemned it on this score, particularly with their eyes upon the forms of communistic ownership and distribution that distinguish many primitive tribes. As a matter of fact, the vast amount of historical and anthropological documentation now assembled, plus its largely generalized or abstract nature, makes certain that any trend of history, no matter what it may be, will show marked similarity with the past, and hence may be denigrated as a reversion at a time when the prestige of progress is still intact. Our point is simply that a philosophy corrective to the technological rationalization can advocate its correctives only by taking human needs as its point of reference (the kind of human needs, perhaps, whose permanency arises from the permanency of the neurological structure itself). Perhaps the word "coöperative" (as distinct from the "competitive" which flourished when the acquisitions of science were backed by the stimuli of business enterprise) would replace the word "communicant" as the pivotal term of the new rationalization. And a restoration of homogeneity in the means of *communication* is sought in the Marxian emphasis upon one unifying ideology that will inform the Marxian culture.

3) In the first and second editions, the "Conclusions" of "The Poetry of Action" (part 3, chapter 7) is missing a paragraph from page 268. The previous paragraph, continued from 267, ends with "and entails the ideal denial of his own methods." The 1935 edition includes the following paragraph:

[344] Communism is a coöperative rationalization, or perspective, which fulfills the requirements suggested by the poetic metaphor. It is fundamentally humanistic, as poetry is. Its ethics is referable to the socio-biologic genius of man (the economic conquest of the machine being conceived within such a frame). Its underlying concept of vocation is radical—for it does not permit our sense of duty to arise simply from the contingencies which our ways of production and distribution force upon us, but offers a point of view from which these contingencies themselves may be criticized. Under capitalism, man must accommodate his efforts to the genius of machinery—under Communism he may accommodate machinery to the genius of his funda- [345] mental needs as an active and communicating organism.

4) In the first and second editions, a subsection of the "Conclusions" of "The Poetry of Action" (part 3, chapter 7) ends with "economic patterns which reduce the coöperative aspects of action to a minimum" (271). In the 1935 edition the subsection continues with:

[347] And there seems far too little likelihood that those who have control of our economy will peacefully relinquish this control in the interests of culture. Rather, they will continue to degrade people, and to contemn them for being

degraded. Their [348] very "morality" is involved in their privileges; their means and purposes are adjusted to them; their concepts of the "good life" are grounded in them; their fabulous possessions are their tools and shelter; their incapacity is their training. Hence it is not likely that we can expect a better day until the opportunity to persist in their kinds of effort has been taken away from them.

Notes

Chapter 1—The Formation of a Critic

1. Matthew Josephson, *Life among the Surrealists, A Memoir* (New York: Holt, Rinehart and Winston, 1962), 30. For a fuller description of this episode, see David E. Shi, *Matthew Josephson, Bourgeois Bohemian* (New Haven: Yale University Press, 1981), 24–25.

2. Burke's poetry has been collected in *Book of Moments,* later expanded in *Collected Poems.* His major works of fiction are *The White Oxen and Other Stories,* 1924, republished with additional material in *The Complete White Oxen,* and *Towards a Better Life.* Burke did publish one new story in 1957 in the *Kenyon Review* and reissued his books of fiction in the 1960s.

3. Kenneth Burke, Afterword, *ATH,* 377. See also *CS,* 216. "Curve of development" and "position" are terms Burke uses in that postscript, p. 213. See also Paul Jay, ed., *The Selected Correspondence of Kenneth Burke and Malcolm Cowley, 1915–1981* (New York: Viking, 1988), 291.

4. I borrow the phrase from Harvey Klehr, *The Heyday of American Communism: The Depression Decade* (New York: Basic Books, 1984).

5. See Frederick J. Hoffman, Charles Allen, and Caroline F. Ulrich, eds., *The Little Magazine: A History and a Bibliography* (Princeton: Princeton University Press, 1947).

6. Burke received at least six honorary degrees. For more on Burke's life, see Richard Kostelanetz, "A Mind That Cannot Stop Exploding," *New York Times Book Review,* 15 March 1981, 11 ff.

7. Not much biographical material concerning Burke has been published. I cannot offer an exact account, especially of his early years, because published sources provide little material, dates are often omitted, and many statements are vague. Several articles and books briefly sketch the early years, often saying much the same thing. Jack Selzer, *Kenneth Burke in Greenwich Village: Conversing with the Moderns, 1915–1931* (Madison: University of Wisconsin Press, 1996) has the best coverage. Robert Wess, *Kenneth Burke: Rhetoric, Subjectivity, Postmodernism* (New York: Cambridge University Press, 1996) is good too. My account borrows heavily from Jay, *Selected Correspondence,* 3–7; Shi, *Matthew Josephson,* passim; and Sonja K. Foss, Karen A. Foss, and Robert Trapp, *Contemporary Perspectives on Rhetoric* (Prospect Heights, Ill.: Waveland, 1985), 154–55.

8. Shi, *Matthew Josephson,* 25.

9. Malcolm Cowley, *Exile's Return: A Narrative of Ideas* (New York: Norton, 1934), 26.

10. Shi, *Matthew Josephson,* 27.

11. Daniel Aaron, *Writers on the Left: Episodes in American Literary Communism* (New York: Oxford University Press, 1977), 85. Dorothy Day would eventually become the common-law wife of Burke's brother-in-law.

12. Years later Burke would say that he left Columbia because the program would not let him take the courses he desired.

13. Josephson, *Life,* 51. Shi, *Matthew Josephson,* 36.

14. Shi, *Matthew Josephson,* 31. Burke lived with the Lights, Djuna Barnes, and Berenice Abbott. Richard Kostelanetz says the American painter Stuart Davis also lived there. See Kostelanetz, "Mind," 11.

15. Daniel Bell, *Marxian Socialism in the United States* (Princeton: Princeton University Press, 1967), 104.

16. Ibid., 106.

17. Young was also a cartoonist for *The Masses.*

18. For a description of this event, see Josephson, *Life,* 53–55; and Shi, *Matthew Josephson,* 29–30.

19. See, especially, Burke's discussion of the "communist fiction" in *PC* and his discussion of "collectivism" in *ATH.* See also Kenneth Burke, "My Approach to Communism."

20. Shi, *Matthew Josephson,* 23.

21. Josephson, *Life,* 64.

22. Ibid., 62, 67–68.

23. Hoffman et al., *Little Magazine,* 196. My brief history of the *Dial* borrows heavily from this work.

24. Hoffman et al., *Little Magazine,* 196.

25. Ibid., 196–97. According to Selzer, in *Kenneth Burke,* "*Seven Arts* promoted economic equality and optimistically heralded the creation of an American cultural renaissance" (34). For a fuller discussion, see 33–35.

26. William Wasserstrom, *The Time of the Dial* (Syracuse, N.Y.: Syracuse University Press, 1963), 83.

27. Ibid., 125.

28. I thank Thomas M. Conley for pointing this out to me.

29. "As W. C. Blum has stated the case deftly, 'In identification lies the source of dedications and enslavements, in fact of cooperation'" (Burke, *RM,* xiv).

30. Watson and Moore were not the only ones who took an interest in Burke. In the summer of 1924, "Burke served as Thayer's private secretary and lived in Thayer's cottage on Martha's Vineyard" (Wasserstrom, *Time of the Dial,* 125).

31. This, perhaps, was the beginning of Burke's essay "The Armour of Jules Laforge [*sic*]," published in *Contact* between 1920 and 1923 (the number in which it appears gives no indication of publication date).

32. Kenneth Burke, "Approaches to Rémy de Gourmont," 126–27.

33. Ibid., 129. The example is from 130.

34. Burke had translated Mann's "Loulou" for the *Dial*'s April number.

35. The date of composition of the Pater essay is the least clear. Selzer, in *Kenneth Burke,* discusses this.

36. Kenneth Burke, "The Correspondence of Flaubert," 147.

37. Kenneth Burke, "On Re and Dis."

38. Kenneth Burke, "A 'Logic' of History," 242–48.

39. Josephson arranged the meeting. McAlmon was then an aspiring young poet. Soon, after marrying into wealth, McAlmon started Contacts Editions Press, which published William Carlos Williams, Gertrude Stein, and Ernest Hemingway. See Josephson, *Life,* 72–77.

40. The essay may have been "The Armour of Jules Laforge [*sic*]," which was published sometime between 1920 and 1923 (the exact date is unclear). The poem may have been "*Ver Renatus Orbis Est,*" which was published in 1922. See also Jay, *Selected Correspondence,* 86.

41. I do not mean to imply that Williams was directly responsible for Burke's appearance in the *Little Review.* In fact, Munson intimates that "a Greenwich Village novelist" may have been the spark. See Gorham Munson, "The Fledgling Years, 1916–1924," *Sewanee Review* 40

(Jan.–Mar. 1932): 29. It is true, however, that in such a close community obsessed with literature, influence works in many ways.

42. Hoffman et al., *Little Magazine,* 267. Whether or not *Manuscripts* was the "pamphlet-magazine" Rosenfeld had in mind when he approached Burke is unclear.

43. The essay in the *Dial* was "The Correspondence of Flaubert." "The Armour of Jules Laforge [*sic*]" may also have appeared the same year.

44. "André Gide, Bookman." *The Freeman* 5 (Apr. 1922), 155–57. "Last Words on the Ephebe," *Literary Review of the New York Evening Post,* 2 (Aug. 1922), 897–98.

45. The influence of surrealism and Dada became much stronger later on.

46. Hoffman et al., *Little Magazine,* 97. Burke had previously done editorial work for the *Sansculotte,* the student paper at Ohio State.

47. The evidence indicates that all three arrived at the same idea independently. Munson seems to have taken the greatest initiative. See Munson, "Fledgling Years"; Cowley, *Exile's Return,* 108–15; and Josephson, *Life,* 155–59.

48. Malcolm Cowley, "This Youngest Generation," *Literary Review of the New York Evening Post,* 15 Oct. 1921.

49. Cowley, *Exile's Return,* 108–12.

50. Gorham B. Munson, "The Fledgling Years, 1916–1924," *Sewanee Review* 40 (Jan.–Mar. 1932): 30.

51. This quotation comes from a circular-announcement by Munson, cited in "Fledgling Years," 32.

52. Munson, "Fledgling Years," 34–35.

53. Josephson, *Life,* 233.

54. Jack Selzer, in *Kenneth Burke,* gives a thorough account of Burke's involvement with the little magazines. Discussions of this appear throughout the book.

55. Wasserstrom, *Time of the Dial,* 59–60, 125. For the fullest account of Burke and the *Dial,* see Selzer, *Kenneth Burke,* 115–36.

56. Burke's position on this is a bit unclear. Although he makes a strong claim about the "unsensitivity" of the general public, I think he is being hyperbolic.

57. "Psychology and Form" first appeared in the *Dial* in the July 1925 number. "The Poetic Process" first appeared in the *Guardian* in the May–June 1925 number. They were subsequently reprinted in *CS.* See Jay, 233.

58. "Rhetoric" appears, quite insignificantly, in "Poetic Process," 289.

59. Both remarks are quoted in Wasserstrom, *Time of the Dial,* 125. They are from letters from Burke to Alyse Gregory dated 20 Nov. and 23 Dec. 1924.

60. Both "Lexicon Rhetoricae" and "Applications of the Terminology" were written exclusively for *CS.*

61. Though, again, the term "rhetoric" does not appear often in these books.

Chapter 2—*Counter-Statement:* Aesthetics, Meaning, and Social Reform

1. After *Towards a Better Life,* he did not publish any more fiction until 1957.

2. Biographical information comes from a thorough study of Burke's early life in New York: Jack Selzer, *Kenneth Burke in Greenwich Village: Conversing with the Moderns, 1915–1931* (Madison: University of Wisconsin Press, 1996). Although this book is primarily an intellectual history of Burke's place in the modernist conversations of the 1920, Selzer provides excellent biographical

detail. He relies heavily on readily available published sources, such as Paul Jay's *Selected Correspondence of Kenneth Burke and Malcolm Cowley, 1915–1981* (New York: Viking, 1988) and Matthew Josephson's *Life among the Surrealists, A Memoir* (New York: Holt, Rinehart and Winston, 1962), for example. He also incorporates material from a variety of rare publications, holdings in archives, and interviews. For information about Burke's career and life through 1931 there is no better source.

3. Frank Lentricchia, *Criticism and Social Change* (Chicago: University of Chicago Press, 1983); Selzer, *Kenneth Burke.*

4. Selzer, *Kenneth Burke,* 138–43.

5. Burke stated (1 Dec. 1940) that he wrote this essay in winter 1924. See Jay, *Selected Correspondence,* 233. "Psychology and Form" was first published in the *Dial* in 1925.

6. See Jay, *Selected Correspondence,* 233. "The Poetic Process" was first published in the *Guardian* in 1925.

7. Kenneth Burke, "On Re and Dis."

8. Compare pages 77 and 78 of "The Status of Art" to pages 166–67 and 168 of "On Re and Dis."

9. Kenneth Burke, "A New Poetics," 154.

10. Kenneth Burke, "A `Logic' of History."

11. This is an enduring concern—as valid in the era of Reagan and the "New Conservatism," for instance, as it was in the 1930s.

12. That is, one quarter of what is contained in the original 1931 edition (which does not have the preface to the second edition or the "Curriculum Criticum").

13. The idea of perfection is central to the section on "Dialectic in General"; see *GM,* 402–43. And it is especially central to the section on "Pure Persuasion"; see *RM,* 267–94.

14. For instance, p. 14 of "Three Adepts" leaves out the "deeper contemporaneity" of Pater. Page 15 of "Three Adepts" leaves out the discussion of impressionism and relativism that appears on p. 58 of "Pater."

15. I am sure he means not the conditions of that specific year but rather post-Crash conditions.

16. That is, of course, if those closing pages were from "Applications." There is no reason to think not.

17. This quotation explains Burke's view of the terms of the pentad. They should not be fixed and perfected, he says, but used as foci for understanding the points at which different perspectives are similar.

18. See Thomas Bender, *New York Intellect: A History of Intellectual Life in New York City, from 1750 to the Beginnings of Our Own Time* (Baltimore: Johns Hopkins University Press, 1988). Further page references to Bender appear within parentheses in the text.

19. Gorham B. Munson, "In and About the Workshop of Kenneth Burke," in *Destinations: A Canvass of American Literature since 1900* (New York: J. H. Sears, 1928), 153.

20. John Chamberlain, "Rhetoric Finds a Champion in Mr. Kenneth Burke," *New York Times Book Review,* 25 Oct. 1931, 2.

21. By "cult of vacillation" Chamberlain refers to Burke's "urging the artist to be skeptical of all values."

22. Granville Hicks, "A Defense of Eloquence," *New Republic,* 2 Dec. 1931, 75.

23. See Kenneth Burke, "Counterblasts on 'Counter-Statement,'" 101.

24. See Granville Hicks, letter, *New Republic,* 9 Dec. 1931, 101.

25. Isidor Schneider, "A New View of Rhetoric," *New York Herald Tribune Books,* 13 Dec. 1931, 22. Further page references to Schneider appear within parentheses in the text.

26. Harold Rosenberg, review of *CS, Symposium* 3 (Jan. 1932): 117. Further page references to Rosenberg appear within parentheses in the text.

27. Joshua Kunitz, "Counter-Statement," *New Masses* (Apr. 1932): 19. Further page references to Kunitz appear within parentheses in the text.

Chapter 3—*Permanence and Change:* Ideals of Cooperation

1. It is important to keep in mind that "On Interpretation" has appeared in three versions. It originally appeared in *Plowshare* in 1934, it was revised for inclusion in the first edition of *PC* (1935), and it was revised again for the second edition of *PC* (1954).

2. "Program" and "Applications of the Terminology" were written in the early 1930s. See also Kenneth Burke, "The Allies of Humanism Abroad"; "Waste—The Future of Prosperity"; "Bankers Arise"; "War, Response, and Contradiction"; and "My Approach to Communism."

3. Albert Halper, *Good-bye, Union Square: A Writer's Memoir of the Thirties* (Chicago: Quadrangle, 1970), 95–96.

4. See Halper, *Good-bye, Union Square,* 96. At the time, the party considered Trotsky's interest in theoretical and political clarity quite dangerous. As Trotsky became more critical of Stalin, the sense of danger intensified.

5. See Halper, *Good-bye, Union Square,* 89–97; and Harvey Klehr, *The Heyday of American Communism: The Depression Decade* (New York: Basic Books, 1984), 73–75. Earlier, representatives of the John Reed Clubs and *New Masses* (including Mike Gold, William Gropper, Joshua Kunitz, A. B. Magil, and Harry Alan Potamkin) went to Kharkov, Russia, to affiliate with the Second World Plenum of the International Bureau of Revolutionary Literature. At that meeting, which was more about politics than literature, the bureau forced the Americans to accept a program that "called for attracting proletarians, 'radicalized intellectuals,' and blacks to their ranks, organizing 'agitprop troupes,' securing more translations of Marxist classics, and so on" (Klehr, *Heyday,* 73). At the same meeting the bureau attacked and ostracized Diego Rivera. "Among other sins," Harvey Klehr points out, "he was flirting with Trotskyism" (Klehr, *Heydey,* 75). The murals for capitalists just made matters worse.

6. Kenneth Burke, "Thirty Years Later: Memories of the First American Writers' Congress," *American Scholar* 10 (Summer 1966): 507.

7. For a good discussion of academic cultures, see Richard H. Pells, *The Liberal Mind in a Conservative Age: American Intellectuals in the 1940s and 1950s* (New York: Harper, 1985), 96–150.

8. "Psychology and Form" and "The Poetic Process" were written in winter 1924 and published in 1925.

9. These are the major figures Burke discusses. He does mention other psychologists.

10. Austin Warren, "The Sceptic's Progress," *American Review* 6 (1935–36): 203.

11. Burke's mention of social deviance is not mere chance. After the *Dial* ceased publication in 1929, he was a researcher for the Laura Spelman Rockefeller Memorial Foundation. Later, as an editorial assistant to Col. Arthur Woods, he researched drug addiction for the Bureau of Social Hygiene (Paul Jay, ed., *The Selected Correspondence of Kenneth Burke and Malcolm Cowley, 1915–1981* [New York: Viking, 1988], 152). Also, for most of his life Burke overindulged in alcohol (which in 1932, he said, resulted in "social damage"; see Jay, *Selected Correspondence,* 203).

12. The text of the third edition (1984), with the exception of the afterword, is the same as the text of the second edition (1954). In the appendix I have quoted the most important sections of the first edition deleted from later editions. The first edition of *PC* was published as *Permanence and Change: An Anatomy of Purpose* (New York: New Republic, 1935). For a thorough description of the differences in the three editions, see Edward Schiappa and Mary F. Keehner, "The 'Lost' Passages of *Permanence and Change*," *Communication Studies* 42 (Fall 1991): 191–98.

13. See, for instance, the closing remarks concerning the "pathetic fallacy" (*PC*, 215).

14. I do not mean to imply that Burke believed in a simple environmentalism, though his references to Pavlov and others may lead some readers of *PC* to think so. Readers of *PC* must understand the intellectual context in which such references occurred. Burke was simply pointing out that traditional ideas of motives were deficient.

15. Terry A. Cooney, *The Rise of the New York Intellectuals: Partisan Review and Its Circle* (Madison: University of Wisconsin Press, 1986), 14–17.

16. Edgar Johnson, "Society and the Poetic Method," *Saturday Review of Literature*, 26 Oct. 1935, 22.

17. Terry Eagleton, *Literary Theory: An Introduction* (Minneapolis: University of Minnesota Press, 1996), 39.

18. Johnson, "Society and the Poetic Method," 22.

19. Ernest Sutherland Bates, "A Spendthrift with Ideas," *New York Herald Tribune Books,* 12 May 1935, 8.

20. Ibid. This kind of criticism will be leveled against Burke throughout his career. A notable example is Sidney Hook's attack against *Attitudes,* discussed in chapter 4.

21. Henry Hazlitt, "Kenneth Burke's Metaphysics," *New York Times Book Review,* 5 June 1935, 19.

22. Harold Rosenberg, "Meaning and Communication," *Poetry* 47 (Mar. 1936): 347–49. Further page references to Rosenberg appear within parentheses in the text.

23. T. D. Eliot, review of *PC, American Sociological Review* 2 (Feb. 1937): 114–15; Louis Wirth, review of *PC, American Journal of Sociology* 43 (Nov. 1937): 483–86; and Irving J. Lee, review of *PC, Quarterly Journal of Speech* 25 (Dec. 1939): 688. Lee begins his review with this statement: "Students of public speaking should know this book."

Chapter 4—*Attitudes toward History:* Conflict in Human Association

1. Perhaps it was a marketing decision. *Attitudes* appeared in the *New Republic's* "Dollar Series," which had previously published Burke (*PC*) and was known for producing well-manufactured case-bound editions of sophisticated criticism at a reasonable cost. Even in 1937 a publisher could hardly make a profit on a single long book priced at only one dollar (*Attitudes* retailed for one dollar per volume). I have seen two first editions of *Attitudes,* and neither seemed well produced. Both were printed on relatively cheap paper, and one of them had pages of varying height (with virtually all of the octavos uncut on the top). By the way, the latter copy supports my claim that the dictionary is largely ignored. In vol. 1 of that copy many of the pages were separated; the ragged and careless cuts were made by readers, I presume. Vol. 2 did not have a single readable octavo. No one cared to cut those pages apart.

2. Control is a half-page in length. Bridging Device, Cluster, Forensic, Salvation, Sect, Stealing Back and Forth of Symbols, and Symbolic Mergers are one to two pages in length. Alienation, Bureaucratization of the Imaginative, Casuistic Stretching, Discounting, Efficiency, "Good Life," "Heads I Win, Tails You Lose," Lexicological, Perspective by Incongruity, and

Secular Prayer range from four to slightly more than eight pages. The longer entries are: Neo-Malthusian Principle (eleven pages), Identity, Identification (fifteen pages), Symbolic Authority (fifteen pages—this figure is somewhat misleading because the text of that entry is mostly footnotes that are densely printed), and Imagery (twenty-four pages). The longest entry is Cues (thirty pages). These figures are approximations, based on the text of the first edition.

3. Burke began writing *Attitudes* in the summer of 1936. Though the exact date of completion is unclear, it was finished within a year. See Paul Jay, ed., *The Selected Correspondence of Kenneth Burke and Malcolm Cowley, 1915–1981* (New York: Viking, 1988), 212–20.

4. In 1916 eight people were killed and forty injured when a bomb exploded during a Preparedness Day parade in San Francisco. Tom Mooney was sentenced to death in 1917 for the bombing, sparking worldwide protests. President Wilson then commuted the sentence to life imprisonment. See Daniel Bell, *Marxian Socialism in the United States* (Princeton: Princeton University Press, 1967), 103–4.

5. Frederick J. Hoffman, Charles Allen, and Caroline F. Ulrich, eds., *The Little Magazine: A History and a Bibliography* (Princeton: Princeton University Press, 1947), 105–7. I have found no record of the exact passage that so irritated the censor, but it was probably this one: "and when the auctioneer had shouted Who buys these women? Llan answered I buy these w—— and flung down the money inasmuch as they were dear girls they were lovely girls nor were they afraid by God of him. Their breasts were tight up beneath their shoulders. Their breasts, they stood out firm like pegs. When they walked, one could note their sitters, how they undulated. And taking each girl by an arm, so that his thumbs were pressed carefully into their armpits, Prince Llan started with them out into life." This passage appears in Kenneth Burke, *The Complete White Oxen: Collected Short Fiction of Kenneth Burke,* 222 (the reissued version, with additions, of *The White Oxen and Other Stories* [1924]). The censorship of *Broom* is discussed in Selzer, *Kenneth Burke,* chapter 5, passim.

6. Stalin's excesses and the anti-Stalinism they fueled have a complex history. I shall point out a few of the factors important to the intellectual Left in New York in the 1930s. Perhaps the earliest attacks against Stalin generally available to Americans were conducted by Max Eastman, who released Lenin's last two letters (known as the "Suppressed Testament"), which attacked Stalin and suggested that Trotsky replace him as party secretary. Eastman then published *Since Lenin Died* (1925) and *Leon Trotsky: Portrait of a Youth* (1926). See Alan M. Wald, *The New York Intellectuals: The Rise and Decline of the Anti-Stalinist Left from the 1930s to the 1980s* (Chapel Hill: University of North Carolina Press, 1987), 112–13. In the next ten years anti-Stalinism existed principally as a theoretical critique. The Moscow Trials, which began in 1936, marked the beginning of widespread questions about Stalin's tyranny. His refusal to intervene in the Spanish Civil War, a conflict which captured the hearts of American Communists and leftists, supported the perception that Stalin was more interested in his own position than realizing the goal of world communism. Also, in early 1937 André Gide published *Return from the U.S.S.R.,* a report critical of Russian society. Gide was harshly criticized, leading him to publish a response to his critics, *Second Thoughts on the U.S.S.R.* (July 1937, in French). The *Partisan Review* published excerpts of *Second Thoughts* in Jan. 1938. See Terry A. Cooney, *The Rise of the New York Intellectuals: Partisan Review and Its Circle* (Madison: University of Wisconsin Press, 1986), 121–23.

7. After 1933 *Modern Quarterly* became *Modern Monthly.*

8. See Daniel Aaron, *Writers on the Left: Episodes in American Literary Communism* (New York: Oxford University Press, 1977), 322–33; and Wald, *New York Intellectuals,* 111–12.

9. This comment appears on p. 506 of the transcript of a discussion held 8 Dec. 1965, sponsored by the *American Scholar* at the suggestion of Kenneth Burke and Malcolm Cowley, and published as "Thirty Years Later: Memories of the First American Writers' Congress," *American Scholar* 35 (Summer 1966): 495–516. The discussants included Malcolm Cowley, Kenneth Burke, Granville Hicks, and William Phillips. Daniel Aaron moderated.

10. See the 8 Dec. 1965 transcript, p. 508. Malcolm Cowley gives much the same report in *The Dream of the Golden Mountains: Remembering the 1930s* (New York: Viking, 1980), 276–79.

11. Groff Conklin, "The Science of Symbology," *New Masses*, 10 Aug. 1937, 25. Further page references to Conklin appear within parentheses in the text.

12. Crane Brinton, "What Is History?" *Saturday Review of Literature*, 14 Aug. 1937, 3. Further page references to Brinton appear within parentheses in the text.

13. His beat is "The Curve of History." The "philosophers of history" include Oswald Spengler, Vilfredo Pareto, Pitirim A. Sorokin, Charles A. Beard, and Arnold Toynbee.

14. Schlaugh cites the section on "Cues," in "The Dictionary of Pivotal Terms." Even Burke was unhappy with this section. He called it "the most vulnerable section" (Jay, *Selected Correspondence*, 219).

15. Margaret Schlaugh, review of *ATH, Science and Society* 2 (Winter 1937): 130. Further page references to Schlaugh appear within parentheses in the text.

16. This aspect of "acceptance" and "rejection" is similar to ideas Burke developed in his earlier books. In *CS*, for instance, Burke spoke of "yea-saying" and "nay-saying" ("Applications of the Terminology," in *CS*, 185–86). In *ATH*, Burke virtually began his analysis of "acceptance" and "rejection" (*ATH*, 3) by tracing these terms to Schopenhauer's "Bejahung und Verneinung"—terms stemming etymologically from the German "yes" and "no." Burke even suggests a connection. In a letter to Cowley dated 6 Oct. 1936, Burke wrote that the early part of *ATH* "focuses on 'frames of acceptance and rejection' (our reworking of Schopenhauer's 'Bejahung und Verneinung' formula?)" (Jay, *Selected Correspondence*, 214). Also, in *PC* "trained incapacity" and "occupational psychosis" were examples of how "acceptance" and "rejection" are cultivated by experience.

17. Arthur E. DuBois, "Accepting and Rejecting Kenneth Burke," *Sewanee Review* 45 (July–Sept. 1937): 343–57.

18. Ibid. DuBois uses these terms on p. 349.

19. Ibid. DuBois (343) cites Charles I. Glicksberg, "Kenneth Burke: The Critic's Critic," *South Atlantic Quarterly* 36 (1937): 74–84. DuBois also reveals some knowledge of Burke's background (345).

20. *Avenue* was published semimonthly from Jan. 1934 until Apr. 1935. *Alentour* lasted from spring 1935 until winter 1942–43. *Chameleon* was a mimeographed quarterly published from Sept. 1936 until summer 1937. See Hoffman et al., *Little Magazine*, 317, 329, 332.

21. The discussion of "the best part" comprises the last three paragraphs of the review (355–56).

22. Arthur E. DuBois, review of *ATH, Southwest Review* 23 (Jan. 1938): 224. Further page references to DuBois appear within parentheses in the text.

23. Henry Bamford Parkes, "Attitudes toward History," *Southern Review* 3 (Spring 1938): 699. Further page references to Parkes appear within parentheses in the text.

24. Sidney Hook, "The Technique of Mystification," *Partisan Review* 4 (Dec. 1937): 57–62. Further page references to Hook appear within parentheses in the text. Burke had received more

emotionally taxing criticism at the 1935 American Writers' Congress, in response to his address "Revolutionary Symbolism in America." But this criticism came orally. The published proceedings of the congress supply texts of the papers presented (which do not comment on Burke's address) and some quotations from the discussion/attack of "Revolutionary Symbolism." These quotations are generally thoughtful and tame—lacking the vitriolic temper elsewhere reported of the discussion. This lacuna may be explained by the desire of the editor of the congress proceedings to present in writing a sense of unity. Or perhaps Burke had a hand in it, since he at least helped edit the papers for publication. See Henry Hart, ed., *American Writers' Congress* (New York: International, 1935), 17, 165–71.

25. For "stinko" see Jay, *Selected Correspondence,* 367; for "hatchetman job" see "Thirty Years Later," 514. Also, Burke said, "I myself, for instance, had begged to have the Hook ones included." This stems in part from Burke's desire that the book "go back over the things that were said pro and con, o'er the years, and make a document of them" (Jay, *Selected Correspondence,* 367).

26. Kenneth Burke, "Is Mr. Hook a Socialist?" *Partisan Review* 4 (Jan. 1938): 40–44; Sidney Hook, "Is Mr. Burke Serious?" *Partisan Review* 4 (Jan. 1938): 44–47. Further page references to these works appear within parentheses in the text.

27. Burke has published some commentary on reviews of his books (for instance, "Counterblasts on 'Counter-Statement'" and "Intuitive or Scientific?"), but these statements are substantially briefer than the *Partisan Review* piece. Burke's longest response to a critic is his response to Margaret Schlaugh's review of *ATH*. See Kenneth Burke, "Twelve Propositions by Kenneth Burke on the Relation between Economy and Psychology," 242–49.

28. Kenneth Burke, letter to Benjamin De Mott, 2 Feb. 1963, James Sibley Watson/Dial Papers, in the Henry W. and Albert A. Berg Collection of English and American Literature, the New York Public Library.

Chapter 5—*The Philosophy of Literary Form:* Literature as Equipment for Living

1. "The Rhetoric of Hitler's 'Battle'" is Burke's most frequently cited piece of criticism on a single book. The essay has gained attention more for what it says about Hitler and his rhetoric than for Burke's particular critical methods. It is true that the concept of "scapegoating," largely because of this essay, has become a topos in the secondary literature. However, for the past fifty years the kind of analysis Burke used in this essay has seldom been repeated by others.

2. René Wellek, "Kenneth Burke," in René Wellek, *A History of Modern Criticism: 1750–1950,* vol. 6: *American Criticism, 1900–1950* (New Haven: Yale University Press, 1986), 235–56. This chapter is based on René Wellek, "Kenneth Burke and Literary Criticism," *Sewanee Review* 79 (Apr.–June 1971): 171–88. Further page references to Wellek appear within parentheses in the text.

3. There are more than a dozen citations to *PLF.* Only three of these are to other essays in the book.

4. Although Burke's response came in 1972 and he refers to works after *PLF,* the point applies to the rest of the book too.

5. William H. Rueckert, *Kenneth Burke and the Drama of Human Relations* (Minneapolis: University of Minnesota Press, 1963), 56–59. Rueckert focuses on how symbol action is "representative of the self" and "has a compensating function for the self" (58). See Burke's discussion of Samuel Taylor Coleridge for how such elements obtain in symbolic action. On another matter

Rueckert points out, quite appropriately, that symbolic acts are not impractical; rather, he says, the difference is between an "act" and an "accident" (59).

6. For more on debunking, see "Corrosive without Corrective" (review of Arnold's *The Folklore of Capitalism* in *PLF,* 400–404) and "Semantics in Demotic" (review of Stuart Chase's *The Tyranny of Words* in *PLF,* 396–99).

7. William S. Knickerbocker, "Wam for Maw: Dogma Versus Discursiveness in Criticism," *Sewanee Review* 49 (Oct.–Dec. 1941): 520–36; Harry Slochower, review of *PLF, University Review* (University of Kansas City) 8 (Winter 1941): 119–23.

8. This is the subtitle of the essay (*CS,* 123).

9. Burke had long argued against a simple quality-quantity distinction, contending that changes in quantity induce changes in quality. Note also "Quantity and Quality," in *PLF,* 394–96.

10. Kenneth Burke, "As I Was Saying," *Michigan Quarterly Review* 11 (Winter 1972): 26.

11. Frank Lentricchia, *Criticism and Social Change* (Chicago: University of Chicago Press, 1983), 69. Further page references to Lentricchia appear within parentheses in the text.

12. The date of composition of "The Philosophy of Literary Form" is unclear. As early as Dec. 1940 Burke indicated that it had been completed (Paul Jay, ed., *The Selected Correspondence of Kenneth Burke and Malcolm Cowley, 1915–1981* [New York: Viking, 1988], 233).

13. "On the Sublime" was the third, unfinished, essay (Jay, *Selected Correspondence,* 233). When Burke turned his gaze back to his literary roots, he also looked forward. In the 1940 letter cited earlier (Jay, *Selected Correspondence,* 233), Burke also spoke of working on a "Human Relations book" (which, after many changes, eventually became *GM* and perhaps part of *RM*). He believed, moreover, that "a very neat monograph" on the five key terms "might prove to be as fertile an essay for me personally as my 'Psychology and Form'" (Jay, *Selected Correspondence,* 233). A decade later, reviewing for Cowley the genesis of his books, Burke commented that the proposed third volume of his motives trilogy, "A Symbolic of Motives," would "carry further the sort of problem treated in *The Philosophy of Literary Form*" (Jay, *Selected Correspondence,* 292). Thus, *PLF* anticipates one key element of the problem of motives in human conduct.

14. Burke speaks of "statistical motives" in "The Search for Motives." See *PC,* 218–20.

15. Burke should have seen the criticism coming. His entry "Cues" in "The Dictionary of Pivotal Terms" in *ATH* was attacked on similar grounds.

16. Or, one might even say, Aristotelian rhetoric over Aristotelian dialectic. I hesitate to bring Aristotle into the matter, since for too long too much has been made of Burke's purported Aristotelianism. For an illuminating discussion of the issue, see Michael Leff, "Burke's Ciceronianism," in Herbert W. Simons and Trevor Melia, eds., *The Legacy of Kenneth Burke* (Madison: University of Wisconsin Press, 1989), 115–27.

17. Malcolm Cowley, "A Critic's First Principle," *New Republic* 14 (Sept. 1953): 17.

18. The *Faust* piece, I gather, is "Goethe's *Faust, Part I,*" *Chicago Review* 8 (Fall 1954). A decade later Burke followed this with "*Faust II*—The Ideas behind the Imagery," *Centennial Review* 9 (Fall 1965): 367–97. Both are reprinted in *LASA*. The essay on *Othello,* I gather, is "Othello: An Essay To Illustrate a Method," *Hudson Review* 4 (Summer 1951): 165–203. This was reprinted in Stanley Edgar Hyman, ed., *Perspectives by Incongruity* (Bloomington: Indiana University Press, 1964). Burke also suggests to Cowley that a superior essay is "Form and Persecution in the *Oresteia,*" *Sewanee Review* 60 (Summer 1952): 377–96. This too is reprinted in *LASA*.

19. Rhetorical form establishes the nature of symbolic appeal on the individual level. "Eloquence" suggests that the proliferation of rhetorical forms is the means through which sym-

bolic appeal is effected. And the Lexicon is an extended compilation of instances of that mechanism's workings.

20. Piety is much like the expectation-satisfaction curve of *CS*. Perspective by incongruity is analogous to eloquence—the proliferation of form.

Part III—The Tactics of Motivation

1. In the 1935 edition of *PC,* Burke uses the term "communist corrective." Burke deleted some references to communism and changed the language of others for the 1954 edition. This is discussed in more detail in chapter 3.

2. There are reports of drafts of "A Symbolic of Motives." In his letters to Malcolm Cowley and James Sibley Watson Jr., Burke talks about drafts, though what they were composed of is not clear from primary sources. For some of Burke's comments about the "Symbolic," see *CS,* 217–19 and the "Addendum" in the same volume. In addition, see William H. Rueckert, *Kenneth Burke and the Drama of Human Relations,* 2d ed. (Berkeley: University of California Press, 1963), 230–37, 288–92. See also Herbert W. Simons and Trevor Melia, eds., *The Legacy of Kenneth Burke* (Madison: University of Wisconsin Press, 1989), 251–52.

3. Burke did not get along with the staff and writers of the *Partisan Review.* Sidney Hook, who had much influence on the journal, had been particularly critical of both Burke and Cowley—hence "Fartisan."

4. Kenneth Burke, *Dramatism and Development,* Heinz Werner Series, vol. 6 (Barre, Mass.: Clark University Press, 1972), 23–24.

5. Ibid., 21.

6. The series appeared in two issues, with three articles in the Jan.–Feb. issue and the other four in the Mar.–Apr. issue. Included in "The New Failure of Nerve, Part I," *Partisan Review* 10 (Jan.–Feb. 1943): 2–57, are "The New Failure of Nerve," by Sidney Hook; "Anti-Naturalism in Extremis," by John Dewey; and "Malicious Philosophies of Science," by Ernest Nagel. Page references to Hook, Dewey, and Nagel appear within parentheses in the text. Included in "The New Failure of Nerve, Part II," *Partisan Review* 10 (Mar.–Apr. 1943): 134–77, are "Neither-Nor," by Norbert Guterman; "The Huxley-Heard Paradise," by Richard V. Chase; "Human Nature Is Not a Trap," by Ruth Benedict; and "The Failure of the Left," by Sidney Hook. "The New Failure of Nerve" elicited responses and rejoinders. For instance, see David Merian, "The Nerve of Sidney Hook," *Partisan Review* 10 (May–June 1943): 248–57; Sidney Hook, "The Politics of Wonderland," *Partisan Review* 10 (May–June 1943): 258–62; Philip Wheelwright, "Dogmatism—New Style," *Chimera* 4 (Spring 1943): 7–16; Ernest Nagel, "Mr. Wheelwright's Wisdom," *Partisan Review* 11 (Winter 1944): 37–42.

7. Kenneth Burke, "The Tactics of Motivation." Page references to this work appear within parentheses in the text. The essays by Wheelwright and Auden appeared in *The Chimera.* I do not know if Maritain wrote a response. If he did, it was not published with the others.

Chapter 6—*A Grammar of Motives: Ad Bellum Purification* through "Dialectic"

1. Kenneth Burke, "Dramatism." This is a shortened version of "Dramatism," which appeared in Lee Thayer, ed., *Communication: Concepts and Perspectives* (Washington, D.C.: Spartan, 1967), 327–52.

2. Ibid., 445.

3. Burke discusses this in "The Tactics of Motivation," 23–27.

4. See "Semantic and Poetic Meaning," *PLF,* 138–67.

5. Burke would certainly admit that some philosophies are rhetoric in the traditional sense, designed to advance the interests of their creators. However, in casting philosophy as casuistry, he refers to a philosophy's nature as a structure of ideas.

6. A representative anecdote is essentially the same as a paradigm case. Although drama is the representative anecdote for dramatism, Burke discusses other representative anecdotes in *GM.* The most significant is political constitution, which is largely the anecdote for the last third of the book. Burke had considered a variety of other representative anecdotes for that section, including Grand Central Station, tribal festivals, warfare, and peace. Burke analyzes these alternatives under the classes in which they fall, including "metonymic," "synecdochic," "concentric," "constitutive," "admonitory," and "directive" (*GM,* 325 ff.).

7. With dramatism founded on a representative anecdote, we see why Max Black's criticisms are so harsh. Not only does he spurn what he takes to be Burke's metaphysical and ontological assumptions, he is well known for rejecting the idea of a paradigm case.

8. In an addendum Burke points out that if he were writing *GM* now, he would posit a "hexad" instead of a pentad. The sixth term would be "attitude."

9. The discussion of Darwin occurs in "The Philosophic Schools," 152–58.

10. "Stasis theory was designed to enable one both to locate the relevant points at issue in a dispute and to discover applicable arguments drawn from the appropriate 'places' (loci, the Latin equivalent of the Greek *topoi*)" (Thomas M. Conley, Rhetoric in the European Tradition [New York: Longman, 1990], 32).

11. With dramatism being an act-centered perspective, Burke expends much effort examining how we interpret acts as arising from the other terms. Given the prominence of a variety of materialist and other scenic perspectives in the world, Burke also expends much effort analyzing ratios involving scene.

12. "Rationalism is, in one sense, intrinsic to philosophy as a medium, since every philosophy attempts to propound a rationale of its position, even if it is a philosophy of the irrational" (GM, 129).

13. "The fiction of positive law," he cautions, "has generally served to set up the values, traditions, and trends of business as the Constitution-behind-the-Constitution that is to be consulted as criterion" (GM, 363).

14. See the discussion of this in chapter 5.

15. In the collections of essays (CS and PLF), the credo occurs generally in distinct sections; in the books conceived as singular entities (PC and ATH), the functions remain analytically clear, though organizationally less distinct.

16. The attack against science and positivism is most explicit in PC and CS. Writing to Malcolm Cowley in 1947 concerning neo-substantiveness and terminologies of essence in RM, Burke said: "It is all part of my continuing battle against positivism. . . . Positivists, in the formal sense, are not very ubiquitous enemies. But positivism, in the half-assed sense, is all about us, and thus is properly one of my major concerns" (Paul Jay, ed., The Selected Correspondence of Kenneth Burke and Malcolm Cowley, 1915–1981 [New York: Viking, 1988], 277). Regarding another matter, Burke's later writings in the period from 1925 to 1945 tend to conflate the credo.

So "The Philosophy of Literary Form" serves all three functions to some extent, whereas the essays written in the early to middle 1930s that appear in PLF tend to be more singular.

17. Max Black, review of *GM, Philosophical Review* 40 (July 1946): 487. Further page references to Black appear within parentheses in the text.

18. Abraham Kaplan, review of *GM, Journal of Aesthetics and Art Criticism* 5 (March 1947): 233. Further page references to Kaplan appear within parentheses in the text.

Chapter 7—*A Rhetoric of Motives:* Communication, Hierarchy, and Formal Appeal

1. Hugh Dalziel Duncan, review of *RM, American Journal of Sociology* 56 (May 1951): 593.

2. For instance, see the following passage: "In particular, as regards the teaching of literature, the insistence upon 'autonomy' reflects a vigorous concern with the all-importance of the text that happens to be under scrutiny. This cult of patient textual analysis (though it has excesses of its own) is helpful as a reaction against the excesses of extreme historicism (a leftover of the nineteenth century) whereby a work became so subordinated to its background that the student's appreciation of first-rate texts was lost behind his involvement with the collateral documents of fifth-rate literary historians" (*RM*, 28). In a roughly similar case, Burke comments that anthropology and literary criticism are not mutually exclusive, that each may benefit from the discoveries of the other (*RM*, 40–41).

3. Burke elaborates on the meaning and function of ultimate terms in the third part of *RM*, "Order" (see 183–97).

4. See, for instance, Foss, Karen A., and Cindy L. White, "'Being' and the Promise of Trinity: A Feminist Addition to Burke's Theory of Dramatism," in *Kenneth Burke and the Twenty-first Century*, ed. Bernard L. Brock (Albany, N.Y.: State University of New York Press, 1999), 102–5. For a broader discussion of feminist criticisms of Burke, see Condit, "Framing Kenneth Burke" and "Post-Burke."

5. I borrow this phrase from Stanley Cavell, *The Claim of Reason: Wittgenstein, Skepticism, Morality, and Tragedy* (New York: Oxford University Press, 1982), 318–26.

6. See, for instance, Foss, Sonja K., and Cindy L. Griffin, "A Feminist Perspective on Rhetorical Theory: Toward a Classification of Boundaries," *Western Journal of Communication* 56 (Fall 1992): 29–45.

7. The best overview of the intellectual currents that led to Ramus's theories and their impact appears in Walter Ong, S. J., *Ramus, Method, and the Decay of Dialogue: From the Art of Discourse to the Art of Reason* (Cambridge: Harvard University Press, 1958).

8. Note that Burke is reaffirming here the position he took in *PC* that communication is a matter of ethics. See chapter 3 on *PC*.

9. Aristotle lists twenty-eight common topics. Among them are arguments from: opposites, different grammatical forms, correlatives, the more and less, time, turning what has been said against oneself upon the one who said it, definition, the varied meanings of a word, division, induction, a previous judgment about the same or a similar or opposite matter, parts, and consequences. Burke offers the following as an example of how a common topic is used (in this case, "dividing an assertion"): "there were three motives for the offense; two were impossible, not even the accusers have asserted the third" (*GM*, 57).

10. See, for instance, Booth, *Modern Dogma*, 17–21, 101–6.

11. See the discussion of *PC* in chapter 2.

12. As malign and exploitative as these relations sometimes are, Burke does not seem to be referring to the kind of masculine-feminine distinction between the leader and the masses that he noted in Hitler's *Mein Kampf.*

13. For instance, see Burke's qualifications regarding his aesthetic program in *CS* (121–22). He argues that his aesthetic program—a corrective to capitalist profit motives—may not be necessary under "a kindlier cluster of conditions."

14. Few persons—other than proponents of racial segregation—complained about affirmative action when there were plenty of jobs to be had in what was thought to be an ever-growing economy.

Chapter 8—*The Rhetoric of Religion* and *Language as Symbolic Action:* Burke in the 1950s and 1960s

1. Richard Kostelanetz, "A Mind That Cannot Stop Exploding," *New York Times Book Review,* 15 Mar. 1981, 11, 24–26.

2. René Wellek, "Kenneth Burke and Literary Criticism," *Sewanee Review* 79 (Apr.–June 1971): 171–88; R. P. Blackmur, "A Critic's Job of Work." In *Language as Gesture: Essays in Poetry* (New York: Harcourt, Brace, 1952), 393.

3. William H. Rueckert, *Kenneth Burke and the Drama of Human Relations,* 2d ed. (Berkeley: University of California Press, 1982), 241. Further page references to Rueckert appear within parentheses in the text.

4. Robert Wess, *Kenneth Burke: Rhetoric, Subjectivity, Postmodernism* (New York: Cambridge University Press, 1996), 218, 217.

5. Robert E. Garlitz, "The Sacrificial Word in Kenneth Burke's Logology," *Recherches Anglaises et Américaines* 12 (1979): 33–44. Further page references to Garlitz appear within parentheses in the text.

6. Joseph Frank, "Symbols and Civilization," *Sewanee Review* 72 (Summer 1964): 485. Burke responds in *Sewanee Review* 73 (Winter 1965): 173–75.

7. I borrow the term "alchemic moment" from *GM.*

8. Daniel Hughes, review of *LASA, Criticism* 10 (Summer 1968): 252. Further page references to Hughes appear within parentheses in the text.

9. Denis Donoghue, *Ferocious Alphabets* (Boston: Little, Brown, 1981), 118.

10. Decades earlier Yvor Winters criticized *CS* (especially "Program") for Burke's alleged slighting of the individual. See Yvor Winters, "Primitivism and Decadence: A Study of American Experimental Poetry." In *In Defense of Reason* (New York: Morrow, 1947), 30–89.73.

11. I disagree with the rest of the quotation, which suggests that dramatism and logology are completely worked-out systems.

Bibliography

The most complete bibliography of Kenneth Burke's writings and of critical responses to him is Armin Paul Frank and Methchild Frank's in *Critical Responses to Kenneth Burke, 1924–1966,* edited by William H. Rueckert. The most complete set of additions and corrections (through 1986) is Richard H. Thames's in *The Legacy of Kenneth Burke,* edited by Herbert W. Simons and Trevor Melia.

This list includes a few items that are not mentioned in this book but which were consulted and contributed to the text's argument.

Books by Kenneth Burke

Attitudes toward History. 2 vols. New York: New Republic, 1937. 2d ed., rev., Los Altos, Calif.: Hermes Publications, 1959. Paperback ed., Indianapolis: Bobbs-Merrill, 1965. 3d ed., rev., Berkeley: University of California Press, 1984.

Book of Moments: Poems 1915–1954. Los Altos, Calif.: Hermes, 1955.

Collected Poems: 1915–1967. Berkeley: University of California Press, 1968.

Counter-Statement. New York: Harcourt, Brace, 1931. 2d ed., rev., Los Altos, Calif.: Hermes Publications, 1954. Berkeley: University of California Press, 1968.

Dramatism and Development. Heinz Werner Series, vol. 6. Barre, Mass.: Clark University Press, 1972.

A Grammar of Motives. New York: Prentice-Hall, 1945. 2d ed., New York: George Braziller, 1955. Berkeley: University of California Press, 1969.

Language as Symbolic Action: Essays on Life, Literature, and Method. Berkeley: University of California Press, 1966.

Permanence and Change: An Anatomy of Purpose. New York: New Republic, 1935. 2d ed., rev., Los Altos, Calif.: Hermes, 1954; Indianapolis: Bobbs-Merrill, 1965. 3rd ed., rev., Berkeley: University of California Press, 1984.

The Philosophy of Literary Form: Studies in Symbolic Action. Baton Rouge: Louisiana State University Press, 1941. 2d ed., New York: Vintage, 1957. 3rd ed., Berkeley: University of California Press, 1973.

A Rhetoric of Motives. New York: Prentice-Hall, 1950. 2d ed., New York: George Braziller, 1955; Berkeley: University of California Press, 1969.

Towards a Better Life: Being a Series of Epistles, or Declamations. New York: Harcourt, Brace, 1932. 2d ed., Berkeley: University of California Press, 1966.

The White Oxen and Other Stories. New York: Albert and Charles Boni, 1924. Reissued, with additions, as *The Complete White Oxen: Collected Short Fiction of Kenneth Burke.* Berkeley: University of California Press, 1968.

Other Works by Kenneth Burke

"Acceptance and Rejection." *Southern Review* 2 (Winter 1937): 600–632.

"The Allies of Humanism Abroad." In *The Critique of Humanism: A Symposium,* edited by C. Hartley Grattan, 169–92. New York: Brewer and Warren, 1930.

"The Anaesthetic Revelation of Herone Liddell." *Kenyon Review* 19 (Autumn 1957): 505–59.

"André Gide, Bookman." *Freeman* 5 (April 1922): 155–57.

"Approaches to Rémy de Gourmont." *Dial* 70 (February 1921): 125–38.

"The Armour of Jules Laforge [*sic*]." *Contact,* issue unknown, probably no. 3 of early series (1920–23): 9–10.

"As I Was Saying." *Michigan Quarterly Review* 11 (Winter 1972): 9–27.

"Bankers Arise." *Americana, Satire and Humor* 1 (May 1933): 4.

"Chicago and Our National Gesture." *Bookman* 57 (July 1923): 497–501.

"The Correspondence of Flaubert." *Dial* 72 (February 1922): 147–55.

"Counterblasts on 'Counter-Statement.'" *New Republic,* 9 December 1931, 101.

"Dramatism." In *International Encyclopedia of the Social Sciences,* vol. 7, 445–52. New York: Macmillan and Free Press, 1968.

"In Response to Booth: Dancing with Tears in My Eyes." *Critical Inquiry* 1 (September 1974): 23–31.

"Intuitive or Scientific?" *Nation* 146 (January 1938): 139–40.

"Is Mr. Hook a Socialist?" *Partisan Review* 4 (January 1938): 40–44.

"A 'Logic' of History." Rev. of *The Decline of the West,* by Oswald Spengler. *Dial* 81 (September 1926): 242–48.

"Methodological Repression and/or Strategies of Containment." *Critical Inquiry* 5 (Winter 1978): 401–16.

"Mrs. Maecenas." *Dial* 68 (March 1920): 346–58.

"Munsoniana." *New Republic* 69 (25 November 1931): 46.

"My Approach to Communism." *New Masses* 10 (20 March 1934): 16, 18–20.

"A New Poetics." Rev. of *Principles of Literary Criticism,* by I. A. Richards. *Saturday Review of Literature* 2 (September 1925): 154–55.

"Notes on Walter Pater." *1924,* no. 2 (1924): 53–58.

"Olympians." *Manuscripts,* no. 1 (February 1922): 5–7.

"On Interpretation." *Plowshare* 10 (February 1934): 3–79.

"On Re and Dis." Rev. of *The Newer Spirit: A Sociological Criticism of Literature,* by V. F. Calverton. *Dial* 79 (August 1925): 165–69.

"The Poetic Process." *Guardian* 2 (May–June 1925): 281–94.

"Prince Llan: An Ethical Masque in Seven Parts, Including a Prologue and a Coda." *Broom* 6 (January 1924): 12–22.

"Psychology and Form." *Dial* 79 (July 1925): 34–46.

"Revolutionary Symbolism in America." In *American Writers' Congress,* edited by Henry Hart, 87–94. New York: International, 1935.

"Scherzando." *Manuscripts,* no. 1 (February 1922): 7–8.

"The Soul of Kajn Tafha." *Dial* 69 (July 1920): 29–32.

"The Tactics of Motivation." *The Chimera* 1 (Spring 1943): 21–33; 2 (Summer 1943): 37–53.

"Thomas Mann and André Gide." *Bookman* 71 (June 1930): 257–64.

"Twelve Propositions by Kenneth Burke on the Relation between Economy and Psychology." *Science and Society* 2 (Spring 1938): 242–49.

"*Ver Renatus Orbis Est.*" *Contact,* no. 4 (1922): 9.

"War, Response, and Contradiction." *Symposium* 4 (October 1933): 458–82.

"Waste—the Future of Prosperity." *New Republic* 73 (July 1930): 228–31.

Translations by Kenneth Burke

Mann, Thomas. "Loulou." *Dial* 70 (April 1921): 428–42.

———. "Tristan." Trans. with Scofield Thayer. *Dial* 73 (December 1922): 593–610; continued in 74 (January 1923): 57–76.

Mombert, Alfred. "Lullaby." *Sansculotte* 1 (January 1917): 4.

Reviews of Kenneth Burke's Books

Bacon, Wallace. Review of *Language as Symbolic Action*. *Quarterly Journal of Speech* 53 (October 1967): 295–96.

Bates, Ernest Sutherland. "A Spendthrift with Ideas." Review of *Permanence and Change*. *New York Herald Tribune Books*, 12 May 1935, 8.

Black, Max. Review of *A Grammar of Motives*. *Philosophical Review* 40 (July 1946): 487–90.

Brinton, Crane. "What Is History?" Review of *Attitudes toward History*. *Saturday Review of Literature*, 14 August 1937, 3–4, 11.

Chamberlain, John. "Rhetoric Finds a Champion in Kenneth Burke." Review of *Counter-Statement*. *New York Times Book Review*, 25 October 1931, 2.

Chase, Richard. "Rhetoric of Rhetoric." Review of *A Rhetoric of Motives*. *Partisan Review* 17 (September–October 1950): 736–39.

Conklin, Groff. "The Science of Symbology." Review of *Attitudes toward History*. *New Masses*, 10 August 1937, 25–26.

Cowley, Malcolm. "A Critic's First Principle." Review of *Counter-Statement*, 2d ed. *New Republic*, 14 September 1953, 16–17.

Dineen, F. P., S.J. Review of *The Rhetoric of Religion*. *General Linguistics* 13 (1973): 176–95.

DuBois, Arthur E. "Accepting and Rejecting Kenneth Burke." Review of "Acceptance and Rejection," as published in the *Southern Review*. *Sewanee Review* 45 (July–September 1937): 343–57.

———. Review of *Attitudes toward History*. *Southwest Review* 23 (January 1938): 224–31.

Duncan, Hugh Dalziel. "Communication in Society." Review of *The Rhetoric of Religion* and other books. *Arts in Society* 3 (1964): 93–106.

Eliot, T. D. Review of *Permanence and Change*. *American Sociological Review* 2 (February 1937): 114–15.

Frank, Joseph. "Symbols and Civilization." Review of *The Rhetoric of Religion* and other books. *Sewanee Review* 72 (Summer 1964 [or July–September 1964]): 479–89.

Hazlitt, Henry. "Kenneth Burke's Metaphysics." Review of *Permanence and Change*. *New York Times Book Review*, 5 June 1935, 19.

———. "Two Critics." Review of *Counter-Statement*. *Nation*, 6 January 1932, 76–77.

Hicks, Granville. "A Defense of Eloquence." Review of *Counter-Statement*. *New Republic*, 2 December 1931, 75–76.

Hook, Sidney. "The Technique of Mystification." Review of *Attitudes toward History*. *Partisan Review* 4 (December 1937): 57–62. Burke's reply to this review is "Is Mr. Hook a Socialist?" *Partisan Review* 4 (January 1938): 40–44. Hook's rejoinder is "Is Mr. Burke Serious?" *Partisan Review* 4 (January 1938): 44–47.

Hughes, Daniel. Review of *Language as Symbolic Action*. *Criticism* 10 (Summer 1968): 251–53.

Hymes, Dell. Review of *Language as Symbolic Action*. *Language* 44 (September 1968): 664–69.

Johnson, Edgar. "Society and the Poetic Method." Review of *Permanence and Change*. *Saturday Review of Literature*, 26 October 1935, 22.

Knickerbocker, William S. "Wam for Maw: Dogma Versus Discursiveness in Criticism." Review of *The Philosophy of Literary Form* and other books. *Sewanee Review* 49 (October–December 1941): 520–36.

Kunitz, Joshua. "Counter-Statement." Review of *Counter-Statement*. *New Masses* (April 1932): 19–20.

Le Brun, Philip. Review of *Language as Symbolic Action*. *Review of English Studies* 20 (May 1969): 243–46.

Lee, Irving J. Review of *Permanence and Change*. *Quarterly Journal of Speech* 25 (December 1939): 688.

Parkes, Henry Bamford. "Attitudes toward History." Review of *Attitudes toward History*. *Southern Review* 3 (Spring 1938): 693–706.

Rosenberg, Harold. "Meaning and Communication." Review of *Permanence and Change*. *Poetry* 47 (March 1936): 347–49.

———. Review of *Counter-Statement*. *Symposium* 3 (January 1932): 116–22.

Schlaugh, Margaret. "A Reply to Kenneth Burke." Commentary on Burke's "Twelve Propositions by Kenneth Burke on the Relation between Economy and Psychology." *Science and Society* 2 (1937–38): 250–53.

———. Review of *Attitudes to History* [*sic*]. *Science and Society* 2 (Winter 1937): 128–32.

Schneider, Isidor. "A New View of Rhetoric." Review of *Counter-Statement*. *New York Herald Tribune Books*, 13 December 1931, 4. Rpt. in *Critical Responses to Kenneth Burke: 1924–1966*, edited by William H. Rueckert, 22–26. Minneapolis: University of Minnesota Press, 1969.

Slochower, Harry. Review of *The Philosophy of Literary Form*. *University Review* (University of Kansas City) 8 (Winter 1941): 119–23.

Vivas, Eliseo. "Toward and Improved Strategy." Review of *Attitudes toward History*. *Nation*, 25 December 1937, 723.

Warren, Austin. "The Sceptic's Progress." Review of *Permanence and Change*. *American Review* 6 (1935–36): 193–213.

Wirth, Louis. Review of *Permanence and Change*. *American Journal of Sociology* 43 (November 1937): 483–86.

Other Sources

Aaron, Daniel. *Writers on the Left: Episodes in American Literary Communism*. New York: Oxford University Press, 1977.

Abbott, Don. "Marxist Influences on the Rhetorical Theory of Kenneth Burke." *Philosophy and Rhetoric* 7 (Fall 1974): 217–33.

Abel, Lionel. *The Intellectual Follies: A Memoir of the Literary Venture in New York and Paris*. New York: Norton, 1984.

"Announcement." *Dial* 86 (January 1929): 90. An announcement of Kenneth Burke's "*Dial* Award."

Bell, Daniel. *Marxian Socialism in the United States*. Princeton: Princeton University Press, 1967.

Bender, Thomas. *New York Intellect: A History of Intellectual Life in New York City, From 1750 to the Beginnings of Our Own Time*. Baltimore: Johns Hopkins University Press, 1988.

Bizzell, Patricia, and Bruce Herzberg, eds. *The Rhetorical Tradition: Reading from Classical Times to the Present*. Boston: Bedford, 1990.

Blackmur, R. P. "A Critic's Job of Work." *Language as Gesture: Essays in Poetry*. New York: Harcourt, Brace, 1952, 372–99.

Booth, Wayne C. "Kenneth Burke's Way of Knowing." *Critical Inquiry* 1 (September 1974): 1–22.

Buckley, Michael J., S.J. "Philosophic Method in Cicero." *Journal of the History of Philosophy* 8 (April 1970): 143–54.

Carter, C. Allen. "Logology and Religion: Kenneth Burke on the Metalinguistic Dimension of Language." *Journal of Religion* 72 (January 1992): 1–18.

Cavell, Stanley. *The Claim of Reason: Wittgenstein, Skepticism, Morality, and Tragedy*. New York: Oxford University Press, 1982.

Chesebro, James W., ed. *Extensions of the Burkeian System*. Tuscaloosa: University of Alabama Press, 1993.

Conley, Thomas M. *Rhetoric in the European Tradition*. New York: Longman, 1990.

Cooney, Terry A. *The Rise of the New York Intellectuals: Partisan Review and Its Circle*. Madison: University of Wisconsin Press, 1986.

Cowley, Malcolm. *The Dream of the Golden Mountains: Remembering the 1930s*. New York: Viking, 1980.

———. *Exile's Return: A Narrative of Ideas*. New York: Norton, 1934. Revised and reissued as *Exile's Return: A Literary Odyssey of the 1920's*. New York: Viking, 1951.

———. "This Youngest Generation." *Literary Review of the New York Evening Post*, 15 October 1921, 81–82.

Crusius, Timothy W. "A Case for Kenneth Burke's Dialectic and Rhetoric." *Philosophy and Rhetoric* 19 (January 1986): 23–37.

———. "Kenneth Burke's *Auscultation:* A 'De-struction' of Marxist Dialectic and Rhetoric." *Rhetorica* 6 (Autumn 1988): 355–79.

Desilet, Gregory. "Nietzsche Contra Burke: The Melodrama in Dramatism." *Quarterly Journal of Speech* 75 (February 1989): 65–83.

Donoghue, Denis. *Ferocious Alphabets*. Boston: Little, Brown, 1981.

Eagleton, Terry. *Literary Theory: An Introduction*. Minneapolis: University of Minnesota Press, 1996.

Feehan, Michael. "Kenneth Burke's Discovery of Dramatism." *Quarterly Journal of Speech* 65 (December 1979): 405–11.

Foss, Sonja K., Karen A. Foss, and Robert Trapp. *Contemporary Perspectives on Rhetoric*. Prospect Heights, Ill.: Waveland, 1985.

Glicksberg, Charles I. "Kenneth Burke: The Critic's Critic." *South Atlantic Quarterly* 36 (1937): 74–84.

Gregg, Richard B. "Kenneth Burke's Prolegomena to the Study of the Rhetoric of Form." *Communication Quarterly* 26 (1978): 3–13.

Halper, Albert. *Good-bye, Union Square: A Writer's Memoir of the Thirties*. Chicago: Quadrangle, 1970.

Hart, Henry, ed. *American Writers' Congress*. New York: International, 1935.

Heath, Robert L. "Kenneth Burke on Form." *Quarterly Journal of Speech* 65 (December 1979): 392–404.

————. "Kenneth Burke's Break with Formalism." *Quarterly Journal of Speech* 70 (May 1984): 132–43.

————. *Realism and Relativism: A Perspective on Kenneth Burke.* Macon, Ga.: Mercer University Press, 1986.

Henderson, Greig E. *Kenneth Burke: Literature and Language as Symbolic Action.* Athens: University of Georgia Press, 1988.

Hoffman, Frederick J., Charles Allen, and Caroline F. Ulrich, eds. *The Little Magazine: A History and a Bibliography.* Princeton: Princeton University Press, 1947.

Hook, Sidney. *Out of Step: An Unquiet Life in the Twentieth Century.* New York: Harper, 1987.

Hyman, Stanley Edgar. *The Armed Vision: A Study in the Method of Modern Literary Criticism.* New York: Vintage, 1955.

————. *The Tangled Bank: Darwin, Marx, Frazer and Freud as Imaginative Writers.* New York: Antheneum, 1974.

Jameson, Fredric. "Critical Response: Ideology and Symbolic Action." *Critical Inquiry* (Spring 1978): 417–22.

————. "The Symbolic Inference; or, Kenneth Burke and Ideological Analysis." *Critical Inquiry* 4 (Spring 1978): 507–23.

Jay, Paul, ed. *The Selected Correspondence of Kenneth Burke and Malcolm Cowley, 1915–1981.* New York: Viking, 1988.

Josephson, Matthew. *Life among the Surrealists, A Memoir.* New York: Holt, Rinehart and Winston, 1962.

King, Robert L. "Transforming Scandal into Tragedy: A Rhetoric of Political Apology." *Quarterly Journal of Speech* 71 (August 1985): 289–301.

Klehr, Harvey. *The Heyday of American Communism: The Depression Decade.* New York: Basic Books, 1984.

Kostelanetz, Richard. "A Mind That Cannot Stop Exploding." *New York Times Book Review,* 15 March 1981, 11, 24–26.

Lentricchia, Frank. *Criticism and Social Change.* Chicago: University of Chicago Press, 1983.

Ling, David L. "A Pentadic Analysis of Senator Edward Kennedy's Address to the People of Massachusetts, July 25, 1969." *Central States Speech Journal* 21 (Summer 1970): 81–86. Reprinted in *Methods of Rhetorical Criticism: A Twentieth Century Perspective,* comp. Robert L. Scott and Bernard L. Brock, 327–35. New York: Harper and Row, 1972.

Mumford, Lewis. *The Golden Day: A Study in American Literature and Culture.* New York: Dover, 1968.

Munson, Gorham B. "The Fledgling Years, 1916–1924." *Sewanee Review* 40 (January–March 1932): 24–54.

————. "In and About the Workshop of Kenneth Burke." In *Destinations: A Canvass of American Literature since 1900,* 139–59. New York: J. H. Sears, 1928.

Pells, Richard H. *The Liberal Mind in a Conservative Age: American Intellectuals in the 1940s and 1950s.* New York: Harper, 1985.

————. *Radical Visions and American Dreams: Culture and Thought in the Depression Years.* New York: Harper, 1974.

Phillips, William. *A Partisan View: Five Decades of the Literary Life.* New York: Stein, 1983.

Recherches Anglaises et Americaines 12 (1979).

Rueckert, William H., ed. *Critical Responses to Kenneth Burke.* Minneapolis: University of Minnesota Press, 1969.

————. *Kenneth Burke and the Drama of Human Relations.* 2d ed. Berkeley: University of California Press, 1982.

Schiappa, Edward, and Mary F. Keehner. "The 'Lost' Passages of *Permanence and Change.*" *Communication Studies* 42 (Fall 1991): 191–98.

Scott, Robert L., and Bernard L. Brock, comps. *Methods of Rhetorical Criticism: A Twentieth Century Perspective.* New York: Harper and Row, 1972.

Selzer, Jack. *Kenneth Burke: Conversing with the Moderns, 1915–1931.* Madison: University of Wisconsin Press, 1996.

Shi, David E. *Matthew Josephson, Bourgeois Bohemian.* New Haven: Yale University Press, 1981.

Simons, Herbert W., and Trevor Melia, eds. *The Legacy of Kenneth Burke.* Madison: University of Wisconsin Press, 1989.

Wald, Alan M. *The New York Intellectuals: The Rise and Decline of the Anti-Stalinist Left from the 1930s to the 1980s.* Chapel Hill: University of North Carolina Press, 1987.

Wasserstrom, William. *The Time of the Dial.* Syracuse, N.Y.: Syracuse University Press, 1963.

Wellek, René. *A History of Modern Criticism, 1750–1950.* Vol. 6: *American Criticism, 1900–1950.* New Haven: Yale University Press, 1986.

————. "Kenneth Burke and Literary Criticism." *Sewanee Review* 79 (April–June 1971): 171–88.

Wess, Robert. *Kenneth Burke: Rhetoric, Subjectivity, Postmodernism.* New York: Cambridge University Press, 1996.

White, Hayden, and Margaret Brose, eds. *Representing Kenneth Burke: Selected Papers from the English Institute,* n.s., 6. Baltimore: Johns Hopkins University Press, 1982.

Wilson, Edmund. *The American Earthquake: A Documentary of the Twenties and Thirties.* 1958. Reprint, New York: Farrar, 1979.

————. *The American Jitters: A Year of the Slump.* Essay Index Reprint Series. Freeport, N.Y.: Books for Libraries Press, 1968.

————. *The Shores of Light: A Literary Chronicle of the Twenties and Thirties.* New York: Farrar, 1979.

————. *The Thirties: From Notebooks and Diaries of the Period.* New York: Farrar, 1980.

————. *The Twenties: From Notebooks and Diaries of the Period.* New York: Farrar, 1975.

Winters, Yvor. *In Defense of Reason.* New York: Morrow, 1947.

Index